D0343154

CP 6ᵃ

LIFE HISTORIES
OF NORTH AMERICAN
WOODPECKERS

LIFE HISTORIES
OF NORTH AMERICAN
WOODPECKERS

by

Arthur Cleveland Bent

Dover Publications, Inc.

New York

Published in Canada by General Publishing Company, Ltd., 30 Lesmill Road, Don Mills, Toronto,
Ontario.
Published in the United Kingdom by Constable
and Company, Ltd., 10 Orange Street, London WC 2.

This Dover edition, first published in 1964, is an
unabridged and unaltered republication of the work
originally published in 1939 by the United States
Government Printing Office, as Smithsonian Institution United States National Museum *Bulletin 174*.

Standard Book Number: 486-21083-9
Library of Congress Catalog Card Number: 64-20879

Manufactured in the United States of America
Dover Publications, Inc.
180 Varick Street
New York, N. Y. 10014

ADVERTISEMENT

The scientific publications of the National Museum include two series, known, respectively, as *Proceedings* and *Bulletin.*

The *Proceedings* series, begun in 1878, is intended primarily as a medium for the publication of original papers, based on the collections of the National Museum, that set forth newly acquired facts in biology, anthropology, and geology, with descriptions of new forms and revisions of limited groups. Copies of each paper, in pamphlet form, are distributed as published to libraries and scientific organizations and to specialists and others interested in the different subjects. The dates at which these separate papers are published are recorded in the table of contents of each of the volumes.

The series of *Bulletins*, the first of which was issued in 1875, contains separate publications comprising monographs of large zoological groups and other general systematic treatises (occasionally in several volumes), faunal works, reports of expeditions, catalogs of type specimens, special collections, and other material of similar nature. The majority of the volumes are octavo in size, but a quarto size has been adopted in a few instances in which large plates were regarded as indispensable. In the *Bulletin* series appear volumes under the heading *Contributions from the United States National Herbarium*, in octavo form, published by the National Museum since 1902, which contain papers relating to the botanical collections of the Museum.

The present work forms No. 174 of the *Bulletin* series.

ALEXANDER WETMORE,
Assistant Secretary, Smithsonian Institution.

WASHINGTON, D. C., *March 22, 1939.*

CONTENTS

INTRODUCTION

This is the twelfth in a series of bulletins of the United States National Museum on the life histories of North American birds. Previous numbers have been issued as follows;

107. Life Histories of North American Diving Birds, August 1, 1919.
113. Life Histories of North American Gulls and Terns, August 27, 1921.
121. Life Histories of North American Petrels and Pelicans and their Allies, October 19, 1922.
126. Life Histories of North American Wild Fowl (part), May 25, 1923.
130. Life Histories of North American Wild Fowl (part), June 27, 1925.
135. Life Histories of North American Marsh Birds, March 11, 1927.
142. Life Histories of North American Shore Birds (pt. 1), December 31, 1927.
146. Life Histories of North American Shore Birds (pt. 2), March 24, 1929.
162. Life Histories of North American Gallinaceous Birds, May 25, 1932.
167. Life Histories of North American Birds of Prey (pt. 1), May 3, 1937.
170. Life Histories of North American Birds of Prey (pt. 2), August 8, 1938.

The same general plan has been followed, as explained in previous bulletins, and the same sources of information have been utilized. The nomenclature of the 1931 check list of the American Ornithologists' Union has been followed, but it has seemed best to continue in the same order of arrangement of families and species as given in the old check list (1910).

An attempt has been made to give as full a life history as possible of the best-known subspecies and to avoid duplication by writing briefly of the others and giving only the characters of the subspecies, its range, and any habits peculiar to it. In many cases certain habits, probably common to the species as a whole, have been recorded for only one subspecies; such habits are mentioned under the subspecies on which the observations were made. The distribution gives the range of the species as a whole, with only rough outlines of the ranges of the subspecies, which cannot be accurately defined in many cases.

The egg dates are the condensed results of a mass of records taken from the data in a large number of the best egg collections in the country, as well as from contributed field notes and from a few published sources. They indicate the dates on which eggs have been actually found in various parts of the country, showing the earliest and latest dates and the limits between which half the dates fall, the height of the season.

The plumages are described in only enough detail to enable the reader to trace the sequence of molts and plumages from birth to maturity and to recognize the birds in the different stages and at the different seasons. No attempt has been made to describe fully the adult plumages; this has been done very well in the many manuals and State bird books that are now available. The names of colors, when in quotation marks, are taken from Ridgway's Color Standards and Color Nomenclature (1912), and the terms used to describe the shapes of eggs are taken from his Nomenclature of Colors (1886). The boldface type in the measurements of eggs indicates the four extremes of the measurements.

Many of those who contributed material for previous bulletins have continued to cooperate. Receipt of material from more than 430 contributors has been acknowledged previously. In addition to these, our thanks are due to the following new contributors: Dean Amadon, E. R. Forrest, Allen Frost, J. J. Hickey, Joseph Janiec, Melvin Johansen, M. B. Meanley, Jr., R. L. Meredith, E. E. Murphey, A. G. Nye, Jr., R. T. Orr, R. S. Palmer, Cordelia J. Stanwood, Wendell Taber, A. E. Thompson, and Mrs. L. J. Webster. If any contributor fails to find his name in this or in one of the previous lists, the author would be glad to be advised.

Egg measurements were furnished especially for this volume by Dean Amadon, A. M. Bailey, C. E. Doe, J. R. Gillin, W. C. Hanna, H. L. Harllee, R. C. Harlow, R. T. Orr, J. H. Riley, G. H. Stuart, 3d, and Miss M. W. Wythe.

Through the courtesy of the Bureau of Biological Survey, the services of Frederick C. Lincoln were again obtained to compile the distribution paragraphs. With the matchless reference files of the Biological Survey at his disposal, his many hours of careful work have produced results far more satisfactory than could have been attained by the author, who claims no credit and assumes no responsibility for this part of the work.

Dr. Winsor M. Tyler rendered valuable assistance in reading and indexing, for this group, the greater part of the leading periodicals relating to North American birds, which saved the author many hours of tedious work and for which he is very grateful. Dr. Tyler contributed the life histories of the northern downy woodpecker and yellow-bellied sapsucker, Dr. Arthur A. Allen wrote the life history of the ivory-billed woodpecker, Bayard H. Christy that of the northern pileated woodpecker, and Dr. Eugene E. Murphey that of the red-cockaded woodpecker. Thanks are due also to F. Seymour Hersey for figuring the egg measurements.

The manuscript for this volume was completed in June 1938. Contributions received since then will be acknowledged later. Only information of great importance could be added. The reader is reminded again that this is a cooperative work; if he fails to find in these volumes anything that he knows about the birds, he can blame himself for not having sent the information to—

THE AUTHOR.

LIFE HISTORIES OF NORTH AMERICAN WOODPECKERS

ORDER PICIFORMES

By Arthur Cleveland Bent

Taunton, Mass.

Order PICIFORMES

Family PICIDAE: American Woodpeckers

CAMPEPHILUS PRINCIPALIS (Linnaeus)

IVORY-BILLED WOODPECKER

PLATES 1, 2

HABITS

Contributed by Arthur Augustus Allen

THE LARGE size and striking color pattern, the mystery of its habitat, and the tragedy of its possible extinction combine to make the ivory-billed woodpecker one of peculiar interest to all Americans who have any pride in the natural resources of their country.

Ever since the days of Mark Catesby (1731) this species has attracted popular attention, and even at that time, as he stated in his Natural History of Carolina, Florida, and the Bahama Islands: "The bills of these Birds are much valued by the *Canada Indians*, who made Coronets of 'em for their Princes and great warriors, by fixing them round a Wreath, with their points outward. The Northern Indians having none of these Birds in their cold country, purchase them of the *Southern People* at the price of two, and sometimes three, Buck-skins a Bill." At that time the species was found throughout the Gulf States as far north as North Carolina and up the Mississippi Valley as far as southern Ohio and Illinois.

Today it is almost extinct, and indeed during the past 50 years long periods have elapsed when no individuals have been reported from any part of its range. It apparently has been exterminated from all but a few isolated localities in Louisiana, Florida, and South Carolina, where it still clings on in a precarious position.

1

The ivorybill is primarily a bird of the great moss-hung southern swamps, where mature timber with its dying branches provides a bounteous food supply of wood-boring larvae, but its habits apparently vary in different parts of its range, for the birds I observed in Florida, although nesting in a cypress swamp, did most of their feeding along its borders on recently killed young pines that were infested with beetle larvae. They even got down on the ground like flickers to feed among palmetto roots on a recent burn. In Louisiana, on the other hand, the nesting birds observed confined their activities to a mature forest of oak, sweetgum, and hackberry, and paid little attention to the cypress trees along the lagoons.

Spring.—At what time the winter groups of ivorybills break up and spring activities commence is rather difficult to state, for there seems to be considerable irregularity to the breeding season. Judged from published records of its nests, the period of greatest activity would seem to be late March and early April. According to Audubon (1842): "The ivory-billed woodpecker nestles earlier in spring than any other species of its tribe. I have observed it boring a hole for that purpose in the beginning of March." Scott (1881) reports taking an incubating female in Florida on January 20, 1880, and (1888) of finding a nest containing one young female about one-third grown on March 17, 1887. Ridgway (1898) likewise speaks of shooting a male that left its nest hole February 15, 1898, and Hoyt (1905) states that "in Florida they begin building the latter part of January, and if undisturbed the eggs are laid by February 10th." In 1937 James Tanner (MS.) discovered a nest in Louisiana from which the fledgling left on March 30, fully 2 months earlier than any previous records from the same locality, and in 1938 apparently the same pair of birds had young the last week in February. In contrast to these dates we find 10 records of April nesting, 5 for May, and 1 (Beyer, 1900) of a young bird just out of the nest in July. The latter records might well constitute second attempts at nesting. The Florida birds, in general, start earlier than those in Louisiana, but at best there seems to be less regularity to the commencement of the nesting period than is found with most of our North American woodpeckers. In this, the ivorybill may register its affinity with tropical birds in general, the ivorybill being the most northern representative of an otherwise tropical or semitropical genus. There is some evidence for believing that ivorybills wander over considerably larger territories in winter than those to which they confine their activities in the spring, but little definite information has thus far been recorded on any of their before and after breeding activities.

Courtship.—Nothing seems to have been written on the courtship of the ivorybill except the observations of Allen and Kellogg (1937):

Our only observations were made in Florida about 6 a. m., on April 13, 1924. We had discovered this pair of ivorybills at about the same time the preceding morning when they came out of the cypress swamp and preened their feathers and called a few times from the top of a dead pine before going off together to feed. They had made such a long flight the previous day that we were unable to find them again, but that night, still traveling together, they had returned to the same group of medium-sized cypress trees which they had apparently left in the morning and in which there was one fresh hole in addition to four or five other old ones in the near vicinity. On the morning of the 13th, they called as they left these cypress trees and flew to the top of a dead pine at the edge of the swamp, where they called and preened. Finally the female climbed up directly below the male and when she approached him closely he bent his head downward and clasped bills with her. The next instant they both flew out on to the "burn," where we followed their feeding operations for about an hour.

Nesting.—As before stated, while there are a few records of February nesting, the most definite records are for March, April, and early May, as follows:

April 6, ——. M. Thompson, Okefinokee swamp, Georgia. Laying.

April 9, 1892. E. A. McIlhenny, Avery swamp, Louisiana. Three fresh eggs.

April 10, ——. Dr. S. W. Wilson, Altamaha swamp, Georgia. Four eggs.

April 15, 1893. A. Wayne, Florida. A young female about 2 weeks out of the nest.

April 19, 1893. Ralph Collection, Lafayette County, Fla. Three eggs.

May 2, 1892. E. A. McIlhenny, Avery swamp, Louisiana. Three eggs.

May 19, 1892. E. A. McIlhenny, Avery swamp, Louisiana. Four eggs, a second laying.

May (early) 1894. E. A. McIlhenny, Avery swamp., Louisiana. Five young, 3 days old.

May 3, 1885. Capt. B. F. Goss, Jasper County, Tex. Three eggs.

July 1897. George G. Beyer, Franklin Parish, La.

March 4, 1904. Brown brothers (Hoyt), feeding young.

March 16, 1904. R. D. Hoyt, Taylor County, Fla. Large young.

March 4, 1905. R. D. Hoyt, Claremont County, Fla. Two eggs, incubation advanced.

March 24, 1905. R. D. Hoyt, Claremont County, Fla. Two eggs slightly incubated (second laying of the preceding).

April 13, 1924. A. A. Allen, Taylor Creek, Fla. Nest completed. Incubation not yet started.

April (early) 1931. J. J. Kuhn, northern Louisiana. Incubating.

May 13, 1934. J. J. Kuhn, northern Louisiana. Probably small young.

April 6, 1935. A. A. Allen and P. P. Kellogg, northern Louisiana. Incubating.

April 9, 1935. A. A. Allen and P. P. Kellogg, northern Louisiana. Building.

April 25, 1935. A. A. Allen and P. P. Kellogg, northern Louisiana. Incubating.

May 10, 1935. A. A. Allen and P. P. Kellogg, northern Louisiana. Small young.

Again quoting from the report of Allen and Kellogg (1937):

The site of the Ivorybill's nest seems to vary considerably. Audubon states: "The hole is, I believe, always made in the trunk of a live tree, generally an ash or a hackberry, and is at a great height." There are, however, records of their nesting in live cypress, partially dead oaks, a dead royal-palm stub, "an old and nearly rotten white elm stump," etc., indicating about as great a variety as shown by the pileated woodpecker. The lowest authentic nest of which we have found a record, was that described by Beyer (1900) "about 25 feet up in a living over-cup oak," although Scott (1881) mentions what he considered "an old nest evidently of this species," in a palmetto stub only fifteen feet from the ground. The nest which we discovered in Florida, in 1924, was about thirty feet up in a live cypress and there were other holes in the vicinity in similar trees that had apparently been used in years past. The bark had healed over in some cases and scar tissue was apparently trying to close the wounds. Of the four nests examined in Louisiana, three were in oaks and one in a swamp maple. The maple, seven and a half feet in circumference (breast high), was partially alive, but the top where the nest was located, 43 feet from the ground, was dead and pithy. Of those in oak trees, one was in a dead pin-oak stub about ten feet in circumference and about fifty feet high, standing in more or less of a clearing. The nest was 47 feet 8 inches from the ground. The other two were not measured accurately but were certainly over forty feet from the ground. About the middle of May when it was determined that the first two trees had been deserted, they were cut down, careful measurements taken, and the contents of the holes preserved. The hole in the maple was 5 inches in vertical diameter and 4⅛ inches laterally, and was slightly irregular at the bottom, as shown in the photographs; that in the oak was more symmetrical with a similar vertical diameter of 5 inches and a transverse diameter of 4 inches. The depth of the maple nest from the top of the entrance hole was 19⅛ inches, of which 3 inches was filled with chips and "sawdust." This nest cavity was 8⅛ inches in diameter at the egg level, and the tree itself 18½ inches in diameter at the level of the hole. The nest cavity in the oak was 20 inches from top to bottom with a diameter of 8¼ inches at the egg level. The entrance hole went in 3 inches before it turned abruptly downward; the tree at this point was 22 inches in diameter. There was a stub just above the hole in the maple about 4 inches long representing a branch that had apparently died and been broken off years before and started to heal over. The oak was perfectly smooth at the entrance hole, but on either side, slightly above, were the bases of two large branches that could not have given the opening any protection from the weather. The opening in the maple faced north, two of those in the oaks east, and one west. Audubon states: "The birds pay great regard to the particular situation of the tree and the inclination of the trunk; first, because they prefer retirement, and, again, because they are anxious to secure the aperture against the access of water during beating rains. To prevent such a calamity the hole is generally dug immediately under the juncture of a large branch with the trunk." None of the nests examined by us showed this desire for protection from rain, and the chips at the bottom of the cavity were perfectly dry, though we had had some very heavy rains shortly before they were examined.

Audubon further states: "The average diameter of the different nests which I examined was about 7 inches within, although the entrance, which is perfectly round, is only just large enough to admit the bird." Beyer (1900) says: "The entrance measures exactly 4½ inches in height and 3⅞ inches in width," and McIlhenny (Bendire, 1895) gives the measurements of a typical hole as "oval and measures 4⅛ by 5¾ inches," and Scott (1888) as "3½ inches wide and 4½ inches high." The corresponding measurements of the nests of Pileated Woodpeckers are given by Bendire (1895) as follows: "The entrance measures from 3 to 3½ inches in diameter, and it often goes 5 inches straight into the trunk before it is worked downward." The additional one to two inches in diameter of the nest hole should be kept in mind when searching for reasons why the Ivorybill has proven less successful than the Pileated Woodpecker in its struggle for existence. Thompson (1885) states: "The depth of the hole varies from three to seven feet, as a rule, but I found one that was nearly nine feet deep and another that was less than two." He also claims that they are always jug-shaped at the lower end.

Of two nests discovered by Hoyt (1905) in Claremont County, Fla., one was 58 feet up in a live cypress about 20 yards from a nest discovered in 1904 by the Brown brothers; the second nest built by the same pair after the first eggs had been taken was in a cypress stub about 70 yards distant from the first and 47 feet from the ground. The opening of the first nest was 6¾ inches by 3¼ inches, with the trunk of the tree 15 inches in diameter at the nest cavity, which was 14 inches deep. The second nest hole measured 6 by 3¾ inches and was likewise 14 inches deep. "The opening in both nests was uneven and rough, and just inside the hollow was much enlarged, being 9 inches across, and unlike the nests of other woodpeckers, was smaller at the bottom than at the top. * * * One marked feature of the nest tree of which I have seen no mention made is that the outer bark of those I have examined was torn to shreds from a point some distance below the nest site to 15 or 20 feet above it. This made the nest tree noticeable for quite a distance. The last nest taken this season had little of this work done."

Allen and Kellogg (1937) say further:

According to McIlhenny (Bendire, 1895) the female does all the work of excavation, requiring from eight to fourteen days, while the male sits around and chips the bark from neighboring trees. Audubon, however, states that "both birds work most assiduously at this excavation, one waiting outside to encourage the other." Maurice Thompson (1896) likewise reports that both birds work at the excavation. We had no opportunity to check either statement but certainly both birds take part in incubation and feeding the young. The chips are not removed from the vicinity of the nest for each one that we have examined has had piles of chips directly below the opening though, since most of the trees were standing in water, the chips were not very conspicuous.

We camped within three hundred feet of our first Ivorybill nest in Louisiana, in 1935. A pair of 24-power binoculars set on a tripod was trained on the nest opening, and from daylight, April 10, until 11 a. m., April 14, continuous observations during the hours of daylight were made either by the writers or by James Tanner. The nest had been found the morning of April 6, when the female was incubating, but how far along incubation had proceeded we made no effort to determine for fear of disturbing the birds. Contrary to most published accounts, however, the birds were not particularly wary and soon became so accustomed to our presence that they would enter the nest-hole with one of us standing at the base of the tree and later even when one of us was descending from a blind which we built on April 9 in the top of an adjacent rock elm, twenty feet distant from the nest. On April 9, we located a second pair of Ivorybills in the vicinity of a fresh hole about fifty feet up in a dead oak, some two miles to the south of the nest in the maple. The following morning, however, the nest was occupied by a black squirrel and the birds had disappeared.

Briefly summarizing our five-day vigil at the occupied nest, we learned that the birds took turns sitting on the eggs, working in approximately two-hour shifts when not alarmed, but changing places more frequently when disturbed. Activities usually commenced about six o'clock in the morning, three-quarters of an hour after Cardinals and Carolina Wrens started singing. At this time the female relieved the male after his having spent the night on the eggs. Activities ceased about four o'clock in the afternoon when the male relieved the female on the eggs and went in the nest for the night. This was nearly three hours before dark, which came about seven o'clock.

Eggs.—According to Bendire (1895) :

The eggs of the Ivory-billed Woodpecker are pure china white in color, close grained, and exceedingly glossy, as if enameled. They vary in shape from an elongate ovate to a cylindrical ovate, and are more pointed than the eggs of most of our Woodpeckers. They appear to me to be readily distinguished from those of the Pileated Woodpecker, some of which are fully as large. From three to five eggs are laid to a set, and only one brood is raised in a season. * * *

The average measurement of thirteen eggs is 34.87 by 25.22 millimetres or about 1.37 by 0.99 inches. The largest egg measured 36.83 by 26.92 millimetres, or about 1.45 by 1.06 inches; the smallest, 34.54 by 23.62 millimetres, or about 1.36 by 0.93 inches.

The eggs described by Hoyt (1905) measured 1.46 by 1.09 and 1.43 by 1.07 inches in the first set and 1.43 by 1.10 and 1.43 by 1.08 inches in the second set.

From my own experience and the observation of others, it seems to me that the number of eggs laid by the ivorybill would not normally exceed three, and one or two of these are often infertile. Frequently, if the bird is successful in rearing any offspring at all, a single youngster is the result rather than two or three. Allen and Kellogg (1937) describe three nests in which no young were successfully reared, although at least some of the eggs apparently hatched, while Scott (1888), Beyer (1900), and Tanner (1937 and 1938 MS.) each report single young, and in the type set of three eggs (Ralph collection, Lafayette County, Fla.) two were infertile, and both of Hoyt's sets contained two eggs each. On the other hand, J. J. Kuhn reports seeing one pair of ivorybills with four young in 1931 and again in 1936 in the same forest where Allen and Kellogg made their studies. In 1932, 1933, and 1934 he observed a pair of ivorybills with two young.

Plumages.—So far as I have been able to find, no one has ever published a description of the natal or juvenal plumages of the ivory-billed woodpecker. The probability is that natal down is absent, although Scott (1888), who found a nest containing one young in Florida March 17, 1887, says: "The young bird in the nest was a female, and though one-third grown had *not yet opened its eyes.* The feathers of the first plumage were apparent, beginning to cover the down, and were the same in coloration as those of the adult female bird."

During April 1937, James Tanner, recipient of the Audubon fellowship at Cornell University for the study of the ivory-billed woodpecker (MS.), was able to follow a young ivorybill for over 3 months after it left the nest, and though he never had the bird in his hands, his description is much more complete than Scott's and the most accurate one available: "March 10, 1937: The young ivory-billed woodpecker just out of the nest resembled an adult female in general pattern but with the following differences: The black crest was short and blunt; the tail was short and square; the outer primaries were all tipped with white, instead of being wholly black as in the adult; the bill was shorter than that of an adult and was chalky white instead of ivory; the eye was a dark brown or sepia. One month later the crest was long but still blunt and black, the tail was almost as long and pointed as an adult's, and the eye and bill were beginning to turn color.

"The bird developed gradually from then, until at three and a half months out of the nest (July 14, 1937) its size, proportions, bill, and eye color were the same as those of an adult. By then, scarlet feathers had appeared in the back of the crest. The white wing tips to the outer primaries were almost worn away."

Since Tanner's bird began to show red in the crest when it was three and a half months old, it is probable that the postjuvenal molt is completed by early fall and that thereafter young and adults are similar.

The chief difference between adult male and female ivorybills lies in the crest, which in the male is a brilliant scarlet, not including the uppermost feathers, which are black, like the top of the head, while the somewhat recurved crest of the female is entirely black. Females average somewhat larger than males in most of their measurements, except those of bill and feet, as the following figures (length in millimeters) given by Ridgway (1914) for 15 males and 11 females indicate:

ADULT MALES: Skins, 420–493 (454); wing, 240–263 (255.8); tail, 147–160.5 (154.4); culmen, 63–72.5 (68.2); tarsus, 42.5–46 (44.2); outer anterior toe, 30–34 (32.1).

ADULT FEMALES: Skins, 452–488 (471); wing, 240–262 (256.4); tail, 151–166 (159.5); culmen, 61–67.5 (64.3); tarsus, 40.5–44 (42.6); outer anterior toe, 30–33.5 (31.7).

In both sexes the general color is a glossy blue-black, with the tail and primaries duller or with the gloss less distinct. A narrow stripe on each side of the neck, starting below the eye and continuing down to the folded secondaries, is conspicuously white, as are also the secondaries, all but five or six of the outermost primaries, and the under wing coverts. The white nasal plumes and anterior edges of the lores more or less match the ivory-white bill and help to emphasize its size. The iris is pale, clear lemon-yellow in both sexes, and the tarsi and toes are light gray.

Food.—Audubon (1842) mentions grapes, persimmons, and hackberries as food of the ivorybills in addition to beetles, larvae, and large grubs. McIlhenny, in his communication to Bendire (1895), mentions their feeding on acorns, but Maurice Thompson (1885) asserts that "it is only woodpeckers which eat insects and larvae (dug out of rotten wood) exclusively." Allen and Kellogg (1937) report:

We were never able to follow a bird continuously through the forest of either Louisiana or Florida for more than an hour before it would make a long flight and we would be unable to find it again. Ordinarily upon leaving the nest-tree or its immediate environs the bird would fly at least a hundred yards before stopping. Then it would feed for from a few minutes to as long as half an hour on a dead tree or dead branch before making a short flight to another tree. It might make a dozen such short flights and then, without any warning and for no apparent reason, it would start off on a long flight through the forest that would take it entirely out of sight.

Audubon states that "it seldom comes near the ground"; but the birds we have watched behave no differently from pileated woodpeckers in this respect, sometimes working high up in the trees but at other times within five or ten feet of the ground. The female of the Florida pair which we watched for over an hour on a "burn" sometimes got down on the ground around the seared, prostrate trunks of the saw palmettos, hopping like a Flicker, while her mate stayed on the trunks of the pines five to ten feet up. We never saw the Louisiana birds on the ground but there was plenty of evidence, both in Florida and Louisiana, that a bird will continue scaling the bark from recently killed trees for the beetle larvae beneath, clear to the base of the tree, until the tree stands absolutely naked with the bark piled around its base.

Frequently they return again and again to the same tree until they have entirely stripped it. At one time we thought this was their chief method of feeding, but we have since watched them digging for borers exactly like hairy or pileated woodpeckers. At one time we watched the female working at a deep gash in the tall stub of a dead gum, which was apparently a favorite feeding place. She clung to the spot for about five minutes, occasionally picking hard, but never chipping off any large flakes that would account for the depth of the hole which was exactly like that made by pileated woodpeckers,—about four inches deep and eighteen inches long. Finally she flew and disappeared in the direction of the nest which was about two hundred yards away. In a few minutes the male ivorybill came to the same spot where the female had been working and he, too, picked at the hole and stayed there for several minutes. At the time we decided that either the ivorybills or perhaps the pileateds had made the gash in the tree for carpenter ants and that the ivorybills were returning each time for more ants. Since the stub was rather rotten and full of woodpecker drillings, we decided to cut it down the next day and make certain of what the ivorybills were securing. Upon examining the hole made by the birds there was, however, no evidence of carpenter ants, and the deep gash followed the tunnels of large, wood-boring beetle larvae (Cerambycidae) of which there were a great many in the tree; the only other available woodpecker food was termites of which there were comparatively few.

Certainly the ivorybills did not do enough digging while we were watching them to uncover any additional borers, so they may have been picking up such termites as appeared in the gash. The birds, while we watched them in Louisiana, divided their time between dead branches of live trees and completely dead trees, but more time was spent knocking off the bark for whatever could be found immediately beneath it than was spent digging deeply for borers. The forest was made up primarily of oak, gum and hackberry, and the woodpeckers showed no preference for species so far as we could determine. In Florida, while the nest was located in a cypress swamp in a live cypress tree, the birds apparently did most of their feeding in the dead pines at the edge of the swamp, scaling off the bark of those small and medium-sized pines that had been killed by fire, or actually getting down on the ground like Flickers, as already described.

The ivorybills are, therefore, apparently somewhat adaptable in their food and feeding habits, but forests of mature trees with their dying branches seem to give them the best habitat for securing their food. The fruits of these trees may likewise add considerably to their attractiveness. The only definite stomach analyses published are of two birds examined by the United States Biological Survey, and reported upon by Beal (1911) : "One stomach contained 32 and the other 20 of the wood-boring cerambycid larvae, which live by boring into trees. These constituted 37.5 per cent of the whole food. The remainder of the animal food consisted of engraver beetles (*Scolytidae*) found in one stomach. Of these, three species were identified— *Tomicus avulsus*, *T. calligraphus*, and *T. grandicollis*. The total animal food amounted to 38.5 per cent. The vegetable food consisted of fruit of *Magnolia foetida* in one stomach, and of pecan nuts in the other. The average for the two was 61.5 percent."

The ivory-billed woodpecker is represented in the Biological Survey's collection by the stomachs of three birds. Two of these were males collected on November 26, 1904, at Tarkington, Tex., by Vernon Bailey, and the third was shot at Bowling Green, West Carroll Parish, La., on August 19, 1903, by E. L. Moseley.

The first two stomachs were well filled, and though only the content of the third was received it was apparently well filled also. This last stomach alone contained a trace of gravel. Forty-six percent of the food was animal in origin, long-horned beetles (Cerambycidae, including *Parandra polita* and *Stenodontus dasystomus*) comprising 45.33 percent, while the remaining 0.67 percent consisted of 3 different species of engraver beetles (*Tomicus* spp.). Southern magnolia seeds (*Magnolia grandiflora*) formed 14 percent of the vegetable food, hickory (*Hicoria* sp.) and pecan (*Hicoria pecan*) nuts formed 27 percent, and poison ivy (*Rhus radicans*) equaled 12.67 percent. Fragments of an unidentified gall formed 1 percent of the content.

Behavior.—The uniform direct flight of the ivorybill resembles that of the red-headed woodpecker more than it does the swooping undulating flight of the pileated, and this general resemblance is emphasized by the large amount of white in the wings. When viewed from below, the long pointed tail is quite conspicuous and the wings seem very narrow because the black portion is so much more conspicuous than the white, which apparently cuts off the whole rear of the wing. This is perhaps not so conspicuous when viewed from the side, but even so it is remarkable how ducklike the bird can appear as it flies swiftly and directly up a lagoon, so much so in fact that certain Louisiana hunters have told me that they have even shot at them under such circumstances, mistaking them for ducks. In this connection Audubon's (1842) description of the flight of the ivorybill is quite misleading: "The flight of this bird is graceful in the extreme, although seldom prolonged to more than a few hundred yards at a time, unless when it has to cross a large river, which it does in deep undulations, opening its wings at first to their full extent and nearly closing them to renew the propelling impulse. The transit from one tree to another, even should the distance be as much as a hundred yards, is performed by a single sweep, and the bird appears as if merely swinging itself from the top of the one tree to that of the other, forming an elegantly curved line."

Voice.—Concerning the voice of the ivorybill there seems to be considerable agreement in that the ordinary note sounds like a single blast from a tin trumpet or a clarinet. In the words of Audubon, "Its notes are clear, loud, and yet rather plaintive. They are heard at a considerable distance, perhaps half a mile, and resemble the false, high note of a clarionet." According to Hoyt (1905): "It is a single note and resembles the word Schwenk, at times keyed very high, again soft and plaintive, it lacks carrying capacity and can rarely be heard over 100 yards on a still morning, while the harsh notes of the pileated woodpecker can be heard a full mile." Allen and Kellogg (1937) state that anyone can produce the sound very accurately by using only the mouthpiece of the clarinet. They question whether the loudest calls can be heard half a mile:

It is doubtful, however, if the loudest calls can be heard, under normal conditions, for a quarter of a mile, and some of the weaker ones are scarcely audible at 300 yards. However, when we tested the carrying power of one of our recordings of the common alarm note, *kent*, amplified until it sounded to our ears normal at about one hundred feet, the call was distinctly recognizable at a distance of 2,500 feet directly in front of the amplifier with no trees or buildings intervening. At a 45-degree angle the sound was not recognizable at half this distance. The birds are so often quiet for such long periods that we can scarcely agree with Audubon's statement that "the bird spends few minutes of the day without uttering them." They seem much more likely to call when they are alarmed, as when they discover an intruder in their haunts. Both birds give the call, but that of the female is somewhat weaker. In addition to this *kent* note, as it is called by the natives of Louisiana, and because of which they call the birds "Kents," they have a variety of low conversational notes when they exchange places at the nest, which are suggestive of similar notes of the Flicker; but they never, so far as we know, give a call at all similar to the *pup-pup-pup*! of the pileated, nor have we ever heard them sound a real tatoo like other woodpeckers, such as described by Thompson (1885), and which McIlhenny (Bendire, 1895) compares to the "roll of a snare drum." The birds in Florida and all those in Louisiana telegraphed to each other by single or double resounding whacks on the trunk or dead branches. Mr. Kuhn who has had years of experience with them, likewise has never heard any notes or tatoos that were comparable with those of the Pileated. Our observations agree with Audubon's, rather than with those of some others, in that "it never utters any sound while on the wing."

Tanner (MS.) reports, however, that in his studies during 1937 he occasionally heard a rapid succession of "kents" given on the wing as one bird flew in to join another.

The calls of the two large species of woodpeckers are so distinct that they should not be confused with each other or with those of any other birds. The fact, however, that ivorybills are continually being reported, even from the Northern States, indicates how unobservant many people are and how necessary it is to stress even such conspicuous differences as those mentioned above.

Winter.—Ivory-billed woodpeckers are apparently not only non-migratory but also sedentary and perhaps spend their entire lives within a few miles of the spot where they were hatched. At least, once a pair has established a territory it seems to cling to that area winter and summer, and Tanner (MS.) reports one pair using the same roosting hole in December that they used the preceding April. These territories are doubtless several miles in diameter, but the tendency was for the birds to build up small communities in certain areas until in former years, when their distribution was normal, they were reported as fairly common by observers who happened upon one of these communities. On the other hand, there were perhaps always large areas of similar timber uninhabited by them, so that with equal truth by equally competent observers they were called extremely rare. How much farther they range during the winter than during the nesting season has not yet been worked out, but doubtless the area covered at such times is considerably larger, and this accounts for sporadic records of birds in the nonbreeding seasons in areas where no nests have been located and where no one has been able to find the birds subsequently.

The family groups apparently keep together until the following nesting season, and Mr. Kuhn has reported seeing groups of from three to five birds even as late as early March. Hoyt (1905) states that "after the young leave the nest in April they and the parents remain together until the mating season in December. During the summer they are always found in bands of three to five, and I have never seen more than the latter number."

Conservation.—Arthur T. Wayne (1910) records having "encountered more than two hundred of these rare birds [in Florida] during the years 1892, 1893, and 1894." Today it is doubtful if there are a fourth of that number left alive in its entire range.

A number of theories have been advanced for the increasing scarcity of the ivorybill, that most often mentioned being the destruction of its natural habitat, the virgin cypress and bottomland forests of the South. Commercialization, avarice of collectors, shooting for food by natives, predation by natural enemies that can enter its hole (but not the pileated) are likewise suggested, while Allen and Kellogg (1937) suggest that with increasing scarcity because of their sedentary habits, inbreeding and lack of sex rhythm resulting in weak young and infertile eggs have become increasingly important. At this writing the National Association of Audubon Societies has established a Fellowship at Cornell University for the study of the ivorybill, and it is hoped that the incumbent, James Tanner, may ascertain such facts regarding the bird and its habits that constructive measures for its preservation can be undertaken.

DISTRIBUTION

Range.—The Southeastern United States; nonmigratory.

The range of the ivory-billed woodpecker extends **north** to northeastern Texas (Gainesville); southeastern Oklahoma (Caddo); northeastern Arkansas (Newport and Osceola); southeastern Missouri (Little River); southeastern Illinois (Mount Carmel); southern Indiana (Monroe County and Franklin County); and southeastern North Carolina (Wilmington). **East** along the coast from North Carolina (Wilmington) to southeastern Florida (Cape Florida). From this point the southern limits of the range extend westward along the Gulf coast to Texas (Guadalupe and New Braunfels). **West** to eastern Texas (New Braunfels, San Marcos, Brazos River, and Gainesville).

The range of the species has been so restricted in modern times that periodically it is feared the bird is on the verge of extinction. It is now known to exist only in a very few remote areas, chiefly in Louisiana.

Egg dates.—Florida: 4 records, March 4 to April 19.

Louisiana: 5 records, March 6 to May 19.

Georgia: 2 records, April 6 and 10.

Texas: 2 records, April 11 and May 3.

DRYOBATES VILLOSUS VILLOSUS (Linnaeus)

EASTERN HAIRY WOODPECKER

PLATE 3

HABITS

The hairy woodpecker, with its various subspecies, ranges through-out practically all the timbered regions in North America, but the type race, the subject of this sketch, is confined, during the breeding season at least, to the Transition and Upper Austral Zones of North-eastern United States and extreme southern Canada.

In the region where I am most familiar with it, southern New England, it is not an abundant bird at any season, quite rare in summer and oftener seen in winter. It is essentially a retiring, for-est-loving bird, being found with us in summer in the dry deciduous woods, or occasionally in rural districts in old orchards near the borders of wooded areas. In winter, it is given more to wandering into villages and towns, or may be seen even in the shade trees in larger cities.

I remember having found it only twice in swampy woods, but Dr. George M. Sutton (1928b), in his paper on the birds of Pymatuning Swamp, Crawford County, Pa., says: "The hairy woodpecker occurs only rarely in the higher deciduous woods outside the borders of Pymatuning during the nesting season, but it is abundant everywhere in the wooded Swamp, and in the restricted area, closely examined in 1922, was considered one of the most numerous species."

Courtship.—Francis H. Allen has sent me the following notes on this subject: "The courtship dance consists of a weaving motion of the head, as with the flicker, accompanied by a high-pitched *ch'weech*, *ch'weech*, *ch'weech*, repeated over and over vociferously. The note is much like that of the flicker, but higher-pitched and more rapidly delivered. Three and sometimes four birds may be seen so engaged together, but I have no observation as to the sexes. In quiet inter-vals in courtship, the head is held with bill parallel with the axis of the body, not at right angles as in feeding."

Edward H. Forbush (1927) writes:

On bright March days this bird begins to practise what is either a love song, a challenge, a call to its mate, or all combined. This is no vocal music but instead a loud drumming on some resonant dead tree, branch, or pole. This long roll or tattoo is louder than that of the downy woodpecker, not quite so long, and with a slightly greater interval between each succeeding stroke. It takes a practiced ear, however, to distinguish between the drumming of these two species. In courtship the male chases the female from tree to tree with coaxing calls, and there is much dodging about among the branches and bowing to each other before the union is consummated.

Rex Brasher (1926) writes:

Seated under a cluster of small maples, one day in early May, I watched the interesting courting antics of the pair. The jaunty male's favorite position was one in which he appeared to be almost standing on his tail. With bill upright, wings thrown forward, and tail wide-spread he repeated over and over what was undoubtedly intended for a love-song, a series of notes divided between chuckles and whistles. But the strangest, most mystifying performance was a series of backward drops on the under side of a limb inclined about forty-five degrees. * * * Why didn't the little acrobat fall when he released his claws? Studying his movements carefully through the binoculars, I came to the conclusion that at the instant of releasing his grip he jerked his body toward the limb with sufficient impetus to catch the bark six inches or so below.

Lewis O. Shelley says in his notes: "I have watched the act of copulation of the hairy woodpecker and noted its dissimilarity to the downy. For the hairy invariably instills a follow-up procedure to the display, the male coming to her call and, soon thereafter, hopping up the branch toward her with a short jerking movement, in which he calls *wick-up*, *wick-up*, *wick-up*, wings agitating, this immediately followed by copulation."

Nesting.—The hairy woodpecker is rather rare, as a breeding bird, in my home territory in southeastern Massachusetts, but I have the records of 12 local nests. It shows a decided preference for deciduous woodlands, six of the nests being in dry, upland woods and two in maple swamps; of the other four nests, three were in apple orchards, close to extensive woodlots, and the fourth was in a small, living, red maple in a swampy meadow, some distance from any woods. The birds showed no decided preference for any one species of tree; three nests each were found in maples and apple trees, two each in chestnuts and poplars, and one each in a dead oak and a dead beech. Only four nests were in dead trees or dead branches; the others were all in living hardwoods. The heights from the ground varied from 5 feet in a dead poplar stub to 30 feet, or more, in tall chestnuts or maples. The entrance to the nesting cavity often appears nearly, or quite, circular, but on careful measurement will usually be shown to be more or less elliptical, higher than broad; a typical entrance hole that I measured was 1⅞ high by 1½ inches wide. The depth of the cavity was found to vary from 10 to 12 inches, but Mr. Shelley (1933) measured one that was 15 inches deep, and even deeper holes have been reported. Owen Durfee's notes give some very careful measurements of two of our local nests, one of which is worth quoting as showing an unusually elliptical entrance: "The entrance to the nest was on the northeast side of the trunk of a live chestnut and 22½ feet from the ground. The tree leaned toward the east about 2 feet. At the butt it was 9 inches in diameter and at the opening about 6½ inches. The opening had the usual elongated appearance, 2⅝ high by 1⅞ inches wide. The top of the hole went straight in across the cavity for 4½ inches, the bottom edge of the opening slanting up ¾ of an inch while going in 1½ inches. Then the cavity went nearly straight down below the hole for 12 inches, enlarging only a trifle, so that the base was about 4½ inches in diameter. The shell of the tree was only about ⅞ inch thick on one side but on the other was 2 inches thick."

Dr. Sutton (1928b) says of the nests in Pymatuning Swamp, Pa.: "The cavities were drilled near the tops of dead trees which nearly always stood in water. It was impossible to climb many of them because their bases were weak; but the clamoring of the young birds could be heard some distance away. On May 30, 1922, I located six nests within a half hour by watching the parent birds and listening for the young. * * * The twenty-six nests averaged roughly over thirty feet from the ground."

T. E. McMullen mentions in his notes a Pennsylvania nest that was 50 feet from the ground in a large maple in some woods. J. Claire Wood (1905) reports some very high nests in Michigan; one was in the "trunk of very large barkless dead elm about 50 feet above ground"; another was in the trunk of a "dead beech 55 feet up and just under a large limb."

The female probably selects the nesting site, but both sexes work alternately at the labor of excavating the cavity. This work requires one to three weeks, depending on how hard the wood is; a cavity in the soft wood of a poplar, which is a favorite with this species in some localities, might be excavated in a very short time, but I have known a pair to take over three weeks to excavate a nest in a hard maple; the trunk of a living tree may have a soft center, and some of the birds seem to be clever enough to select such a tree. A new nest may often be recognized by the presence of fresh chips on the ground around the tree, as the birds are not very particular about removing them.

The male sometimes digs out another shallower hole near the nesting tree, which he uses as a sleeping place. Usually a fresh hole is made each season, but I have seen occupied holes that were very much weathered, as if they had been occupied for more than one season; in such cases, the cavity may be deepened somewhat and the bottom covered with fresh chips. I once found a pair of these woodpeckers excavating their domicile, which they later abandoned, as I found on a later visit that the hole was partly full of water and sap. They are not always successful in their first attempt, for this and other reasons, and may have to start two or three holes before they find just the conditions they want. The eggs are laid on a soft bed of fresh chips at the bottom of the cavity and are usually half buried in it; no nesting material is carried in.

Eggs.—The hairy woodpecker lays three to six eggs, but four seems to be the commonest number. The eggs vary in shape from oval to elliptical-oval, usually more nearly oval. The shell is smooth and often quite glossy. The color is pure white, but in fresh eggs the yolk shows through the translucent shell, giving the egg a beautiful orange-pink color. The measurements of 47 eggs average 23.81 by 18.04 millimeters; the eggs showing the four extremes measure 29.50 by 18.80, 28.70 by 18.90, and 20.57 by 16.26 millimeters.

Young.—Only one brood is raised in a season, but, if the nest is robbed, the female will lay a second set after an interval of 12 or 14 days, and sometimes even a third set; often subsequent layings may ◂be in the same nest hole.

Bendire (1895) says:

The duties of incubation are divided between the sexes and last about two weeks. The young when first hatched are repulsive-looking creatures, blind and naked, with enormously large heads, and ugly protuberances at the base of the bill, resembling a reptile more than a bird. They are totally helpless for some days, and can not stand; but they soon learn to climb. They are fed by the parents by regurgitation of their food, which is the usual way in which the young of most Woodpeckers are fed when first hatched. * * * The young remain in the nest about three weeks. When disturbed they utter a low, purring noise, which reminds me somewhat of that made by bees when swarming, and when a little older they utter a soft "puirr, puirr." Even after leaving the nest they are assiduously cared for by both parents for several weeks, until able to provide for themselves.

Plumages.—The young hairy, like all other young woodpeckers, is hatched naked, and the juvenal plumage is assumed while in the nest, so that when the young birds emerge they are fully fledged. In the juvenal plumage the sexes are sometimes much alike, though oftener there is a decided difference. In both sexes the bill is decidedly smaller, weaker, and more pointed than in the adult; the color pattern is almost exactly like that of the adult, but the plumage is softer and fluffier; the white markings are more or less tinged with yellowish, the two inner primaries are dwarfed, and the innermost white tail feather is usually tipped with black. The colored markings in the crowns of both sexes are very variable in color and in extent. L. L. Snyder (1923) has made a careful study of the crown markings of young hairy and downy woodpeckers of both sexes. He found that 90 percent of the young male hairies had more or less red, pinkish, or yellowish markings in the crowns, and only about 14 percent of the young females were so marked. But only 10 percent of the young males and about 43 percent of the young females had white markings only on a black crown; and about 43 percent of the young females had the entire crown black. There is great individual variation in the amount and in the distribution of these colors; the white spots are often mixed with the other colors; the reddish and yellowish colors may invade nearly the whole crown, exist in one or two large patches, or appear on only a few scattered feathers.

The juvenal plumage is worn but a short time; the molt into the first winter plumage is accomplished between July and October. This first winter plumage is much like that of the adult in both sexes, but the white spots are not quite so pure white, and the red nuchal patch of the male is duller and often interrupted. Adults have a complete postnuptial molt in August and September and perhaps a partial prenuptial molt in spring.

Food.—Various studies of the food habits of the hairy woodpeckers show that these birds are among our most useful birds and especially valuable as protectors of our forest and shade trees and orchards. More than 75 percent of their food consists of injurious insects, while the amount of useful insects and cultivated fruits that they destroy is insignificant. Prof. F. E. L. Beal (1911) has published the most exhaustive report on this subject, based on the study of 382 stomachs collected during every month in the year and from many parts of the range of the species, including practically all of the races. He says: "In the first analysis the food divides into 77.67 percent of animal matter and 22.33 of vegetable. The animal food consists of insects, with a few spiders and millepeds; the vegetable part is made up of fruit, seeds, and a number of miscellaneous substances." Of the animal food, he says: "The largest item in the annual diet of the hairy woodpecker consists of the larvae of cerambycid and buprestid beetles, with a few lucanids and perhaps some other wood borers. These insects constitute over 31 percent of the food and are eaten in every month of the year. * * * One stomach contained 100 of these larvae and 83 and 50, respectively, were taken from two others. Of the 382 stomachs, 204, or 53 percent, contained these grubs, and 27 of them held no other food. Other beetles amount to a little more than 9 percent."

Ants rank second in importance, amounting to a little more than 17 percent, and are taken every month in the year; other Hymenoptera are eaten in very small quantities and irregularly. Caterpillars are the next most important item, many of them wood-boring species, amounting to a little less than 10 percent. "Prof. F. M. Webster states that he has seen a hairy woodpecker successfully peck a hole through the parchment-like covering of the cocoon of a Cecropia moth and devour the contents. On examining more than 20 cocoons in a grove of box elders, he found only 2 uninjured," according to Professor Beal (1911), who adds that bugs (Hemiptera) and plant lice (aphids) form only a small part of the food, and says: "Orthoptera, that is, grasshoppers, crickets, and cockroaches, are rarely eaten by the hairy. A few eggs, probably those of tree crickets, and the egg cases (oötheca) of cockroaches, constitute the bulk of this food. These with a few miscellaneous insects amount to a little more than

2 percent for the year. Spiders with their cocoons of eggs, including one jointed spider (Solpugidae), and a few millepeds, were eaten to the extent of about 3.5 percent, which completes the quota of animal food."

He says further:

The vegetable food of the hairy woodpecker may be considered under four heads: Fruit, grain, seeds, and miscellaneous vegetable substances. Fruit amounts to 5.22 percent of the food, and was contained in 54 stomachs, of which 13 held what was diagnosed as domestic varieties, and 41 contained wild species. Rubus seeds (blackberries or raspberries) were identified in 4 stomachs, and were counted as domestic fruit, but it is perhaps more probable that they were wild. * * * Of wild fruit 18 species were identified. It constitutes the great bulk of the fruit eaten, and is nearly all of varieties not useful to man.

Corn was the only grain discovered in the food. It was found in 10 stomachs, and amounted to 1.37 percent. * * * The seed of poison ivy and poison sumac (*Rhus radicans* and *R. vernix*) were found in 17 stomachs, and as they usually pass through the alimentary canal uninjured, the birds do some harm by scattering the seeds of these noxious plants. * * * Cambium, or the inner bark of trees, was identified in 23 stomachs. Evidently the hairy does but little damage by denuding trees of their bark. Mast, made up of acorns, hazelnuts, and beechnuts, was found in 50 stomachs. It was mostly taken in the fall and winter months, and appears to be quite a favorite food during the cooler part of the year.

Illustrating the quantities of insects eaten by individual birds, F. H. King (1883), Wisconsin, writes: "Of twenty-one specimens examined, eleven had eaten fifty-two wood-boring larvae; five, thirteen geometrid caterpillars; ten, one hundred and five ants; six, ten beetles; two, two cockroaches; two, nine oötheca of cockroaches; two, two moths; one, a small snail; one, green corn; one, a wild cherry; and one, red elder berries. * * * One of the above birds had in its stomach eleven wood-boring larvae (Lamides?) and twelve geometers; another, thirteen larvae of long-horn beetles and four cockroach oötheca; another, nine wood-boring larvae; and two others together had three wood-boring larvae, and nine larvae not coleopterous."

V. A. Alderson (1890) published the following interesting note: "Last summer, potato bugs covered every patch of potatoes in Marathon County, (being my home county,) Wis. One of my friends here, found his patch an exception, and therefore took pains to find the reason, and observed a hairy woodpecker, making frequent visits to the potato field and going from there to a large pine stub a little distance away.

"After observing this for about six weeks, he made a visit to the pine stub and found, on inspection, a large hole in its side about fifteen feet up. He took his axe and cut down the stub, split it open, and found inside, over two bushels of bugs. All had their heads off and bodies intact."

The woodpecker's method of locating tree-boring larvae and its specialized apparatus for extracting them are so well described by Dr. Thomas S. Roberts (1932) that I cannot do better than to quote him, as follows:

The hairy woodpecker possesses in its tongue one of the most remarkably developed and perfectly adapted instruments for extracting the tree larvae from their tunnels. The tip is a rigid, barbed spear and can be thrust out to an astonishing distance by reason of greatly elongated, posterior horns which pass up over the back and top of the head and run together down in front of the right eye, around which they are coiled for almost the entire circumference of the socket! So that, the drilling into the tunnel accomplished, the tongue darts out, the inner ends uncoil, the spear transfixes the grub, and with little ado the larva is dragged from its retreat into the bill of the bird, pounded perhaps for a moment or two, swallowed forthwith or carried to the young, and this most perfectly contrived and highly efficient engine is once more ready for action. There has been considerable discussion as to how the woodpeckers locate the larvae, active or dormant, which are hidden deeply in the wood and for which they drill so unerringly. All the special senses of birds are very highly developed, and it seems probable that in this case hearing, touch, and smell all may play a part. The active grub, as it crunches the wood, makes a sound that would surely be audible to a bird with its keen sense of hearing. The tunnel produces a cavity which would give both a different sound and feeling on tapping over it. Such things as grubs have a strong odor, and it is probable that this plays a part also.

Forbush (1927) says: "Maurice Thompson asserts that the hairy woodpecker strikes its bill into the wood and then holds the point of one mandible for a moment in the dent thus made. He believes that the vibrations produced by the insect in the wood are then conveyed through the beak and skull of the bird to its brain."

In winter this woodpecker comes readily to suet or meat bones hung up on our trees or feeding stations to attract birds. It is also said to feed on the carcasses of animals left in the woods by trappers or hunters and to pick the fat from fresh skins that the trapper has hung up to dry. Although often called a sapsucker, there is practically no evidence that it ever does any injury to trees in this way; any sap or cambium eaten is probably taken incidentally in its search for insects.

Behavior.—The hairy woodpecker is a much shier, more retiring bird than the confiding little downy; it is also more active and noisier; it usually will not allow such close approach but will dodge around the trunk of a tree or fly away, if an intruder comes too near, bounding through the air in a series of graceful dips and rebounds. Rex Brasher (1926) followed one for four hours that alighted "on two hundred and eighteen different trees, an average of nearly one a minute! The longest time he remained on one tree was seven minutes. This was a dead chestnut with most of the bark still adhering. By far the larger proportion of the trees were old chestnuts, and under their loosely attached covering he found most successful hunting. Rough-bark species were preferred—chestnuts, oaks, old maples and hickories, about in the order named. Smooth-barked ones received little notice."

Dr. Morris Gibbs (1902) says: "Have my readers carefully watched a Woodpecker leave its perch on the trunk or limb? The bird throws itself backward from its vertical position by a leg spring, together with a tail movement, turns in the air in the fraction of a second and is sweeping away to the next perch. Arriving at the next resting place it makes a single counteracting stroke of the wings against the air, and perches lightly on the bark of limb or trunk."

Like all woodpeckers, the hairy is an expert climber, perfectly at home on the trunk of a tree, or even on the under side of a branch, where its strong claws enable it to cling in almost any position or to move about with astonishing rapidity and skill in any direction. Its stiff tail feathers act as a prop and help to support it while hammering away at the bark with its powerful beak. Forbush (1927) says that it "is the embodiment of sturdy energy and persistent industry. Active, cheerful, ever busy, its life of arduous toil brings but one reward, a liberal sustenance. It sometimes spends nearly an hour of hard labor in digging out a single borer, but commonly reaches the object of its quest in much less time."

Voice.—The ordinary call of the hairy woodpecker is louder and shriller than that of the downy. Francis H. Allen says, in his notes, that it bears "about the same relation to it as the solitary sandpiper's *peet-weet* does to that of the spotted sandpiper. I hear it most frequently from the female. In fact, a female of the species that visits my place at all times of the year often utters this note continually, as if calling for a mate or claiming territory, but she never nests very near."

Bendire (1895) describes its ordinary note as "a shrill, rattling note, *triii, triii;*" and again as several loud notes uttered on the wing, like *huip, huip.* Forbush (1927) calls the ordinary note "a high, sharp, rather metallic *chink* or *click.*" Aretas A. Saunders (1929) says: "The call is a loud 'keep,' like that of the downy woodpecker, but louder. Another call is a loud rattle, suggesting that of the Kingfisher, but slurring down the scale. Another call, 'kuweek kuweek kuweek kuweek,' is used during the mating season, and suggests the Flicker's 'oweeka.'"

Field marks.—The hairy woodpecker is a large edition of the downy woodpecker, a black and white woodpecker, white below and black above, spotted with white on the wings, and with a broad white stripe down the center of the back. Only the male has the red patch on the back of the neck. It can be distinguished from the downy by its much larger size, its more restless behavior, its relatively longer and larger bill, and by the lateral tail feathers, which are pure white in the hairy and somewhat barred with black in the downy.

Enemies.—B. T. Gault, in his notes from Marshall County, Ill., states: "The hairy woodpecker is now a very rare breeder here owing to the fact that the English sparrow appropriates almost every nest hole as soon as it is excavated. I once saw one of these sparrows enter the hole of one of these birds, take a newly hatched bird out in its bill, flutter for an instant over the water (the nest was in a dead willow snag standing in the overflowed Illinois River bottoms), and drop the young bird into the water to drown. It then returned into the nest and soon appeared with another newly hatched woodpecker in its bill. As it fluttered over the water for an instant, my gun cracked and the sparrow died."

Verdi Burtch (1923) writes: "April 16, 1922, when in a thin wood I heard a female hairy woodpecker making a great fuss as they do when one invades the vicinity of their nest. As I neared the place I saw the nest hole about twenty feet up in an elm stub. About ten feet away, sitting erect on a limb of another tree, was a red squirrel eating something that it held in its fore-paws. My 8-power binoculars showed this to be a naked baby bird, presumably a hairy woodpecker and not more than two or three days old."

Mr. Shelley (1933) tells of a pair of hairy woodpeckers that were twice, in the same season, driven out of their nest by starlings and their eggs destroyed.

Fall.—The hairy woodpecker has often been said to be a permanent resident on its breeding grounds, but this is not strictly true. The species may be present all through the year over much of its range, but there is evidence to indicate a general southward movement in fall; the individuals seen in winter are probably not the same as those seen in summer. Moreover, there is a noticeable increase in numbers in certain localities in winter.

Lewis O. Shelley has sent me some full notes on the migration of hairy woodpeckers, as he has observed it near East Westmoreland, N. H., from which I quote as follows: "For four years I have watched, in the autumn months, passing hairies that go through, some dropping down into the valley to feed as they go along, but others passing over the valley from hill to hill (2 miles) without stopping. In passing through, they traverse in general the same route each year. They come from an eastern and continue on in a western direction at an oblique angle to the Connecticut River, which they must cross in the vicinity of Brattleboro, Vt.

"These migrants usually appear here late in August or early in September and continue to arrive at irregular intervals until late in October. It is common for one, or two, rarely more, to pass together; but such occurrences have happened, as on October 24, 1934, when, beginning soon after noon and lasting until four o'clock, the birds continued to pass through. At least 12 were seen as I walked up a roadway parallel to their course; and other moving birds were heard. It was also noticed that they kept spaced 40 to 50 yards apart, keeping abreast of one another, traversing in a leisurely manner; and as they approached a rock maple woods, the tendency was to close in like passing through the neck of a bottle and, once through the woods, again to spread out. Their progress was rather fast; and they fed little, if at all. They often called, as though to locate each other, since they were keeping about 40 yards apart, as was easily noted when they crossed pasture and mowing land.

"I followed and watched in particular a male that continued keeping along ahead of me. He repeatedly crossed the road in a zigzag manner. Climbing to the top of a fence post or stump, he made lengthy observations, probably noting the progress of the other birds, and often answered their ringing calls. He, as well as the others, gave the appearance of a stranger in a new environment, truly a migrant. I noted how low the birds were passing, quite frequently flying not over 2 feet from the ground over open spaces, where long, bounding flights were made."

L. McI. Terrill told Mr. Forbush (1927) that the few local breeding birds disappear from the vicinity of Montreal early in autumn, and others, in a very noticeable wave, appear toward the end of October or early in November.

Winter.—Aside from the regular migratory movements, the hairy woodpecker is much more given to wandering about in winter. It is apt to forsake its woodland haunts and travel about in search of food, coming frequently into the farmer's orchard, into rural villages, and even into thickly settled communities in some of our larger cities. Here it often joins the merry parties at our winter feeding stations, feeding readily on the suet or scraps of meat provided for our insect-eating birds; and here the smaller birds show due respect for its larger size, or perhaps for its formidable beak, and it is usually allowed to eat alone. It seems to be a solitary bird at this season, for we seldom see more than one at a time. I find it not so constant and regular a visitor to my feeding station as the downy woodpecker and some other birds; it probably wanders about more.

Mr. Forbush (1927) writes: "During the inclement season it is said to require a sheltered place in which to sleep and, like the downy woodpecker, to excavate a hole in a tree for a sleeping chamber, but there is evidence that it does not always seek such shelter, as the late Charles E. Bailey and myself watched one for several winter evenings in a grove, clinging upright against a tree trunk in the usual woodpecker position. Night after night, the bird was there at dusk, remained there until dark, and was there also at daybreak each morning in precisely the same place."

Joseph J. Hickey tells me that, around the lower Hudson River Valley in winter, woodpeckers obtain much of their food by deliberately scaling the bark off trees in search for their insect food. The Arctic three-toed woodpeckers work mainly on pines and hemlocks, but the hairies appear to confine their work to the hemlocks, using the same methods as the three-toed.

DISTRIBUTION

Range.—Northern and Central America; not regularly migratory.

The range of the hairy woodpecker extends **north** to Alaska (Kenai Peninsula, Fairbanks, and Fort Egbert); Yukon (Forty Mile, Fort Reliance, and Macmillan River); Mackenzie (Fort Wrigley, Lake Hardisty, and Fort Resolution); northern Saskatchewan (mouth of the Charlot River and Poplar Point); northern Manitoba (Grand Rapids, probably Fort Churchill, and probably York Factory); Ontario (Hat Island and Cobalt); Quebec (Blue Sea Lake, Quebec City, Godbout, Eskimo Bay, and Anticosti Island); and Newfoundland (Nicholsville and Raleigh). From this point the range extends **southward** along the Atlantic coast to southern Florida (Eau Gallie); the western Bahama Islands (Great Bahama, Abaco, and Andros); and Panama (Boquete). The **southern** boundary of the range extends westward from Panama (Boquete); Nicaragua (San Rafael); western Guatemala (Tecpam); Chiapas (San Cristobal); to Guerrero (Chilpancingo and Omilteme). From this point, **northward** through the mountains of western Mexico, northern Baja California (Sierra San Pedro Martir and Sierra Juarez); and the coastal districts of California, Oregon, Washington, and British Columbia, to Alaska (Chilkoot, Chitina Moraine, and the Kenai Peninsula).

As outlined, the range is for the entire species, which has, however, been so divided that no less than 13 subspecies are currently recognized as occupying the range north of Mexico, while still others occur in Central American countries. The typical eastern hairy woodpecker (*D. v. villosus*), occurs in the Eastern United States and southern Canada west to Manitoba, North Dakota, and Colorado and south to North Caralina and central Texas. The northern hairy woodpecker (*D. v. septentrionalis*) occupies the zone to the north, from southeastern Quebec, northwestward to western Mackenzie, Yukon, and central Alaska. The Newfoundland woodpecker (*D. v. terraenovae*) is found only on the island of that name. The southern hairy woodpecker (*D. v. auduboni*) occupies the southeastern part of the range from Missouri, Illinois, and western Virginia south to southeastern Texas and southern Florida. The Sitka hairy woodpecker (*D. v. sitkensis*) is found in southeastern Alaska and northern British Columbia. The Queen Charlotte woodpecker (*D. v. picoideus*) is found only on the group of islands of that name off the coast of British Columbia. Harris's woodpecker (*D. v. harrisi*) occupies the coastal regions of southern British Columbia south to northwestern California. Cabanis's woodpecker (*D. v. hyloscopus*) is confined to certain coastal and mountain areas of California, chiefly in the southern part. The Lower California hairy woodpecker (*D. v. scrippsae*) is restricted to the Sierra Juarez and the Sierra San Pedro Martir of Baja California. The Modoc woodpecker (*D. v. orius*) is found in the Sierra Nevada of central California north to Oregon and Washington and east to Nevada. The Rocky Mountain hairy woodpecker (*D. v. monticola*) is found through the Rocky Mountain region from central British Columbia south to northern New Mexico and east (in winter) to western South Dakota and Nebraska. The white-breasted woodpecker (*D. v. leucothorectis*) is found chiefly in Arizona and New Mexico but also east to central Texas and north to southern Utah. The Chihuahua woodpecker (*D. v. icastus*) occurs principally in western Mexico but occurs also in southern Arizona and southwestern New Mexico.

Migration.—As stated above, the hairy woodpeckers are generally nonmigratory and may be found in midwinter even in the northern parts of their range, as Alaska, Mackenzie (Fort Simpson), and Manitoba (Aweme, Minnedosa, and Roseau River). Nevertheless, some individuals are given to a certain amount of wandering during the winter months, which explains the occasional records of some subspecies far outside of their normal range. There also is more or less vertical migration in the mountainous regions of the north and west, the birds descending into the lower valleys during the winter season. This is noted particularly in the Rocky Mountain form, which in winter has been taken east to Nebraska and South Dakota.

Despite the fact that during the past 18 years several hundred individuals of this species have been marked with numbered bands, and many have been subsequently recaptured, there is no evidence that any of these moved at any time more than a few miles from the point of banding.

Egg dates.—British Columbia: 8 records, April 27 to June 24.

California: 43 records, March 23 to June 21; 22 records, April 28 to May 29, indicating the height of the season.

Colorado: 10 records, May 5 to June 18.

Florida: 18 records, April 10 to May 16; 9 records, April 22 to 28.

Illinois: 8 records, May 1 to 23.

Iowa: 8 records, April 21 to May 15.

Labrador: 5 records, May 26 to 30.

Massachusetts: 17 records, May 1 to June 5; 9 records, May 10 to 19.

Ontario: 8 records, May 6 to June 16.

DRYOBATES VILLOSUS SEPTENTRIONALIS (Nuttall)

NORTHERN HAIRY WOODPECKER

HABITS

This large northern race of the hairy woodpecker inhabits the Canadian Zone of northern North America, north almost to the limit of trees, from central Alaska and northern Canada southward. In the eastern portions of southern Canada it intergrades with typical *villosus*, and in northwestern Montana with *monticola*, where the ranges of these races meet. Specimens have been taken as far north as Fort Simpson, on the Mackenzie River, in latitude 62° N., and at Fort Reliance, on the upper Yukon River, Alaska, in about latitude 66° N. It may occur as a straggler farther north, where it can find sufficient tree growth, but it is said to be rare north of latitude 56° N., and apparently it does not reach the Arctic coast or the coast of Bering Sea. It is a decidedly larger bird than typical *villosus*, the white markings average rather larger, and the white is purer. In the southern portion of its range, where it begins to intergrade with *villosus*, these characters are, of course, less pronounced and many individuals are difficult to name.

Living in a region over much of which coniferous forests predominate, this woodpecker frequents and breeds in this type of forest. Winton and Donald Weydemeyer (1928) say that it is an abundant permanent resident in Lincoln County, Mont., where it intergrades with *monticola*. They also say:

In the valleys it is most numerous, during summer, in forests containing a large percentage stand of western larch (*Larix occidentalis*). The next trees in attractiveness seem to be Douglas fir (*Pseudotsuga taxifolia*), western yellow pine (*Pinus ponderosa*), and Engelmann spruce (*Picea engelmanni*), in the order named. In the Hudsonian zone it frequents trees of white-bark pine (*Pinus albicaulis*) and alpine larch (*Larix lyallii*). The species is noticeably rare or absent in forests containing nearly pure stands of western white pine (*Pinus monticola*), arborvitae (*Thuja plicata*), or lodgepole pine (*Pinus contorta*), except where the woods have been logged or injured by fire.

Nesting.—The same observers say: "In Lincoln County this species uses a wide variety of nesting sites. Of eight nests included in our records, three were in live aspens; one in a live cottonwood; one in a live larch; one in a dead larch, one in a dead Douglas fir; and one in a woodpecker nesting box."

Ernest Thompson Seton (1890) found a nest in a tall poplar tree about 30 feet from the ground, in Manitoba; the hole was about a foot deep, 3 inches wide inside and 2 inches at the entrance. John Macoun (1909) quotes Rev. C. J. Young as saying: "Most of the nests I have seen have been in wet places or near water, and almost all were in white ash trees, from thirty to fifty feet from the ground. Two nests were in elm trees and one in a telegraph pole by the roadside not more than ten feet from the ground."

Roderick MacFarlane (1908) writes: "On the 6th of May, 1885, Mr. Reid discovered a nest in a hole in a dry standing poplar tree near Fort Providence. There were eight eggs therein, and the parent was seen and shot. * * * At Fort St. James, Stuart's Lake, on the 25th of May, 1889, a native hunter found a nest holding four fresh eggs in a similar position. Both parents in this instance were also observed near by and shot. On 4th June, in the same locality, an Indian girl brought us four eggs. * * * The nest was found in a hole in a dry pine tree, at a height of several feet above the ground."

Henry Mousley (1916) says that near Hatley, Quebec, "as a rule the nest hole is somewhat high up but on one occasion I found one which was only three feet above the ground in a birch stub, containing four eggs, the entrance hole being two inches in diameter, extreme depth eleven inches and average width two and three quarters inches."

P. B. Philipp and B. S. Bowdish (1919), referring to northern New Brunswick, say: "A nest with young was found in a dead maple stub in a burnt barren, on May 29, 1917. On May 30 of the same year another nest about fifteen feet up in a dead maple stub in a similar situation, contained four eggs, very slightly incubated. On June 9, 1917, a third nest in a cedar telephone pole beside a public road was examined. It was at a height of about nine feet; cavity 14½ inches deep; entrance 2⅛ inches in height by 2¼ inches in width. This nest contained four nearly fresh eggs."

Eggs.—The northern hairy woodpecker lays three to five eggs; the eight eggs mentioned above by MacFarlane may have been the product of two females or eggs of the boreal flicker; in the latter case the collector may have shot the wrong parent. The eggs are like those of the eastern hairy woodpecker but average slightly larger. The measurements of 41 eggs average 25.39 by 20.10 millimeters; the eggs showing the four extremes measure 28.45 by 22.10, 27.43 by 22.35, and 21.5 by 16.6 millimeters.

The plumage changes, food, behavior, voice, and other habits apparently do not differ materially from those of its southern relative. It is said to be a permanent resident throughout its range, but there

is probably some southward migration or wandering from at least
the northern portion of its range and perhaps from the southern
parts also. That some individuals remain far north in winter is
shown by the fact that the Fort Simpson specimen was taken on
December 29, 1860. The Weydemeyers (1928) say that during winter, in northwestern Montana, "this woodpecker is commonly found
in mixed broad-leaf and conifer associations along streams, but it is
most abundant at that season in the larch woods of the valleys."

DRYOBATES VILLOSUS AUDUBONI (Swainson)

SOUTHERN HAIRY WOODPECKER

PLATE 5

HABITS

In the Lower Austral Zone of the South Atlantic and Gulf States
we find this small race of the hairy woodpecker. In addition to being
decidedly smaller than its northern relative, the white of the under
parts is less pure, and the white markings of the upper parts are
somewhat smaller.

Arthur H. Howell (1932) says of its haunts in Florida: "The
southern hairy woodpecker, though not particularly shy, prefers the
wilder sections for its home. It occurs in a variety of situations—
the open pine forests, oak hammocks, and the hardwoods of the deep
river swamps. The birds are of a rather solitary disposition, and
rarely is more than a single bird or a pair found near together."

Nesting.—Mr. Howell (1932) says that "the nests are located 12 to
45 feet from the ground in holes excavated in dead oaks or willow
stubs, or in cypresses growing on the edge of a swamp." S. A.
Grimes (1932) says: "A nest thirty feet up in a live cypress near
Eastport [Florida] held three eggs on April 13. Two well feathered
young were found in a hole fifteen feet up in a dead sweet gum in
southern Duval County on May 13. A nest eight feet up in a pine
stub in northern St. Johns County contained three heavily incubated
eggs on May 11."

Arthur T. Wayne (1910) says that in South Carolina "the nest
is very hard to find; indeed I have found but six nests, two which
contained eggs, and four which contained young. I have known
this species to excavate a hole and raise a brood in a limb of a living
live oak tree, but it generally excavates its hole in a dead tree and at
a great height. A set of three fresh eggs was taken April 7, 1898,
from a hole 40 feet from the ground in a dead pine. This hole was
14 inches deep. The young remain in the hole for more than a
month after they are hatched."

Harold H. Bailey (1913) says that in Virginia "dead stubs of gum
and poplar treetops seem to be their favorite location for a nesting

site, varying from 25 to 60 feet up, the cavity from eight to twelve inches deep. They are one of our earliest breeding birds, the drilling of the nesting cavity beginning the last week in March, and by April 10th to 15th finds a full complement or set of eggs, numbering from four to six."

J. G. Suthard writes to me of a nest he found near Madisonville, Ky. The cavity was "excavated in a dead crab apple stub in open woodland. Only the female was observed excavating the hole and caring for the eggs, which proved to be infertile. No male was ever observed near the nesting stub, though it was carefully observed." M. G. Vaiden tells me of a nest 9 feet up in a chinaberry tree in a yard at Rosedale, Miss., and another that was 23 feet up in a pecan tree and 3 feet out in a dead snag.

Eggs.—The southern hairy woodpecker is said to lay three to six eggs. The latter number must be unusual, as the set generally consists of three or four eggs. The eggs are scarcely distinguishable from those of other hairy woodpeckers, though they average somewhat smaller than those of the more northern races. The measurements of 42 eggs average 21.29 by 18.29 millimeters; the eggs showing the four extremes measure **26.1** by 19.2, 25.8 by **19.8, 21** by 19, and 23.8 by **16.6** millimeters.

Food.—Major Bendire (1895) says that this subspecies seems to be fonder of fruit and berries than are the northern races and that "the young are fed largely on figs." Audubon (1842) says that in the salt marshes about the mouths of the Mississippi "it alights against the stalks of the largest and tallest reeds, and perforates them as it is wont to bore into trees. * * * I have often observed it clinging to the stalks of the sugar-cane, boring them, and apparently greatly enjoying the sweet juices of that plant; and when I have seen it, in severe winter weather, attempting to bore the dried stalks of maize, I have thought it expected to find in them something equally pleasing to its taste."

Milton P. Skinner (1928) says of these birds, in the sandhills of North Carolina: "In winter the hairy woodpeckers vary their diet of insects with various berries and dried wild fruits. They are particularly fond of the small black berries of the sour gum (*Nyssa silvatica*). Soon after the early frosts the birds flock to these swamp trees and feast as long as the berries last."

The main food supply of this and other woodpeckers consists of insects and their larvae, which are obtained by searching in the crevices in the bark of whatever trees are available, or drilling into the trunks and branches to find the grubs. Mr. Skinner (1928) saw one working on "a charred and dead stub of a shrub oak. Here it worked steadily for fifteen minutes pulling out small white grubs and borers. It drove its bill for three or four strokes up under a bit of bark and then pried the bark off with its bill as a lever. Then it attacked the semi-rotten wood so uncovered, directly. It did not seem to work so fast as a downy woodpecker, but then it was so busy eating grubs that it did not have to dig much."

Behavior.—The same observer says:

They do not show a preference for any one kind of tree but are found on both living and dead shrub oaks, long-leafed pines, loblolly pine, sycamore, sour gum and sweet gum. They work on both trunks and limbs but usually at low heights, from the ground up to twenty feet above. On a vertical surface these birds work up, spiraling it and tapping it as they go. They move by a series of short hops, propping themselves each time with their tails. When hopping lightly along a horizontal limb they still use their tails as props. Perhaps their most astonishing feat is to spiral horizontal limbs, and to cling beneath them and hammer them with their backs down. Sometimes they work their way up to the very tip of slender shoots.

Even in a heavy wind they cling to the violently swaying twigs while eating, but they stay only a short time before flying to a tree trunk to perch and rest before trying it again. * * *

The flight of these birds is strong and undulating, with fast beating wings, and generally only from one tree to the next. Where the trees are not very close together, they swoop down to within a few feet of the ground and then fly with nearly level flight until they glide up to their next stopping place. Where they have to fly out across intervening open fields their flight becomes more undulatory, at times deeply so.

DRYOBATES VILLOSUS HARRISI (Audubon)

HARRIS'S WOODPECKER

PLATES 4, 5

HABITS

The range of this well-marked subspecies is now restricted to the humid coast belt from southern British Columbia southward to Humboldt County, Calif. In 1895, Bendire wrote:

Until within the last few years all the Hairy Woodpeckers from the eastern slopes of the Rocky Mountains to the Pacific coast have been considered as belonging to this subspecies. * * *

The breeding range of this race, as now considered, is a very limited one, and is probably coextensive with its geographical distribution. It is apparently confined to the immediate vicinity of the coast, and is not found at any great distance inland. Among the specimens collected by me at Fort Klamath, Oregon (mostly winter birds), there are two which might be called intermediates between this and the more recently separated *Dryobates villosus hyloscopus*, but the majority are clearly referable to the latter. In the typical Harris's woodpecker the under parts are much darker, a smoky brown, in fact; it is also somewhat larger and very readily distinguishable from the much lighter-colored and somewhat smaller Cabanis's woodpecker.

Dawson and Bowles (1909) say: "Doctor Cooper judged the Harris to be the most abundant Woodpecker in Western Washington; and this, with the possible exception of the Flicker (*Colaptes cafer saturatior*), is still true. The bird ventures well out upon the eastern slopes of the Cascade Mountains, and is found sparingly in the higher mountain valleys; but its favorite resorts are burns and the edges of clearings, rather than the depths of the woods."

Johnson A. Neff (1928) quotes Dr. I. N. Gabrielson as saying: "The Harris woodpecker is found throughout western Oregon from the western slope of the Cascades to the coast, altho in the Rogue River Valley some specimens which are close to 'orius' have been taken. I have one labeled 'orius' by Dr. H. C. Oberholser, also have typical Harris from this district, so that this is probably the region of inter-gradation between these two forms."

Harris's woodpecker, like many other races of the humid Northwest coast region, is darkly colored, one of the most easily recognized of all the hairy woodpeckers. Even in Audubon's day it was recognized, described, figured, and named by him in honor of his friend Edward Harris. Ridgway (1914) describes it as "similar to *D. v. hyloscopus*, but under parts (including lateral rectrices) light drab or buffy drab-gray, instead of white or nearly white, the head-stripes and stripe on back also usually more or less suffused with the same color, often uniformly light drab; average size slightly larger."

Courtship.—Theed Pearse (1934) gives us the following interesting description of the courtship display of this woodpecker:

There were two males on the limb of a small cedar and my attention was first drawn to them by their note, which is very similar to the flicker's "wickety" note but softer, and might almost be described as "caressingly soft." Both birds were calling.

The displaying bird would draw in its head so that no neck was apparent, with beak pointed outwards and upwards and would then slowly swing the upper part of the body from side to side, thereby bringing into play the red nape marking. Once the bird very rapidly lifted its wings into an upright position, at other times there was a quivering flicking motion of the wings as they lay against the sides.

The two birds flew to another branch, settling side by side and instantly each froze, the neck drawn in and the beak pointed upwards. They were perched sideways on the branch and were displaying the white markings in the tail which each of them would slightly spread and turn out (to one side). The feathers of the back were at the same time hunched up as though to show up the white markings there also. They did this several times before flying off together.

Nesting.—Although this is evidently a common bird within its restricted range, surprisingly little has appeared in print regarding its nesting habits. Authentic eggs seem to be very rare in collections; most of the eggs in collections, of which I have the records, that are labeled *harrisi*, prove to be referable to one of the neighboring sub-species.

D. E. Brown writes to me:

Its nesting cavities may be at any height from 4 feet to well over 100 feet from the ground. I found a nest 8 feet up in an 8-inch dead fir stub in a dry open locality. The female flushed from the nest, and the date was just right for fresh eggs, May 6. The cavity was carefully opened. It was 16 inches deep and contained a single egg. This egg was so fresh and the shell so clear that the yolk could be plainly seen. The cavity was carefully repaired with bark from the stub, held in place with black thread. Both birds were near all this time, complaining loudly. I returned in five days. The bark was still in place, but the egg was gone. The dust from the decaying stub, where the egg had been, was very dry, and I am of the opinion that the parent bird had removed the egg.

G. D. Sprot has sent me a beautiful photograph (pl. 4) of a nesting site of this woodpecker in a dead alder stump in a coniferous forest clearing, near Mill Bay, Vancouver Island, taken May 23, 1928.

Dawson and Bowles (1909) say:

The nest of this bird is usually placed well up in a small dead fir tree in some burn or slashing on dry ground. It is about ten inches deep and has no lining save fine chips, among which the crystal white eggs, four or five in number, lie partially imbedded. Incubation is begun from the last week in April to the last week in May, according to altitude, and but one brood is raised in a season. These Woodpeckers are exceptionally valiant in defense of their young, the male in particular becoming almost beside himself with rage at the appearance of an enemy near the home nest.

S. F. Rathbun sends me the following note on a Harris's woodpecker that made an attempt to dig a nesting hole in a small young fir topped about 10 feet up: "The tree had been cut off so that it could be used as one of the supports of a cross piece to which a swing was attached. The woodpecker began to dig a hole in the topped upright, and the owner of the place called me up and wanted to know what the bird was and what it was up to. I told him all about it and suggested that he keep away from the stub. Two weeks later, I asked him how the bird was getting on. He said at first the bird was busy digging away every day, but of late seemed to have something the matter with it, for 'lately every day it just sat with its head sticking out of the hole and did no work on it.' I cut a piece from the edge of the entrance and quickly found out. When the crossbar for the swing had been nailed to the sapling, a 10-inch spike was used to hold it; and this had gone nearly through the sapling. The woodpecker ran into this spike, as it was digging the hole, after progressing 6 inches or so downward. It did not seem able to go around the spike, although it had enlarged the cavity an inch on each side of the heavy nail and had cut away the wood for 2 inches or more below the spike. But the job proved to be too much for the bird, and it eventually gave up and disappeared. I told my friend to pull the spike and maybe next year the bird would be back. He followed my suggestion, and, the following spring, a Harris's woodpecker showed up, dug a hole in the stub, and raised its young. This was repeated the next spring after, and then no return of the bird. So quite likely it may have been the same woodpecker."

Eggs.—Harris's woodpecker apparently lays four or five eggs, probably seldom fewer or more. Bendire (1895) was evidently unable to locate any properly identified eggs of this race, and I have not fared much better. The eggs are probably indistinguishable from the eggs of other hairy woodpeckers of similar size. The measurements of 34 eggs average 25.29 by 18.91 millimeters; the eggs showing the four extremes measure **27.9** by 19.6, 25.46 by **20.32, 22.86** by 18.29, and 23.5 by **17.5** millimeters.

Food.—J. A. Neff (1928) says:

A total of 57 stomachs of hairy woodpeckers were taken for the present study, over three fourths of them of the Harris type. The months were represented by fairly even numbers of specimens. Analysis of these stomachs shows a considerable variation from the results of Professor Beal's California studies. The total animal food averaged 82.00 percent, while vegetable matter made up the other 18.00 percent. * * *

The larvae of wood-boring beetles, Cerambycids and Buprestids, composed 49.00 percent of the total. This total is unexceeded in Federal studies of birds. Since these two groups of borers include species doing enormous damage to both forest and ornamental trees, as well as to orchards, this item of food alone almost settles the question of the utility of having woodpeckers. * * *

The vegetable food was of little value economically. Fruits, of small wild varieties, totaled 6.00 percent, and seeds, mostly of coniferous trees, averaged 12.00 percent.

Behavior.—Taylor and Shaw (1927) made the following interesting observation:

As is well known, western Washington is a region of copious rainfall. During the frequent downpours one can not help speculating on the manner in which the different birds and mammals avoid injury from the damp and chill of the storm. The thick foliage of firs and hemlocks is well suited, in many instances, to serve as a thatched roof; and in the deep woods there are many big branches and large logs under which birds—and mammals too—find dry retreats. During the heaviest rain of the summer a Harris woodpecker was frightened from its shelter beneath a huge log in the heavy forest of Tahoma Creek Canyon. Here the bird was keeping perfectly dry. One can imagine its displeasure at being driven out from its comfortable refuge into the drenching rain.

Winter.—D. E. Brown says in his notes: "Early in fall Harris's woodpecker very often excavates a cavity that is its winter home. It can be found there every night and quite often in the daytime on stormy days. It is not always secure in this retreat. Such a cavity was made in a partly dead stub, about 20 feet high, just back of my house. Frequent visits were made to find out how much the nest was used. At first the bird, a male, would fly to a nearby tree when I rapped on the stub, but soon it contented itself with just coming to the opening. One time, while I was in plain sight of the stub, a western pileated woodpecker alighted at the cavity and proceeded to open it up, which it did clear to the bottom in less than three minutes. It had taken the Harris about a week to dig it out."

Dawson and Bowles (1909) say: "The Harris woodpecker visits the winter troupes only in a patronizing way. He is far too restless and independent to be counted a constant member of any little gossip club, and, except briefly during the mating season and in the family circle, he is rarely to be seen in the company of his own kind."

DRYOBATES VILLOSUS HYLOSCOPUS Cabanis and Heine

CABANIS'S WOODPECKER

HABITS

The hairy woodpeckers of the coast district of California from Mendocino County southward, the mountains of southern California, and the southern Sierra Nevada, as far east as White Mountains of California, are now known by the above name. This race is somewhat smaller than *harrisi* and decidedly smaller than *orius*, its neighboring races to the northward; its under parts are much lighter colored than in *harrisi*; these parts are described by Ridgway (1914) as "dull grayish or brownish white or pale drab-grayish or buffy grayish." This and the Sierra woodpecker (*orius*) seem to form connecting links between the dark-breasted *harrisi* and the white-breasted Rocky Mountain forms, *monticola* and *leucothorectis*, both of which are decidedly larger also.

Dr. Joseph Grinnell (1908) says of the distribution of this woodpecker in the San Bernardino Mountains in southern California: "This was the most widely distributed species of woodpecker in the region, occurring throughout the timbered portions, irrespective of zones. It was common from Santa Ana Cañon to the summit of Sugarloaf, 9,800 feet, and nearly to timber line on San Gorgonio peak. On the desert side the species was noted as low as Cactus Flat, 6,000 feet, where one was seen in some golden oaks in a ravine, August 16, 1905."

Courtship.—The drumming of woodpeckers in the spring on some resonant limb or tree trunk is an important part of the courtship urge, as a warning to any rival, or as a call to a possible mate. Dr. Grinnell (1908) shows how the manner of drumming may also serve as a recognition call; he says: "The resonant rattling drum identified this species from any other of this region. Near Dry lake, 9,000 feet altitude, dead tamarack pines were selected for this purpose, and on June 23, 1905, I listened for many minutes to a remarkable demonstration of this kind. Different branches were tattoed in rapid succession, so that a xylophone-like variety of tones was produced, very impressive and far-carrying through the otherwise quiet forest."

Nesting.—Major Bendire (1895) writes:

In California Cabanis' Woodpecker is common in the mountains, but in the lowlands in the southern part of this State Mr. F. Stephens considers it a rather rare summer resident. He found it breeding in a cottonwood tree, near San Bernardino, on March 21, 1885. Mr. Lyman Belding took several nests of this subspecies in Calaveras County, in the Sierra Nevadas; in one, found on June 6, 1879, which had been excavated in a dead pine stump, 12 feet from the ground, the eggs, three in number, were on the point of hatching. In his notes he says: "I scared the female from it and prevented her return by inserting a stick, the end of which protruded for several feet. When she found she could not enter she gave several cries, which brought the male, who hopped up and down the stick a few times, striking it with his bill and screaming angrily, pausing occasionally, and apparently deliberating on the best method of extracting it." Another nest, found by him on July 10, 1880, was located only 3 feet from the ground, and contained young which were still in the nest on the 20th. Mr. Charles A. Allen informs me that along the Sacramento River, in California, it breeds in sycamores and willows, but that it is not common there.

Eggs.—Major Bendire (1895) says:

The number of eggs laid to a set varies from three to six; those of four are by far the most common; sets of five are only occasionally met with, while sets of six are very unusual. * * * The eggs lie on the fine chips left in the bottom of the cavity, and are occasionally well packed into these, so that only about one-half of the egg is visible. They resemble the eggs of *Dryobates villosus* in color, but those of an elliptical ovate shape are more common than the oval and elliptical ovals, averaging, therefore, more in length, while there is proportionally less difference in their short diameter.

The measurements of 23 eggs average 24.49 by 18.38 millimeters; the eggs showing the four extremes measure 25.7 by 18.2, 24.2 by 19.7, 22.8 by 18.1, and 24.9 by 16.5 millimeters.

Young.—Mrs. Irene G. Wheelock (1904) says: "Both sexes share the labors of excavating, brooding the eggs, and feeding the young. Incubation lasts about fifteen days, and the young remain nearly four weeks in the nest, being fed most of that time by regurgitation. After leaving they are fed by the parents for at least two weeks, and usually return to the nest at night to sleep."

Food.—W. Leon Dawson (1923) writes: "Nearly half of the Cabanis Woodpecker's food consists of the larvae of wood-boring beetles (the *Cerambycidae* and *Buprestidae*); and of the remainder the caterpillars of various injurious moths form a large per cent. Wild raspberries and blackberries are eaten in summer, and certain hardy fruits, such as cornel berries, acorns, and the pits of the islay, or evergreen cherry (*Prunus ilicifolia*), eke out the winter sustenance."

Referring to its manner of feeding, Milton P. Skinner says in his notes: "On August 10, 1933, I saw a Cabanis working on both the trunk and the limbs of a small Douglas fir. It worked all around a horizontal limb and really seemed to be under the limb more than above. It also worked on upright branches as well. I have also seen a Cabanis feeding on the bark of a lodgepole pine. One day I found one on a dead black oak, scaling off dead bark to get at the insects beneath. So far as I can tell, these birds, in the Sequoia National Park, seem to prefer to pick food from the surface and furrows in the bark, and do not bore into the bark and wood as much as other woodpeckers. During my work among the Big Trees, I noticed that these birds seem to avoid the sequoia's bark; but at one place I found a living tree with many holes bored in the old wood of its charred base, where it was unprotected by bark."

Behavior.—Mr. Skinner's notes say that "this woodpecker has quite a few mannerisms of its own. One, seen flying across a meadow, went first to the limbs of Douglas firs, then to a small dead limb of a sequoia, then to the limb of a fir, and then to the trunk of the same fir. It perched lengthwise of limb and trunk each time. And this procedure was followed again and again on different days. Usually the Cabanis perches crosswise on a horizontal limb, especially when resting or preening, but lengthwise on erect, or nearly erect, trunks and limbs when feeding.

"Although this woodpecker almost always flies to the exact spot it selects, its flight through the forest is undulatory. The undulations are due to the fact that it progresses by a series of wing beats. At the end of each series, it seems to actually close its wings and shoot forward with the impetus gained."

DRYOBATES VILLOSUS MONTICOLA Anthony

ROCKY MOUNTAIN HAIRY WOODPECKER

HABITS

This large, white-breasted hairy woodpecker inhabits the Rocky Mountain region, in the Canadian and Transition Zones, from central British Columbia and Montana southward to eastern Utah and northern New Mexico, and eastward to western South Dakota and western Nebraska. Ridgway (1914) characterizes it as "similar, in large size and whiteness of under parts, to *D. v. septentrionalis*, but with white spots on wing-coverts much reduced in size or number, or altogether wanting." It evidently intergrades with *septentrionalis* in Montana and Wyoming and probably with the more western races west of the Rocky Mountains.

Milton P. Skinner tells me that in the Yellowstone National Park it "occurs at all elevations from the lowest at 5,500 feet to timberline at 9,500 feet above sea level, but never far from a tree of some kind. It is a resident bird here but moves down from the mountain heights at the approach of winter."

Aretas A. Saunders (1921) says of its status in Montana: "A common permanent resident throughout the western half of the state in the mountains. Winters mainly in the valleys in cottonwood groves, but does not breed there. * * * The eastern limits of its range are evidently in the eastern foothills of the mountains. Just what form breeds in the more eastern mountain ranges is not definitely determined. In the mountains this bird has been recorded by all observers. It is common everywhere, and usually the commonest of the mountain woodpeckers."

Nesting.—The following remarks by Major Bendire (1895), under *hyloscopus*, evidently refer to this subspecies: "Mr. Denis Gale found it breeding in Boulder County, Colorado, on May 28, 1886, in a live aspen tree, at an altitude of about 8,500 feet. The nest contained five eggs, in which incubation was somewhat advanced. Mr. William G. Smith also reports it as common in Colorado, coming down into the valleys in winter. He says it is the earliest of the Woodpeckers to breed, that it commences nesting in the latter part of April, and usually excavates its holes in old dead pines, frequently at a considerable distance from the ground, and that he has seen full-grown young by June 1."

J. K. Jensen (1923) says of this woodpecker, in northern Santa Fe County, N. Mex.:

Quite common in the Sangre de Cristo Mountains, from 8,000 to 11,000 feet. June 21, 1920, I found a nest thirty feet up in a large quaking aspen. This tree stands on the edge of a place where an avalanche has plowed its way down through the timber on the mountain side, depositing trees and rocks in a great heap for hundreds of feet around the tree. The nest contained young, and judging from the noise they made, were quite well developed. The parent birds were very noisy.

May 22, 1921, I made my way through four feet of snow to the same tree. A new nest had been made, and the female flew off when I was about 150 feet away. I cut into the nest and found a set of four eggs on which incubation had just commenced. The altitude at this point is 11,000 feet. May 26, 1922, I found a nest with young about seventy-five feet up in an aspen. This was in Santa Fe Canyon at an altitude of 8,000 feet.

Eggs.—The eggs of the Rocky Mountain hairy woodpecker are similar to the eggs of other hairy woodpeckers of similar size. The measurements of 33 eggs average 24.89 by 18.49 millimeters; the eggs showing the four extremes measure 28.08 by 18.03, 27.0 by 20.1, 23.37 by 17.78, and 24.38 by 17.27 millimeters.

Food.—Mr. Skinner says, in his notes, that this woodpecker "seeks its food on the trunks of lodgepole and *flexilis* pines, cedars, firs, aspens, willows, and even electric-light and telephone poles; it prefers dead and diseased trees and stubs to work on, probably because of more borers and grubs. At Basin, and over 7,000 feet elevation, I found a female where I could watch her, only 5 feet away from the lodgepole trunk on which she was working. She worked down, tapping here and there as she went. Whenever a tap revealed a borer, she scaled off the bark with quick right and left strokes, having a slight lever motion at the end, and always secured from one to six bark-borer grubs. Evidently the tap told her whether it was worth while to search further, for she never made a mistake and performed no useless labor."

J. A. Munro (1930) writes: "During the winter of 1928–29 a male hairy woodpecker frequently was seen feeding on Virginia creeper berries in competition with several red-shafted flickers. On one occasion the same bird visited an apple tree, attracted by a few apples that still clung to the bare branches. Standing crossways on a branch, in the ordinary position of a perching bird, he rapidly stabbed his bill downward into the top of an apple. After doing this several times he flew to another portion of the tree and repeated the performance."

DRYOBATES VILLOSUS PICOIDEUS Osgood

QUEEN CHARLOTTE WOODPECKER

HABITS

Dr. Wilfred H. Osgood (1901) described the hairy woodpecker of the Queen Charlotte Islands, as a full species, *Dryobates picoideus.* He says it can be distinguished from all other members of the *villosus* group by the black markings on the back and characterizes it as "similar in general to *Dryobates v. harrisi;* bill slightly smaller; middle of back barred and spotted with black; flanks streaked with black." He says that this woodpecker is not abundant on the islands; during a period of over a month spent in active collecting he saw only six, all of which were collected.

I cannot find that anything has been published on the habits of the Queen Charlotte woodpecker, which probably do not differ essentially from those of *harrisi*, to which it is closely related and which inhabits a similar, humid coast environment. There are a number of skins of this race in various collections, but, so far as I know, no authentic eggs have ever found their way into any American collection. Very little exploration has been done in the interior of the Queen Charlotte Islands, and we know very little about the habits of its birds.

DRYOBATES VILLOSUS TERRAENOVAE Batchelder

NEWFOUNDLAND WOODPECKER

HABITS

Charles F. Batchelder (1908), who discovered and described this race of the hairy woodpecker, characterized it as—

Similar to typical *Dryobates villosus*, but slightly larger, the black areas of the upper parts increased, the white areas reduced both in number and in size, especially in the remiges and wing coverts. * * * *Dryobates villosus terraenovae* is much smaller than *D. v. leucomelas*, and is, of course, even more remote from it in coloring than from true *villosus*. Between it and *D. v. hyloscopus* and *D. v. monticola* there is a striking resemblance in coloring, but the wide area—occupied throughout its extent either by *villosus* or by *leucomelas*—that intervenes between the ranges of these two Western subspecies and that of *terraenovae*, precludes the possibility of immediate intergradation, while the utter dissimilarity of the climatic conditions of their respective habitats forbids the supposition that like causes in environment have developed like characters; apparently this is a case where superficial resemblances have arisen entirely independently of climatic influences.

I found the Newfoundland woodpecker fairly common in the heavily timbered valleys of the Fox Island and Sandy Rivers in Newfoundland in 1912. The timber in the flat river bottom and on the islands in the Fox Island River is almost wholly made up of deciduous trees, mainly poplar, canoe birch, ash, mountain ash (which grows to a very large size), and alder, mixed with a few spruces. On the surrounding hillsides the forest growth consists mainly of firs and spruces, with plenty of canoe and yellow birches, poplars, larches, and mountain ashes. The Sandy River runs through a fairly level and heavily timbered region, with forests of large firs, red, white, and black spruces, mixed with some birches and poplars. These two regions were the only places where we found this and the downy woodpecker, nesting in the deciduous trees. It has been observed by others in other places, and doubtless it occurs wherever there is heavy timber, with a fair sprinkling of deciduous trees, mainly along the streams and about the shores of lakes.

I can find nothing noted on its habits that is in any way different from those of the other eastern races. So far as I know, its eggs have never been taken.

DRYOBATES VILLOSUS ICASTUS Oberholser

CHIHUAHUA WOODPECKER

PLATE 6

HABITS

The hairy woodpeckers of the Canadian and Transition Zones in the mountains of northwestern Mexico, southern Arizona, and southern New Mexico are referable to this race. In describing and naming it, Dr. H. C. Oberholser (1911a) characterized it as "similar to *Dryobates villosus hyloscopus*, but bill much smaller, and wing slightly longer. * * * This bird is decidedly smaller than *Dryobates villosus leucothorectis*, as well as noticeably smoky-tinged on the under surface, instead of pure white; and it is in size so very much inferior to *Dryobates villosus orius*, that it is readily distinguishable."

Harry S. Swarth (1904) says of the haunts of this woodpecker in the Huachuca Mountains, Arizona: "Fairly abundant in the higher parts of the mountains, from 7,000 feet upward. They may be seen almost anywhere in that region, but for breeding purposes, seem to particularly favor the dense thickets of quaking asp." In 1922, Frank C. Willard and I found them breeding mainly among the tall pines near the summit of these mountains, above 7,500 feet. From here to the summit, about 9,000 feet, the land is rolling, mostly in gentle slopes, and covered with a fine, open, parklike forest of tall pines of two or three species, many of them from 80 to 100 feet high. The many dead, standing trees and stumps offered suitable nesting sites for pygmy nuthatches, Mexican creepers, and Chihuahua woodpeckers. We did not see any of these woodpeckers in the spruce and fir belt, below 7,000 feet.

Nesting.—On May 7, 1922, in the pine region near the summit of the Huachuca Mountains, described above, we located two pairs of Chihuahua woodpeckers and saw some new excavations in the dead pine stubs, in which they seemed to be preparing to nest, but they evidently had not yet laid their eggs. On May 15 we returned and found two of the nests occupied (pl. 6). The first nest was about 40 feet from the ground in a dead pine stub at an elevation of about 7,900 feet; the cavity was about 15 inches deep and contained four fresh eggs. Farther up, near the summit, at about 8,500 feet, we found the second nest; this was only about 15 feet up in a large dead pine, in a hole we had previously passed by as an old one; but we saw the female enter the hole and stay there, so we chopped it out and found three heavily incubated eggs in a cavity about 12 inches deep. Frank C. Willard (1918) tells of a pair of these woodpeckers that "had nested for several seasons in the dead top of a tall pine. One winter, this broke off and lodged in the top of an adjoining pine. Even with their nest site in this apparently insecure position the woodpeckers were unwilling to leave it, and their new nest was found dug in the same old tree top in its inverted position."

Eggs.—The eggs of the Chihuahua woodpecker do not differ materially from those of other hairy woodpeckers of similar size. The measurements of three eggs in the author's collection are 24.6 by 17.2, 24.5 by 17.7, and 24.6 by 18.0 millimeters.

Winter.—Mr. Swarth (1904) says: "They do not seem to remain through the winter months; at any rate I saw none during February, 1903 nor did any appear until March 17, when I secured two and saw one other. Ten days later they were quite abundant. The winter of 1902–1903 was quite cold, with a great deal of snow on the ground, and it is possible that with a milder winter they might remain the year through. There does not seem to be any vertical migration on the part of this woodpecker, for I saw none below 7,000 feet, and but very few as low as that." Bendire (1895), however, writes: "In southern Arizona it does not appear to breed in the lower valleys, but I have shot several near Tucson in winter."

DRYOBATES VILLOSUS SITKENSIS Swarth

SITKA HAIRY WOODPECKER

HABITS

In the coast region of southeastern Alaska and northern British Columbia we find a race that Harry S. Swarth (1911b) says, in describing and naming it, "differs from *D. v. harrisi* mainly in the very much paler, less smoky hue of the lower parts, and the more buffy coloration of the nasal tufts. Somewhat like *D. v. picoideus*, but paler colored below, and lacking the barred rectrices of that race." He says elsewhere (1922):

Sitkensis, in its relatively light ventral coloration, is intermediate between the extremely dark *harrisi* and the white-breasted *monticola*. The dark-breasted type of coloration reaches its extreme development in *picoideus* of the Queen Charlotte Islands, interposed between the ranges of *harrisi* and *sitkensis*. Thus, while specimens of *sitkensis* as laid out in trays may be arranged to illustrate a step between *harrisi* and *monticola*, the geographical distribution of the several forms is not in accordance with this idea. The geographical chains appear to lie as follows: Starting with the white-breasted races of the interior of the northwest, *septentrionalis* and *monticola*, there is an extension westward on the coast of a slightly darker breasted race, *sitkensis*. Starting again with the dark breasted type, *harrisi*, of the Puget Sound region, and going northward, we reach the extremely dark colored *picoideus*. Thus, *sitkensis* and *harrisi* are really far apart genetically, and the appearance of *sitkensis* as a seeming intergrade between *monticola* and *harrisi* must be explained on grounds other than those of such actual intermediate relationship. *Sitkensis*, as an offshoot of the white-breasted type of the interior, may have arrived at the humid coast at too recent date to be yet affected by its surroundings to the extent that *harrisi* and *picoideus* have been; or it may be more resistant to such an environment. In either case the slight modification of the clear white breast of *monticola* produced by the humid surroundings would result in an apparent intergrade toward *harrisi*.

On the habits of this subspecies, which probably do not differ materially from those of other hairy woodpeckers, I can find only the following brief comment by Joseph Dixon, quoted by Dr. Joseph Grinnell (1909): "At the three lakes back of Mole Harbor I saw more of these birds than at all other places put together. Their slow drumming sounded so similar to the clicking of a telegraph instrument that we dubbed them 'telegraph woodpeckers' to distinguish them from the sapsuckers." So far as I know, the nest of this woodpecker has never been reported. It is probably resident throughout its breeding range.

DRYOBATES VILLOSUS ORIUS Oberholser

MODOC WOODPECKER

HABITS

This race of the hairy woodpecker occupies a rather extensive range in the interior of California, Oregon, and Washington, west of the range of *monticola* in the Rocky Mountains, north of the range of *hyloscopus* in southern California, and east of the range of *harrisi* in the above States. As might be expected, it is more or less intermediate in size or coloration between the surrounding races. Dr. H. C. Oberholser (1911a), who described and named it, characterized it as "resembling *Dryobates villosus leucothorectis*, but larger; lower parts usually brownish white, instead of pure white."

Grinnell and Storer (1924) say of its haunts in the Yosemite region: "As with most of the allied forms, the present race ranges through several life zones, from the scattered digger pines at Pleasant Valley eastward through the main forest belt to the sparse tracts of Jeffrey pines in the vicinity of Mono Lake. It is nowhere really common, even for a woodpecker; it reaches its greatest numbers in the upper part of the Transition Zone and in the Canadian Zone."

In the Lassen Peak region, according to Grinnell, Dixon, and Linsdale (1930), "this woodpecker foraged over the trunks and larger limbs of many kinds of trees both in the forests proper and where there were a few trees or restricted tracts of trees in the mainly unforested parts of the section. Much of each bird's time was spent on coniferous trees, either living or dead ones, but nesting excavations were many of them in trunks of deciduous trees."

Bendire (1895) says that, at Fort Klamath, Oreg., "it appears to be especially abundant in tracts in which the timber has been killed by fire, and where many of the slowly rotting trunks still remain standing. Such burnings are frequently met with in the mountains, and seem to attract several species of Woodpeckers, presumably on account of the abundance of suitable food to be found."

Courtship.—Grinnell and Storer (1924) say: "At Chinquapin, on May 19, 1919, a pair of these woodpeckers was seen going through their courting antics. A male was in a large yellow pine at the edge of a logged-over area, calling almost incessantly. His usual *speenk* had become *spenk-ter-ter-ter*, a staccato run repeated every few seconds. The female answered in like voice but uttered the trill less often. The male changed his location many times, and after protracted calling on his part, the female flew to the same tree."

Nesting.—Bendire (1895) writes:

I took my first nest near Camp Harney, Oregon, on May 29, 1875, in a canyon on the southern slopes of the Blue Mountains, at an altitude of about 5,000 feet. The cavity was excavated in the main trunk of a nearly dead aspen, about 12 feet from the ground. The entrance hole was about 1¾ inches in diameter, and the cavity about 9 inches deep. It contained four much incubated eggs. The female was in the hole, and stayed there looking out until I had struck the tree several times with a hatchet, when she flew off and alighted on one of the limbs of the tree, uttering cries of distress, which brought the male, who was still more demonstrative, hopping from limb to limb, squealing and scolding at me and pecking at the limbs on which he perched. At Fort Klamath, Oregon, it was somewhat more common, and here I took several of its nests. * * * Dead or badly decayed trees are preferred to live ones for nesting purposes, and deciduous trees to conifers; it also nests occasionally in firs and madrone trees.

Milton P. Skinner says, in his notes, that "in the Yosemite National Park, one nested in a living willow trunk about ten feet above the ground." Grinnell, Dixon, and Linsdale (1930) say that, in the Lassen Peak region, "aspens and cottonwoods, dead at core, seemed to be preferred nesting trees, although other kinds were also used. Nest holes, when in conifers, were made in dead and decaying trunks or stubs."

Eggs.—Three or four eggs make up the usual set for this woodpecker. They are indistinguishable from the eggs of other hairy woodpeckers, though Bendire (1895) says that "those of an elliptical ovate shape are more common than the oval and elliptical ovals." The measurements of 15 eggs average 24.70 by 18.80 millimeters; the eggs showing the four extremes measure 26.4 by 20.6 and 21.5 by 16.2 millimeters.

Young.—Grinnell, Dixon, and Linsdale (1930) write: "Near Eagle Lake Resort on June 12, 1929, an adult was feeding a nestful of young woodpeckers in a cavity three meters up in a yellow-pine stub close to the lake. The nest hole had been freshly cut. Only the female was seen to carry food. The young were large enough to be fed without the parent entirely entering the cavity. When the observer walked near the nest stub the parent became much excited and flew about calling loudly for several minutes. The young birds called when the parent came with food."

Food.—Grinnell and Storer (1924) say:

The Modoc Woodpecker forages on both evergreen and deciduous trees, favoring the latter, perhaps, during the winter months. In summer it is usually rather quiet, particularly so as compared with the noisy California Woodpecker. It gains much of its food in the outer portions of the bark, where a few strokes of moderate intensity enable it to secure any insect or grub living near the surface of the tree.

At the margin of the forest above Coulterville, May 31, 1915, a Modoc Woodpecker was seen foraging in a yellow pine. The tree in question had recently been killed by the boring beetles which were common in the western forests that year. The woodpecker was going over the tree in systematic manner, working out and in along one branch, then ascending the trunk to the next branch where it would repeat the performance. The bird was flaking off the outer layers of the bark without much evident expenditure of effort, for little noise of tapping was heard; it was feeding presumably on the boring beetles or their larvae.

Bendire (1895) writes: "It is one of our most active Woodpeckers, always busy searching for food, which consists principally of injurious larvæ and eggs of insects, varied occasionally with a diet of small berries and seeds, and in winter sometimes of piñon nuts, pine seeds, and acorns. At this season I have often seen this species around slaughter houses, picking up stray bits of meat or fat, and have also seen it pecking at haunches of venison hung up in the open air."

Behavior.—Mr. Skinner says, in his notes, that "the Modoc hairy seems very unsociable. One that was feeding on a cottonwood chased a visiting red-breasted sapsucker away from that tree to another, and then from tree to tree. But, when a California woodpecker came to its tree, the Modoc hairy promptly flew away."

Voice.—Major Bendire (1895) says that this woodpecker "is very noisy, especially in the early spring. It likewise is a great drummer, and utters a variety of notes, some of which sound like 'kick-kick, whitoo, whitoo, whit-whit, wi-wi-wi-wi,' and a hoarse guttural one, somewhat like 'kheak-kheak' or 'khack-khack'."

DRYOBATES VILLOSUS SCRIPPSAE Huey

LOWER CALIFORNIA HAIRY WOODPECKER

HABITS

Laurence M. Huey (1927) who described and named this wood-pecker, characterized it as "similar to *Dryobates villosus hyloscopus* Cabanis and Heine, but decidedly smaller. In fully adult birds, the dusky white of the breast extends farther down on the breast than does that on examples from the northern mountains." He gives, as its range, "the pine clad slopes of the Sierra Juarez and Sierra San Pedro Martir, Lower California, Mexico. * * * The range of this south-ern race does not extend north of the International Boundary, as speci-mens examined from the mountains of San Diego County, California, are in no way inclined toward the race *D. v. scrippsae*, but are counter-parts of typical *D. v. hyloscopus* from the northern localities. In fact, the only variation that could point toward a 'blending' is found in the Sierra Juarez birds, but their average falls so near that of the birds from the Sierra San Pedro Martir that the name proposed herewith should apply."

This southern race probably does not differ materially in its habits from other hairy woodpeckers, except in so far as it is affected by its environment.

DRYOBATES VILLOSUS LEUCOTHORECTIS Oberholser

WHITE-BREASTED WOODPECKER

HABITS

Northward and eastward from the range of the Chihuahua wood-pecker (*icastus*) and southward from the range of the Rocky Moun-tain hairy woodpecker (*monticola*) lies the range of this white-breasted race of the hairy woodpecker, extending from southern Utah, through Arizona and New Mexico, into central western Texas. It is evidently a smaller edition of *monticola*, for Dr. Harry C. Ober-holser (1911a), in describing and naming it, says that it is "much like *Dryobates villosus monticola*, but decidedly smaller; wing coverts practically always without white spots."

Dr. Edgar A. Mearns (1890b) says of its haunts in the mountains of northern Arizona:

Breeds commonly throughout the pine belt, often ascending higher in sum-mer, then preferring aspens to the fir and spruce woods of higher altitudes. It very rarely descends to the cottonwoods of the Verde Valley to fraternize with its smaller relative, Baird's woodpecker, and only when the mountain timber is icy or the weather uncommonly fierce; then it is usually accompanied by flocks of Cassin's Purple Finches, Red-backed Juncos, and its boon com-panions, the Slender-billed Nuthatches. About the middle of June the young leave their nests, and soon after make a partial migration downward towards the lower border of the pine belt, in common with many other birds that breed at high levels.

Nesting.—I can find no references to the nesting habits or eggs of this subspecies, which probably do not differ materially from those of the Chihuahua woodpecker, except that J. S. Ligon told Mrs. Florence M. Bailey (1928) that it nests "generally in small trees in canyon beds."

Eggs.—The eggs of this subspecies are apparently similar to those of other hairy woodpeckers. They seem to be scarce in collections; I have been able to locate only two sets of eggs, one set of four and one set of three. These seven eggs show average measurements of 24.66 by 17.91 millimeters; the eggs showing the four extremes measure 25.3 by 18.2, 24.6 by 18.6, 24.2 by 18.2, and 24.6 by 17.2 millimeters.

Food.—Mrs. Bailey (1928) quotes Maj. E. A. Goldman as follows:

One afternoon I found one pecking at a hole near the ground in the trunk of an oak. It worked for a second or two and then paused long enough to look in my direction, beginning work again immediately. This was repeated several times and it seemed disinclined to leave the spot, allowing me to approach to within ten feet, when, instead of flying off, it slid around to the opposite side of the trunk while I examined the place and found the hole inhabited by numerous small black beetles which were running excitedly about. I moved off a short distance and watched the Woodpecker return to the hole which seemed to be a rich find.

She goes on to say:

On Chloride Creek in May, 1916, when Mr. Ligon was standing by a half dead box elder containing a woodpecker nest, the mother came with her bill for half its length jammed full of wood ants for the squawking young inside the hole. One that Mr. Kellogg took at Silver City had recently eaten two woodboring larvae, six caterpillars, and at least ten moth pupae, besides other insects and mast.

DRYOBATES PUBESCENS PUBESCENS (Linnaeus)

SOUTHERN DOWNY WOODPECKER

HABITS

Because the Linnaean name *Picus pubescens* was based on Catesby's smallest spotted woodpecker, of South Carolina, the southern bird becomes the type race of the species, and the above scientific name, which for many years was used for the more northern bird, is now restricted to the downy woodpeckers of the Lower Austral Zone of the South Atlantic and Gulf States, from North Carolina to eastern Texas. William Brewster (1897) has given us a full review of the changes that have taken place in the nomenclature of the downy woodpeckers of eastern North America, to which the reader is referred.

The southern downy woodpecker, *D. p. pubescens*, is smaller, from the more southern parts of its range decidedly smaller, than the more northern bird, *D. p. medianus*, intergrading with it where the two ranges meet; the under parts are more brownish, and the white markings of the wings and tail will average of less extent.

The haunts of this woodpecker are similar to those of its northern relative, due allowance being made for the difference in environment. It is a more sociable species than the hairy woodpecker and less of a woodland bird.

In Florida, according to Arthur H. Howell (1932), "it occurs alike in pine woods, hammocks, orchards, roadside hedges, and dooryards."

Nesting.—Mr. Howell (1932) says that, in Florida, "the nest of the downy is usually dug in a decaying limb of a tree or occasionally in a fence post, and may be anywhere from 5 to 50 feet above the ground." Harold H. Bailey (1925) says that "for the nesting site, they usually select a dead stub of some live tree, preferring a hard one to a soft or decayed wood. The cavity is drilled each year anew by the birds, the hole being about one and a quarter inches in diameter and eight to twelve inches deep, varying in height from twenty to sixty feet above ground." John Helton, Jr., tells me of a nest he found on April 20, near Troy, Ala., that "was drilled in a rotten oak limb, which had fallen, been caught, and was suspended among the branches of a pine. It contained three small young and one infertile egg. The mother bird fed the young with great regularity every three minutes." M. G. Vaiden, of Rosedale, Miss., writes to me of a nest 35 feet up in a dead snag of a pecan tree; the limb was four inches in diameter and the cavity only five inches deep. George Finlay Simmons (1925) says that, in Texas, it nests "10 to 20 feet from ground in small dead deciduous trees, or in old stumps or telegraph poles."

Eggs.—The eggs are like those of the northern downy but slightly smaller. The measurements of 25 eggs average 19.43 by 15.24 millimeters; the eggs showing the four extremes measure 20.8 by 14.9, 20.6 by 16.7, and 17.78 by 13.46 millimeters.

Behavior.—Writing of the habits of these woodpeckers in the sandhills of North Carolina, Milton P. Skinner (1928) says:

They are seen at times with Chickadees, red-cockaded woodpeckers, Brownheaded Nuthatches, Kinglets and Juncos. And these associations seem to be actual and usual, and not temporary and accidental ones as they are between most birds of different species. The downy woodpeckers are peaceable little fellows but other birds will impose on them. I have seen a yellow-bellied sapsucker and a mob of three or four English Sparrows near Pine Bluff chasing one about. But downy was a fast flier and outflew all his tormentors each time. Their flight is undulating and typical of the woodpecker family. These woodpeckers have one trait of the Brown Creepers—they prefer to work *up* a tree and fly *down* to the base of the next one.

Perhaps a downy woodpecker does not really work any harder or faster for its food than any other bird, but somehow it seems that it does. I found one once on an inclined limb of a catalpa near the Highland Pines Inn and watched it work up ten feet in thirteen minutes. During that time downy's blows fell good and hard at the average of a hundred strokes each minute except for a dozen momentary stops when a big bird flew over, or the downy scratched its head. It was feeding on small white grubs which it secured at an average rate of four per minute. * * *

These woodpeckers have the habit in the Sandhills of digging holes in which to sleep. One found a suitable place in the end of a dead limb of a large gum standing in a flooded swamp near Mid Pines Club. This limb had been broken and left a stub sticking out about five feet long at right angles to the trunk of the gum and about forty feet above the ground. It was about five inches in diameter where the woodpecker began work on it. Work was started on the under side of the limb about nine inches from the outer end on February 11, 1927, and the bird dug at it for forty-five minutes to such good purpose that the hole would then admit all its bill and half its head. As it worked it clung head down under the limb. Then it left its work to go foraging but came back in thirty minutes to resume work. During the next three days this woodpecker must have worked steadily for it then had a hole into which it could completely disappear. But the hole was not large enough nor deep enough, and the bird was still at work, continually popping in and out (backward) of its hole; usually when it backed out it carried a bill full of chips and shavings that it threw over its shoulder. As it did so, it glanced once or twice to either side as if to assure itself that all was well. Then back into the hole for another period of steady hammering. Apparently this woodpecker worked thus from thirty minutes to an hour after each half hour's foraging trip. Two more days of work completed the sleeping quarters in a snug cozy retreat. When finished, the hole was six inches deep, and the limb around it was a mere shell. The opening being beneath the limb, it was sheltered from storms, and from any water running into it.

DISTRIBUTION

Range.—North America; nonmigratory.

The range of the downy woodpecker is **north** to Alaska (Russian Mission, Tanana, and Fort Egbert); southwestern Mackenzie (Fort Simpson and Fort Providence); northern Alberta (Fort McMurray); central Saskatchewan (Big River and Prince Albert); southern Manitoba (Lake St. Martin, Shoal Lake, and Indian Bay); Ontario (Lac Seul, Gargantua, and Sudbury); Quebec (Lake Mistassini, Godbout, and Natashguan River); and Newfoundland (Nicholsville and probably St. Johns). The **eastern** limit of the range extends **south** along the Atlantic coast from this point to southern Florida (Miami, Royal Palm Hammock, and Flamingo). From this southeastern point the species is found westward along the Gulf coast to Mississippi (Biloxi) and Louisiana (New Orleans), thence in the interior to south-central Texas (Giddings and Pecos); southern New Mexico (Mayhill, Cloudcroft, and Silver City); Arizona (San Francisco Mountain and Fort Valley); and southern California (Escondido). The **western** limits extend nearly or quite to the Pacific coast north through California, Oregon, Washington, and British Columbia to Alaska (Sitka, Sitka- lidak Island, Bethel, and Russian Mission).

The range as above outlined is for the entire species, which has been separated into six subspecies. The typical form, the southern downy woodpecker (*D. p. pubescens*), is found in the South Atlantic and Gulf States north to North Carolina and Oklahoma; the northern downy woodpecker (*D. p. medianus*) ranges north from Virginia, Tennessee, and Kansas (casually eastern Colorado) north to southern Alberta, Manitoba, Quebec, and Newfoundland; Nelson's downy woodpecker (*D. p. nelsoni*) ranges southeast from northwestern Alaska to central Alberta and is found casually even farther east; Batchelder's woodpecker (*D. p. leucurus*) is the Rocky Mountain form and is found from the Kenai Peninsula of Alaska south to New Mexico and Arizona, casually east to Nebraska and on the coast of British Columbia; Gairdner's woodpecker (*D. p. gairdneri*) is found on the Pacific coast from British Columbia south to northern California; and the willow woodpecker (*D. p. turati*) is confined to California, being distributed rather generally over the State except in the desert areas and the northwestern part.

While the downy woodpecker is not migratory in the accepted sense of the term, and during the months of November and December has been recorded north to Mackenzie (Fort Simpson) and central Quebec (Lake Mistassini), it appears to have some local movements and seems given to a certain amount of wandering after the close of the breeding season. In some of the more northern areas it is commoner in winter than in summer, while in the mountainous regions of the West there is apparently a vertical movement in winter to the valley floors.

While the files of the Biological Survey contain the data for more than 4,600 of these birds that have been marked with numbered bands, many of which have been subsequently recovered, only one of these indicates a flight of any distance from the point of banding. This bird (83460), banded on February 2, 1925, at Elkader, Iowa, was found dead at Balsam Lake, Wis., on October 25, 1925. The distance between the two points is about 185 miles.

Egg dates.—Alberta: 12 records, May 25 to June 14.

California: 82 records, April 7 to June 9; 41 records, April 24 to May 13, indicating the height of the season.

Colorado: 9 records, May 4 to June 30.

Florida: 7 records, April 2 to May 14.

Illinois: 16 records, April 3 to June 3; 8 records, May 12 to 20.

New York: 12 records, May 10 to June 2.

Washington: 8 records, May 1 to June 2.

DRYOBATES PUBESCENS GAIRDNERI (Audubon)

GAIRDNER'S WOODPECKER

HABITS

This subspecies of our well-known downy woodpecker is one of those well-marked dark-colored races that occur in the humid Northwest coast region, ranging in the Transition Zone from southern British Columbia to Mendocino County, Calif. It is practically a small edition of the equally dark Harris's woodpecker, which inhabits the same region. Its characters are so well marked that it was recognized and named by Audubon (1842). Ridgway (1914) describes it as "similar to *D. p. turati*, but color of under parts darker (often light brownish gray or drab), the white of back often tinged with brownish gray."

D. E. Brown, in his notes from western Washington, says: "Gairdner's woodpecker is next to the commonest woodpecker in western Washington, the northwestern flicker being the only one that outnumbers it. This, the smallest of the woodpeckers in this locality, is fond of old river beds, willow swamps, and the deciduous trees along streams. It is found here at all times of year but seems to be more in evidence in winter, probably because the leaves are off the trees where it is usually found."

Nesting.—Mr. Brown states further that "it digs its nesting cavity usually in a dead willow stub of small size, but at times it excavates, with much labor, a cavity in a growing tree. Nests have been found as low as 3 feet from the ground, and they are seldom more than 30 feet up. Three to six eggs are laid, five being the usual number. The first week in May is the best time for fresh eggs. The incubating bird has a habit that, I think, saves its eggs many times; when the stub that contains the eggs is rapped, the sitting bird comes to the opening with its bill full of chips from the bottom of the nest; these are dropped outside, and the bird drops back into the nest, only to repeat this action when the rapping is repeated. I have seen this performance not once but many times, and I think it a regular occurrence when the eggs are well incubated."

Dawson and Bowles (1909) write: "Gairdners place their nests at inconsiderable heights in deciduous trees, and those, if possible, among thick growths on moist ground. Both sexes assist in excavation, as in incubation. Partially decayed wood is selected and an opening made about an inch and a quarter in diameter. After driving straight in an inch or two, the passage turns down and widens two or three diameters. At a depth of a foot or so the crystal white eggs are deposited on a neat bed of fine chips. Incubation lasts twelve days and the young are hatched about the 1st of June."

Eggs.—The eggs of Gairdner's woodpecker resemble those of the northern downy (*medianus*) in every respect but average slightly smaller. The measurements of 34 eggs average 18.71 by 14.51 millimeters; the eggs showing the four extremes measure 20.83 by 15.24, 20.32 by 16.0, 17.27 by 14.22, and 17.78 by 12.95 millimeters.

Food.—Johnson A. Neff (1928) had 68 stomachs available for study, mostly Gairdner's woodpeckers from the Willamette Valley, Oreg., and states that—

the animal food items averaged 82.07 percent of the annual food, and vegetable matter, 17.93 percent. * * *

At Peyton, in August, the Gairdner Woodpeckers were observed working busily for several days removing the larvae, pupae, and adults of weevils from the stems of common mullen, *Verbascum thapsus*. * * *

During July, 1925, whole families of the Gairdner Woodpecker were observed in the huge cottonwoods which abound near the Willamette River, feeding on aphids and scale. They often numbered as high as ten birds in one tree, and worked from the lowest limb to the highest leaf. While paying some attention to the branches, their chief interest was in the clusters of leaves; they clambered out each small branch to the group of leaves at the tip, peered under each leaf intently, even swinging around sidewise and up-side down in their efforts. Through the binoculars it was easy to see them remove small objects and, later, stomach analysis showed that most of the objects were scale insects. * * *

These woodpeckers have yet to be observed doing any injury to a living tree; the writer has been unable to find any evidence of their doing so in this area. While they nested abundantly in the river-bottom lands in very close companionship with true sapsuckers, they were never seen to visit the flowing sap pits. * * *

Fruit was hardly touched by these birds; elderberry (*Sambucus*) and Madrona (*Arbutus*) were the only kinds found, averaging only 0.46 percent of the diet. * * *

The Gairdner, Willow, and Batchelder Woodpeckers in the orchard are worth their weight in gold to the fruit grower. They should be strictly protected, and every known means of attraction should be used in the attempt to persuade them to remain about the ranches.

Winter.—Anderson and Grinnell (1903) say that, in the Siskiyou Mountains, Calif., "the Gairdner woodpecker is usually to be found in company with the flocks of mountain chickadees which frequent the black oak groves all winter. The oaks are their favorite working places, but they are also to be seen among the pines and spruces. Six specimens brought home are all quite near *gairdneri*. The smokiness of the lower surface is not so intense as in skins from western Oregon, but the size, especially of the feet, is decidedly that of the northwest coast form."

DRYOBATES PUBESCENS LEUCURUS (Hartlaub)

BATCHELDER'S WOODPECKER

HABITS

The downy woodpecker inhabiting the Rocky Mountains and adjacent regions from southern Alaska to Arizona and New Mexico is described by Ridgway (1914) as "similar in large size and whiteness of under parts to *D. p. nelsoni*, but with less of white on wing-coverts, sometimes with none, the spots, when present, only on terminal or (usually) subterminal portion, and on only a few of the covert features." It also differs from it in a "tendency to reduction or absence of bars on lateral rectrices."

The common name of this woodpecker is in honor of Charles F. Batchelder, who first (1889) called the attention of American ornithologists to the characters of this race under the name *D. p. oreoecus*. Batchelder's name was used in the 1895 A. O. U. Check-List, but it was later found to be antedated by *Dryobates homorus* of Cabanis and Heine, which was adopted in the 1910 Check-List. This was found to be still further antedated by the name *Picus leucurus*, given to the downy woodpecker of the Rocky Mountains by Hartlaub in 1852. It seems rather strange that this race remained so long unrecognized in this country. This may be due to the fact that this woodpecker seems to be a comparatively rare bird throughout most of its range.

The Weydemeyers (1928) say of its occurrence in northwestern Montana:

A rather rare permanent resident, irregular in winter. Occurs throughout the county, but is rare at high elevations. It frequents mixed broad-leaf and conifer woods along the lower streams, where it undoubtedly breeds in preference to other locations. During winter it is often seen about farmsteads and pastures, and in bordering woods of Douglas fir, yellow pine, and larch. In the Canadian zone it occurs sparingly in lodgepole pine and alpine fir (*Abies lasiocarpa*) woods, usually along streams.

In the western half of the county, an observer may consider himself fortunate to see an individual of this species twice a week. In the eastern portion, during July and August, along Transition zone streams, one or two birds may be seen nearly every day.

We have obtained no definite nesting dates for this species, although it evidently breeds in suitable locations. On July 22, 1923, a brood of young on the wing was seen near Fortine in woods of spruce and aspen, in the Transition zone, at 2,960 feet altitude.

Major Bendire (1895) writes:

Dr. Edgar A. Mearns, United States Army, reports it breeding sparingly throughout the *Pinus ponderosa* belt, ascending into the Spruce zone, on the San Francisco cone, and considers it the rarest of the woodpeckers found in Arizona. Mr. Denis Gale took a nest and eggs of this subspecies in Boulder County, Colorado, on June 12, 1889. The excavation was found in a half-dead aspen, 30 feet from the ground, and presumably well up in the mountains, as Mr.

William G. Smith informs me that it is only a winter visitor in the lower valleys, and is never seen there during warm weather. I found it rare near Fort Custer, Montana, and only obtained a single male specimen, on November 23, 1884, among the willows and cottonwoods on the Little Horn River. Dr. James C. Merrill, United States Army, met with it breeding at Fort Shaw, Mont., early in June, 1879, and tells me that five or six eggs are generally laid to a set, and that the nesting habits are just like those of the downy woodpecker.

Lee R. Dice (1918) says that, in southeastern Washington, it is "numerous throughout the year in the timber along the Touchet River near Prescott.

"* * * On June 11, 1908, a nest containing young was found four feet from the ground in an apple tree near Prescott. The female was seen gathering large, red aphids from nearby golden-rod. She would gather all her mouth could hold and until the aphids stuck out like a fringe all around the edges of the bill. Then she flew in a direct line toward the nest. This female was also seen to gather aphids from apple trees."

A set of four eggs in the Thayer collection was taken near Fort Shaw, Mont., on June 8, 1879; the nesting cavity was 12 feet from the ground in a dead tree and was excavated to a depth of 10 inches. The eggs are characteristic of the species, short-ovate in shape, dull white in color, and only slightly glossy.

The measurements of 28 eggs average 19.86 by 15.29 millimeters; the eggs showing the four extremes measure **23.37** by **16.00, 19.0** by 14.8, and 18.4 by **14.4** millimeters.

DRYOBATES PUBESCENS MEDIANUS (Swainson)

NORTHERN DOWNY WOODPECKER

PLATES 7, 8

HABITS

CONTRIBUTED BY WINSOR MARRETT TYLER

The downy woodpecker, including six geographical forms, inhabits nearly the whole of the wooded parts of North America. It is absent or rare on the arid deserts and less common in the densely forested regions than some of the larger woodpeckers; its favorite country is the open woodland that covers a large part of the United States.

When civilized man invaded their territory, the downy woodpeckers of the Atlantic coast—the northern and southern races—did not retreat before his advance but accepted as a home the orchards and shade trees with which man replaced the forest. At the present time it builds its nest sometimes within sight from our windows and often in the parks of our large cities. It is one of the best known of our permanent residents.

The ornithologists of a century ago show unanimity in their characterization of the bird. Audubon (1842) remarks that it "is perhaps not surpassed by any of its tribe in hardiness, industry, or vivacity"; Wilson (1832) says that "the principal characteristics of this little bird are diligence, familiarity, perseverance" and speaks of a pair of the birds working at their nest "with the most indefatigable diligence"; and Nuttall (1832) characteristically shares Wilson's opinion even to the extent of employing his exact words, "indefatigable diligence," in his own account of the building of the nest. Nearly a hundred years later Forbush (1927), when near the end of his long life, put the seal of his approval upon this sentiment, expressed long ago, by summarizing the downy as a "model of patient industry and perseverance."

Backed by these authorities we may regard the downy woodpecker as a bird with a stable and well-balanced nature, a bird which, unconcerned by the rush and traffic "of these most brisk and giddy-paced times," still perseveres in its "indefatigable diligence."

Spring and courtship.—As spring advances, the downy woodpecker seems to wake up; it attracts our notice by its more frequent notes and increased activity. During the cold months of the year the bird has been comparatively silent, although even in the depth of winter we may occasionally hear its single *chip* and even the long whinny, but in April, for so sedate a bird, it becomes a lively personality; it moves about quickly—sometimes with lightninglike agility—and takes a voluble interest in the members of its own species.

Francis H. Allen, in his notes, gives the two following graphic accounts of the initial stage of the bird's courtship: "April 10, 1904. West Roxbury, Mass. I found two downy woodpeckers courting— at least, I suppose that was what they were up to. They acted like mating flickers, chasing each other about from tree to tree, keeping almost constantly on the move and only pausing now and then to execute a sort of dance, spreading their wings and tails. From time to time I heard from them a long call resembling the flicker's *whick, whick whick whick*, etc., but higher pitched than the flicker's and, of course, not so loud. Less often I heard another note—a softer, slighter, more hurried call, similar in quality. I did not make out whether these two calls were made by different sexes, nor did I positively make out that the birds were a pair, they kept in such constant motion. At least once one lit crosswise of a twig. At last one flew off, and then the familiar and characteristic long call of a downy sounded from another direction, and the remaining bird flew over to the third bird, which was clinging to the trunk of an elm. Then these two stayed in each other's company but did not conduct so elaborate a dance as the first couple.

·"All this time a fourth bird had been drumming on a tree not far away. I went up to the place and timed the drum calls, finding each roll to last about two seconds. I could not count the taps, but thought they numbered eight or ten to each roll. While I watched this bird, another downy came along, sounding the flickerlike call, but rather faintly, and the drummer flew to join her. They flew off together. I believe it is only the male that drums, and I think it probable that the bird that answered the drummer was the one that had taken part in the dance before described, for that bird when she left her partner had flown off in this direction.

"April 8, 1917. West Roxbury. Watched a pair courting this morning for several minutes. Both sexes had a curious 'weaving' action, moving the head and whole body from side to side on the tip of the tail as a pivot with the neck stretched out and bill pointed on a line with the body, and the whole body elongated. They did this both when clinging to the side of a trunk and when on a horizontal or slanting branch. They were silent but very active, flitting one after the other from branch to branch and tree to tree, but making only short flights. The waving, or 'weaving,' motion of the head was rather rapid, perhaps two waves, that is from left to right and back again, in about a second—but this is stated from general impressions and memory only. These birds did not spread the wings and tail as did the courting pair observed on April 10, 1904, and, as stated, they uttered no note."

My notes refer to a bit of courtship observed during the actual breeding season, May 11, 1911, in a wooded swamp in Lexington, Mass., where the species used to nest every year. The female bird was perched motionless along a horizontal limb of a tree, and the male was poised in the air just behind and a little above her. He was hovering. His wings were more than half spread, I should say, and waving slowly up and down, a maneuver which displayed finely the rows of white spots on the flight feathers and coverts.

William Brewster (1936), in his Concord journal under date of May 5, 1905, notes another form of courtship. He says: "At 8 A. M. saw a pair of Downy Woodpeckers in young oaks behind Ball's Hill, behaving very strangely. They kept flying from tree to tree, flapping their wings slowly and feebly like butterflies, sometimes moving on a level plane, sometimes in long loops, occasionally sailing from tree to tree in a long *deep* loop. Their wings had a strange fin-like appearance due, probably, to the way they were held or flexed. They both uttered a low, harsh, chattering cry, almost incessantly. No doubt this was a love performance, but they were male and female and both 'showed off' in the same way."

Lewis O. Shelley (1932), who, at East Westmoreland, N. H., has had an extensive experience with banded birds throughout the year, describes the courtship thus:

Courtship activities begin rather early with the male's tattooing commencing in the warm days of March. I believe the most active mating display is given by a new male that desires a mate, not by a male mated the previous year whose mate is still living. The latter male seems to give a protective display to its rival, seemingly just enough to hold his mate's trust.

- In the spring of 1931, father and son * * * fought for and sought the favor of the young female * * * the son finally winning after days of courtship in our yard and vicinity. * * * Courting lasted for upwards of two weeks, or perhaps longer, before the female made her choice. Of the two rivals the son finally was accepted, the older male shortly disappearing. * * * The courtship display of these three birds was the same as I have observed with other mating Downy Woodpeckers elsewhere in past seasons. At my station the mating activities began when the birds first met and was continued more or less regularly thereafter. The female is usually rather quiet, sometimes giving a *week, week, week, week*, or again a squeaking note. The males give forth a loud *wick, wick, wick, wick, wick, wick*, sometimes with a rolling *k-k-k-k-k* at the end. Very little drumming on resonant objects is done by the male, once a female is located, and in this case almost none was done except when one male was out of sight and hearing of the female and the other courting bird. To the casual observer, the chasing of the female by the male to a tree, and from tree to tree, in a seemingly idle manner (often, but not always, by both males) is in reality a part of the mating manoeuvres.

When it happens that both males are in pursuit, the activities take on an added impetus. I have a number of times seen one male dash headlong across a fifty-yard opening to where the other two birds were, loudly uttering his cry, and, when alighting, dash at his adversary, the female squeaking intermittently, and swinging her body from side to side. The display also consists of spread wings nervously fluttered; raising and lowering of the scarlet patch; mad dashes from one tree to another at the fleeing female, who dodges to the opposite side of the tree as the pursuing bird alights; loud calls at intervals when he stops in his mad hopping up the limbs and smaller branches. This activity may last from five to thirty minutes, from the large elm in our yard, where the birds feed, to a larger area either south or east of the house. When two birds are alone together, it is common to find them perching near together and motionless for considerable periods of time, but let the second male appear and the first male will drive the female from the tree and the round is begun again. When two males come face to face in a headlong rush, wings spread, crest raised, and beak open in a challenging attitude, it is mostly sham, for they soon quiet down unless one advances up the tree toward the female clinging immovable above.

There is a period when the male is very active in his rushing of the female— I suppose to make sure of his desire, a mate—but this phase of courtship plays no part in the act of copulation, which I have seen enacted early in the morning, a quiet, matter-of-fact performance.

The first and last paragraphs of this quotation are taken from Mr. Shelley's manuscript notes.

Nesting.—The downy woodpecker nests in a cavity that the birds themselves drill in a branch or stub 8 feet (rarely less) to 50 feet (rarely more) above the ground, generally in dead or dying wood, sometimes in a solid branch. The entrance, one and a quarter inches in diameter, is just large enough to admit the bird's body, and is perfectly circular unless some bits of soft wood chip off. The cavity is roughly gourd-shaped, turning downward and widening soon after penetrating the wood and extends to a depth varying normally from eight to twelve inches. Generally a few chips are left in the bottom of the cavity.

Lewis O. Shelley says (MS.) that according to his experience "the female selects the nest site on her winter, or year-round, territory." He speaks of a female that in the fall "partly dug out a cavity, supposedly for her winter quarters, but the following summer I found a brood of young of this same bird occupying the nest."

Writers are almost unanimously of the opinion that both birds of the pair excavate the nest, but Shelley (MS.) states: "Of a number of nests observed, I have never known the male downy to assist in excavating. He often comes near when the female is working, but this seems to be an understood signal for her to cease work and go off in his company."

A. Dawes DuBois, in a letter to Mr. Bent, describes the behavior of a pair working jointly on a nest in Ithaca, N. Y., about 15 feet up in an old stub. He says: "These birds were working the lower depths. The partners worked alternately. First the female lighted on the stub and disappeared within the cavity. Immediately she thrust out her head, and, with a quick shake, disposed of a billful of chips. She repeated this a number of times. She was throwing out the loose chips from the bottom of the cavity. Soon she began to chisel, remaining inside where we could not see her. After she had been working for five or six minutes, her mate flew to the stub and uttered a chirp, whereupon the female came out and flew away.

"The male went in to continue the work by a somewhat different method. He was never entirely lost to view—his tail was always visible—and he backed out of the hole to dispose of the chips. He ruffled his feathers considerably in squirming out backward, as his body was a snug fit in the entrance hole. He threw out a quantity of loose chips in this manner and then began chiseling, his tail meanwhile protruding from the doorway. He worked for 22 minutes; then his mate came back.

"She went inside and came out with her mouth quite full of chips; but instead of tossing the chips to the ground, she flew off with them to another tree. She stayed away for several minutes, then returned and went to work in her accustomed way, staying within the cavity, and thrusting only her head outside. When she had worked about 15 minutes the male came again to the entrance. She put her head out of the doorway; they rubbed their bills together and chirped a few remarks. The female then flew away and the male took up the task again."

Audubon (1842) says: "About the middle of April it begins to form its nest, shewing little care as to the kind of tree it selects for the purpose, although it generally chooses a sound one, sometimes, however, taking one that is partially decayed. The pair work together for several days before the hole is completed, sometimes perhaps a whole week, as they dig it to a depth of a foot or sixteen inches. The direction is sometimes perpendicularly downwards from the commencement, sometimes transverse to the tree for four or five inches, and then longitudinal. The hole is rendered smooth and conveniently large throughout, the entrance being perfectly round, and just large enough to admit one bird at a time."

A. Dawes DuBois (MS.) writes that the male bird of a pair was caught in a nest 6 feet from the ground, evidently incubating the six eggs well advanced in development. This observation is in accord with the general belief that the male takes his share in incubation.

Mrs. Alice Hall Walter (1912) states that "in the North, only one brood is raised during a season; but it is not uncommon in the South for one brood to be raised in May and a second in August."

Eggs.—[AUTHOR'S NOTE: The northern downy woodpecker lays ordinarily four or five eggs, though sets of three or six are not rare, and as many as seven or even eight eggs have been found in a nest. The eggs are pure white, either dull white or more or less glossy, and they vary in shape from ovate to rounded-ovate. The measurements of 55 eggs average 19.35 by 15.05 millimeters; the eggs showing the four extremes measure **22.35** by **16.26, 17.78** by 14.73, and 18.80 by **13.97** millimeters.]

Young.—The incubation period of the downy woodpecker is 12 days, according to Frank L. Burns (1915) and Dr. Arthur A. Allen (1928).

Whether in their earliest days the young birds, hidden in the depths of their dark chamber, are fed by regurgitation has not been determined, but very soon after they leave the egg food is brought directly to them. Dr. Allen (MS.) says: "Certainly by the time the young are four or five days old entire insects are brought in the parents' bills and given to the young; I have photographic proof of this."

Craig S. Thoms (1927), in a study of the nesting habits in South Dakota, says: "On June 9 the young were beginning to come up to the door of their excavation to receive food. Presumably the largest and strongest sticks his head clear out. When he fed he subsided and the next came up, but not quite so far. He in his turn subsided and the parent entered to feed the weaker ones still farther down. * * *

"On June 12 the last of the young left the nest, which upon being measured was found to be 10 inches deep."

A. Dawes DuBois (MS.) tells of the flight of the young birds from the nest: "The young chattered most of the time during the last two days of nest life. One at a time they looked out a great deal at the strange outer world. They left the nest on June 11. The last two, a male and a female, left during the afternoon, each after being fed at the entrance and seeing the parent fly away. The young male flew from the nest hole straight to a tree 60 feet away. His sister quickly followed, lighting on the trunk of the same tree and following her parent up the bole in the hitching manner of their kind as though she had been practicing this vertical locomotion all her life."

Plumages.—[AUTHOR'S NOTE: Young downy woodpeckers are hatched naked and blind, but the juvenal plumage is acquired before the young leave the nest. In this first plumage, the young male is much like the adult male, except that the red nuchal patch is lacking; the forehead is black, spotted with white, but the crown and occiput are more or less marked with various shades of red, pinkish, or yellowish, as well as spotted with white; the black portions of the plumage are duller than in the adult; the sides of the breast are streaked and the flanks obscurely spotted with dusky; the white areas, underparts, and white spots elsewhere, as well as the rectrices, are tinged with yellowish.

The young female is like the young male, except that there is no red on the head, and the crown is clear black, or black spotted with white. L. L. Snyder (1923) has shown that young males sometimes have only white markings on a black crown and that young females sometimes have reddish, pinkish, or yellowish markings on the crown.

The juvenal plumage is worn but a short time, for a complete molt, beginning in September or earlier, produces a first winter plumage, which is practically adult. Adults have a complete annual molt from July to September. Both adults and young show a tinge of yellowish in the white areas in fresh fall plumage, which gradually fades away.]

Food.—F. E. L. Beal (1911) in an examination of the contents of 723 stomachs of the downy woodpecker found that 76.05 percent was animal matter, the remaining 23.95 percent vegetable matter. The following quotations are from his exhaustive report.

Beetles taken collectively amount to 21.55 percent, and are the largest item of the food. Of these, a little less than 14 percent are wood-boring larvae. * * * They were found in 289 stomachs, or about 40 percent of all, and 10 contained no other food. This is only about half the amount found in the stomachs of the hairy woodpecker, and shows that the downy pecks wood much less than the hairy. These larvae are eaten at all times of the year, though the most are taken in the cooler months. * * * The economic value of the destruction of these larvae is very great.

Weevils amount to a little more than 3 percent, but appear to be a rather favorite food, as they were found in 107 stomachs. * * *

Ants are eaten by the downy to the extent of 21.36 percent of its diet, and are taken more regularly than any other element of the food. * * *

Caterpillars appear to be a very acceptable food for the downy woodpecker, as they constitute 16.50 percent of the yearly diet. * * *

Fruit was eaten to the extent of 5.85 percent of the whole food. Most of it is of useless wild varieties. * * *

The charge sometimes made that the downy injures trees by eating the inner bark is disproved. It eats cambium rarely and in small quantities.

Beal gives a list of 20 seeds and fruits found in the downy's food. Summarizing his findings, he says: "The foregoing discussion of the food of the downy woodpecker shows it to be one of our most useful species. The only complaint against the bird is on the score of disseminating the poisonous species of Rhus. However, it is fortunate that the bird can live on this food when it is difficult to procure anything else. The insect food selected by the downy is almost all of species economically harmful."

Forbush (1927) lays stress on the usefulness of the downy to man; he says that it "searches out the pine weevil which kills the topmost shoot of the young white pine and so causes a crook in the trunk of the tree, unfitting it for the lumber market."

Mrs. Alice Hall Walter (1912) shows how well the downy is equipped to secure its food. She says that the feet, two toes in front and two behind, "serve to *clamp* the bird to the tree." She continues:

Additional support is furnished by the stiff, sharply pointed tail-feathers, that act as a brace when the bird delivers heavy blows with its beak. Effective as this tool is for the work of *hammer, wedge, drill* and *pick-axe*, it could not obtain the deeply hidden grubs known as "borers," from their tortuous, tunneled grooves, without the aid of the long, slender, extensile tongue. In the case of the Hairy and Downy, as well as some others of the family, this remarkable tool is provided with barbs, converting it into a spear, which may be hurled one inch, two inches or even more, beyond the tip of the beak.

A. Dawes DuBois says in his notes: "I have seen a downy woodpecker industriously applying the percussion test to the dried stalks of the previous summer's horse weeds, which grow to prodigious size in the creek bottoms near Springfield, Illinois. He went up each stalk, tapping it lightly, and frequently stopping to pierce the shell and extract a worm from the pith. I found that the weed stems he had visited were punctured and splintered in numerous places."

The following note by Elliott R. Tibbets (1911) shows how agile the downy is on the wing. He was watching some birds at a feeding shelf. "I was told," he says, "to throw a cracked nut into the air and see what followed—I did so, and, to my surprise, the Downy darted after it, not allowing it to touch the ground, and then returned to the evergreen, where he proceeded to pick the kernel from the hard shell."

Henry D. Minot (1877) also mentions that they "catch insects on the wing."

Behavior.—The downy woodpecker sits very still as it digs out a grub from under the bark of a tree, or from the wood under the bark, or as it dislodges a bit of bark in its hunt for a cocoon or a bundle of insects' eggs. We hear the gentle taps of its bill, and when our eyes, led by the sound, catch sight of the bird, perched on a branch or the trunk of a tree, we understand why it has been called industrious. It is concentrated on its work; it works patiently, seriously, like a carpenter working earnestly with his chisel, spending a full minute, sometimes more, to secure a bit of food.

As it sits there quietly, working painstakingly at the bark, it gives the impression of a rather sedentary bird, deliberate and staid, but when it begins to move about—taking short flights among the the branches—alighting on little swaying twigs and flitting off again— we see it in another mood. It is lively now; all deliberateness is gone. It hops upward over the branches with quick jerky hops, rearing back a little after each one; it may descend a little way by backward hitches; it winds about the smaller branches, peering at the right side, the left side, and around at the back; it flits to a twig no thicker than a pencil for the space of a single peck, and then is off with the speed of an arrow, weaving and undulating through a maze of branchlets, cutting the air audibly with its wings.

We can watch the downy woodpecker best in winter when the trees and shrubs are bare. But even in such an exposed situation as a leafless tree, we do not find it a conspicuous bird—one hop and it is hidden behind a branch, seeming almost to glide out of our sight. At the slightest alarm it disappears; it uses a branch as a shield— slipping behind it, safe from observation or attack.

The bird is at home also in shrubbery, moving easily among the smaller branches, hitching along their slender length, picking at the bark, and leaping from one branch to another with the aid of a flip of the wings. It sits crosswise on a perch scarcely bigger than a twig, leaning forward a little, bill outstretched, suggesting in position and outline a tiny kingfisher.

Here, at close range, on a level with our eyes, we realize how rapid the bird's motions are. The beak strikes and draws back—the two movements a single flash. The head turns to one side, to the other side, bringing first one dark shining eye, then the other, to bear on the bark; we see the head in the two positions, although we get only a hint of the motion between.

Thus the day's work goes on, until the downy, replete with the results of its industry, rests motionless for a while on a high, sunny branch, taking its ease.

The downy woodpecker, like most of its family, has an undulating flight when flying any considerable distance. The undulations are not deep, as in the plunging flight of a goldfinch; it gives rather the effect of a ship pitching slightly in a head sea. A few strokes carry the bird up to the crest of the wave—the wings clapping close to the sides of the body—then, at the crest, with the wings shut, the bird tilts slightly forward, and slides down into the next trough.

Besides employing its strong beak and the powerful muscles of its neck to secure food and dig out a cavity for its nest, the downy woodpecker makes use of them to beat a loud tattoo on the branch of a tree or some other resonant object. This habit is oftenest noticed in spring, when it appears to form a part of courtship or a prelude to it, but Lewis O. Shelley says in his notes that "on February 3, 1934, a male downy commenced its drumming on a dead elm branch near the house. A few hours earlier the temperature had been 5° below zero. On the 6th, 8th, and 9th he was tattooing at the usual hour, about 8 a. m. On the 8th the temperature registered zero, and on the 9th 18° below zero!"

Dr. Charles W. Townsend, in his Ipswich manuscript notes, under date of March 16, 1930, speaks of "a male bird hammering a *rat-at-at-too* on the apex of a telephone pole for three seconds. He then paused, hunching up a little and looking about for from five to twelve seconds, before resuming the hammering. He made a small round dent in the pole, but there were no chips."

A. Dawes DuBois tells in his notes the following anecdote: "One April day I watched this avian drummer as he entertained himself by beating on the wooden insulator-pins of an unused cross-arm on a telegraph pole. From each pin he rang out a different tone—loud, clear, and high-pitched. It was evident that this pleased him, for he hopped from one pin to another to repeat the variations."

I have found in the books no mention of drumming by the female downy, but at the end of the extract from William Brewster's notes, quoted under "Courtship," in which he describes a mutual display by a pair of birds, he adds: "Both sexes drum, also."

William Brewster (1876b) points out the difference between the tattoo of the downy woodpecker and that of the hairy woodpecker and the yellow-bellied sapsucker. He says: "*P. pubescens* has a long unbroken roll, *P. villosus* a shorter and louder one with a greater interval between each stroke: while *S. varius* commencing with a short roll ends very emphatically with five or six distinct disconnected taps."

R. Owen Merriam (1920) gives, from Hamilton, Canada, an instance of "snow bathing." He says:

This morning a female Downy Woodpecker that I was watching flew to a horizontal branch and proceeded vigorously to bathe in the loose snow lying there. Like a Robin in a puddle, Mrs. Downy ducked her head, ruffled her feathers, and fluttered her wings, throwing some of the snow over her back and scattering the rest to the winds. As all the snow fell off one part of the branch, she moved along to another, until she had cleared a place about two feet long. Two forks held more snow than the straight limb, and apparently Mrs. Downy enjoyed herself immensely when she came to them.

Dr. Arthur A. Allen (1928) in his admirable "Downy Woodpecker's Story," published in the School Department of Bird-Lore, says, letting the bird tell its own story: "When cold weather sets in, * * * I begin drilling roosting-holes where I can spend the nights. I usually have to drill quite a number for they seem to be quite popular with other birds like the Chickadees and Nuthatches, and sometimes when I get ready to retire I find my hole occupied by a flying squirrel or a whole family of deer mice, and it is easier to drill a new hole than to drive them out. One winter I got tired of drilling holes and every night retired to a bird-house and perched on an old Wren's nest that was in it."

Many ornithologists, even as long ago as the time of Wilson and Nuttall, have believed that the rows of small holes, such as we commonly see in the bark of our orchard trees, are drilled by the downy woodpecker. These little holes, about three-eighths of an inch across, circular when old, but oval when fresh, are arranged in fairly regular rows parallel to the ground, and sometimes in tiers, when they have the appearance of a waffle. In settled regions they are found oftenest in the trunks and the larger branches of trees belonging to the rose family—most commonly of all in apple trees. The holes may be within 3 feet of the ground or as high as 20 feet or more above it, depending on the height of the tree. Oftentimes they are very close together; I have counted as many as six of them in the space of an inch and a half. The question has arisen whether the downy woodpecker ever makes these holes.

We know now, what the older ornithologists did not know, that it is a regular habit of the yellow-bellied sapsucker to drill such holes, but there are plenty of statements in the ornithological literature today ascribing the work to the downy woodpecker as well.

Dr. Charles W. Townsend (1932) gives an able summary of the literature on this question and, after carefully weighing the evidence, comes "to the conclusion that these well known and characteristic circles of holes are made by true sapsuckers and not by downy or hairy woodpeckers."

He throws a good deal of doubt on some seemingly definite observations from correspondents quoted by Forbush in his "Birds of
Massachusetts," when he says that "many leave one in considerable
uncertainty as to whether the correspondents actually saw the downy
woodpecker making the rings of holes, or merely tapping in the same
region, or drinking the sap, or eating cambium from holes whose
origin was not ascertained. It may be that some of the correspondents
were unable to distinguish the true species of woodpecker."

Dr. Townsend cites several observations, two of which are quoted
below. If the first of these had not been correctly interpreted, and if
the other had not been seen in its entirety, they might have led to
error. He says:

There is one observation, however, which should be quoted here, as it is of
considerable interest in this discussion, an observation made by a capable
observer with great care. Forbush says, *loc. cit.*, vol. II, p. 268: "The first trust-
worthy evidence, however, that I obtained regarding the tapping of trees for sap
by the Downy Woodpecker was in 1899, when my assistant, the late Charles E.
Bailey, on April 6 watched one for several hours. His report reads: 'At 12:30
I found a Downy Woodpecker, and watched him till 2:45; he took three larvae
from a maple stub, just under the bark. He next tapped two small swamp
maples, four and six feet from the ground, and spent most of the time taking
sap. He tapped the tree by picking it a few times very lightly; it looked like
a slight cut, slanting a little. The bird would sit and peck the sap out of the
lower part of the cut. The cut was so small the sap did not collect very fast.
The bird would go and sit for a long time in a large tree and not move, then
it would come back and take more sap. It did this three times while I was
watching it. It did not care to take any food but the sap.' * * * Mr. Bailey
cut off and brought me the limb, the bark of which was perforated by the bird.
* * * The perforations passed through the bark to the wood, but did not enter
it and they do not in the least resemble in shape those made by the Yellow-bellied
Sapsucker." Here is just what we should expect in a woodpecker not specialized
as a sapsucker. * * *

The next record is of considerable significance in this discussion, and had I
seen only the latter half of the drama, my conclusions might have been different.
In the Wenham swamp on May 11, 1906, my notes state that Glover M. Allen and
I found a Yellow-bellied Sapsucker drilling holes in a white pine. His movements were slow and he paid little attention to us standing below him at the
foot of the tree. When he departed, a female Downy Woodpecker visited the
holes.

Speaking of his own observations, Dr. Townsend says: "I may state
that, although I have long watched Downy Woodpeckers gleaning
insects on and in the bark and wood of trees at all seasons of the year,
I have never seen them dig circles of holes in the bark. * * * I
have never found fresh rings of holes except during the time of the
sapsucker migrations."

Voice.—The downy woodpecker is by no means a noisy bird; compared to the red-headed woodpecker, with its loud rattling calls, or to
the shouting, boisterous flicker, it is quiet and demure. Nevertheless,

we cannot be for long near one of these little birds, hidden high among leafy branches, before we learn of its presence. Within a few minutes, long before we catch sight of it, we are almost certain to hear its voice.

Its call note is a single abrupt syllable, like *tchick*. Although this note is of sufficient volume to carry a considerable distance, it is not a loud note even when heard at short range. As in the case of many bird notes, it is recognizable from the voice of any other bird hereabouts once we have become familiar with it, yet it is not easy to say how it differs from numerous other calls that might be suggested by the same letters. I believe one characteristic of the note that helps us distinguish it is its shortness—it is over almost as soon as begun, like a dot in the telegraph code. But in spite of being sharp, it is a modest little sound; it does not ring through the woods like the wild call of the hairy woodpecker.

Another note is a long whinny made up of a dozen or more *tchicks*. These increase in rapidity soon after the beginning of the series, and the pitch drops rather sharply. Near the close, the volume diminishes, and the whinny ends with a "dying fall."

Elizabeth Sampson (1934) brings this note very clearly to our mind when she speaks of it as "a handful of his staccato notes * * * flung out in a rapid run, gaining speed as they came, till they almost tumbled over each other at the end."

This whinny is also given, although not often, without any fall in pitch.

The downy woodpecker has other notes in its vocabulary, some of which are described under courtship, but, compared to the two noted above, they are rarely heard. It may be that some of these notes are only modifications of the call note, uttered with a slightly changed inflection. One, a single short note, has a distinct vocal quality.

Of the young birds in the nest, Dr. Arthur A. Allen (1928) says that they "keep up an incessant chippering, especially when they get the least bit hungry, and at times they sound almost like a bee-hive, from the ground."

After the young birds have left the nest, I have often heard them give a series of *tchicks* similar to the whinny of the adults, but in a weaker voice and *all on the same pitch*. However, this note evidently varies, for Francis H. Allen says in his notes that the young have also a rattle resembling the kingfisher rattle of *D. villosus*, but fainter and falling in pitch like the similar note of the adult.

Field marks.—The downy, the smallest of our woodpeckers, may be separated at once from any other woodpecker, except the hairy, by the broad white stripe down the back.

The hairy is half again as large as the downy, but in situations where comparative size counts little, the downy may be recognized by its short bill—no longer than its head. The hairy's bill is longer even in proportion to the size of the bird.

Enemies.—Lewis O. Shelley, who as a bird bander has handled many downy woodpeckers, says in his notes: "I find this species practically free from parasites, but I have found among the feathers the two bird flies, *Ornithoica confluenta* and *Ornithomyia anchineuria.*"

Alexander Wilson (1832) shows that the house wren, although not an open enemy of the downy, causes it a good deal of annoyance by stealing its nest sometimes. He says:

> The house wren, who also builds in the hollow of a tree, but who is neither furnished with the necessary tools nor strength for excavating such an apartment for himself, allows the woodpeckers to go on, till he thinks it will answer his purpose, then attacks them with violence, and generally succeeds in driving them off. I saw some weeks ago a striking example of this, where the woodpeckers we are now describing, after commencing in a cherry-tree within a few yards of the house, and having made considerable progress, were turned out by the wren; the former began again on a pear-tree in the garden, fifteen or twenty yards off, whence, after digging out a most complete apartment, and one egg being laid, they were once more assaulted by the same impertinent intruder, and finally forced to abandon the place.

Maurice Thompson (1885) describes thus the bird's defense against the attack of a goshawk:

> I once saw a goshawk pursuing a downy woodpecker, when the latter darted through a tuft of foliage and flattened itself close upon the body of a thick oak bough, where it remained as motionless as the bark itself. The hawk alighted on the same bough within two feet of its intended victim, and remained sitting there for some minutes, evidently looking in vain for it, with nothing but thin air between monster and morsel. The woodpecker was stretched longitudinally on the bough, its tail and beak close to the bark, its black and white speckled feathers looking like a continuation of the wrinkles and lichen.

More commonly, when attacked by a hawk, the downy dodges behind a branch and, if the hawk catch sight of it again, either winds round the branch or dives behind another one. By this adroit defense the downy has a fair chance of eluding the hawk's attack.

Fall and winter.—We see little change in the behavior of the downy woodpecker at the approach of autumn, at the time when many of the migratory birds are beginning to show a daily increasing restlessness, seeming on tiptoe to start on their long journey, moving about actively in their new feathers, and breaking out sometimes with a phrase of postnuptial song. In the role of permanent resident, the downy remains calm in the midst of the bustle of travel; it may join the hurrying groups for a time, or become surrounded by them, but it does not catch the contagion of departure, and soon drops behind to continue its local round.

The downy is not forced to seek the sun and warmth and the inexhaustible food of the Tropics, for the woodlands of New England and southeastern Canada are stored with food that, with a roosting hole, enables the bird to withstand the severest winter. But this food is limited; the insects that have been multiplying all summer, thus adding continually to the woodpeckers' supply of food, stop multiplying when the frosts come, and will add no more until spring.

The downy is not a bird that ranges widely in search of food; moreover, for protection against the weather it is held to the vicinity of its roosting hole. Therefore each bird, in order to be sure of sufficient food for itself during the cold months, must maintain dominion over a territory large enough to support it through the winter.

Thus it comes about that in autumn the downy *does* perforce change its habits, or rather its attitude toward other birds of its species. The families disperse, and until the next breeding season each individual becomes a solitary bird, living in a restricted region, which it defends against trespass, resenting and repelling the approach of any other downy woodpecker.

This reversal of attitude or character—the change from a member of a family to an anchorite in fall, and back again in spring—takes place gradually, we may suppose, and not exactly at the same time in every bird. Hence one bird meeting another in autumn, while the change is in progress, may underestimate the degree to which it has drawn away from its fellows, or, in the spring, may overestimate the amount of cordiality that has returned to the wintering anchorite. This lack of understanding may give rise to behavior difficult or impossible for us to interpret.

Sometimes the relationship between two downies is clear enough, as when, on September 20, 1910, I saw a male fly repeatedly at a female in a menacing way and drive her off; and when on November 3, 1935, I saw a female bird fly toward a male, which was perched near a hole in an electric-light pole, from which he did not retire, as a perched bird commonly does when approached by a bird on the wing, but held his ground while she flew away; and when Lewis O. Shelley (MS.) tells of a female bird "rushing with antagonistic attitude at her two daughters" and also driving off her granddaughters whenever they invaded her winter territory in autumn, all these birds being identified by bands.

There are cases, however, in which the relationship between the birds is very puzzling. In the following scene, from my notes, there is a hint of hostility or remonstrance, but a suggestion of courtship also—out of place, it seems, in autumn between two female birds. "October 15, 1935. Two birds are in a large, bare maple tree; one is noticeably larger than the other, but neither one has a red occipital patch. They keep near each other, one following the other by short, quick flights. They perch perfectly motionless for a moment a foot or two apart; then both together sway their heads, swinging them quickly down and up to one side, down and up to the other side. The swing is very rapid, like the wink of an eye. They flit their wings upward and outward, also with the speed of a wink, over and over—all this without a sound. They fly behind a branch sometimes but keep mostly in sight of each other, and, although neither attacks, each seems wary of attack and dodges away when approached. They sometimes alight on very slender branches, and once a bird goes to the ground where it stands with its head held high up. They move very actively and lightly, with never the slightest blundering, flitting silently and easily from branch to branch."

The following astonishing story, taken from William Brewster's Concord journal (1937), tells of a case in which antagonism of unknown cause leads to the killing with brutal violence of a female downy by a male:

March 20, 1911. We were in the dining-room, consulting about the day's work, when we heard the *tchick* note of the Downy Woodpecker repeated almost incessantly and very rapidly just outside. For a moment or more we paid no attention to it. But something unusual in its quality and its insistence soon led me to look out and this was what I saw:

On the snow, among the outermost stems of the lilacs on one side of the dense thicket that they form was a female Downy with extended and quivering wings. About her hopped or rather danced a handsome male, showing the red on his occiput very conspicuously. He kept striking at her head with his bill and occasionally he held on for a few seconds, when the two birds fluttered about together and perhaps rolled over once or twice, closely united. At first I thought it an amatory encounter and I am still almost certain that the male attempted to secure sexual contact with the female once or twice. But if so it could not have been his primary or at least sole object. For he continued to peck her head even when she was lying almost motionless on the snow. For a time she seemed to be trying to escape and for fully two minutes her cries were piteous and incessant. At length he left her and flew up into an elm where he clung for a moment or two, making what seemed to me a very unusual display of the red on his occiput. Then of a sudden he swooped down on the female, who had meanwhile been cowering in the middle of a cluster of lilac stems, on the snow. Dragging her forth from this slight shelter into an open space, he attacked her again, this time with obvious fury, fairly raining a shower of blows on the back of her head. She seemed too weak to make any further attempt to escape and her cries, although continued, were so faint that we could only just hear them. I now realized for the first time that he was inspired by the *lust of killing* and not by sexual ardor. It was very hard to refrain from rushing out and driving him away but I restrained the impulse, not being willing to interrupt a tragedy of such extraordinary, if repulsive, interest. It would have made no difference any·way, for this final onslaught lasted only a very few seconds. During its continuance the male Downy seemed literally beside himself with rage. No

Butcher Bird that I have ever watched has shown, while dealing with a Mouse or Sparrow, more murderous energy. After finishing the foul deed he left the female lying perfectly motionless and flew up again into the elm. We now went out and picked up the female. She was still living but unable to move. The [back] of her head was soaked in blood and her bare skull showed in places. She died a little later. I skinned her and preserved her skull which I have attached to the skin. It is *punctured in 10 or 12 places.* The bird was in normal condition physically with healthy-looking ovary the ovules undeveloped. The only injuries were to the skull.

Doubtless a few downy woodpeckers move southward in autumn or early in winter, especially from the northern part of the bird's range. Dr. Charles W. Townsend in his Ipswich notes (MS.) says that he sees "evident migrants not uncommonly in October and November." But most of our birds spend the whole year round with us, and in autumn we may watch them as they make provision for winter. Even before the leaves are off the trees—in September here in New England—we may hear, day after day as we pass a certain tree, the tapping of a downy woodpecker where, invisible from the ground, high up on a branch, it is digging out a cavity, its roosting hole, in which it will sleep alone through the long winer nights, and into which it may retreat in the daytime whenever "the frost-wind blows."

DRYOBATES PUBESCENS NELSONI Oberholser

NELSON'S DOWNY WOODPECKER

HABITS

This large race of the downy woodpecker inhabits the wooded regions of northern Alaska and northern Canada, intergrading with *Dryobates pubescens medianus* in southern Canada and possibly in northern New England.

Dr. H. C. Oberholser (1896a), in describing and naming it, characterizes it as "similar to *Dryobates pubescens* [=*medianus*], but averaging larger; the under parts pure white instead of brownish; the lower tail-coverts and outer tail-feathers averaging with much less of black markings; red nuchal band of male averaging somewhat wider."

Swainson and Richardson (1831) say: "This diminutive but exceedingly industrious Woodpecker is a constant inhabitant of the fur-countries up to the fifty-eighth parallel. It seeks its food principally on the maple, elm, and ash, and, north of latitude 54°, where these trees terminate, on the aspen and birch. Its researches are made mostly, if not wholly, on live trees."

Dr. E. W. Nelson (1887) writes:

Throughout the Territory [Alaska] where woodland or a growth of bushes and small trees occurs the present bird is certain to be found, and is a resident winter and summer. It has been taken along the entire course of the Yukon as well as at various points on the coast of Bering Sea, and thence south at Kadiak and Sitka. In autumn it is a rather common visitant to the coast of Norton Sound in spite of the lack of timber, and it was not uncommon to see it clinging to the sides of the houses, or to the flagstaff, and other similar supports; after resting awhile, and, perhaps, tapping a few times on the unproductive logs, they would leave for a more promising field. They were seen at times passing from one alder patch to another, on the hill-sides, and they follow the spruces and other trees to the shore of the sea.

While I was camping in spring, at the Yukon mouth, these birds were rather common in the dense bushes along this stream and its tributaries. Their holes were frequently found in the decaying stubs, although I did not find a nest containing eggs. This species appears to frequent deciduous thickets and trees by preference, as, in addition to the various times which I saw it in the interior in winter, while at the Yukon mouth, I always found it about locations where only deciduous trees and bushes were found, and its holes were always made in cottonwood or birch-stubs.

Judged from what little is known about them, the nesting, food, and other habits of Nelson's downy woodpecker do not differ materially from those of its more southern relatives, except as influenced by its different environment. Living in the far north, where trees are small and scarce, it has to be content to excavate its nest in small trees or low stumps. There are very few eggs in collections; a set of five eggs in the Thayer collection was taken from a hole 4 feet from the ground in a rotten stump, near Fort Saskatchewan, Canada, on June 10, 1898. These eggs are like other eggs of the species, pure white, ovate in shape, and somewhat glossy. The measurements of 31 eggs average 19.54 by 15.43 millimeters; the eggs showing the four extremes measure 21.9 by 16.1, 19.4 by 16.4, 17.5 by 15.0, and 18.65 by 14.28 millimeters.

DRYOBATES PUBESCENS TURATI (Malherbe)

WILLOW WOODPECKER

HABITS

The downy woodpeckers of California were for many years all called *D. p. gairdneri*, until Dr. Walter K. Fisher (1902) called attention to the smaller and lighter-colored race, which inhabits much of the coast region and nearly all the lowlands of southern California. For this race, he very properly revived Malherbe's name, as given above, for this name was based on birds taken near Monterey. He gives as the characters of the willow woodpecker:

Smaller than *Dryobates pubescens gairdneri*, with smaller feet; under parts lighter; the elongated superciliary patch and rictal stripe extending over sides of neck, pure white, instead of smoky white of *gairdneri;* tertials always more or less spotted with white. * * *

Dryobates pubescens turati is a southern representative of *gairdneri*, which it resembles in the smoky under parts and restricted areas of white on the wings, and from which it differs in its smaller size, much smaller feet, and clearer white markings of head. The present form is near true *pubescens* of the Southern States, but differs from it in having much less white on the wings, the coverts and tertials of *pubescens* being conspicuously and often heavily marked with white. * * *

The willow woodpecker in a typical form breeds from Los Angeles and San Bernardino counties north in the coast ranges to San Francisco Bay, and along the west slope of the Sierra Nevada at least to Yuba County. Intergradation with *gairdneri* occurs over the coast region north of San Francisco Bay and in the mountains at the head of the Sacramento Valley.

Grinnell, Dixon, and Linsdale (1930) say of the haunts of the willow woodpecker in the Lassen Peak region: "Downy woodpeckers were seen most often close to streams and in orchards. Their forage places included the limbs or small trunks of willow, alder, cottonwood, sycamore, valley oak, blue oak, digger pine, and yellow pine trees."

Nesting.—Major Bendire (1895) writes: "Mr. Charles A. Allen informs me that it breeds in the oaks and willows along the Sacramento River, Calif., but that it is not common. Its breeding sites seem to be confined to deciduous trees, preferably dead ones, or old stumps, and besides those already mentioned, sycamore and cottonwoods are occasionally used. Their nesting sites are rarely found at any great distance from the ground, usually ranging from 4 to 20 feet up and rarely higher."

W. L. Dawson (1923) says: "Willow woodpeckers, in the wild, place their nests at considerable heights in deciduous trees, and those, if possible, among thick growths on moist ground. Both sexes assist in excavation, as in incubation. Partially decayed wood is selected, and an opening made about an inch and a quarter in diameter. After driving straight in for an inch or two, the passage turns down and widens two or three diameters. At the depth of a foot or so the crystal white eggs are deposited on a neat bed of fine chips. Incubation lasts twelve days, and the young are hatched some time in May."

Eggs.—The willow woodpecker lays three to six eggs, more commonly four or five; it may occasionally lay seven, as some of the other western races have been known to do. The eggs are typical of the species. The measurements of 40 eggs average 18.74 by 15.20 millimeters; the eggs showing the four extremes measure **22.3** by 15.7, 18.4 by **16.3**, **17.3** by 14.5, and 18.0 by **14.4** millimeters.

Food.—Mr. Dawson (1923) writes:

It is as an orchardist that the Willow Woodpecker deserves the most careful consideration. Bird-lovers are, perhaps prone to superlatives in commending their friends, but it is safe to say that a more useful bird *for his ounces* than the downy woodpecker does not exist. He eats not only ants and the larvae of wood-boring beetles, but scale insects, plant lice, and the pupae of the detestable coddling moth. The evidence is clear that these incomparable tree experts, together with their friends, the nuthatches, the chickadees, and the creepers, would insure the health of our orchards if they were numerous enough. It becomes of the highest importance, then, to study their welfare in turn. In the northern and more elevated valleys of the State, it may be worth while to offer them nuts or to hang out a bit of suet in winter. In the South no such precautions are necessary. A fundamental consideration, however, is the provision of suitable nesting sites. Experiment has shown that the downy's forage range during the breeding season is not extensive. The clamoring young are fed by the product of nearby trees (fed, it may be, a thousand insects a day). Their services, therefore, must be secured in the orchard; and to this end the orchardist must consent to leave certain dead branches—a foot or so at the base of the larger ones will do—for a nesting site. Dead wood, of course, invites insects; but the most serious and frequent mistake which our California orchardists make is to trim out all the dead wood from the fruit trees. A pair of Willow Woodpeckers, or of Slender-billed Nuthatches, will clean out all the dangerous pests from a dead tree, and sixteen live ones to boot.

Grinnell and Storer (1924) made some studies of the feeding habits of the willow woodpecker in the Yosemite region, of which they say:

A pair of Willow Woodpeckers proved to be regular tenants of Curry's apple orchard on the floor of the Yosemite Valley. They, or their ancestors, had evidently worked there for some years, with the result that most of the 150 trees in the orchard showed marks of their attention, and many of the trunks were fairly riddled with drillings somewhat like those of the sapsucker. * * *

However destructive this drilling may seem to be, it does not seriously affect the vitality of the trees; the pits are but 4 to 5 mm. deep, penetrating only those outer layers of the bark which after a time scale off. We should judge that all evidence of this woodpecker's work is thus removed through natural process within about three years. The heartwood of the tree therefore seems not to be damaged at all by the woodpecker's work; it *is* damaged, however, by the work of the true sapsucker. Our inference from these facts is that the willow woodpecker feeds on the inner layers of bark, which the bird exposes through the perforations described above. We watched a bird at work; moreover, bits of inner bark-fibers were found adhering to the bristles around the bill of a bird shot.

Evidently this observation and report started the same old controversy that arose in connection with the eastern bird, which has been referred to under that subspecies. Charles W. Michael intimated, in course of conversation with Dr. Grinnell, that they were mistaken in ascribing these drillings to willow woodpeckers rather than to red-breasted sapsuckers. This led to the publication, by Dr. Grinnell (1928a), of the evidence produced by Mr. Michael and himself, to which the reader is referred. In spite of some evidence, and more supposed evidence, to the contrary, it now seems to be generally conceded that the downy woodpeckers seldom, if ever, drill these holes for themselves, but that they often feed from holes drilled by sapsuckers. The small amount of drilling done by the downy woodpeckers seems to do the trees no great harm.

Behavior.—Grinnell and Storer (1924) write:

The quietness of the willow woodpecker, as compared with most other species in its family, is noteworthy. We heard no single call note from it, and only at long intervals did we hear the indescribable short trill characteristic of this bird. Individuals are much restricted in range, foraging along a relatively short line of cottonwoods or willows day after day. Once a bird is located, it can usually be found in the same place regularly. When foraging it moves about with very little commotion, and even when drilling for insects works so quietly that only a keen auditor can detect its presence. No matter what the season of the year, a pair of these birds is to be found usually within hearing of each other. The bird's close adherence to deciduous trees makes it more conspicuous and easier to observe in late fall and winter than in the summertime when the trees are fully leaved out; but even in winter, our experience with the willow woodpecker led us to consider it about the most elusive of all the diurnal birds of the Yosemite region.

We had always supposed that the rapid series of notes uttered by this species were given only by the adult male and hence constituted a sort of song. But on June 24, 1920, in Yosemite Valley a juvenile male was found, with his head out of a nest hole eight feet above the ground in a dead branch of a live willow, giving every few moments this very series of notes. The large *crown* patch of red on this bird established its age and sex clearly. There was every indication that the notes were being given as a food call.

M. P. Skinner contributes the following note:

One seen in Sequoia National Park in August was drilling at the bases of willow shoots near a river. It perched lengthwise of the stems. It managed to keep well hidden, but worked industriously and did not change its position much during the short time that I could see it. Later, I caught a glimpse occasionally of the woodpecker's red head, although the bird kept hidden most of the time. This reminded me that I had often wondered why red usually marked a woodpecker's head. Certainly it makes a wonderful recognition mark. In that way it might well be that red on the constantly moving head of the woodpecker would be of value to the race.

DRYOBATES BOREALIS (Vieillot)

RED-COCKADED WOODPECKER

PLATES 9, 10

HABITS

CONTRIBUTED BY EUGENE EDMUND MURPHEY

Introduced to ornithology by Wilson under the name of *Picus querulus*, the red-cockaded woodpecker is locally common throughout the open pine country of the South Atlantic and Gulf States and extends its range into the pine country of Oklahoma and Missouri. Its preference is very definitely for the open woods, shunning the dense thickets of second-growth pine and the deep recesses of the cypress swamps even when the latter are only a few hundred yards away from its chosen environment. These open pine woods, which abound both in the Austro-Riparian and Carolinian Zones of the South Atlantic and Gulf States, represent not a normal growth of pine forest but an original pine forest modified by the pernicious custom of annually burning the woods under the impression that in that way next year's pasturage will be improved.

As a result, the younger trees and seedlings are killed off. Only the hardier and more resistant survivors remain, so that there is little or no underbrush and the general appearance of these woods is more that of an open glade or park than of typical pine forest. William Brewster (1882) comments on the character of these forests as follows: "The pine lands of the South have an open park-like character that is a continual surprise to one accustomed only to New England forests. The trees rarely stand in close proximity to one another, and they are often so widely scattered that the general effect is that of an opening rather than a forest." These pines are chiefly *Pinus palustris* Miller, *Pinus ellioti* Engelmann, and *Pinus taeda* Linnaeus.

From many sections of the South where it was formerly common, the red-cockaded woodpecker has disappeared by reason of the ruthless destruction of pine forests by the lumbermen. When the large timber is cut out, the birds leave the locality and apparently do not return. However, there is still a considerable amount of pine forest suitable for its nesting that is held in private hands and not about to be destroyed. In fact, such timber holdings are largely on the increase, particularly in the "low country" of South Carolina and Georgia and in certain zones around Thomasville, Ga., and Aiken, S. C., where vast tracts are being conserved by private ownership as game refuges and shooting preserves.

There is also a very considerable amount of intelligent reforestation being carried out, which in time will also furnish adequate and suitable breeding grounds. This species is so highly specialized at least in the South Atlantic States in its habits and its choice of environment that the destruction of the pine forests would probably put its existence in serious jeopardy.

Nesting.—Audubon (1842) stated that "the nest is not unfrequently bored in a decayed stump about thirty feet high." G. W. Morse (1927) found the bird nesting in a willow tree in a pasture in Oklahoma. M. G. Vaiden (MS.) reports from Collins, Miss., the taking of a nest from a pine tree, the top of which was dead and the nest hole about 8 feet from the top. Arthur T. Wayne (1906), who has probably had more intimate experience with this bird than any other observer, states:

I have seen perhaps a thousand holes in which this woodpecker had bred or was breeding, and *every one* was excavated in a *living* pine tree, ranging from eighteen to one hundred feet above the ground. This bird never lays its eggs until the pine gum pours freely from beneath and around the hole, and in order to accelerate the flow the birds puncture the bark to the "skin" of the tree thereby causing the gum to exude freely. This species, unlike the Pileated Woodpecker, returns to the same hole year after year until it can no longer make the gum exude. But like the Pileated Woodpecker, it is much attached to the tree in which it has first made its nest, and as long as it can find a suitable spot it will continue to excavate new holes until the tree is *killed* by this process of boring. I have frequently counted as many as four holes in one tree, and in two instances I have seen as many as eight. These birds seem to know by instinct that the center of the tree is rotten, or what lumber men call "blackheart," and they never make a mistake when selecting a tree! The hole is bored through the solid wood, generally a little upward, and to the center of the tree (which is always rotten).

The overwhelming majority of observers who have studied the red-cockaded woodpecker in its normal habitat concur in the opinion that the site of selection for the nest hole is in a living pine that, however, has begun to rot at the core, and this condition of the heart of the tree the birds seem to be able to discern with unfailing accuracy. All the nests I have seen and studied were in living pines, and other ornithologists have made similar observations. T. Gilbert Pearson (1909) says: "So far as I have observed, always excavated in the trunk of a living pine tree. The site chosen varies from twenty-five to fifty feet from the earth." H. L. Harllee (MS.), of Florence, S. C., writes: "It nests in the same hole each year in close proximity to several pairs, usually from two to four." The observations of Gilbert R. Rossignol (MS.), writing from Savannah, Ga., agree with the foregoing. He states: "Before the lumberman invaded our great pine forests, the red-cockaded was fairly common, for I have found 10 or 12 pairs nesting in a 50-acre tract, provided, of course, that the pine trees were not too close to one another. These little woodpeckers did not like dark heavily timbered forests. The bird drills a hole in a living pine ranging from 25 to 80 or more feet high, and it is almost impossible to get the eggs without full equipment. It takes a brace and bit to bore holes a little above where you think the bottom of the nest is located, and then sometimes you strike below it, or again right into it on an incomplete set or no eggs at all. The eggs I have found were always more or less sticky with pine gum. This bird will nest in the same hole for several years and use the same tree probably during its entire life, but if the tree dies, or the gum does not flow freely, the birds will desert their old home." Henry Nehrling (1882), writing from Texas, states that "it usually excavates its nesting sites in deciduous trees," and E. A. McIlhenny (Bendire, 1895) that "in southern Louisiana it generally nests in willow and china trees." The nesting hole is bored usually slightly upward for several inches then straight through into the softer unsound heart of the tree and downward for 8 inches to a foot or more. The nest cavity is gourd-shaped, and the eggs are laid upon fine chips and debris in the bottom of the cavity. The most striking thing about the nesting site, however, is due to the bird's custom of drilling numerous small holes through the bark of the tree until the resin exudes freely. This glazed patch of gum around the nesting hole is unmistakable and when once seen becomes an easy landmark for the location of the nests, inasmuch as it may be discerned through the open woods for a distance of several hundred yards. During the period of incubation, the birds are a sorry spectacle, the abdomen being largely denuded of feathers, as is customary with many birds, and the breast feathers from the clavicle to the end of the sternum begaumed and matted together with resin, and, in fact, they remain permanently unfit to be taken as specimens until the next molting has been completed.

The nidification is earlier along the coast and southward than in the interior and toward the northern limits of its range, beginning sometimes as early as February, but the major nesting season may be said to be the last week in April and the first week in May.

S. A. Grimes tells us that old nests of this species are used by red-bellied and red-headed woodpeckers, white-breasted nuthatches, bluebirds, crested flycatchers, and flying squirrels.

Eggs.—The eggs vary from three to five in number, the latter being unusual; they are elliptically ovate in shape, pure glossy white, and semitranslucent when fresh. Not infrequently they are stained or smeared with resin from the breast feathers of the incubating bird. As a rule only one brood is raised in a season unless the first set has been taken, and both parents participate in incubation. There is some evidence tending to show that the eggs and even the unfledged young are sometimes thrown out of the nest by the birds when it has been disturbed.

The measurements of 50 eggs average 24.04 by 17.86 millimeters; the eggs showing the four extremes measure **26.42** by 18.54, 26.4 by **19.8, 21.38** by 17.46, and 23.77 by **16.66** millimeters.

Plumages.—The young in their first plumage bear the general color pattern of the adults with this important exception—the young male has a dull crimson oval central crown patch. However, while the pattern is identical with that of adult birds, the black is replaced by a dark sepia merging at times into an aniline black, and the bluish gloss evident on the crowns of the mature birds is lacking. Similarly, the feathers of the cheek patch in both sexes lack the fine silky gloss and texture that are later attained. The underparts show uniformly a buffy or ochraceous wash everywhere, and the barring of the tail is more pronounced. During this phase, the plumage is much softer and looser than it subsequently becomes.

With the first molt, the red crown patch is lost.

It is the belief of the writer, without sufficient specimens properly to verify it, that the cockades of the full adult male plumage are not attained until at least the third molt. Without careful dissection and sex determination of the immature birds, a fact notoriously difficult to the average ornithologist, the young of both sexes, after the crown patch is lost and the cockades have not appeared, would be indistinguishable.

Food.—The food, like that of most woodpeckers, consists primarily of larvae of various wood-boring insects, although beetles and grubs of other kinds as well as ants, grasshoppers, crickets, and caterpillars are frequently taken. An interesting habit of the red-cockaded woodpecker is that of going into the cornfields throughout the South at the time when the corn is at the roasting-ear stage and when many of the ears are infested with a worm that damages the grain to a very considerable extent. This habit is reported by Billy Ward (1930), of Timmonsville, S. C., and by Edward Dingle (1926), of Mount Pleasant, S. C., who says, "The Red-cockaded Woodpecker (*Phrenopicus borealis*) is very commonly found in cornfields during the time the corn is in the ear; in fact, the bird spends a large part of its time at this season in extracting the worms that bore into the ears of corn. I have often, at short distance, watched them engaged in this valuable work." They also feed on pine mast, the small wild grape, pokeberries, and other small wild fruit. I have never seen them in orchards or in fig trees, where the red-headed woodpecker is frequently found feeding.

As far as is known, this species does not visit cultivated fields, except as above referred to, or orchards and is not destructive to fruit and deserves to be regarded as wholly beneficial. This statement takes into account the fact that a number of observers say that they will continue to bore into certain pines that they have selected for a nesting site until the tree is killed. The fact is, however, that the tree is diseased and unsound before the woodpecker begins to utilize it and is already worthless for lumber, so that this species seems worthy of complete protection.

Behavior.—The bird is strikingly gregarious as compared with other woodpeckers and is ordinarily to be found in small groups of six, eight, or even ten individuals, which seem to keep in continuous touch with one another, calling back and forth, sounding their drum roll on resonant timber and apparently not satisfied unless assured of the near presence of the group.

This behavior is no doubt due to the fact that the family remains together until early in winter, although family groups are probably joined by other individuals until the number above referred to is attained. Numerous observers speak of the frequent association of the red-cockaded woodpecker with other birds. This to the mind of the writer, however, is purely accidental and is due to the fact that there are certain species of birds that inhabit the open pineries and have common feeding ground and habitat. It is true that one often sees bluebirds, tufted titmice, white-breasted and brown-headed nuthatches, and red-cockaded woodpeckers in the same woodland and that when sitting quietly and concealed all the species mentioned pass in review before the observer, but probably it is not a true gregariousness that embraces all these various species; rather the restlessness that so frequently seems to possess the avian population of a given tract of woods communicates itself from one to the other and the entire avifauna of a limited patch of woodland begins to move in a certain direction perhaps because of some alarm which has been communicated from one member of the group to the others.

These woodpeckers are exceedingly active, galloping from one tree to another and rapidly ascending it in quest of food or apparently often merely to secure a better observation point somewhere near the top of the tree. Their usual custom is to ascend the tree in spirals, although they have frequently been observed to continue a straight course up the trunk particularly when feeding. The bird may be described as wary rather than shy and is most adept at the familiar woodpecker trick of keeping the trunk of the tree between an approaching observer and itself.

As a rule they do not feed close to the ground, nor have I ever observed one on the ground even after the burning of a woodland, at which time the flicker and the red-bellied woodpecker may both be observed on the ground searching for grubs and insects killed by the blaze. Dr. Irving Phinizy (MS.) states that he has on several occasions observed the red-cockaded woodpecker descend a tree in a series of backward hops. This the writer has never observed. Arthur H. Howell (1932) states that the ivorybill inches backward down a tree, a somewhat different procedure. Frequently also they are observed, particularly when feeding near the top of a pine and out toward the end of a limb, to descend the hanging limb nuthatch fashion. Much of their feeding is done in the highest branches of the trees, and they seem to have a predilection for remaining there, spending a considerable portion of their time in the very crown of the tree, where they are very difficult to see.

They are exceedingly quarrelsome, particularly during the breeding season, yet their quarrels do not seem to be so serious or so prolonged as those of the red-headed woodpecker; and not infrequently, after the lapse of a very little time, birds that have been scolding one another most extensively again alight on the same pine tree and go about their respective businesses in perfect amity.

C. J. Maynard (1896) states, concerning its habits, as follows:

Wilson called the Cockaded Woodpeckers, *Picus querulus*, and this seems, at first glance, to be a most appropriate name, for, of all the family, these are not only the most noisy, but their notes are given in a decidedly fretful tone as if the birds were constantly in an irritable state of mind. It must have been upon the impulse of the moment, however, that the Pioneer Ornithologist gave them the name of Querulus Woodpeckers, for a close study of their habits gives a very different impression of them. They are, in fact, a most jovial class of birds, being almost contantly engaged in sporting about the tops of tall pines or chasing one another from tree to tree, uttering their peevish sounding notes very frequently when in the best humor. The noise is more noticeable because they congregate in flocks, and it is quite rare to find even a pair without other companions. They are also fond of the company of other members of the family and will even associate with the Jays, Blue Birds, or Warblers. This gregarious instinct does not forsake them during the breeding season, for they build in detached communities. The nests are almost always in living pines, often thirty or forty feet from the ground; thus, as the trunks of these trees are covered with a smooth bark, it is quite difficult to climb them and, when the nests are reached it is not easy to cut the hard wood, especially as the straight trunks afford no foot-hold.

In flight, the cockaded woodpeckers resemble the downy but when they alight they strike the object upon which they wish to rest very hard. Like the preceding species, they are also exceedingly agile, moving spirally up the tall tree trunks with great celerity. Although they will occasionally alight near the ground, yet they spend the greater part of their time in the tops of the lofty pines; in fact, they pass a large portion of their lives there, for they are seldom, if ever, found elsewhere than in the piney woods and they inhabit this kind of woodland even to the extreme southern portion of the main-land of Florida.

The bird is resident throughout its normal range, although David V. Hembree, of Roswell, Ga., in the very foothills of the Appalachian Range, a lifelong student and collector of birds, writes me, "This bird does not breed in this locality. I have never seen a nest. A few are found here, nearly always males in April or May, and I have always thought them to be migrants or strays from their regular range."

In common with the other small black and white woodpeckers, this species carries the vernacular name of sapsucker and in the main is not differentiated from the others, although one astute lumberman once said to me: "Speaking of sapsuckers, there *is* a piney-woods sapsucker which is different from the others, leastways he acts different."

Voice.—The voice is variously described by different observers—"harsh and discordant," "almost exactly resembling the calls of the Brownheaded Nuthatch," "resembling the yank-yank of a White-breasted Nuthatch," "they have sharp calls more like loud sparrow alarms than woodpecker notes," "resembling the querulous cries of young birds."

The bird is noisy, and its call notes and scolding notes are to the ear of the writer quite radically different, the scolding note being more prolonged, somewhat rolling in character and lower in pitch. There is a definite nasal character to a note that to that extent does resemble the notes of the nuthatch. The note is quite characteristic and when once learned is distinguishable with ease from that of the other small woodpeckers. It resembles more the high note of some small woodwind instrument than anything else, having a definite clarinetlike quality.

Descriptions of bird notes are notoriously variable because of the variability of the human ear, and many attempts at phonetic reproduction of the bird notes are unsuccessful, and when, as is so often done, the attempt is directed to reproduction in syllables, the result is usually a futile and meaningless onomatopoeia.

DISTRIBUTION

Range.—Southeastern United States; nonmigratory.

The range of the red-cockaded woodpecker extends **north** to northeastern Oklahoma (Copan); southern Missouri (Shannon County); Tennessee (Beersheba and Allardt); and North Carolina (Red Springs and Beaufort). **East** on the Atlantic coast from North Carolina (Beaufort) to southern Florida (Long Pine Key). **South** on the Gulf coast from the Florida Keys (Long Pine Key) to southeastern Texas (Houston). **West** to Texas (Houston); northwestern Louisiana (Mansfield); probably western Arkansas (Mena); and eastern Oklahoma (Tulsa and Copan).

Casual records.—It seems probable that this species may breed or upon occasion has bred in the vicinity of Raleigh, N. C., as it was noted there several times in April from 1890 to 1898. It also has been reported as seen at Piney Creek, N. C., on July 6, 1932, and on September 12, 1933.

A specimen in the Academy of Natural Sciences of Philadelphia was collected near that city in 1861; one in the collection of the Ohio State University was taken near Columbus, Ohio, on March 15, 1872. According to Stone (1909) the collection of George N. Lawrence contained a specimen taken near Hoboken, N. J.

Egg dates.—Florida: 30 records, April 3 to May 28; 15 records, April 29 to May 20, indicating the height of the season.

South Carolina: 14 records, April 27 to May 28.

DRYOBATES SCALARIS SYMPLECTUS Oberholser

TEXAS WOODPECKER

HABITS

This is the subspecies that was formerly known as Baird's woodpecker, *Dryobates scalaris bairdi*, which was then understood to be the resident bird of Texas, New Mexico, and Arizona. But when Dr. H. C. Oberholser (1911b) revised the *scalaris* group, the name *bairdi* was restricted to the bird of central Mexico, and the Texas bird was described, as a new subspecies, under the above name. It was characterized as follows:

Resembling *Dryobates scalaris cactophilus*, but male smaller; upper parts lighter, the white bars wider, the black bars narrower, and with more white on pileum; and sides of breast less often *streaked* (mostly spotted). * * *

This new subspecies differs from *Dryobates scalaris bairdi*, from Hidalgo, much as does *Dryobates scalaris cactophilus*, except that it is smaller, and still more extensively white on all the upper parts.

This race reaches its extreme development in Texas; and specimens from central Tamaulipas and central Nuevo Leon are not so light above, showing a tendency toward *Dryobates scalaris bairdi*. They are also somewhat more smoky below. There is, however, no difference in size between examples from Texas and Tamaulipas.

The range of the Texas woodpecker extends northward into southeastern Colorado and southward into southern Tamaulipas. George Finlay Simmons (1925) says that in Texas it is "rather general in distribution and in choice of habitat; somewhat open post oak woods and oak upland gravel terraces; mesquite forests; hackberry shade trees in town; mesquite association pasturelands; open woods not far from water; marginal timber along streams. In the hills, cottonwoods and oaks along stream bottoms; wooded slopes of gorges. In winter, leafless city shade hackberry trees."

The Texas woodpecker is widely distributed and fairly common all over Texas, except in the extreme eastern and extreme western portions; it is a well known and familiar bird, just as our eastern downy woodpecker is in the East; it is locally known as the "Texan sapsucker" or "ladder-backed woodpecker." Most of its habits are similar to those of the cactus woodpecker, but it seems to enjoy a somewhat more diversified habitat and is more inclined to forage and nest in larger trees; it is not so strictly confined to the deserts and their environs.

Nesting.—Mr. Simmons (1925) says that the nest is located from "4 to 25, average 12, feet from ground, in rotten stubs or dead and partly decayed branches of oak, mesquite, hackberry, and willow trees, usually alongside lake, river, creek, or ravine; when suitable trees are not to be found, nests in cedar fence posts or telegraph poles along roadsides; when in mesquite tree on mesquite-covered prairie, entrance of cavity on under side of low, drooping limb. * * * Entrance diameter 1.50. Depth of cavity 7 to 8, rarely 10."

Eggs.—The Texas woodpecker lays 2 to 6 eggs, usually 4 or 5, rarely as many as 7. These are indistinguishable from the eggs of the cactus woodpecker. The measurements of 51 eggs average 20.50 by 15.83 millimeters; the eggs showing the four extremes measure 22.86 by 15.75, 20.32 by 17.02, 17.27 by 15.49, and 19.05 by 14.73 millimeters.

Food.—Mr. Simmons (1925) says that it "searches high up on the knotty trunks of oak trees in open groves for larvae and eggs of injurious wood-boring insects, for the adults of similar as well as other insects, and for weevils and ants."

Voice.—Simmons (1925) says that this is "usually a thin, high-pitched, shrill *cheek; tcheek, queep* or *queep-queep,* uttered as the bird gives a hop in its progress up the tree-trunk. Sometimes an incredibly rapid, shrill, ringing, even, not-so-high-pitched *cheeky-cheeky - cheeky - cheeky - cheeky* or *tchee-dee-dee-dee-dee-dee-dee-dee-dee-deet;* less commonly, *chickp, chickp, chick-chick-chick-chick-chick-chick-chick-chick.* Drums rapidly with its bill on dead limb of tree at any time of year."

DISTRIBUTION

Range.—Southwestern United States, Mexico, and British Honduras; nonmigratory.

The range of this woodpecker extends **north** to southern California (Hesperia and Needles); southern Nevada (Upper Cottonwood Springs); southern Utah (Virgin River Valley); and probably southeastern Colorado (Swink). **East** to probably southeastern Colorado (Swink and Springfield); western Oklahoma (Kenton and Hollis); Texas (San Angelo, Kerrville, Boerne, San Antonio, Corpus Christi, and Brownsville); Tamaulipas (Presas and Ciudad Victoria); Yucatan (Chichen-Itza); Quintana Roo (Cozumel Island); and British Honduras (Manatee Lagoon and Ycacos Lagoon). **South** to British Honduras (Ycacos Lagoon); Jalisco (Zapotlan); Nayarit (Tres Marias Islands); and Baja California (Cape San Lucas). **West** to Baja California (Cape San Lucas, San Jose del Cabo, El Sauz, San Fernando, and Cocopah); and southern California (Paint Canyon, White Water, and Hesperia).

The range as above outlined applies to the entire species, which has, however, been divided into 15 or more subspecies or geographic races. Most of these, including the typical variety (*Dryobates scalaris scalaris*), are found only in regions south of the Rio Grande. The four races found in North America are distributed as follows: The Texas woodpecker (*D. s. symplectus*) is found from southeastern Colorado south and east through east-central Texas to Coahuila, Tamaulipas, and Nuevo Leon. The cactus woodpecker (*D. s. cactophilus*) ranges from western Texas through New Mexico, Arizona, and southern Utah and Nevada south to northern Durango. The western edge of the range of this race cuts across southeastern California and northeastern Baja California. The San Fernando woodpecker (*D. s. eremicus*) is found in northern Baja California except for the northeastern part. The San Lucas woodpecker (*D. s. lucasa-*

nus) occurs in southern part of Baja California north to about latitude 29° N.

Egg dates.—California: 7 records, April 11 to May 9.

Baja California: 12 records, April 16 to June 2.

Texas: 45 records, April 14 to June 22; 23 records, April 20 to May 7, indicating the height of the season.

DRYOBATES SCALARIS LUCASANUS (Xantus)

SAN LUCAS WOODPECKER

HABITS

The ladder-backed woodpecker of the southern half of the peninsula of Baja California, Mexico, has long been recognized as a distinct subspecies under the above name. It inhabits the Lower Austral deserts from Cape San Lucas north to about latitude 29° N. William Brewster (1902) says: "Mr. Frazar considers this woodpecker 'rather common and generally distributed in the cape region, except on the mountains, where it was not met with.' He found it most numerous about La Paz, but did not see it anywhere to the northward of that place during his trip along the Gulf coast."

This is a smaller bird than *Dryobates scalaris eremicus* from the northern half of Baja California; both upper and lower surfaces are lighter in color, with the white bars on the back broader and with the sides of the breast spotted. Mr. Brewster (1902) writes:

All the characters which have been proposed for this Woodpecker are shown by the large series before me to be subject to much variation, but this, as in the case of *Melanerpes angustifrons*, is confined within limits which do not overlap, if, indeed, they quite reach those of the bird's nearest allies. The restriction of the black on the outer tail feathers is perhaps its best distinguishing feature, although this is not at all uniform, for many of my specimens have three complete dark bars crossing both webs of the outer tail feathers, while in one a fourth bar is only broken by a small space near the middle of the feather. The width of the dark bars on the back is also variable, although these bars are usually wider than in any of the allied forms. The feet average larger than those of *bairdi*, but they are by no means *always* larger. A difference which I do not find mentioned in descriptions, but which is shown by my series to be quite as constant as most of the characters that have been proposed, is that the white spots on the top of the head are much larger and more numerous than in *bairdi*, while the red is less vivid and more nearly restricted to the crown and occiput.

Griffing Bancroft (1930) writes of this woodpecker, in central Lower California, near the northern limit of its supposed range:

This little denizen of brush and thick undergrowth requires a heavy stand of low cactuses in which to feed and rest. It occurs from the shores of the Gulf to the mouth of José María Cañon. Though the rarest of the resident Picidae it is still fairly common. Its nesting instincts are quite distinct from other *Dryobates scalaris*. They, similarly situated, would utilize sahuaro, it is true, but they would also be prone to add such substitutes as dry mescal stalks, telephone poles, tree yucca and mesquite and would, more often than not, chose one of these other sites by preference. But *lucasanus* confines itself to the cardón, at least in the district we were studying, selecting a single-stalked giant cactus and drilling its hole very near the top of the plant. As a result the nest-cavity is rather uniformly twenty feet above ground. The entrance hole is at the top of a cavity typically five inches in diameter by fifteen in depth. No foreign material is brought in for a nest. The eggs lie on the chips that fall in the process of excavating.

The number of eggs in a clutch is two, three, or rarely four. The first two weeks in May find almost all the San Lucas Woodpeckers at the peak of laying. After the middle of the month nests with young may be expected. The parent bird will ordinarily flush, especially if the cardón be tapped, but it is not very nervous about its home. It is too busy with family duties to waste much attention on strangers.

The eggs are similar to those of the other subspecies. Bancroft (1930) gives the average measurements of 23 eggs as 22.9 by 18.1 millimeters. The measurements of 10 other eggs average 21.30 by 16.61 millimeters; the eggs, in this series, showing the four extremes measure **24.40** by 18.70, 23.70 by **18.80, 19.50** by 16.80, and 21.43 by **15.42** millimeters.

DRYOBATES SCALARIS CACTOPHILUS Oberholser

CACTUS WOODPECKER

HABITS

The ladder-backed woodpeckers are quite widely distributed in the Southwestern United States and in nearly all Mexico and in British Honduras, chiefly in the Lower Austral and Tropical Zones. When Dr. Harry C. Oberholser (1911b) wrote his revision of this group, he split the species *Dryobates scalaris* into 15 subspecies, 9 of which he described and named as new subspecies. Only two of these subspecies are found within the limits of the United States, and only two in Baja California, giving us four on our Check-List.

The name *Dryobates scalaris bairdi*, which was for a long time used to designate the ladder-backed woodpeckers of the United States, was restricted by Oberholser to a Mexican form. He gave as the characters of *cactophilus*, "much like *Dryobates scalaris eremicus*, but smaller, particularly the tail and bill; lower surface lighter, laterally almost always *streaked* with black; upper parts lighter—the black bars on back and scapulars narrower; wing-quills with larger spots and broader bars of white; outer long rectrices with exterior webs barred throughout with black; black bars on posterior lower surface narrower."

Ridgway (1914) compares it with *symplectus*, the Texas bird, as "slightly larger, and with black bars on back, etc., decidedly broader."

The cactus woodpecker ranges, according to the 1931 A. O. U. Check-List, from "central western Texas through New Mexico and Arizona to extreme northeastern Lower California and southeastern

California, north to extreme southern Nevada and southwestern
Utah, and south to northern Durango." It frequents the deserts, or
the borders of the deserts, and the lower slopes of the mountains in
the Sonoran Zone, a hot, dry region where there are no trees of any
size and where this is about the only species of woodpecker found.
We never found it in the giant-cactus, or saguaro, region, where it
seemed to be replaced by the noisy Gila woodpecker and Mearns's
gilded flicker. W. Leon Dawson (1923) says:

Of course it must not be understood that the Cactus Woodpecker tries to
live in the central wastes of the desert; for however much it may forage
over the creosote and cholla patches, on occasion, it requires something of
more ample girth for a nesting site. Hence its breeding range is confined
to the more fruitful upper edges of the Lower Sonoran zone, and to the moister
bottoms. In the former situation the dried stalks of the agave and the lesser
yucca (whipplei), or of the Joshua tree (Yucca arborescens), and the Mohave
Yucca offer asylum. In the valley of the Colorado, fearing no rivalry from
D. pubescens turati, the Cactus Woodpecker is able to monopolize the willows
which grow so rankly along the lagoons.

Referring to Arizona, Harry S. Swarth (1904) says: "This woodpecker is seldom seen above 5,500 feet, and rarely ventures into the
canyons. On the plains below, wherever there is brush or trees, and
all along the San Pedro River it is very common, as in fact, I have
found it in all similar places I have visited in southern Arizona."

Swarth says elsewhere (1929):

In southeastern Arizona, east of the Santa Rita Mountains, the vast areas
of prairie land are for the most part unsuitable to this species. Wherever even
a scanty growth of chaparral has found a foothold, though, the Cactus Woodpecker is pretty sure to occur, for it does not require large trees. Along the
streams and washes in this same area, as elsewhere, it does frequent the sycamores and other larger growths, but these do not form the preferred habitat.
In the lowlands west of the Santa Rita Mountains this woodpecker is in the
surroundings that suit it best. It does not frequent the giant cactus (I do
not believe that there is a known instance of its nesting in one), but stays
nearer the ground, in cholla cactus, creosote bush, catclaw or other low-
growing vegetation.

Nesting.—Major Bendire (1895) writes:

In southern New Mexico and Arizona it nests sometimes in the flowering
stems of the agave plant and also in yucca trees, and I have found it nesting
on Rillito Creek, Arizona, in a small dead willow sapling not over 3½ inches
in diameter. The cavity was about 12 feet from the ground and 10 inches
in depth, and the entrance hole a trifle over 1½ inches in diameter. This
nest was found on June 8, 1872, and contained only two eggs, in which incubation was about one-half advanced; the eggs laid on fine chips. The nesting
sites are placed at various distances from the ground, from 3 to 30, usually
from 6 to 14 feet. Dead branches of trees or partly decayed ones seem to be
preferred to live ones. * * * It nests by preference in mesquite trees, one
of our hardest woods, and it must require a long time to chisel out a nesting
site in one of these trees. While it is true that the heart is usually more or
less decayed, the birds have first to work through an inch or two of solid
wood which is almost impervious to a sharp ax.

Mrs. Florence M. Bailey (1928) says that in New Mexico the nests are "from 2 to 30 feet from the ground in holes in mesquite, screw bean, palo verde, hackberry, and China trees, willows, cotton-woods, walnuts, oaks, and other trees, telegraph poles, fence posts, and stalks of agave, yucca, and cactus."

While collecting with Frank C. Willard, in southern Arizona, we found the cactus woodpecker fairly common about Tombstone and near Fairbanks on the San Pedro River. Near the former place, one nest was 6½ feet up in a fence post; the cavity was about 10 inches deep and 3¼ inches in diameter at the bottom; another nest was in a cavity 12 inches deep in the dry stalk of a mescal about 5 feet from the ground. In the valley of the San Pedro River, we found a nest about 12 feet from the ground in a willow stub; and another nest was located in a stump of a willow beside a fence; it was only 6 feet up in the solid part of the stub, and so well concealed behind a bunch of sprouts that we had passed it many times without seeing it.

Mr. Willard (1918) says:

Along the San Pedro River the Cactus Woodpecker (*Dryobates s. cactophilus*) is the only one nesting at all commonly. In the lines of willows bordering the irrigation ditches and in all the small groups found along the river banks, I had quite a list of pairs whose nests I could count upon finding within certain circumscribed areas. They exhibited individual characteristics. One pair never dug its nest lower than twenty feet from the ground and usually selected a site that overhung the water. Another liked short stubs not over five or six feet tall. Another was partial to fence posts. While these selections were not invariably followed they were so usual that I always began my search by examining all the available sites of that character before looking at others and was usually successful in my first search."

Eggs.—The cactus woodpecker lays 2 to 6 eggs, usually 4 or 5. These are usually oval or short oval, sometimes elliptical-oval or elliptical-ovate. They are pure white and more or less glossy. The measurements of 18 eggs average 21.48 by 16.18 millimeters; the eggs showing the four extremes measure 23.02 by 16.67, 22.5 by 17.0, and 19.2 by 15.1 millimeters. Bendire (1895) says that incubation lasts for about 13 days and is shared by both sexes.

Plumages.—The young are probably hatched naked (I have not seen any), as is the case with other woodpeckers, but the juvenal plumage is acquired before the young bird leaves the nest. This first plumage is much like that of the adult male, but the sexes are not quite alike. In the young male, the forehead, sides of the occiput, and the nape are uniform black; only the crown is scarlet, more or less dotted with white. The young female is similar to the young male, except that there is usually much less scarlet on the crown, often only a few scarlet tips. In both sexes the back is barred with dull black and grayish white, instead of the clear black and white of the adult; the under parts are "vinaceous-buff," faintly spotted on the sides and flanks; the plumage is softer and the markings are not so clearly defined as in the adult. Just how long this plumage is worn I have not been able to determine, but July birds show signs of body molt and an increasing amount of the clear black streaks of the adult plumage on the sides and flanks. Probably a plumage that is practically adult is assumed by the first fall at the latest. Adults apparently have a complete annual molt in summer, mainly in August.

Food.—The cactus woodpecker lives mainly on the larvae of woodboring beetles, which it gleans from the trunks and branches of trees. It also eats the larvae of the coddling moth and other Lepidoptera, ants, caterpillars, and cotton worms. It usually forages at low elevations on small trees, shrubs, and various cacti and is often seen feeding on the ground. Major Bendire (1895) says that this woodpecker, "like several other species, is very fond of the ripe figlike fruit of the giant cactus, and I have met it more than once in Sahuarito Pass, Arizona, eating it on the ground."

Voice.—Ralph Hoffmann (1927) compares the notes of the cactus woodpecker with those of the downy woodpecker and says that "the common notes are a single high-pitched *tschik* or a longer rattling call with a slight fall toward the end. It often calls as it flies, and like other woodpeckers drums in spring on dry limbs." Dawson (1923) refers to the notes as "his *plink, plink,* and his long rolling chirrup."

Field marks.—A small woodpecker with the upper parts distinctly and extensively barred with black and white is either one of the races of *Dryobates scalaris*, commonly called ladderbacks, or *Dryobates nuttalli*. These two species are very much alike in superficial appearance and might be easily confused; but fortunately their ranges do not overlap, except to a slight extent in some of the mountain passes of southeastern California. Mr. Dawson (1923) says that the cactus woodpecker "is browner above, more strikingly, heavily, and numerously barred, with less of black on sides of head, and red (of adult male) pervading crown as well as nape."

Winter.— W. E. D. Scott (1886) says that these woodpeckers "are at times gregarious. I particularly noticed this in December, 1885, when I frequently met the species in flocks of from four to a dozen, on the plains at an altitude of 3,000 feet."

DRYOBATES SCALARIS EREMICUS Oberholser

SAN FERNANDO WOODPECKER

HABITS

This race of ladder-backed woodpeckers occupies the northern half of Baja California, north of the range of *Dryobates scalaris lucasanus*, with which it intergrades about midway the peninsular. It is described by Dr. H. C. Oberholser (1911b) as "similar to *Dryo-*

bates scalaris lucasanus, but larger; lower surface darker; upper parts darker, the white bars on back averaging narrower and less regular, the black bars wider; black bars on posterior lower parts averaging somewhat wider."

Very little seems to have appeared in print about this woodpecker, but, as it lives in a similar habitat to that occupied by the San Lucas woodpecker, it probably does not differ materially from it in habits. It lives in the lowland, desert regions and nests in the giant cactus. Both races are said to be rather shy. It is replaced in extreme northwestern Baja California by Nuttall's woodpecker and in the extreme northeast by the cactus woodpecker.

Griffing Bancroft (1930) states that the measurements of nine eggs of this subspecies average 21.7 by 16.7 millimeters.

DRYOBATES NUTTALLI (Gambel)

NUTTALL'S WOODPECKER

PLATES 11, 12

HABITS

Though closely resembling, superficially, the ladder-backed woodpeckers of the *scalaris* group, Nuttall's woodpecker is a very distinct species; the ranges of the two species come together at several points but do not overlap; and the habitats of the two are in different types of environment. The 1931 A. O. U. Check-List gives the range of *nuttalli* as "Upper Austral Zone west of the southern Cascade Mountains and the Sierra Nevada from southern Oregon to northwestern Lower California."

W. Leon Dawson (1923) described the haunts of this woodpecker very well, as follows:

Although one who is forming the acquaintance of the Nuttall Woodpecker soon learns where to look for him, his range is hard to characterize in terms of associations. Upper Sonoran, foothill, oak, live oak, chaparral, deciduous trees bordering narrow stream beds—all these apply to *nuttalli* well enough, but they are not exhaustive, save for the first, which is all inclusive. Within Upper Sonoran limits it is, perhaps, easier to tell where he will not be found; thus, not (or only occasionally) in pine timber; not in stands of pure willow (which are given over to *D. pubescens turati*); not in orchards, nor about cultures of any sort; not, most decidedly, "nesting in giant cactus." Least of all, is it "seldom found along streams," as one precocious authority avers. A narrow canyon whose floor harbors sycamores and alders and bay trees, nourished by a purling stream, and whose sides are lined with live oaks which run up into ceanothus chaparral, is precisely the best place to look for *D. nuttalli*.

Nesting.—Major Bendire (1895) quotes the following contribution from B. T. Gault:

I had been out on the bowlder plain [in the San Bernardino Valley] several hours, on the morning of April 23, 1883, collecting birds, and spying a clump of elder bushes in the distance, not far from the brook, the thought occurred to me that I might take a rest beneath their shade and at the same time be ready for any bird that put in an appearance. These bushes, or more properly trees, are a great deal larger shrub than our eastern plant, their trunks growing from 4 to 8 inches through; and if they are not the same species, their umbellate blossoms are strikingly similar, if not identical, to those of our common eastern shrub (*Sambucus canadensis*). I had hardly seated myself on an arm of the shrub when my attention was attracted to a hole in the main trunk, directly above my head. At almost the same instant a bird appeared at the opening from within, and dodged back again as soon as she saw me. The movement was executed so quickly that I was unable to tell whether it was a wren or a woodpecker, but concluded that it was the latter. Upon examination of the aperture it seemed to have been lately made. Of course I thought that there would be no trouble in dislodging her, and commenced to rap on the trunk of the shrub with the butt of my gun; but this seemed to have no effect. I then walked back about 50 feet, and taking a stand, waited from ten to fifteen minutes in the hope that she would come out, affording me an opportunity to secure her and thus solve the mystery, but in this maneuver I was also baffled. I then went up to the bush and shouted with all my might, but this did not shake her nervous system in the least, when I finally resorted to my jackknife in order to enlarge the orifice, but, from its being such a tedious job, gave it up in disgust. The next morning I took a hatchet along with me, for I desired very much to know what that hole contained. It did not take me very long to cut a place large enough for me to get my hand in, and I was thoroughly surprised to learn that the bird was still on her nest. I pulled her out, and she appeared to be stupefied— dead, apparently—but soon revived. Upon further inspection I found that the nest contained eggs. The bird proved to be a female Nuttall's woodpecker, and the eggs were pretty well advanced in incubation and would have hatched in a few days.

The nest, which was about 5½ feet from the ground, was nearly a foot deep and about 5 inches wide. The hole at the entrance to the nest was but a little larger than a silver half dollar. The eggs were six in number.

Mr. Dawson's (1923) remarks on the nesting of this woodpecker are rather cryptic, but I infer from them that it nests in willows, alders, elders, cottonwoods, sycamores, live oaks, and other oaks and at heights varying from 2½ to 60 feet above ground. The only nest of this species that I have seen was shown to me by A. M. Ingersoll, while collecting with him and James B. Dixon, in San Diego County, Calif., on April 9, 1929; the nest, which the birds had not quite finished excavating, was about 30 feet from the ground in a leaning, dead cottonwood tree (pl. 11). A set of four eggs in my collection was taken by Henry W. Carriger, on April 23, 1897, in Sonoma County, Calif.; the nest was in a dead limb of a large laurel along a creek; he had taken a set of six eggs from the same tree the previous year.

Eggs.—Nuttall's woodpecker lays three to six eggs, most commonly four and often five. These are ovate, or rarely short-ovate or elliptical-ovate. The color is dull creamy white or pure white, and sometimes rather glossy. The measurements of 47 eggs average 21.75 by

16.27 millimeters; the eggs showing the four extremes measure 25.0 by 16.0, 23.3 by **17.0, 19.30** by 15.75, and 19.7 by **14.6** millimeters.

Young.—The period of incubation is said to be about 14 days, and to be shared by both sexes. Mr. Dawson (1923) says:

The male Nuttall not only takes a lively interest in all matters connected with the nesting, but it is believed that he monopolizes the task of excavation. Certainly he takes his turn at incubating, and he is invariably, in my experience, the more valiant of the two in defense of young. The female, however, is probably the closer sitter, as there are several instances in which she has submitted to the hand rather than forsake her trust. * * * When the chicks are astir the father is fairly beside himself with joy and apprehension. In fact, if you ever require a symbol of doting solicitude, picture a male Nuttall woodpecker thrusting his head into a dark hole to make sure that nothing has spilled out of it since his last inspection—which occurred exactly three seconds ago.

Plumages.—The young are hatched naked, as with other woodpeckers, but the juvenal plumage is acquired before the young leave the nest. The young male, in juvenal plumage, has the forehead, occiput, and nape uniform dull black, leaving only the crown scarlet, spotted or speckled with white dots; the black bars on the back are dull black and the white bars are grayish white, instead of clear black and pure white, as in the adult; these bars are also less clearly defined than in the adult; the under parts are yellowish white, spotted on the sides and flanks less distinctly than in the adult, and with pale dusky, instead of clear black; the wings and tail are as in the adult.

The young female is similar to the young male, except that the red of the crown is more restricted and the forehead is streaked with white. This plumage is, apparently, worn all through the first summer; I have seen young birds in this plumage as late as August 30. Probably early in fall a postjuvenal molt produces a plumage that is practically adult. I have been unable to learn anything about the molts of adults. Ridgway (1914) says that spring males have the "white streaks on forehead and crown much reduced in size, sometimes obsolete, and red nuchal area more restricted, through wearing off of red tips of feathers." The white streaks on the crown of the adult female also wear away almost entirely during winter, leaving the crown clear black.

Food.—The food of Nuttall's woodpecker is very similar to that of the downy and other small woodpeckers. Prof. F. E. L. Beal (1911) summarizes it by saying: "In its animal food the Nuttall woodpecker is beyond criticism. Practically all of the insects eaten are either pests or of no positive benefit. While some fruit is eaten, it consists largely, and perhaps entirely, of wild varieties. Probably the worst that can be said of the bird is that it helps in the distribution of poison-oak seeds."

Among the insect food, the most prominent items seem to be the larvae of the very harmful wood-boring beetles Cerambycidae and Elateridae; other beetles are eaten largely, as well as ants and other Hymenoptera, scales, plant lice and other bugs, weevils, caterpillars, spiders, flies, and millipeds. Prof. Beal (1911) says: "Two stomachs contained each between 30 and 40 box-elder bugs (*Leptocoris trivittatus*). These insects have a way of becoming very abundant at times and making a nuisance of themselves by invading buildings in search of winter quarters."

The vegetable food consists mainly of wild fruits, such as blackberries, elderberries, and the seeds of poison-oaks; a few acorns and some grain are occasionally eaten. Grinnell, Dixon, and Linsdale (1930) write: "Trees that this woodpecker foraged over were sycamore, cotton, valley oak, blue oak (most frequently), digger pine, yellow pine (rarely), and orchard trees. On June 3, 1926, one was seen feeding on cherries in an orchard near Manton."

Behavior.—Florence M. Bailey (1902) says of this little woodpecker:

It has a nuthatch-like way of flying up to light on the underside of a limb, and when hanging upside down turns itself around with as much ease as a fly on a ceiling. * * *

He is a sturdy little fellow, and in flight will sometimes rise high in air and fly long and steadily, dipping only slightly over the brush. He has the full strength of his convictions and will drive a big flicker from a sycamore and then stretch up on a branch and call out triumphantly. Two Nuttalls trying to decide whether to fight are an amusing sight. They shake their feathers and scold and dance about as if they were aching to fly at each other, but couldn't quite make up their minds to so grave a matter.

Voice.—The same writer says of the voice of Nuttall's woodpecker: "At times the small Nuttall waxes excited, and shakes his wings as he gives his thin, rattling call. All his notes are thin, and his *quee-quee-quee-quee'p* has a sharp quality. His *chit' tah* is a diminutive of the *ja' cob* of the California woodpecker."

Ralph Hoffmann (1927) says: "One cannot remain long near a grove of live oaks in the foothills of California without hearing from some tree a hoarse ringing call *prrip*, often lengthened to a rattling *prrrrrrt*. It has the exclamatory quality of the Hairy Woodpecker's, but is less clear and metallic, with more burr. * * * Like the other woodpeckers the Nuttall, particularly in spring, drums on resonant timber or telephone poles; it also gives at that season a rapid, squealing *quee quee quee quee*."

Mr. Dawson (1923) says that this woodpecker "always has a grouch on, and you are sure to be challenged as you pass, by repetition of his double notes of distrust, *ticket, ticket—ticket it*."

Field marks.—Nuttall's woodpecker closely resembles the cactus woodpecker, and where the ranges of the two species come together, in southeastern California, there is a chance for confusion; but their ranges barely touch each other, and fortunately the habitats of the two species are quite different and mainly well separated. Nuttall's is somewhat lighter colored on the under parts, and the black bands on the back are slightly wider than in the cactus woodpecker; but the best distinguishing mark, if the observer is near enough to see it, is the black forehead and front of the crown, which in the male cactus woodpecker is spotted with white and red. It is only slightly larger than the downy woodpeckers but can be readily distinguished from that species by the conspicuous, transverse barring of black and white on the back, instead of the broad, white, longitudinal band of the downies; there are also more white spots in the wings than in the western races of the downy.

DISTRIBUTION

Range.—Southwestern Oregon, California, and northern Baja California; nonmigratory.

The range of Nuttall's woodpecker extends **north** to southwestern Oregon (probably Ashland); and northern California (Weed and Lassen Peak). **East** to California (Lassen Peak, Oroville, probably Florence Lake, Owens Lake, and Redlands); and Baja California (San Rafael and San Domingo). **South** to northern Baja California (San Domingo and Ensenada). **West** to northwestern Baja California (Ensenada); western California (San Diego, San Onofre, Santa Barbara, Morro, Monterey, and East Park); and southwestern Oregon (probably Ashland).

Egg dates.—California: 82 records, March 25 to June 14; 41 records, April 21 to May 6, indicating the height of the season.

DRYOBATES ARIZONAE ARIZONAE (Hargitt)

ARIZONA WOODPECKER

HABITS

Strickland's woodpecker (*Dryobates stricklandi*), a Mexican species, was formerly recorded from southern Arizona by some of the early writers; but Edward Hargitt (1886) discovered that the Arizona bird was specifically distinct, described it, and named it as a new species, *Picus arizonae*. He gave it the following diagnosis: "*P. similis P. stricklandi,* sed dorso uniformi nec albofasciato distinguendus." The two species are quite similar in general appearance, but *stricklandi* has the median portion of the back and the whole rump broadly barred or transversely spotted with white, whereas in *arizonae* these parts are uniformly plain brown, and the markings on the under parts are in the form of large rounded or subcordate spots, instead of streaks.

The range of the Arizona woodpecker includes southeastern Arizona, southwestern New Mexico, Sonora, Chihuahua, and northwestern Durango; it is another one of those Mexican species that barely crosses our southwestern border.

Henry W. Henshaw (1875) was the first to report this woodpecker, under the name of Strickland's woodpecker, as entitled to a place in our fauna; he writes: "This rare woodpecker is a common species on the foothills of the Chiricahua Mountains, where it was one of the first birds that met my eye when the section where it abounds was first entered. Whether it extends upward, and finds its home during a portion of the year among the pines that here begin at an altitude of about 1,000 [10,000?] feet, I do not know. So far as I could ascertain, at this season at least [August], it is confined to the region of the oaks, ranging from about 4,000 to 7,000 feet, thus inhabiting a region about midway between the low valleys and the mountain districts proper."

Harry S. Swarth (1904) writes: "Although the Arizona Woodpecker is resident the year through in the Huachucas, it is singular how the birds seem to disappear in the breeding season, that is from the middle of April to the middle of June, when the young birds begin to leave the nest. During this time their loud shrill call may be occasionally heard from some wooded hillside, but the birds themselves are seldom seen. I have taken specimens from the base of the mountains, about 4,500 feet altitude, up to 8,000 feet, but they are not often seen above 7,000 feet."

Nesting.—We found the Arizona woodpecker well distributed in Ramsay Canyon in the Huachuca Mountains from the base of the mountains up to 7,500 feet, but nowhere common. On April 15, 1922, while exploring the lower part of the canyon, which is quite heavily wooded with giant sycamores, various oaks, ash, maples, black walnut, and locusts, we saw an Arizona woodpecker excavating a nest hole in a solid dead stub, about 50 feet up near the top of one of the big sycamores. The hole was on the under side of the stub and deep enough to take in all the bird but the tail. A red-shafted flicker was "yuckering" in the top of another big tree, and I think it had designs on this nest, for it subsequently drove away the Arizona woodpecker; and later on the nest was found to have been deserted. We found only one occupied nest; this was at an altitude of about 7,500 feet in a branch of Ramsay Canyon; it was about 20 feet from the ground in a dead branch of a small walnut tree, which was growing up through an oak on the steep mountain side; the entrance to the cavity, which was about 12 inches deep, was well hidden; it contained three eggs well advanced in incubation on May 16, 1922. The birds were heard in the vicinity, and one was seen to relieve the other on the nest. Frank C. Willard's notes record the finding of two nests of this woodpecker in the same region on May 24, 1899; these were both in dead branches of oak trees; one was 15 and one 18 feet from the ground, and the nesting cavities were both 12 inches deep; "one bird was seen to leave the nest and the other one entered it; after it got in, it stuck its head out and uttered one sharp note, like a grosbeak's, which was answered by its mate."

Major Bendire (1895) mentions a nest, found by Dr. A. K. Fisher in Garden Canyon in the Huachuca Mountains, on May 14, that was "in a large maple which overhung a stream. The cavity was situated in a dry branch, about 20 feet from the ground, and was about a foot in depth. It contained four young, which were still naked." There are two sets of four eggs each in the Thayer collection; one was taken by O. W. Howard in the Huachuca Mountains on April 24, 1902, from a nest in a mescal stalk, 8 feet from the ground; the other was collected by Virgil W. Owen in the Chiricahua Mountains, on April 22, 1906; the entrance to the cavity was 9 feet up on the under side of a slightly leaning, dead and decaying stub of an oak limb in a dead tree.

Eggs.—The Arizona woodpecker apparently lays either three or four eggs; we have no record of more or fewer. The few that I have seen are practically ovate; they are pure white and some are quite glossy, others less so. The measurements of 27 eggs average 22.82 by 17.33 millimeters; the eggs showing the four extremes measure **24.0 by 18.0, 19.9** by 16.7, and 22.5 by **16.5** millimeters.

Young.—The period of incubation does not seem to have been definitely determined, but it is probably about 14 days, as with other *Dryobates*. Both sexes assist in this task, and probably in the care of the young.

H. S. Swarth (1904) writes:

About the third week in April they commence laying their eggs, and after the middle of June the young birds begin to leave the nest, and soon become quite abundant. I have never had any difficulty in approaching these birds as they are usually quite tame and unsuspicious; far more so than the generality of woodpeckers, and the young birds are noticeably so. I have several times stood within ten feet of a young bird, easily distinguishable by his red cap, as he was industriously pounding on a limb without seeming in the least disturbed by my presence, or showing any inclination to leave. On one occasion the confiding, and in this case inquiring nature of the bird occasioned rather a laughable scene. An acquaintance in the mountains, passing the camp one day stopped to lead his horse down to the well which supplied us with water. A young Arizona Woodpecker was sitting in an oak tree close by, and soon after the horse began drinking he flew down, and lighting on the animal's hind leg as on the side of a tree, hit it a vigorous rap or two. The horse and its owner appeared equally surprised, and both moving a little the bird retreated to his tree. It wasn't a minute before he was back again, this time on a front leg, where he went to work with such energy as to start the horse plunging and kicking in an effort to get rid of its curious assailant. The woodpecker left but did not seem to be particularly frightened, as he sat on the wooden curb of the well until he was left alone again.

Plumages.—The young are hatched naked but acquire the juvenal plumage before leaving the nest. In three young males in my collection, taken on June 20, August 4, and August 30, the upper parts are much like those of the adult male, but the crown is more or less invaded with scarlet or vermilion-tipped feathers, sometimes with only a few scattered feathers and sometimes covering the whole crown and nape; they are more heavily spotted on the breast and more heavily barred on the belly than are the fall adults, and these markings are dark sepia, instead of black, and less well defined than in adults; the bills are smaller and weaker. Mr. Swarth (1904) says: "In the young female, besides occupying a less extensive surface, the red is less intense than in the male, and not as solid, that is there is always more or less brown showing through. The red cap of the juvenile bird seems to be worn but a short time, as a young female taken September 4 has hardly a trace of it remaining."

Apparently the juvenal plumage is molted, including the wings and tail, late in August or September, when the first winter plumage, which is practically indistinguishable from that of the adult, is acquired. Mr. Swarth (1904) says of the molt of the adult:

The Arizona woodpecker commences to moult about the middle of July, and by the first week in September the new plumage is almost completely acquired. The plumage of the breast, abdomen, and lower parts generally, seems to be the first to be renewed, while the remiges, rectrices and feathers of the interscapular region are the last to get their growth. An old female shot on September 3 had practically completed its moult, with the exception of the tail feathers, none of which were over half an inch long; while several specimens of both sexes, taken during the last two weeks in August, are in nearly perfect autumnal plumage, except for some small patches of old feathers in the interscapular region. Fall specimens are considerably darker on the back than birds taken during the spring and summer, but the change is undoubtedly due to fading of the plumage, as birds taken in the late winter and early spring, show not the slightest traces of moult, and a series of birds taken from February to July, show plainly the gradual change of coloration. Singularly enough the pileum and back of the neck does not seem to fade as the dorsum does, and consequently, while birds in fresh fall plumage are of practically uniform coloration on the upper parts, specimens taken in the late spring and summer have the head and neck abruptly darker than the back and exposed portion of the wings. * * * Of twenty-four specimens from this region [Arizona] four show more or less traces of white bars across the rump; one of these is a male in nuptial plumage, one a male in freshly acquired autumnal plumage, one a female in nuptial plumage (this specimen has some faint indications of white bars on some of the scapulars as well), and one is a young male. Another spring female has some white bars on the scapulars but none on the rump. Presumably this is a tendency toward the Mexican species *Dryobates stricklandi*.

Food.—Very little seems to be recorded on the food of the Arizona woodpecker, which probably does not differ greatly from that of other members of the *Dryobates* group. It apparently feeds mainly on insects and their larvae, but to some extent on fruits and acorns. Mr. Henshaw (1875) says of its feeding habits: "When in pursuit of food, they almost always alighted near the base of the trees, gradually ascending, and making their way along the smaller limbs, and even out among the foliage, appearing to prefer to secure their food by a careful search rather than by the hard labor of cutting into the wood in the way the hairy woodpecker employs its strength."

Behavior.—The same observer says of their habits:

Here they appeared to be perfectly at home, climbing over the trunks of the oaks with the same ease and rapidity of movement that distinguish the motions of the downy or hairy woodpecker; though their habits, in so far as they are at all peculiar, are, perhaps, best comparable to those of the red-cockaded woodpecker of the South (*P. borealis*), especially their custom of moving about in small companies of from five to fifteen, though they were occasionally found singly or in pairs. * * *

I found them at all times rather shy, and gifted with very little of that prying curiosity which is seen in some of the better known species of this family; and if by chance I surprised a band feeding among the low trees, a sharp warning note, from some member more watchful than the rest, communicated alarm to the whole assembly, when they took flight immediately, showing great dexterity in dodging behind trunks and limbs, and making good their retreat by short flights from one tree to another till they were out of sight.

In the Whetstone Mountains, Ariz., Austin Paul Smith (1908) observed a female Arizona woodpecker—

working on an oak-trunk, not three feet above the base; while the trees around harbored unnumbered Bridled Tits (*Baeolophus wollweberi*), Lead-colored Bushtits (*Psaltriparus plumbeus*) and Rocky Mountain Nuthatches (*Sitta carolinensis nelsoni*). Very often did I run across a similar assemblage, but rarely were there more than one or two Arizona Woodpeckers in it. There is no recollection at hand, of noting above four adult woodpeckers of this species in view at once; more likely to chance upon a solitary individual than a pair at any time. The noisiest occasion I can accredit to the species occurred one spring day when two adult females were located, perched upon a horizontal limb of a madrona, facing each other, and emitting a continuous volume of characteristic woodpecker notes, the effect being heightened by that peculiar muscular movement which accompanies the vocal utterances of some Pici. The continuity was possible by a relay system; and so engrossed were the participants, that I approached to directly under the limb and stood there at least two minutes, without being detected.

F. H. Fowler (1903) writes:

The Arizona woodpecker (*Dryobates arizonae*) is, outside of the alpine three-toed and pileated, the most interesting member of the woodpecker family, that I have ever seen. So far as I have noted, the species is never common, never noisy, and never at rest. I have not found it except in live-oak woods, and at Fort Huachuca; on a good field day I used to see about six on an average. Not even the chickadees are as active as this little woodpecker. He will alight on the main trunk of the tree, or generally one of the largest limbs, and the moment his claws are fastened in the bark he begins an untiring search for insects and grubs. He ascends rapidly in spirals picking and prying away small pieces of bark in search of food; when a promising limb is reached out he goes on it, often on the lower side. The search over in one tree, he wastes no time in looking around, but launches out, with barely a glance to determine the course, in his undulating flight to the next, there to repeat the performance. When closely approached, he works around the tree without paying any especial attention to the intruder, and when thoroughly frightened he will take flight with as little warning as he does when simply in search of food. While going up the tree he gives, from time to time, a characteristic call, much like that of the hairy woodpecker.

Field marks.—The Arizona woodpecker should be easily recognized, as it is the only small woodpecker that has a uniformly brown, unmarked back and crown, and lower parts thickly spotted with black; the adult male has a red patch on the nape, and young birds of both sexes have more or less red in the crown, less in the female than in the male.

Winter.—This woodpecker is a permanent resident in southern Arizona, moving down from the higher parts of the mountains to the lower levels in winter. Mr. Swarth (1904) says that "in the winter they seem to more particularly favor the large groves of live-oaks along the foot-hills and at the mouths of the canyons; scattering over the mountains and ascending to rather a higher elevation upon the advent of the breeding season." W. E. D. Scott (1886) writes: "Rarely have I met with more than two in company, and a family, two parents and three young, were the most I ever saw associated together. But I frequently met in the fall a party composed of Arizona jays, California woodpeckers, various Titmice and Warblers, and a pair of Strickland's [Arizona] woodpeckers. The birds I have met with them appear late in January or early in February, and are apparently already mated."

DISTRIBUTION

Range.—Southwestern New Mexico, southeastern Arizona, and western Mexico; nonmigratory.

The Arizona woodpecker is found **north** to southeastern Arizona (Canada del Oro and the Whetstone Mountains); and southwestern New Mexico (probably the Animas Mountains and the San Luis Mountains). **East** to southwestern New Mexico (San Luis Mountains); Chihuahua (Cajon Bonito, Colonia Garcia, Temosachic, and Apache); Durango (Metalotes and Arroyo del Buey); and Zacatecas (Sierra de Valparaiso). **South** to Zacatecas (Sierra de Valparaiso) and Jalisco (Nevada Volcanoe, Colima Volcanoe, Tonila, and San Marcos.) **West** to Jalisco (San Marcos and Bolanos); eastern Sinaloa (Sierra de Choix); central Sonora (La Chumata mine and Saric); and southeastern Arizona (Huachuca Mountains, Santa

Rita Mountains, Rincón Mountains Pantano, and Canada del Oro).

The range as outlined is for the entire species, which has been divided into two geographic races, the true Arizona woodpecker (*D. a. arizonae*), occupying the northern part of the area south to northwestern Durango, and the Colima woodpecker (*D. a. fraterculus*), occupying the rest of the range in Mexico.

Egg dates.—Arizona: 8 records, April 20 to May 16.

DRYOBATES ALBOLARVATUS ALBOLARVATUS (Cassin)

NORTHERN WHITE-HEADED WOODPECKER

PLATES 13, 14

HABITS

The northern race of the white-headed woodpecker is found in the Cascade Mountains and the Sierra Nevada, from Washington to Kern County, Calif., and eastward into western Idaho and western Nevada.

It is a bird of the pine and fir forests in the mountains, ranging from 4,000 to 9,000 feet during the breeding season, but coming down to lower levels in winter. W. L. Dawson (1923) says: "This woodpecker is essentially a pine-loving species and is, therefore, nearly confined to the slopes of the Sierras and the Transition zones of the southern ranges. Only in winter does it appear at lower levels, and then rarely beyond the pale of the yellow pine. So close is this devotion of bird to tree that the woodpecker's feathers are almost always smeared with pine pitch; and I have found eggs dotted with pitch and soiled to blackness by contact with the sitting bird."

Clarence F. Smith writes to me that he found this woodpecker very common around a camp where he was located from June 25 to July 10, 1935, in Tuolumne County, Calif., in the Transition Zone at an elevation of about 4,000 feet. The camp was at one time a lumbering mill, and there was much dead standing timber nearby. Most of the trees were *Pinus ponderosa* and *Pinus lambertiana*.

Nesting.—The same observer says in his notes: "All the nests observed, except one in a *Quercus kelloggi*, were in dead standing stumps of the pines. The stumps were mostly some 12 to 15 feet in height, and the nests averaged about 8 feet above ground, with an approximate minimum of 6 feet. These nests may not represent a typical situation, as they were undoubtedly the ones that were most obvious to casual observation. Nests in higher locations would more easily escape notice. We had at least 8 nests within a half-mile radius of camp headquarters, and the birds were one of the commonest species in the vicinity. None of the nests opened contained any lining but chips of wood, and the cavities were about 14 inches in depth. None of the nest trees were less than 2 feet in diameter at the point where the nest was located. Many of the stumps had several holes in them, some of which had been nests in previous years, and some of which had been merely abortive attempts at drilling. The one nest in the oak, referred to above, was in a live tree with a decayed heart."

Major Bendire (1895) writes:

Nidification usually begins about the middle of May and continues through June. The sexes relieve each other in the preparation of the nesting site, which is usually located in a dead stub of a pine or fir; one that is partly decayed seems to be preferred as it rarely excavates one in solid, hard wood. The nesting sites are seldom situated over 15 feet from the ground, and sometimes as low as 2 feet. The entrance hole is about 1½ inches wide, perfectly circular, and just large enough to admit the bird; the inner cavity gradually widens towards the bottom, and is usually from 8 to 12 inches deep, the eggs lying on a slight layer of fine chips, in which they become well embedded as incubation advances. Occasionally a rather peculiar site is selected. Mr. Charles A. Allen found a nest of this species in a post in one of the snow sheds on the Central Pacific Railroad, between Blue Canyon and Emigrant Gap, about 40 feet from the entrance of the shed, and some thirty trains passed daily within a few feet of the nest, which contained six eggs when found.

Milton P. Skinner sends me the following notes on nest building by this woodpecker: "On May 10, 1933, I found one at work on a hole in a stub of a tree, about 3 feet above ground. Although this was in the Sequoia National Park beside one of the most used paths, it was deepening the hole for a nest. Chips were scattered on the ground below. After pecking a while, the woodpecker would get into the hole and soon after back out again with a billful of chips. It then opened its bill and let them scatter to the ground; then back to work again. Although this was as public a place as could be found, and though the birds must frequently have been disturbed by the crowds of people and were within reach of hundreds of children, they succeeded in raising their brood of young. In spite of nesting so low, most of these birds are usually seen from 20 to 50 feet, and sometimes as high as 100 feet, above ground, working on the trees."

Of ten nests found by Grinnell and Storer (1924) in the Yosemite region—

the lowest was located only 58 inches (measured) above ground and the highest, 15 feet (estimated). * * * No nest holes of this woodpecker were found in living conifers. Nor, on the other hand, do the birds seek what is commonly known as rotten wood, that is, wood too soft for the nest cavity to be maintained against the incessant wear involved in the birds' passage back and forth, incident to the rearing of a brood. The tree chosen must have been dead a sufficient length of time for the pitch to have hardened or to have descended to the base of the tree, and the outer shell of the tree must still be hard and firm, whereas the interior must have been softened to a moderate degree by decay. These conditions are not to be met with in every standing dead stub; hence the choice of a nest site becomes a matter of rather fine discrimination.

They found plenty of evidence of this discrimination in the many unfinished nesting holes of varying depths that had been abandoned, often several in the same stub. "Some stubs are literally riddled with holes, these probably recording successive years of occupancy. One stub had at least 5 fully excavated holes besides 11 or more prospects. * * * We were led to conclude from all this that the White-headed Woodpecker is either notional or else very particular, in the selection of its home. Evidence points strongly to the birds excavating and occupying a new cavity each year, although one set of eggs was found in a hole which had been dug in earlier years."

They made a number of careful measurements of four nests, at heights varying from about 5 feet to about 10 feet above ground; the internal dimensions varied somewhat, but the size of the entrance hole was "surprisingly constant"; in one case this hole was a perfect circle, 43 by 43 millimeters, and in another 37 by 37 millimeters; in the other two cases the entrance hole measured 47 millimeters in height and 42 in width; translated into inches this shows a variation in the two dimensions of from 1.45 to 1.85 inches, which does not seem to be "surprisingly constant." The total depth of the cavity varied from 275 to 400 millimeters, or from about 10 to 15 inches.

They say further: "Two of the nest cavities we found were in such unusual sites as to call forth comment. One at Hazel Green was in a slanting upright limb on a prostrate dead black oak trunk lying in a grassy meadow, fully 150 feet from the margin of the forest. The hole was excavated on the lower side of the stub. The other nest was at Tamarack Flat, in the butt end of an old log, lifted above the ground when the tree fell over a granite outcrop. This hole was about $7\frac{1}{2}$ feet above the ground, and as with the other there were piles of chips immediately beneath it."

Grinnell, Dixon, and Linsdale (1930) mention a nest they found in the Lassen Peak region that was "four meters up in the trunk of a dead-topped aspen." Bendire (1895) mentions a nest found near Camp Harney, Oreg., that was about 25 feet from the ground in a dead limb of a pine; this nest seems to be at about the limit as to height above ground. A set in my collection was taken from a nest 10 feet up in a dead aspen.

Eggs.—The white-headed woodpecker lays three to seven eggs, four being the commonest number, and five rather often. These vary in shape from ovate to short-ovate. They are pure white and moderately or quite glossy. Grinnell and Storer (1924) say: "The eggs in one set had a wrinkled appearance at the smaller end as though that end had been compressed before the shells had hardened. Eggs which are advanced in incubation are apt to be soiled by pitch; this is doubtless brought in by the parent birds on their bills, feet, or plumage." Sometimes the eggs show tiny black dots, or are profusely smeared with black from the same cause. The measurements of 50 eggs average 24.26 by 18.11 millimeters; the eggs showing the four extremes measure **26.40** by 18.29, 25.40 by **19.50, 21.84** by 17.78, and 22.86 by **16.76** millimeters.

Young.—Incubation is said to last for 14 days and to be shared by both sexes. Both parents also assist in the care and feeding of the young. Clarence F. Smith tells me that "the female at one nest made trips about twice as frequently as the male; her visits were about two minutes apart, while the visits of the male were about five minutes." Grinnell, Dixon, and Linsdale (1930) write:

> On July 1, the young woodpeckers, by this time half-grown, were being fed by the parents, mostly by the female. Food was brought at intervals averaging fifteen minutes each. The birds foraged at distances up to a quarter of a mile away from the nest. The female carried away the feces.
>
> On July 11 the female seemed to be coaxing the young from this nest. When the young woodpeckers stuck their heads out of the cavity, the parent would move away from the entrance and call, although it remained on the tree trunk. When a person shook the stub two of the young birds flew out and went thirty meters before coming to the ground. When placed on a tree trunk the birds could move freely upward or downward. Within a few minutes one of the young birds could fly so well that it successfully evaded capture by the observer.

Plumages.—As with other woodpeckers, the young are hatched naked and blind, but the juvenal plumage is acquired before the young bird leaves the nest. The juvenal plumage is much like that of the adult but duller, and the bill is shorter and weaker; the contour plumage is softer and looser; the lower parts are brownish black instead of clear black, and the back is only a little darker; the white in the primaries is more restricted. In the young male, the posterior half of the crown is largely "vermilion" or "salmon orange"; these reddish colors are much reduced or entirely absent in the young female. Ridgway (1914) says that the feathers of the hind neck and underparts are sometimes, perhaps on younger birds than I have seen, "indistinctly and narrowly margined at tip with grayish, and the hindneck sometimes indistinctly spotted with whitish." By the middle of September this juvenal plumage, including the wings and tail, has been replaced by the first winter plumage, which is like that of the adult, except for somewhat less white in the primaries. Adults have a complete annual molt, which begins in July and is generally completed before the end of September.

Food.—The white-headed woodpecker forages for its food mainly, if not entirely, on the trunks and branches of coniferous trees, living or dead. Mr. Skinner writes to me that he has seen it feeding on the trunks of sequoias, sugar pines, and Douglas firs, searching most diligently and thoroughly in the crevices in the bark for insects and their eggs; it generally begins low down on the tree and progresses upward, working pretty well up to the top of the tree before flying off; occasionally, one has worked horizontally around a tree trunk, but not downward. Dr. J. C. Merrill (1888) describes its method of feeding very well, as follows:

So far as I have observed, and during the winter I watched it carefully, its principal supply of food is obtained in the bark, most of the pines having a very rough bark, scaly and deeply fissured. The bird uses its bill as a crowbar rather than as a hammer or chisel, *prying* off the successive scales and layers of bark in a very characteristic way. This explains the fact of its being such a quiet worker, and as would be expected it is most often seen near the base of the tree where the bark is thickest and roughest.

It must destroy immense numbers of Scolytidae, whose larvae tunnel the bark so extensively, and of other insects that crawl beneath the scales of bark for shelter during winter. I have several times imitated the work of this bird by prying off the successive layers of bark, and have been astonished at the great numbers of insects, and especially of spiders, so exposed.

Prof. F. E. L. Beal (1911) examined only 14 stomachs, but says that "half of the animal food of the white-headed woodpecker (*Xenopicus albolarvatus*) is ants, but the most pronounced characteristic of this bird is its fondness for the seeds of pines, which constitute more than half of the food."

Grinnell and Storer (1924) say: "Stomachs of two adult birds, obtained at Merced Grove Big Trees on June 10, 1915, and at East Fork of Indian Cañon, June 24, 1915, both held ants, some of which were large carpenter ants. The stomach of one of the young birds from the nest mentioned above contained remains of 2 large spiders, a large ant, 2 boring beetles, and a whole fly larva."

Major Bendire (1895) quotes Rollo H. Beck as saying: "I noticed one of these birds on some fallen logs near the road, busily engaged in catching spiders, searching for grubs, and frequently flying after passing insects, catching them in mid-air in the manner of the California Woodpecker."

Behavior.—Dr. Merrill (1888) writes: "Though not shy, and with care generally approachable to within a short distance, it is watchful and suspicious, and seems to know very well what is going on even if it does not see fit to fly away, though it is more apt to do this than to dodge around the trunk. The flight is direct, and rather slow and heavy." Dr. Merrill noted that the skull of the white-headed woodpecker is "noticeably less hard and dense" than the skulls of other woodpeckers; this is probably due to the fact that its method of feeding requires less heavy drilling into hard wood.

Mrs. Florence M. Bailey (1902) says: "*Xenopicus* works with apparent indifference on trunks or branches. Like the Nuttall woodpecker he often lights upside down. In hunting over the bark he easily backs down the trunk, or if he takes the notion will fly, or perhaps drop backwards, a foot or so. He will also light sidewise on a branch and grasp the limb with his tail as if afraid of falling off.

It is interesting to see him explore cracks in the bark. Standing on the edge he pokes his head into the dark cavern, turning it from one side to the other inquiringly."

Grinnell and Storer (1924) write:

At Tamarack Flat, on May 26, 1919, a female white-headed woodpecker was seen to flush from her nest about ten feet above ground in a dead pine stub. Tapping by one of us on a nearby bole had caused her to leave, but she returned to the vicinity almost immediately. Then, for fully 25 minutes, while the observer remained within watching distance the bird foraged, preened, and flew about from one to another of the circle of 8 or 10 trees within a 50-foot radius of the nest, but always kept the nest tree in her sight. About every 5 minutes she would fly to the nest. In approaching it, she would swoop below its level and then glide up to the site with decreasing speed so as to end her flight with little or no momentum. Then, having gained claw-hold, she would poke the fore part of her body into the hole, withdraw it at once and repeat this performance four or five times before flying away again. Finally, after fully half an hour had elapsed, and her suspicions had been allayed, she went in, to remain. During this entire time the male kept out of sight and was heard only twice.

Van Rossem and Pierce (1915) noted its manner of drinking, thus: "White-headed woodpeckers were often observed to drink at a small stream near our camp at Bear Lake, where a pine sapling grew from the edge of a small pool. On this sapling the birds would alight, usually about three feet from the base, 'hitch' quickly backwards down the trunk to the water, and, leaning sharply to one side, drink by quick, nervous dips."

Another method of drinking is described by Grinnell, Dixon, and Linsdale (1930), as follows: "In mid-afternoon one flew down from a yellow pine to some shallow, running water in an open roadside near Mineral. It alighted in a horizontal position on the ground and dipped its bill into the water six times. After each dip the bird raised its bill skyward at an angle of fully eighty degrees from the horizontal. After drinking, the bird flew to a prostrate log, and foraged horizontally along its lower curvature."

Some observers seem to think that the white-headed woodpecker rarely, if ever, drums on tree trunks, but seeks its food more quietly; but Alexander Sprunt, Jr., tells me that the birds he saw in Oregon "drummed and beat upon the tree trunks and telephone poles at the roadside, exactly as any other woodpecker." Clarence F. Smith writes to me that "one male bird was a regular overnight guest, hanging to the ridgepole of our cabin, outside the wall, just beneath the eaves. He never made any attempt to drill the wood there."

Voice.—Grinnell and Storer (1924) say that "the usual call note of this woodpecker is a single *wiek*, but when excited, the female calls *cheep-eep-eep-eep*, very fast, and repeats the call every few seconds. The male, under similar circumstances calls *yip, yip, yip, yip,* in a much shriller tone, but in slower time." Mr. Dawson (1923) once heard "a double or treble call-note, *chick-up* or *chick-it-up*, which reminded me somewhat of the Cabanis's cry." Major Bendire (1895) heard it utter "a sharp, clear *witt-witt*" as it passed from one tree to another; he considered it a rather silent bird.

Field marks.—The white-headed woodpecker could hardly be mistaken for any other bird. It is the only woodpecker with a wholly black body and a wholly white head; while perched it shows a long white stripe in the wing, and while flying a large white patch in the wing is conspicuous; the narrow red band on the nape is not conspicuous and can be seen only at short range and only in the adult male; young birds show more or less red in the crown. One would think that such a strikingly marked bird would be very conspicuous, but such is not the case; its coloration is, in fact, somewhat concealing in its chosen environment; its quiet behavior helps to make it less obvious. For example, Dr. Merrill (1888) writes: "On most of the pines in this vicinity there are many short stubs of small broken branches projecting an inch or two from the main trunk. When the sun is shining these projections are lighted up in such a manner as to appear quite white at a little distance, and they often cast a shadow exactly resembling the black body of the bird. In winter when a little snow has lodged on these stubs the resemblance is even greater, and almost daily I was misled by this deceptive appearance, either mistaking the stub for a bird or the reverse."

Furthermore, Grinnell, Dixon, and Linsdale (1930) state that "it was further observed that in usual pose, either when foraging or when in digging or inspecting a nest hole, the whole back of a bird (either sex) appeared to a nearby observer solidly black, clear to the top of the head. The white showed only as a very narrow rim or border anteriorly around the black of the head. * * * At the same time the concealing black of the bird's dorsal surface must cover all of the area of the bird exposed to the view of the potentially inimical observer at more or less distance."

And again, Mrs. Bailey (1902) says:

Impossible as it would seem at first sight, I have found that the snow-white head often serves the bird as a disguise. It is the disguise of color pattern, for the black body seen against a tree trunk becomes one of the black streaks or shadows of the bark, and the white head is cut off as a detached white spot without bird-like suggestions. On the other hand, when the bird is exploring the light-barked young Shasta firs or gray, barkless tracts of old trees, the white of the head tones in with the gray and is lost, the headless back again becoming only a shadow or scar. But the most surprising thing of all is to see the sun streaming full on the white head and find that the bird form is lost. The white in this case is so glaring that it fills the eye and carries it over to the light streaks on the bark, making the black sink away as insignificant.

The activities of this and other woodpeckers play an important role in the welfare of the forests and the lives of the little furred and feathered denizens of the woods. It is a well-known fact that wood-peckers are most useful in guarding the living trees and destroying the insect pests that injure them; but Grinnell and Storer (1924) have called our attention to the fact that woodpeckers in general, and the white-headed woodpecker in particular, contribute, by their ex-cessive drilling of nest holes, "rather directly toward bringing down the standing dead timber." They continue:

Drilling by woodpeckers results in an increase in the number of entrances through which insects may get at the heart wood of a tree and thus hasten its ultimate disintegration. Water, also, is thus afforded an easier entrance and this hastens decay. Eventually each and every tree must yield its place in the forest to seedlings. The woodpeckers hasten this process of replacement, once the tree is dead.

Many of the wood-inhabiting animals depend upon this woodpecker to furnish them convenient nest holes or retreats. We have found mountain chickadees and slender-billed nuthatches incubating their own eggs in holes drilled in earlier years by the white-headed woodpecker; a Sierra flying squirrel was found occupying an old white-head's hole. Probably, tree-dwelling chipmunks and perhaps California pigmy owls also occupy holes of this woodpecker.

DISTRIBUTION

Range.—Pacific coast of the United States; occurring rarely in southern British Columbia; nonmigratory.

The range of the white-headed woodpecker extends **north** to Wash-ington (Methow River and probably Fort Colville); and northern Idaho (Fort Sherman). **East** to western Idaho (Fort Sherman and Grangeville); eastern Oregon (Hurricane Creek, Powder River Mountains, Anthony, and Camp Harney); western Nevada (Carson); and eastern California (Bijou, Yosemite Valley, Pyramid Peak, San Bernardino Mountains, and Cuyamaca Mountains). **South** to south-ern California (Cuyamaca Mountains and Mount Pinos). **West** to the western slopes of the Sierra Nevadas, Calif. (Mount Pinos, Bear Valley, Fyffe, Butte Lake, and Mount Shasta); western Oregon (Pinehurst, Foley Creek, and The Dalles); and western Washington (Kalama, Cle Elum, and Methow River).

The species has been separated into two subspecies, the northern white-headed woodpecker (*Dryobates a. albolarvatus*), occupying most of the range south to the southern end of the Sierra Nevadas, and the southern white-headed woodpecker (*D. a. gravirostris*), found in the mountain ranges of southern California.

Casual records.—A specimen collected near Point Bonita, Marin County, Calif., on July 20, 1932, is the only coastal record in that State. There is, however, an old record for Grays Harbor, Wash. (previous to 1892), which cannot now be confirmed.

In the Provincial Museum at Victoria, British Columbia, there is an unlabeled specimen said to have been collected in the Similkameen

Valley. Two have been collected at Okanagan, British Columbia, one on December 20, 1911, and the other on January 24, 1914.

Egg dates.—California: 53 records, April 24 to June 16; 27 records, May 22 to June 7, indicating the height of the season.

DRYOBATES ALBOLARVATUS GRAVIROSTRIS (Grinnell)

SOUTHERN WHITE-HEADED WOODPECKER

HABITS

Dr. Joseph Grinnell (1902), in describing and naming the white-headed woodpecker of the mountain ranges of southern California, gave as its characters: "Similar to *Xenopicus albolarvatus* but bill much heavier, and size in general slightly greater." He named it as a distinct species, on the theory that "the material at hand does not justify subspecific treatment of these two forms. Geographical continuity of ranges possibly exists; but it seems quite as likely that there is a broad hiatus in the vicinity of Tehachapi Pass, whence I can find no record of the white-headed woodpecker."

The range of this form includes the San Gabriel, San Bernardino, San Jacinto, Santa Rosa, and Cuyamaca Mountains in southern California. Dr. Grinnell (1908) found this woodpecker rather scarce in the San Bernardino Mountains, and says: "They were seen only in the Transition zone, none being observed above the fir belt, and but very few down into pure yellow pine tracts. In the vicinity of Fish creek, 6,500 feet, a few pairs were breeding in June. On July 5, 1905, I found a nesting hole seven feet up in a dead pine stub, which contained four half-fledged young. We did not see the species anywhere higher than 8,000 feet, except on the south slope of Sugarloaf, where on July 11, 1906, one was seen among the silver firs at about 9,000 feet altitude. About Bluff lake they were more common than anywhere else, and a few were seen on the northern slopes of Sugarloaf at about 8,000 feet, in August."

W. L. Dawson (1923) writes: "In the San Jacinto Mountains, where these white-heads outnumber all other woodpeckers combined, our attention was drawn, on the 6th day of June, by a male who tittered anxiously as we stumbled along the rough trail. We camped on the prospect immediately, but it took a full hour to trace the 'damage' to a hole fifty feet up in a yellow pine stub, which was three feet through at the base. * * *

"We found a clean-cut round hole, one and a half inches in diameter, which gave admission to a cavity ten inches deep, and which had for its outer wall only the thick bark of the tree."

Frank Stephens wrote to Major Bendire (1895) : "*Xenopicus albolarvatus* is a resident of the pine regions of southern California, but is not common excepting possibly in a few localities. I have never observed it below the pines. I have taken incubating birds in June in the Cuyamaca Mountains at altitudes of about 7,000 feet. The nesting sites here were in very large dead pine trees and inaccessible."

This woodpecker seems to show a tendency to nest, at least occasionally, at greater heights above ground than its northern relative, but otherwise its habits seem to be very similar.

The eggs are similar to those of the northern race. The measurements of 20 eggs average 24.67 by 18.60 millimeters; the eggs showing the four extremes measure **26.70** by 19.50, 25.60 by **19.70**, and **22.62** by **16.67** millimeters.

PICOÏDES ARCTICUS (Swainson)

ARCTIC THREE-TOED WOODPECKER

PLATES 15, 16

HABITS

Although not found in the strictly Arctic, treeless regions, this bird is probably well named, for its range as a whole averages farther north than that of any other woodpecker except *P. tridactylus*. It is a bird of the boreal forests of spruces and firs, ranging as far north in Alaska and northern Canada as these trees grow, and extending its range southward throughout the Canadian Zone into the Northern United States and farther southward in some of the higher mountain ranges.

In the eastern portion of its range this woodpecker seems to prefer the dense virgin forests of spruces and balsam fir, but it nests mainly in the more open windfalls or burned-over clearings where there are plenty of dead, standing trees in which to excavate its nest. In New York State, near the southern limit of its breeding range, a typical locality is thus described by Laurence Achilles (1906) : "At three thousand feet or more above the sea, in the denser spruce and balsam forests of the Adirondacks, the Arctic three-toed woodpecker is fairly common. * * *

"The trees near the nest were chiefly spruces, with a few balsams and birches scattered among them. The birds had selected a rather open place for their nesting-site, as, within a radius of ten yards from their nest, there were several windfalls and dead spruces. The ground was carpeted with moss, while linnea, clintonia, wood-sorrel and bunchberry were blossoming in profusion near the base of the tree."

In the Midwestern States and Provinces, the Arctic three-toed shows a decided preference for tamarack swamps, especially where these have been burned over, leaving a few dead or dying trees still standing; these trees not only furnish an abundant food supply but offer many convenient nesting sites. Into such attractive habitats these birds sometimes congregate to form small breeding colonies.

The Weydemeyers (1928) say that in northwestern Montana this woodpecker "is found most frequently in Transition zone woods that have been logged or burned over. In virgin forests it occurs sparingly in yellow pine woods at low elevations; more commonly in mixed broad-leaf and conifer, and Douglas fir, associations; and rarely in alpine fir and lodgepole pine woods of the higher mountains, in the Canadian zone. Its favorite feeding trees are Douglas fir and western larch."

Nesting.—Philipp and Bowdish (1919) found four or five nests of the Arctic three-toed woodpecker in Northumberland County, New Brunswick, in May and June 1917. Most of the nests were in living balsam firs with dead hearts, but one was "in a dead maple stub, near the edge of a large burnt barren, and a short distance from the edge of mixed woods." This was "at a height of about ten feet. The cavity measured 10½ inches from the lower edge of entrance to bottom. The entrance measured 1⅝ inches in height and 1¾ inches in width." They say that—

apparently nest sites are selected indiscriminately, in dead stubs in open cleared ground or burnt barrens, and in the woods, where nests are often in dead-hearted live trees. The birds have a remarkably strong attachment for their nests, as evidenced by re-laying in nest holes from which eggs had been removed, and their disregard of the immediate presence of intruders. The male evidently performs his share of the work of incubation, as well as care of young. New nest holes are apparently dug each year, and these may not be in the immediate vicinity of nests of the previous year. The site selected tends to be low, only one nest having been noted at a height of over ten feet, while one, as noted, was as low as two feet. Entrances to nest holes are strongly beveled at the lower edge, forming a sort of "door-step," and more or less at sides and even top. While this is true in some cases with the Northern Hairy and some other woodpecker excavations which we have examined, it has not proved so frequent or pronounced. With experience, one can usually identify the nest hole of this species with comparative certainty, by this one feature.

Dr. Harrison F. Lewis watched a pair of these woodpeckers excavating their nesting hole on May 27, 1936, in some second-growth woods, chiefly spruce and fir, in Saguenay County, Quebec; he says in his notes: "The Arctic three-toed woodpeckers had a partly excavated nest cavity at a height of about 14 feet on the northwest side of a dead birch stub in a clearing. The stub was about 20 feet high and 1 foot in diameter and stood about 10 feet from the border of the clearing. The nest cavity was guarded almost continually by one bird of the pair. The bird on guard clung to the lower edge of the opening of this cavity. Nine other woodpecker-made openings, many of them only partly completed, were to be seen in the same stub.

"I watched the three-toed woodpeckers, from partial concealment near at hand, for an hour and 25 minutes. Each one of them would spend a period of 15 to 20 minutes at their nest cavity, then be relieved by the other. The periods spent at the cavity by the male

were somewhat longer than those spent there by the female. While
the male was at the cavity, he spent much of his time in excavating,
with only his tail and the region of his rump projecting from the
opening, but at intervals of a few seconds he would withdraw his
body and head from the cavity and look about him. When he was
excavating, very little noise could be heard. He spent some time in
throwing out chips and some time in resting. When the female was
at the cavity, she did very little excavating, so little that it seemed
to be a mere gesture. On one occasion, after she had been clinging
to the edge of the opening for 10 minutes, she drummed repeatedly,
but not loudly, on the outside of the stub beside the opening. I
wondered if she were signaling to the male to come to relieve her in
guarding the cavity. After 5 minutes of such intermittent drumming,
she was relieved at the opening by the male."

Mr. Achilles (1906) describes the nest he found in the Adirondacks
as follows:

The hole, which was in a spruce tree, faced north by northeast, and was
twenty-seven feet one inch from the ground. The spruce retained all its branches
and some twigs, although it had been dead for some time.

The following dimensions of the hole were taken after the young had left
their nest. The entrance to the hole was two inches wide and one and five-
eighths inches high. From the outside of the hole, straight through over the
top of the nest to the back of the hole, the measurement was five and three-fourths
inches. The outside shell, including the bark, was one and three-fourths inches
thick. The diameter of the nest opening was three and one-fourth inches, while
the diameter of the hole on the inside at the bottom of the shaft, was four and
five-eighths inches. The depth of the hole was nine and one-eighth inches.

Dr. C. Hart Merriam sent Major Bendire (1895) some notes on two
nests that he found in the Adirondacks, as follows:

The water of Seventh Lake, Fulton Chain, had been raised by a dam at the foot
of Sixth Lake, flooding a considerable area along the inlet, and the trees killed
by the overflow stood in about 6 feet of water. In 1883 the place was first
visited by me, May 27. Both species of Three-toed Woodpeckers (*Picoides americanus* and *arcticus*) were tolerably common, and one new nest of each was found.
That of *P. arcticus* contained one fresh egg. The nest was 10 inches deep, and
the opening within 5 feet of the surface of the water. It was in a dead spruce,
10 inches in diameter. * * * The place was next visited June 2, but the date
proved still too early. Several unfinished nests of *P. americanus* were found,
and one completed nest with four fresh eggs of *P. arcticus*. Like the one found
on my first visit, it was in a dead spruce and about 5 feet above the water. The
nest was 11 inches deep and the orifice 1¾ inches in diameter.

J. H. Fleming (1901) says that the Arctic three-toed woodpecker is
"a common resident in Parry Sound, rarer in Muskoka. This Woodpecker has a habit of sometimes nesting in colonies. I saw the nests
of such a colony near Sand Lake in 1896; there were six or seven nests,
each cut into the trunk of a living cedar, just below the first branch,
and usually eight or ten feet from the ground. The cedars were in a
dense forest, overlooking a small stream that empties into Sand Lake."

Macoun (1909) reports, on the authority of Spreadborough, that "a pair nested in a telegraph pole quite near Cache lake station of the Parry Sound railway." Major Bendire (1895) writes:

On May 10, 1883, while en route from Fort Klamath to Linkville, Oregon, and only a few miles from the latter place, just where the pine timber ended and the sagebrush commenced, I found a male busily at work on a pine stump, only about 2½ feet high and about 18 inches in diameter, standing within a few feet of the road, and close to a charcoal burner's camp, in quite an open and exposed situation, nearly all the timber in the vicinity having been cut down. The stump was solid, full of pitch, and showed no signs of decay; the entrance hole was about 1½ inches in diameter and 8 inches from the top. The cavity, when first examined, was only about 2 inches deep, and on my return, two days later, it had reached a depth of 4 inches; the female was then at work. To make sure of a full set of eggs, I waited until the 25th. The cavity then was found to be 18 inches deep, and was gradually enlarged toward the bottom. The four eggs it contained had been incubated about four days. The female was on the nest, and uttered a hissing sound as she left it, and might easily have been caught, as she remained in the hole until the stump was struck with a hatchet. The sides of the cavity were quite smooth, and the eggs were partly embedded in a slight layer of pine chips. The locality where this nest was found was near the top of a low divide, not over 4,100 feet in altitude.

Dr. Thomas S. Roberts (1932) calls attention to an interesting feature in the nesting habits of this woodpecker, as observed in two nestings that he saw in Minnesota; he says of the two nests:

The nesting-hole was in a live jack-pine on the edge of a tamarack and spruce swamp, only twenty feet from a traveled road and close by a log house used as a store. The entrance faced south and was twelve feet from the ground, at which point the tree was seven inches in diameter. The outer bark of the tree had been chipped off for a distance of twelve to fifteen inches above and below the hole and half-way around the tree, thus leaving a large, irregular, whitish area.   *   *   *

Another nest, found the same season, was also in a live evergreen tree and the outer bark had been similarly stripped from around the entrance, making a conspicuous, white patch with the dark nesting-hole in the center. Can this be a direction mark for the returning bird among the dark tree trunks around?

As to the height from the ground, P. B. Philipp writes to me that of 26 nesting holes examined by him in New Brunswick two were 15 feet, two 12 feet, three 10 feet, one 8 feet, two 6 feet, two 5 feet, four 4 feet, six 3 feet, and four only 2 feet above ground.

Although the Arctic three-toed woodpecker usually nests at no great height above ground, there are a few exceptions to this rule, mainly in the western portion of its range. Grinnell and Storer (1924) record a nest seen in the Yosemite region that was 50 feet above ground in a dead lodgepole pine. Harry S. Swarth (1924) found, in the Skeena River region, the highest nest of which I can find any record; he says: "A nest of the Arctic three-toed woodpecker was found in Kispiox Valley. It was placed in a dead and charred Engelmann spruce, in a strip of spruce woods bordering a muskeg otherwise surrounded by poplar forest. The nest hole was eighty feet from the ground. It was two and one-half inches in diameter and one foot deep, drilled through an outer sheath of sound, hard wood, and downward through soft, rotten 'punk.'"

Eggs.—The number of eggs laid by the Arctic three-toed woodpecker varies from two to six, four being the commonest number. These vary from ovate to elliptical-ovate, the former shape prevailing. The shell is dull or only slightly glossy and is pure white. The measurements of 39 eggs average 21.32 by 18.94 millimeters; the eggs showing the four extremes measure **25.9** by 18.7, 25.1 by **20.2**, and **22.35** by **17.53** millimeters.

Young.—The period of incubation is about 14 days; both sexes assist in this and in the care of the young. Only one brood is raised in a season, but if the eggs are taken, a second set will be laid, often in the same nest.

Mr. Achilles (1906) watched a nest containing young for 24 consecutive hours, he and a companion taking turns at the vigil and sleeping alternately within ten yards of the tree; he writes:

The parents, when feeding their young, usually alighted within a space of three feet below the hole, and never directly at its entrance. They would pause here for a moment as though fearing they were observed by someone. Then they would hop up to the hole and look in, anywhere from two up to six times, as if accustoming their eyes to the darkness. Once in a while grubs could be seen in their bills, but, from the actions of the birds when feeding their young, they appeared to be regurgitating. During twenty-four hours the female fed the young thirty times, and the male twenty-nine times.

As it grew dusk, the young gradually grew quieter, and their little "peep-peep-peep" greatly resembled those of chicks when crawling beneath their mother's wings. From two o'clock in the afternoon till seven o'clock that evening, two minutes was the longest period during which the young did not utter a single "peep." From seven P. M. until two minutes after four the next morning, the young birds ceased this continuous chattering. The mother was the last to feed them at night, the time being seventeen minutes after seven; but the male was up first in the morning. At four-fifteen in the morning, the young uttered a few sleepy "peeps," and the male alighted three feet below the hole at four-sixteen. The young birds heard him alight and immediately commenced to chatter. The male hopped up to the hole, looked in twice, and then fed them. The young birds' bills were seen, indicating that they were very hungry, and were hanging on to the inner wall of the nest near the entrance. Soon after this their hunger was appeased, their bills were seen no more, and the parents had to go almost into the hole to feed them.

Plumages.—The nestlings are naked and blind at first, but the juvenal plumage is acquired before the young leave the nest. In the juvenal plumage, the young male is similar to the adult male, but the yellow crown patch is smaller and not so sharply defined; the upper parts are duller, browner black, lacking the glossy, bluish edgings; the breast is tinged with dull buffy white; and the flanks are more heavily and less distinctly barred or spotted with dull black. The young female is similar to the young male, but there is no distinct yellow patch on the crown, only scattering yellow feathers in varying amounts, often few or none at all. This plumage is worn through the summer and early fall; the first winter plumage, which is practically indistinguishable from that of the adult, is apparently not fully acquired until November or December. Adults have one complete annual molt, beginning in August.

Food.—More than three-quarters of the food of both species of three-toed woodpeckers consists of the larvae of wood-boring beetles, mainly Cerambycidae and Buprestidae. Referring to the former, Prof. F. E. L. Beal (1911) says:

Stomachs containing 15 to 20 of these grubs are very common, and one held 34. Probably the stomach is filled several times each day, and it does not seem unreasonable to assume that a bird will eat 50 of these insects every 24 hours for 6 months and at least 25 daily for the other half of the year. At this rate one bird will annually destroy 13,675 of these destructive grubs. * * *

Probably there are not many other agencies more destructive to timber than this family of beetles. Nor is timber safe even after it has been cut. Logs lying in the mill yard or forest may be ruined in a single season if these creatures are not prevented from depositing their eggs. * * * A very efficient check upon the undue increase of these insects is found in the woodpeckers, especially the two species of Picoides.

Weevils and other beetles and some ants are eaten, as well as a few other insects and spiders. Vegetable food, wild fruits, mast, and cambium amount to less than 12 percent of the food.

While with us, in southern New England, in winter, this woodpecker shows a decided preference for dead white pine trees (*Pinus strobus*), especially those that have been killed by fire or have been dead long enough for the bark to have partially peeled off. An isolated tree or a group of trees of this type may be visited day after day by one of these woodpeckers, during its stay, with such regularity that many an observer, who has never seen an Arctic three-toed woodpecker, may feel reasonably sure of finding one in such a place, if it has been previously seen there. Its persistent work on such a tree is well described by E. H. Forbush (1927) as follows:

This species very often begins to work on the trunk near the foot of a tree; it sounds the bark with direct blows, and then, turning its head from side to side, strikes its beak slantingly into and under the bark, and flakes it off. It often works long on the same tree and barks the whole trunk in time, only occasionally working on the branches. Thus it exposes channels of bark-beetles and the holes made by borers. When the bird remains motionless, it is well concealed against the blackened bark of the burnt trees. It seems deliberate in its movements and appears to do its work thoroughly, as it often remains five to ten minutes on the same spot and then shifts only a little distance. In early autumn, while the grubs are still at work on the tree, it lays its head against the tree, at times, turning it first to one side and then to the other as if listening.

Grinnell, Dixon, and Linsdale (1930) write of the feeding habits of this woodpecker in the Lassen Peak region:

One of these woodpeckers was watched as it moved slowly up a tree trunk. It stopped to knock off a piece of bark with a sidewise (glancing) blow of the heavy bill. This was repeated several times. Then the bird began to drill in earnest and the tapping could be heard by a person more than thirty meters distant. The blows were delivered rapidly, about two per second. Between three and five minutes were required to bore through the bark, in this instance twenty millimeters thick. Then after a few moments of probing the bill was withdrawn and was seen to hold a white larva which was quickly eaten. * * *

On one tree thirty-five centimeters in diameter an area of bark thirty by sixty centimeters was punctured completely through by twenty-two holes each leading to the tunnel of a wood-borer. * * * The holes were twelve by twelve millimeters across by twenty deep. It appeared to the observer * * * that many of the still living trees in that locality had been saved from complete destruction by the insects, by the activity of this woodpecker.

Manly Hardy wrote to Major Bendire (1895) that, in Maine, "it seems to feed entirely on such wood worms as attack spruce, pine, and other soft-wood timber that has been fire-killed. Specimens are so abundant in such places that I once shot the heads off of six in a few minutes when short of material for a stew."

Some dead pine trees that had been regularly frequented by these woodpeckers, on the Kennard estate, were cut down; and the birds, seeing their favorite trees gone, continued to search for food on the wood piles made from these trees.

Behavior.—Most observers agree that the Arctic three-toed woodpecker is very tame and unsuspicious, working very quietly on a tree trunk for long periods, without moving about much, and allowing a close approach; perhaps, as it lives most of its life in remote northern forests, where men are scarce, it has not learned to fear human beings. Manly Hardy considered it the tamest and stupidest of the woodpeckers found in Maine. Major Bendire (1895) says:

"Like the hairy woodpecker, they are persistent drummers, rattling away for minutes at a time on some dead limb, and are especially active during the mating season, in April. I have located more than one specimen by traveling in the direction of the sound when it was fully half a mile away. * * * Its flight is swift, greatly undulating, and is often protracted for considerable distances."

Dr. Lewis says in his notes: "When one bird relieved the other in guarding the cavity, the bird taking over guard duty flew low toward the stub and swerved sharply upward, with widespread tail, to alight near the opening."

Voice.—Dr. Lewis (MS.) records the common cry of this woodpecker as "*tchuk,* often shortened and sharpened to *kip.*" He also says: "A male mounted a stub, about 25 feet from me, and there, in plain view, scolded me vigorously with a sharp note like *kuk,* repeated about once a second for some minutes. Each time the note was uttered there was a flash of whitish at the bird's eye, as though it winked with each utterance. It was also heard to utter a rattling note, apparently another kind of scolding cry."

Francis H. Allen tells me that the "call-note resembles the *cluck* used in New England to start a horse; it has a 'woodeny' quality." Ralph Hoffmann (1927) says that "in the breeding season the Arctic Three-toed Woodpecker makes a very loud rolling sound by drumming on dry limbs and when concerned about the nest a shrill *kick-er-uck-a-kick*. The ordinary call is *tschick* or *tschuck*." A note of greeting, possibly part of a love-making performance, is thus described by Mr. Achilles (1906) : "Several times when the female was getting grubs in the dead spruce near the hole, the male would fly from some distant tree and alight near her. She would see him coming and, just about as he was about to alight, would spread her wings and utter a 'whe-e-e-e-ee.' This call, which was its loudest at its middle point, rose and then fell to the same pitch at which it was begun."

Rev. C. W. G. Eifrig (1906) heard a queer sound that "was as if produced by pulling out the end of a clock spring and suddenly releasing it, producing a wiry, humming sound. The author of it proved to be a male of this woodpecker. In the course of the half hour that I watched him he showed himself master of quite a repertoire of notes and would-be songs. When flying he would say: *chut chut* and then rattle like a Kingfisher. When hammering on a tree and preening himself, he would intersperse those actions by chuckling: *duck, duck, duck*."

Field marks.—All the three-toed woodpeckers can be easily recognized by the yellow patch on the crown of the adult male and by more or less yellow in the crowns or young birds of both sexes. The crown patch of the adult male *arcticus* is larger and extends farther forward than that of *tridactylus*. But the best field mark for the Arctic three-toed woodpecker is the solid-black back, without any white markings, and in the female the solid-black crown as well; the dorsal aspect, when the bird is clinging to a tree trunk, often appears wholly black. The white stripe on the side of the head, below the eye, is much wider in *arcticus* than in *tridactylus*, and the latter has the back transversely banded with white.

Enemies.—Mr. Achilles (1906) relates the following:

In the course of the morning, two red-breasted nuthatches tormented the woodpeckers for fifteen minutes. * * * They hovered around the hole with drooping wings, holding their tails up like wrens. One of them finally ventured into the hole so far that just his tail was protruding. They would fly away when the parents approached the hole, but would return as soon as the nest was unprotected. After some time the male woodpecker went into the hole, evidently intending to peck them in case they should look into it. During the three minutes he remained in the hole, he managed to keep from looking out for one straight minute. Nevertheless, he was greatly agitated, and would look out every few seconds to see if the nuthatches were approaching,—his crown-patch showing brightly. At last the male nuthatch came to the edge of the hole, whereat the woodpecker made an unsuccessful attempt to peck his opponent, afterward flying out with a rush, and chasing the nuthatch for some distance on the wing.

Soon after that four Canada jays approached, and one of them ventured near the nest hole, but the woodpecker and a hermit thrush succeeded in driving him and his companions away, and they did not return.

Joseph Dixon (1927) tells of an attempt by a black bear to rob a nest of young Arctic three-toed woodpeckers:

This nest was located only four feet above the ground in a large live lodge-pole pine. My attention was first attracted to the locality by the unusually vigorous scolding of the parent woodpeckers. A closer approach revealed the cause of the excitement.

A bear had located the nest, probably through the noise of the young woodpeckers, which were old enough to come to the nest entrance to receive food, and which squealed with anticipation of a meal any time any bird, animal or person came close to the nest tree. In an endeavor to get at the young in the nest, the bear had bitten out slabs of green wood twelve inches long, two inches wide, and one-quarter of an inch thick. The muddy stains around the inside of the nest entrance showed that the bear had thrust his nose into the hole repeatedly. But after gnawing over an area 10 by 10 inches on the tree trunk to a depth of more than an inch, the bear gave it up as a bad job. Had the nest been in an old stump, the outcome would probably have been different. This offers a reasonable explanation of the tendency of certain woodpeckers to nest in living trees.

Mr. Kennard tells in his notes of a female hummingbird that attacked one of these woodpeckers: "Several times she swooped down at the woodpecker, who, quick as a flash, would dodge around the trunk and out of her way."

Winter.—The Arctic three-toed woodpecker is normally mainly resident in winter throughout most of its breeding range; it is a hardy bird and its food supply is available at all seasons, the grubs on which it feeds remaining in the wood for more than one season. Probably a few wander southward nearly every winter, and there have been several heavy flights of these birds into the Northeastern States, which it is not easy to explain. Dr. Josselyn Van Tyne (1926) has given a full account of one of these invasions, to which the reader is referred. Mr. Forbush (1927) writes:

It is difficult to determine exactly what causes these unusual migrations, They are not forced by inclement weather, for one at least has occurred in a mild winter. * * * It seems probable that the unusual invasions of the species into New England follow summers when its food has been unusually abundant. An excessive food supply tends to fecundity, and overbreeding naturally compels expansion and induces migration, whether among the lower animals or human-kind. Since the above was written, Mr. Josselyn Van Tyne has published a paper regarding the unusual flight of this species in 1923 in which he advances a similar explanation. He says that between 1909 and 1914 there was an irruption of the spruce budworm in eastern Canada and Maine which resulted in the death of many trees and a consequent increase of bark-beetles and borers, followed by an increase in the number of these woodpeckers. On the other hand a scarcity of the usual food supply may cause migration. A wet season with few fires in the woods or a scarcity of insects (such as the spruce bud-moth) that kill trees might, later, cause a migration.

Illustrating the length of the sojourn of these woodpeckers during the winter of 1923–24, Dr. Van Tyne (1926) says:

The greatest concentration of these woodpeckers recorded at any one point was on the estate of Mr. F. H. Kennard where scores of dead and dying white pine afforded an abundance of their special food. The first one seen was a male collected on October 17. Another individual appeared by October 20 and during the winter at least three males and two females were accounted for, while all indications point toward the actual presence of perhaps twice as many. The most remarkable fact about this group of birds, however, was the length of their stay, for both males and females were seen as late as the middle of May and at least one male stayed through the early part of June and was last seen on June 12.

Other invasions are recorded by Mr. Forbush (1927) as follows: "A great irruption of these birds occurred in the autumn of 1860. During the following winter Mr. George O. Welch often saw as many as six or eight at once in a piece of fire-killed timber in Lynn. * * * In the autumn of 1925, there was a lesser movement, and many returned through New England in the spring of 1926. In the autumn of 1926 another considerable southward migration occurred."

DISTRIBUTION

Range.—North America south to the Central United States; non-migratory.

The range of the Arctic three-toed woodpecker extends **north** to central Alaska (probably Tocatna Forks and Fairbanks); southern Mackenzie (Fort Wrigley, Fort Providence, and Smith Portage); northern Manitoba (Cochrane River and probably York Factory); Quebec (Richmond Gulf, Godbout, and Madeline River); and Newfoundland (Nicholsville). **East** to Newfoundland (Nicholsville); probably rarely Prince Edward Island (Baddeck); eastern New Brunswick (Tabusintac); probably rarely Nova Scotia (Advocate); Maine (Machias); and probably rarely Massachusetts (Winchendon and Concord). **South** to probably rarely Massachusetts (Concord); central Vermont (Pico Peak); southern Ontario (Ottawa, Algonquin Park, and Sand Lake); northern Michigan (Au Sable Valley, Blaney, and Huron Mountain); probably northern Wisconsin (Kelley Brook and Star Lake); northern Minnesota (North Pacific Junction, Itasca Park, and White Earth); probably southwestern South Dakota (Elk Mountains); northwestern Wyoming (Yel-

lowstone Park) ; northwestern Montana (Glacier National Park and
Fortine) ; northern Idaho (Fort Sherman) ; and central California
(Mona Lake and Bear Valley). **West** to California (Bear Valley,
Lassen Peak, and Mount Shasta) ; Oregon (Pinehurst and Fort Kla-
math) ; Washington (Bumping Lake and probably Tiger) ; British
Columbia (Arrow Lakes, Fort St. James, Kispiox Valley, and Atlin) ;
south-central Yukon (Six-mile River) ; and Alaska (Chitina Moraine
and probably Tocatna Forks).

During the winter season this species has been recorded **north** to
Alaska (Copper River) ; Mackenzie (Fort Simpson, Fort Rae, and
Fort Reliance) ; Manitoba (Grand Rapids) ; Ontario (Arnprior and
Ottawa) ; New Brunswick (Scotch Lake) ; and Nova Scotia (Pictou).
While no regular movements have been detected, individuals have
been recorded at this season **south** to Long Island, N. Y. (East
Hampton and Southampton) ; northern New Jersey (Upper Mont-
clair and Englewood) ; southern New York (Ithaca) ; Ohio (Paines-
ville and Akron) ; Illinois (Rantoul and Peoria) ; Iowa (Big Cedar
River) ; and Nebraska (Omaha and Dakota).

Egg dates.—Laborador : 3 records, May 27 to June 2.

Maine : 3 records, May 19 to June 12.

New Brunswick : 12 records, May 19 to June 30 ; 6 records, May 30
to June 15, indicating the height of the season.

New York : 5 records, May 18 to June 10.

PICOÏDES TRIDACTYLUS BACATUS Bangs

AMERICAN THREE-TOED WOODPECKER

PLATE 17

HABITS

This North American race of the three-toed woodpecker occupies
an extensive range in the Hudsonian and Canadian Zones of approximately the eastern half of Canada, which extends into some
of the Northern States from Minnesota eastward. Two other races
occupy similar zones in western Canada, Alaska, and the Rocky
Mountains. The species is not particularly common anywhere, but
the eastern race seems to be the best known. For a full discussion
of the various races of the North American three-toed woodpeckers,
the reader is referred to an extensive paper on the subject by Outram
Bangs (1900). This woodpecker is not evenly distributed throughout its range but seems to be confined to certain rather limited and
favorable localities. William Brewster (1898) found it breeding in
the eastern part of Coos County, N. H., on the eastern side of a
small pond; "where an elevated ridge approaches the pond the banks
are above the reach of the highest floods and the land in the rear
slopes gently upward. At this point a dense, vigorous forest of

spruces, balsams and arbor vitaes, intermingled with a few deciduous trees, comes quite to the water's edge and here, on June 2d, 1897, I found my first nest of the Banded Three-toed Woodpecker."

In the same county, Charles L. Whittle (1920) found what he called a colony of three-toed woodpeckers in "a single small area of virgin forest containing abundant white spruces and balsams, the former splendid, healthy trees of large size, and the latter also large but having many trees diseased or decayed at the heart. * * * In the area of diseased balsams, a pleasant surprise awaited me, for here Three-toed Woodpeckers of both species, sexes, and all recognizable ages, were distinctly common—a colony, so to speak, temporarily concentrated owing to two factors: (1) The nearly complete destruction in this region of the former virgin forest of large conifers on which and in which they fed and nested; and (2) the presence of abundant food at this locality in the diseased balsam trees."

Elon H. Eaton (1914) says:

In New York it is evidently confined to the Adirondack forests. I have heard of no specimen taken farther from the spruce belt than Waterville, Oneida county. It therefore shares with the Spruce grouse, the Canada jay and the Hudsonian chickadee the distinction of being one of our perfectly nonmigratory species. Within the spruce and balsam forests it is quite uniformly distributed, but is less common than the Black-backed woodpecker, evidently about one-half as common as that species. It inhabits both the spruce swamps and the mountain sides. While making the bird survey of the Mount Marcy district we found this species breeding on the slopes of Marcy just above Skylight camp, an altitude of 4,000 feet, and in the swamp at the Upper Ausable lake at an altitude of 2,000 feet.

Nesting.—Mr. Brewster (1898) describes, in considerable detail, the nest he found in a spruce tree in Coos County, N. H., as follows:

On measuring the spruce I found it to be thirty-nine inches in circumference one foot above the ground, and twenty-nine inches at the nest. The hole was on the west side at a height above the ground of exactly ten feet and eleven inches. The entrance hole was somewhat irregular outwardly measuring about one and three quarters inches in breadth by two inches in height—the greater diameter vertically being due to the fact that the lower edges had been chiselled away rather freely to afford a foothold for the bird; half an inch in, the hole was perfectly round, and measured one and one-half inches in diameter.

The interior or nest cavity was irregularly gourd-shaped and ten and one-eighth inches in depth, its greatest diameter, about four and one-half inches, being midway between the bottom and top. The walls were rough and seamy but this was not, perhaps, the fault of the birds, for the wood, although soft and easily worked, had evidently peeled off in long, stringy fibers.

The eggs lay on a deep mat of these shreds some of which were more than one inch in length.

Dr. C. Hart Merriam informed Major Bendire (1895) that "numerous nests were found in the Adirondacks in June, 1883. Most of them were in the flooded timber bordering the inlet of Seventh Lake, Fulton Chain. They varied from 5 to 12 feet in height above the

water, and were in spruce, tamarack, pine, balsam, and cedar trees."
The nests of this woodpecker are not always so low down as those
mentioned above; Col. John E. Thayer took a set, near Upton, Maine,
on June 9, 1898, that was 20 feet from the ground in an old dead
spruce stub; and the nests that Mr. Eaton (1914) found in the
Adirondacks "were situated in tamaracks and spruces from 25 to
40 feet from the ground."

Eggs.—Four seems to be the usual number of eggs laid by this
woodpecker; I can find no record of either more or fewer in complete
sets. The eggs are ovate, pure white, and only moderately glossy.
The measurements of 43 eggs average 23.32 by 18.01 millimeters; the
eggs showing the four extremes measure 25.5 by 18.2, 23.8 by 19.6,
and 20.1 by 15.0 millimeters.

Young.—The period of incubation is said to be about 14 days,
and it is shared by both sexes. Both parents feed and care for the
young, even after the young leave the nest, as family parties are seen
traveling about together in summer.

Plumages.—The nestlings are probably hatched naked and blind, as
with other woodpeckers, but the juvenal plumage is acquired before
the young leave the nest. In the juvenal plumage, the young male is
similar to the adult male, but the yellow crown patch is smaller and
less sharply defined; the upper parts are duller, brownish black
instead of sooty black; the flanks are more heavily and more extensively banded, or spotted, with sepia instead of clear black; the white
of the throat and breast is tinged with pale buffy. The juvenal
female is similar to the young male, but the yellow crown patch is
smaller, and the amount of yellow in it is very variable, sometimes
only a few scattered feathers and sometimes a well-defined, clear
patch. This plumage is worn at least through August and probably
well into fall. The only molting adults I have seen were taken in
August.

Food.—The feeding habits of the American three-toed woodpecker
are almost identical with that of the Arctic three-toed. Prof.
F. E. L. Beal (1911) says:

The largest item with both species is wood-boring coleopterous larvae. These
amount to 64.25 percent with *arcticus* and 60.66 with *americanus*. Caterpillars,
which in this case are mostly wood-boring species, amount to 12.88 and 14.45
percent for the two birds respectively. The total of wood-boring larvae, including both caterpillars and beetles, is, 77.13 percent for *arcticus* and 75.11
percent for *americanus*, or more than three-fourths of the food of both
species. * * *

Fruit skins were found in only one stomach of *americanus* and mast in but
one stomach of *arcticus*. Cambium was found in 10 stomachs of *arcticus* and
8 of *americanus*. This indicates that these birds do some pecking at the bark
of living trees for other purposes than getting insects, but no complaints have
yet been made, from which we infer that little or no damage is done; in fact
the amount contained in the stomachs is not large a little less than 10 percent.

E. H. Forbush (1927) says that "Miss Caroline E. Hamilton of Greenfield, Massachusetts, observed in late September an individual that remained in a yard from daylight till dark, making the rounds of the trees and remaining longest on the fruit trees at the tiny holes attributed to Sapsuckers. She said that the bird seemed to find good food in these pits, and it may have been eating some of the cambium." He writes further: .

Mr. E. O. Grant, a faithful correspondent of Patten, Maine, travels over considerable region and north into Quebec, spending much time in the woods. On March 6, 1922, he wrote that the spruce budworm had killed about thirty percent of the spruce in that region and nearly all the fir, and that among the dead trees he saw hundreds of both the three-toed species, together with nearly equal numbers of Downy Woodpeckers and Hairy Woodpeckers. Food for the birds was very plentiful, as dark-beetles and spruce-borers were numerous. When an invasion of caterpillars strips coniferous trees and thus exposes their trunks and branches to the hot summer sun, dark-beetles attack and virtually girdle them with numerous tunnels beneath the bark; borers get in and sometimes most of the trees die. The woodpeckers, concentrating on these dead trees from all the forest around about, help to keep down the undue increase of bark-beetles and borers which, if they became too numerous, might attack some live trees.

Behavior.—Lucien M. Turner says in his unpublished notes: "The manner of flight of this species is less vigorous than in *Picoides arcticus*, yet differing in a manner that is difficult to describe; the unfolding of the wings when preparing to make the upward swoop is quicker, the stroke of the wing not so strong, and the plunge not so deep."

Both species of three-toed woodpeckers are fearless birds, tame, and unsuspicious, probably because of their unfamiliarity with man and his hostile intentions; both are less active than most other woodpeckers, this species being particularly quiet in its movements and sedentary in its habits. Mr. Brewster (1898) writes:

My previous impression that *Picoides americanus* is a very much less active and restless bird than *P. arcticus*, was fully confirmed by the behavior of this male who was almost if not quite as slow and lethargic of movement as a sapsucker. He would spend minutes at a time clinging to one spot and when he moved up the tree trunks it was in a singularly slow, deliberate manner. Only when at or near the nest did he show real animation. * * *

I have rarely seen a nesting bird so alert and keen of hearing as was this *Picoides*. The sound of our voices or the slightest noise made by an oar or paddle would bring him at once to the entrance of the hole, even when we were forty or fifty yards away, and every few minutes when we were sitting perfectly still he would look out turning his head in every direction. He would not leave the hole, however, until we were within a few yards of the foot of the tree and after he had drummed awhile he would return to the stub while we were sitting near its base with the camera directed towards it. * * *

On returning to the stub the bird would usually strike against it about two feet below the hole and reaching it by two or three quick, upward hops would cling to its lower edge, alternately looking in and down at us. * * * He did not once enter the nest while we were near the tree, nor did he again attempt to mislead us by pecking at the bark, evidently realizing that this ruse had failed. When he flew back into the woods he always took one of two courses and along each he invariably alighted not only on the same trees but on the same spot on each tree. He had one particular place on the trunk of a large spruce where he would spend ten or fifteen minutes at a time pluming himself and watching us, before returning to the nest.

Major Bendire (1895) quotes the following from Dr. C. Hart Merriam:

We had just crossed the boundary line between Lewis and Herkimer counties, when Mr. Bagg called my attention to a "fresh hole," about 8 feet from the ground, in a spruce tree near by. On approaching the tree a yellow crown appeared in the hole, showing that the male bird was "at home." To prevent his escape I jumped toward the tree and introduced three fingers, which were immediately punctured in a manner so distasteful to their proprietor as to necessitate an immediate withdrawal and exchange for the muzzle of my friend's gun. A handkerchief was next crowded into the hole, but was instantly riddled and driven out by a few blows from his terrible bill. It was then held loosely over the hole, and as the bird emerged I secured and killed him.

Wendell Taber had a good chance to observe one of these woodpeckers at short range in Grafton County, N. H., on May 31, 1937, about which he writes to me: "The bird was intent upon obtaining its food and ignored our presence. Most of the time the bird would fly to a tree and alight at a height of 20 to 25 feet, then work downward, hopping backward. Particularly it seemed to enjoy prodding around on the base of a tree at or within an inch or two of where tree and earth met. Drilling was barely audible, even when the bird was close-to. Both live and dead trees were attacked impartially. There was no strip act—the bark was not peeled off. There was a row of dead trees at the edge of the forest, which might well have been concentrated on, but which, actually, was attacked only in a haphazard manner along with trees alive in the forest. If anything, more attention was given to live trees."

Voice.—The three-toed woodpecker is normally a rather silent bird. Its weak notes have been likened to the squealing notes of the yellow-bellied sapsucker, or the squeak of a small mammal; it also utters a variety of short notes like *queep* or *quip*. Horace W. Wright (1911) says: "The calls of the *americanus* male bird were not excited or loud. The single calls were somewhat like the robin's call at dusk, and the rattling calls resembled a Hairy Woodpecker's rattle, but were less loud and sharp."

Mr. Brewster (1898) writes:

I had abundant opportunities for studying the drumming call today. It varied in duration from one to two seconds (never running over or under these limits) but was usually one and a half to one and three quarters seconds. The intervals between the calls were too irregular to be worth recording. The first three or four taps were slightly slower and more disconnected than the remaining ones but the general effect was that of a uniform roll similar to that made by the Downy and the Hairy Woodpecker, but less loud and penetrating. Still it carried well and under favorable conditions could be heard fully one quarter of a mile away. * * *

After drumming a dozen times or more he gave a long vocal call closely similar to the Kingfisher-like rattle of the Hairy Woodpecker.

Field marks.—The American three-toed woodpecker is the only woodpecker likely to be seen in the northern woods that has a black back transversely barred with white, white under parts banded with black on the flanks, and a black crown, with or without a yellow crown patch; the yellow patch is very prominent in the adult male and less so in the young birds of both sexes, but lacking in the adult female. In flight the "ladderback" is more conspicuous than when the bird. is at rest, and the tail flashes white.

Winter.—Both species of three-toed woodpeckers are mainly resident throughout the year within their breeding ranges, as their normal food supply is as easily available in winter as in summer. Consequently few species of birds are less inclined to migrate than these woodpeckers. However, on rare occasions this woodpecker has been known to appear in winter somewhat south of its summer range. Probably these southward movements have been due to some shortage of food in its summer home, or an unusual supply of it further south, or, possibly, an unusually successful breeding season may have overcrowded the home range and caused an exodus.

DISTRIBUTION

Range.—Northern Europe, Asia, and North America, south through high mountainous regions to about latitude 35° N.; nonmigratory.

In North America the range of the three-toed woodpecker extends **north** to northern Alaska (Kowak River, Tanana, Beaver Creek, Fort Yukon, Circle, and Charlie Creek); northern Yukon (Forty Mile and probably Coal Creek); Mackenzie (Fort McPherson, Fort Goodhope, Fort Anderson, Fort Rae, and Fort Smith); northern Manitoba (Fort Du Brochet and Churchill); northern Ontario (Fort Albany); northern Quebec (Fort Chimo); and Labrador (Okak). **East** to Labrador (Okak and Nain); Newfoundland (South Exploit River); northeastern Maine (Presque Isle); and New Hampshire (Lake Umbagog and Mount Jefferson). **South** to northern New Hampshire (Mount Jefferson); northern New York (Long Lake and Moose River); probably northern Michigan (Isle Royal); northern Minnesota (Lake Itasca); northern New Mexico (Pecos Baldy and Chuska Mountains); Arizona (White Mountains, San Francisco Mountain, and Kaibab Plateau); east-central Nevada (Snake Mountains); and south-western Oregon (Four-mile Lake). **West** to western Oregon (Four-mile Lake); Washington (Blue Mountains, probably Mount Rainier, and Mount Baker); British Columbia (Chilliwack, Clinton, Willow River, and Hazelton); and Alaska (Chicagof Island, Glacier, Copper River, Lake Clark, Mount McKinley, Nulato, and Kowak River).

Several races of this species have been recognized, three of which are included in the range above outlined. The American three-toed woodpecker (*P. t. bacatus*) ranges from Maine, Newfoundland, and Labrador west to northern Manitoba and southern Mackenzie; the Alpine three-toed woodpecker (*P. t. dorsalis*) is the Rocky Mountain form and is found in that region from Montana and Idaho south to the higher mountains of New Mexico and Arizona; the Alaska three-toed woodpecker (*P. t. fasciatus*) is found from Alaska, Yukon, and western Mackenzie south to Oregon, Idaho, and Montana.

While the three-toed woodpecker is not regularly migratory, it appears likely that during severe winters it withdraws somewhat from the northern parts of its range. At this season it is occasionally collected or observed short distances south of its normal range (Massachusetts, southern Wisconsin, southern Minnesota, and southern New Mexico).

Egg dates.—Alberta: 8 records, May 23 to June 16.

Arctic America: 5 records, May 15 to June 9.

Labrador: 3 records, May 26 and 27.

New York: 3 records, May 14 to June 8.

PICOÏDES TRIDACTYLUS FASCIATUS Baird

ALASKA THREE-TOED WOODPECKER

HABITS

The range of this race of the three-toed woodpecker extends throughout the Hudsonian and Canadian Zones of western Canada and Alaska, and a short distance southward into some of the Western States, where it intergrades with the next form in the boreal forests of the Rocky Mountains.

Ridgway (1914) describes it as similar to the eastern race, "but with much more white on back, the white bars much larger and more or less coalesced along median line, forming a more or less continuous longitudinal patch; whitish spots on forehead much larger, sometimes coalesced into a nearly uniform dull white frontal area; upper tail-coverts and lower rump barred or spotted with white; sometimes even the wing-coverts and middle rectrices are spotted with white; black malar stripe narrower and usually less distinct, and black bars on sides and flanks narrower; averaging slightly larger."

Dr. E. W. Nelson (1887) says that this woodpecker occurs "on the headwaters of the Mackenzie River, extending thence north along the course of this stream and the Anderson River, and westward, covering all the wooded portions of Northern Alaska to the northern tree-limit, * * * outnumbering by far the combined numbers of all the other woodpeckers of that region. * * * On the Yukon these birds are said to prefer the groves of poplar and willow to the spruces."

Dr. Joseph Grinnell (1900) says: "This, the only species of woodpecker detected by me in the Kowak region, was resident throughout the year. It could scarcely be called common, though its borings were noticed in nearly every tract of spruces visited." J. A. Munro (1919), referring to the Okanagan Valley, British Columbia, says: "This species is resident and fairly common in Murray pine, Western larch, and spruce forests. I have never found them in yellow pine or Douglas fir country. They prefer the burnt areas of timber, and specimens collected are generally stained with charcoal on the underparts."

Nesting.—The nesting habits of this woodpecker do not differ materially from those of its eastern relative. Bendire (1895) mentions two sets of eggs, collected by MacFarlane in the Anderson River region, of which he says: "A single egg, originally from a set of three taken on May 30, 1863, accompanied by the female bird, was taken from a cavity in a pine tree, 4 feet from the ground, and another set of four, of which there are three eggs remaining, and likewise accompanied by the male bird, was taken on June 5, 1864, from a hole in a dry spruce, situated about 6 feet from the ground. The eggs from the last set were said to have been lying on the decayed dust of the tree, and were perfectly fresh when found."

Laing and Taverner (1929) found an abandoned nest in the Chitina River region, Alaska, of which they say: "Tree, about 15 inches in diameter at butt, had a dead top and nest in this dead portion, about 40 feet aloft. Dimensions as follows: diameter of door barely 2 inches; depth of nest 9½ inches; greatest diameter 3 inches. Barrel of nest quite cylindrical."

There is a set of four eggs in my collection, taken by Richard C. Harlow near Belvedere, Alberta, on May 29, 1926. The nest was about 20 feet above ground in a dead tamarack stub, among a scattered growth of tamaracks, in a muskeg, near a lake; the eggs lay on a bed of chips 10 inches below the entrance.

Mr. Munro (1919) writes: "On May 28, 1917, I found a nest that had just been finished, thirty feet from the ground in a dead Murray pine. The entrance was smaller than would be expected, slightly over one and a half inches, and the hole about fourteen inches deep."

Eggs.—The eggs of the Alaska three-toed woodpecker are indistinguishable from those of the eastern race. The measurements of 12 eggs average 22.08 by 17.09 millimeters; the eggs showing the four extremes measure **23.6** by **18.1, 20.8** by 16.8, and 21.5 by **16.5** milli-meters.

Behavior.—The plumages, feeding habits, and general behavior of this race do not differ materially from those of the species elsewhere, but Maj. Allan Brooks (Dawson and Bowles, 1909) has given a good description of a habit that seems to be shared by both species of *Picoïdes* and that has been referred to by others; he writes:

When shot, even if instantly killed, three-toed woodpeckers of both species have a marvelous faculty of remaining clinging to the tree in death. Where the trunks are draped with *Usnea* moss, it is impossible to bring one down, except when winged—then they attempt to fly, and fall to earth; but when killed outright they remain securely fastened by their strong curved claws. * * * The only chance is to leave the bird and to visit the foot of the tree when the relaxing muscles have at length permitted the body to drop—usually within two days. Once I was fortunate enough to observe the exact position that enabled the bird to maintain its grip. I had shot and killed an Arctic Three-toed Woodpecker on a low stump. On going up I found the bird's feet to be three inches apart by measurement; the tail was firmly braced, and the further the body was tilted back the more firmly the claws held in the bark.

Dr. Grinnell (1900) says: "In the fall and mid-winter these birds are silent and seldom seen. But after the first of March their drumming on some resonant dead tree was heard nearly every morning. This sound could be heard a long distance through the quiet woods, giving notice of the whereabouts of the woodpeckers."

PICOÏDES TRIDACTYLUS DORSALIS Baird

ALPINE THREE-TOED WOODPECKER

HABITS

This race of the three-toed woodpeckers enjoys the most southern distribution of any of the birds of this genus, ranging from northern Montana to northern Arizona and New Mexico, in the boreal forests of the Rocky Mountains. Ridgway (1914) characterizes it as "similar to white-backed examples of *P. a. fasciatus*, but larger; white markings on back usually all longitudinal (very rarely with any transverse bars of black), white supra-auricular streak usually broader, forehead usually with more black and less whitish spotting, white spots or bars on inner web of innermost secondaries larger, and sides and flanks usually less barred with black."

The Weydemeyers (1928) say that in northwestern Montana, "unlike *arcticus*, this species prefers dense, virgin forests to cut-over woods and open woodland pastures. * * * In the higher elevations, this woodpecker may be found in white pine, lodgepole pine, alpine fir, and Engelmann spruce forests. In the Transition zone, it shows a preference for spruce woods, with larch and yellow pine forests as second choice. In the Canadian zone, this species is somewhat commoner than *arcticus;* in the Transition zone, it occurs only about one-third as frequently as does the larger bird."

M. P. Skinner says, in his Yellowstone National Park notes: "This woodpecker is rather uncommon, but I have seen it in coniferous forests between 6,500 and 8,000 feet, in firs, lodgepole pine, and Engelmann spruce. I have also seen it on dead trees and on telephone poles. I have seen this woodpecker in this Park only between May and October."

Nesting.—At an altitude of about 9,000 feet in the mountains of Colorado, in or near Estes Park, John H. Flanagan (1911) collected a set of four eggs of the alpine three-toed woodpecker. "The hole was in an aspen stub, nine feet from the ground and about a foot or eighteen inches from the top, and just before the guide reached the hole the bird flew out. * * *

"The entrance to the nesting cavity was about one and one-half inches in diameter; the cavity itself about nine or ten inches in depth and quite large at the bottom. The eggs were laid on a few chips."

In north-central Colorado, Edwin R. Warren (1912) found a nest of this woodpecker "in a dead Engelmann spruce, which was twenty-five inches in diameter at the base, and twenty at the nest hole, the latter being seven feet above ground. The nest was eight inches deep, the entrance one and three-quarters inches in diameter; the thickness of the wood on the front side of the hole was two and three-quarters inches, and the cavity was five inches from front to back, and three wide. There were a few chips in the bottom, as well as a few of the birds' droppings. There were two young, about ready to fly, though I had no difficulty in posing them on the tree for pictures; they showed little or no fear."

Randolph Jenks (1934) discovered two nests of the alpine three-toed woodpecker on the Kaibab Plateau, near the east rim of the Grand Canyon, in northern Arizona. One was in "a hole in an aspen tree, two and one-half inches in diameter, opening to the southeast, twelve feet from the ground. The cavity was eight inches deep and the nest was lined with a thick layer of maggot-infested sawdust. In spite of the crawling competitors, the nestlings, a male and a female, seemed quite contented." This was on June 30, 1931. Several days later another nest was found, also on the Plateau, at an elevation of 8,100 feet; this nest was "in a hole about sixty feet above the ground in a western yellow pine."

Dr. Edgar A. Mearns (1890b) writes:

The Alpine Three-toed Woodpecker breeds commonly throughout the pine belt, seldom ascending far into the spruce woods of the highest peaks [in the mountains of Arizona]. On the northwestern slope of San Francisco Mountain I discovered a nest of this species on June 8, 1887. The female was seen alone pecking at a large yellow pine, which, although dead, still retained its bark and was quite solid. While feeding she uttered a peculiar, harsh, nasal cry. I shot her, and then noticed a small, neatly bored hole in the south side of the pine trunk, about 30 feet from the ground and away from branches. With the aid of a rope, and taking a start from the saddle, I was scarcely able to climb to the nest, which the male did not quit until I was well up; then he came out and uttered a sudden, sharp "whip-whip-whip" in a menacing tone, remaining hard by while I worked with saw and chisel. It took me nearly half an hour to make an opening sufficiently large to admit the hand, as the burrow was situated so extraordinarily deep. Two young, male and female, with feathers just sprouting, were found on a bed of small chips at the bottom of the burrow, not more than 8 inches lower than the entrance, but in the very heart of the tree, the cavity being oblique and pear-shaped, and having the strong odor characteristic of Woodpeckers' nests in general. Both parents and their progeny were preserved, and are now in the American Museum collection. The irides of the adults were dark cherry red; their feet, claws, and basal half of mandible plumbeous, the rest of the bill being plumbeous black.

Eggs.—The alpine three-toed woodpecker is said to lay five eggs to a set, but probably the set oftener consists of fewer eggs. I have seen no eggs of this subspecies; and the only measurements I have been able to get are those from a set of five eggs, collected by A. Treganza in Salt Lake County, Utah, on June 3, 1916; these are in the P. B. Philipp collection in the American Museum of Natural History. The measurements average 24.52 by 17.52 millimeters, rather large for the species; the eggs showing the four extremes measure 25.3 by 17.7 and 24.1 by 17.4 millimeters.

Food.—Mrs. Bailey (1928) says that the food of this woodpecker consists of "over 75 percent, destructive wood-boring larvae of caterpillars and beetles. The Three-toed Woodpeckers rank high as conservators of the forest, eliminating annually, as Professor Beal has estimated, some 13,675 of the grubs most destructive to forests. The scarcity of these useful woodpeckers makes their protection and encouragement especially important."

SPHYRAPICUS VARIUS VARIUS (Linnaeus)

YELLOW-BELLIED SAPSUCKER

PLATES 18, 19

HABITS

CONTRIBUTED BY WINSOR MARRETT TYLER

Spring.—It is spring in the Transition Zone when in April the yellow-bellied sapsucker passes through on the way from its winter quarters to its breeding ground in the Canadian Zone. If spring is tardy most of the trees may be leafless, but many of them have blossomed, and the sap is running.

At this season the sapsucker is light-hearted and jaunty compared to the sober, quiet bird that visited us the autumn before. The breeding season is near at hand, and if two birds meet they often engage in a sort of game, a precursory courtship, wherein one bird flies at the other in a playful attack; the other eludes the rush of the on-coming bird by a sudden, last-minute retreat—winding around the branch on which it rests, or sliding off into the air. In these pursuits in and out among the branches we are impressed by the agility and grace of the birds and by the easy way they direct their course through the air. They do not appear to impel themselves by strength of wing alone, but, especially in their slanting descents, they let the force of gravity pull them swiftly along, and then, by the impetus of the speed attained, glide upward to a perch. They seem to swing from branch to branch with little effort, slowly opening and closing their wings to guide them on their way. As we watch them we are reminded of trapeze artists in the circus.

But the new sap is running, and the birds quickly tap the supply by drilling into the bark of their favorite trees and drink of the sap as it flows freely from the wounds.

Every spring the birds come to a sturdy yellow birch tree on the Boston Public Garden, a species of tree with which they must be familiar on their breeding grounds in the north. The sap flows plen-teously in mid-April from the many punctures that the birds make; it wets a large portion of the trunk of the tree and often drips to the ground from the branches. The birds stand clear of the tree as they feed at the sap wells with only the feet and the tip of the tail touching the bark. The tail is braced against the trunk at an angle of about 45°, and the feet reach far forward to grasp the bark oppo-site the bend of the wing. I have never seen a sapsucker crouch against this wet bark as a downy woodpecker commonly does when digging out a grub—like a cat hunched up lapping a saucer of milk. When a bird wishes to move to a point below where it is perched, it jumps from the tree and floats in the air, then turning, with its wings held out somewhat, dives head-downward, drifting in an easy, lei-surely manner as if moving under water; then, just before alighting, it rights itself. If you come too near, the sapsucker scrambles around to the rear of the limb, and if you step close up to the tree, the bird starts away in free, sweeping curves, like a skater over the ice, the white in the wing flashing out.

Eaton (1914) notes that "during the migration it is evident that the male birds arrive first, for during 15 years of continuous records which I have kept with this object in view I have found that male birds are the first to be seen each year and no females are seen for several days after the first males arrive."

Audubon (1842) records the following unique observation:

While travelling I observed that they performed their migration by day, in loose parties or families of six or seven individuals, flying at a great height, and at the intervals between their sailings and the flappings of their wings, emitting their remarkable plaintive cries. When alighting towards sunset, they descended with amazing speed in a tortuous manner, and first settled on the tops of the highest trees, where they remained perfectly silent for awhile, after which they betook themselves to the central parts of the thickest trees, and searched along the trunks for abandoned holes of Squirrels or Woodpeckers, in which they spent the night, several together in the same hole.

A. B. Klugh (1909) reports a remarkably large gathering of sapsuckers on their northward migration. He says:

On the morning of April 17th, 1909, the city of Kingston, Ontario, was alive with yellow-bellied sapsuckers.

From my study window I saw some twenty of them on the trees at the lodge of the park and on going out to investigate I found from one to four on nearly every tree. As a conservative estimate I placed the number of birds in the park at three hundred. * * *

The probable cause of this immense wave of yellow-bellied sapsuckers striking Kingston lies in the strong gale from the north which was blowing on the night of April 16th, the birds apparently dropping as soon as they had crossed the lake.

Courtship.—Little has been recorded on the courtship of the yellow-bellied sapsucker, but we may get a hint of its early stages at least as the birds pass northward—the increased interest in each other shown by their lively pursuits and their rapid whirlings among the branches, as noted under "Spring."

George Miksch Sutton (1928b) speaks thus of the birds on their nesting ground in Pennsylvania: "In late May and June the mewing cry was familiar and they occasionally indulged in strange courtship antics, flashing through the tops of the trees, calling excitedly in tones resembling those of a flicker, and dancing about with wings and tail spread in a manner utterly foreign to the usually stolid bearing of migrant individuals."

Of the spring drumming, perhaps a part of courtship, Dr. Harry C. Oberholser (1896b) says:

In spring the drumming of the yellow-bellied sapsucker may usually be easily recognized by the following peculiarities. Four or five taps given in quick succession are followed by a short pause, this being soon succeeded by two short quick taps; then another pause, and two more taps in somewhat less rapid succession than the first; followed by yet another pause, and two additional taps still a little slower. This is sometimes slightly varied with regard to the number of taps; and occasionally also the latter part consists only of single quick taps with an increasing interval toward the last.

The difference between the tapping of the sapsucker and of the hairy and the downy woodpecker is described in the life history of the latter bird. Wendell Taber told Mr. Bent that he succeeded in calling up three of these birds by imitating their drumming with a fountain pen on a dead tree; one of them alighted on the tree on which he was drumming.

Nesting.—William Brewster (1876a), writing of the nesting of the sapsucker at Umbagog Lake, Maine, says:

They arrive from the South, where they spend the winter, from the middle to the last of April, and, pairing being soon effected, commence at once the excavation of their nests. The trees usually selected are large dead birches, and a decided preference is manifested for the vicinity of water, though some nests occur on high ground in the interior of the woods, but never so abundantly there as along the margin of rivers and lakes. Both sexes work alternately, relieving each other at frequent intervals, the bird not employed usually clinging near the hole and encouraging its toiling mate by an occasional low cry. With the deepening of the hole arises the necessity for increased labor, as the rapidly accumulating débris must be removed, and the bird now appears at frequent intervals at the entrance, and, dropping its mouthful of chips, returns to its work. A week or more is occupied in the completion of the nest, the time varying considerably with the relative hardness of the wood. A small quantity of the finer chips are left at the bottom to serve as a bed for the eggs. * * * The labor of incubation, like all other duties, is shared equally by the two sexes. * * *

All nests examined upon this occasion [an occasion when he found half a dozen nests] were of uniform gourd-like shape, with the sides very smoothly and evenly chiselled. They averaged about fourteen inches in depth by five in diameter at the widest point, while the diameter of the exterior hole varied from 1.25 to 1.60 inches. So small, indeed, was this entrance in proportion to the size of the bird, that in many cases they were obliged to struggle violently for several seconds in either going out or in. The nests in most instances were very easily discovered, as the bird was almost always in the immediate vicinity, and if the tree was approached would fly to the hole and utter a few low calls, which would bring out its sitting mate, when both would pass to and from the spot, emitting notes of anxiety and alarm. The bird not employed in incubation has also a peculiar habit of clinging to the trunk just below the hole, in a perfectly motionless and strikingly pensive attitude, apparently looking in, though from the conformation of the interior it would be impossible for it to see its mate or eggs. In this position it will remain without moving for many minutes at a time.

Henry Mousley (1916) states that the bird "often nests year after year in the same tree (but not necessarily in the same hole) the favourite ones here [Hatley, Quebec] being elm, poplar, and butternut. * * * Of two nests examined the average dimensions are as follows, viz.: entrance hole 1⅜ inches in diameter, extreme depth 10¾ inches, and width 2⅞ inches."

Philipp and Bowdish (1917) say of the nesting site in New Brunswick: "The favorite situation was the dead heart of a live poplar, most often on the bank of a stream, and facing same, but some nests were in totally dead trees, of different kinds. They ranged from eight to forty feet from ground."

Bendire (1895) says that the birds "are devoted parents, and when incubation is somewhat advanced, or the young have been recently hatched, the bird on the nest is loath to have it, and will sometimes allow itself to be captured rather than to desert its treasures."

Eggs.—[AUTHOR'S NOTE: The yellow-bellied sapsucker lays four to seven eggs to a set, though five or six eggs are more commonly found. They vary from ovate to elliptical-ovate and sometimes to elliptical-oval. The shell is smooth and either dull or moderately glossy. They are pure white, like all woodpeckers' eggs. The measurements of 52 eggs average 22.44 by 16.92 millimeters; the eggs showing the four extremes measure 24.9 by 17.0, 23.8 by 18.0, 20.57 by 16.26, and 22.1 by 15.5 millimeters.]

Young.—As in the case of most nestling birds reared in a hole in a tree, little is known of the young sapsuckers while they are in the nest.

Frank Bolles (1892) speaks of "a nest filled with noisy fledglings whose squealing sounded afar in the otherwise silent woods. * * * The parent birds came frequently to the tree, and their arrival was always greeted by more vigorous crying from the young."

William Brewster (1876a), in his study of the bird at Umbagog Lake, Maine, says: "The young leave the nest in July, and for a long time the brood remains together, being still fed by the parents. They are very playful, sporting about the tree-trunks and chasing one another continually."

Frank Bolles (1892) has given a very interesting, detailed account of rearing three nestlings, about to be fledged, over a period of three and a half months. The three birds were dissimilar enough in coloring to be distinguished from one another; they proved to be two males and one female; and they soon developed marked differences in conduct and personality. Mr. Bolles at first kept them in a large cage in which they had ample space to climb about and later allowed them to fly around a room. They became very tame, letting him handle them freely. They subsisted almost entirely on maple syrup and water in equal parts, fed by hand at first, but in a few days they drank readily from a basin. They caught a few flies and ate some other insects that entered the cage, attracted by the syrup. Mr. Bolles says, however, that "the number of insects caught by them in this way was small, and I do not think amounted at any time to ten percent of their food."

The birds were lively and apparently in perfect health from the time they were captured, July 7, until October 11, when one of them, the female, began to droop. Two days later she had a convulsion in the morning and died in the afternoon. Autopsy showed that her body was well nourished and that the organs were apparently normal except the liver, which was "very large, deeply bile-stained, and very soft."

A week later the other two birds died after exhibiting the same symptoms as the first bird. The Department of Agriculture examined the body of one of these birds and reported enlargement and fatty degeneration of the liver.

Mr. Bolles remarks that "the most probable cause of this enlargement of the liver, which seems to have been the reason for the death of the three sapsuckers, was an undue proportion of sugar in their diet. In a wild state they would have eaten insects every day and kept their stomachs well filled with the chitinous parts of acid insects. Under restraint they secured fewer and fewer insects, until during the last few weeks of their lives, they had practically no solid food of any kind."

Summarizing his observations, he says:

From these experiments I draw the following conclusions: (1), that the yellow-bellied woodpecker may be successfully kept in captivity for a period corresponding to that during which as a resident bird he taps trees for their sap, sustained during this time upon a diet of which from 90 to 100 per cent is diluted maple syrup; (2), that this fact affords evidence of an extremely strong character, in confirmation and support of the theory that when the yellow-bellied woodpecker taps trees for their sap he uses the sap as his principal article of food, and not primarily as a bait to attract insects.

Winton Weydemeyer (1926) in Montana "observed a pair of red-naped sapsuckers * * * gathering sap to feed their young in the nest. A regular tree-route, followed alternately by the male and female, included a quaking aspen, a larger alder, and a large willow, in which borings had been made. The birds flew directly from the nest to the aspen, and gathered the sap that had accumulated since the last visit; then flew to the alder and to the willow, repeating the process; and finally flew back to the nest, without hunting for insects. Occasionally the male would vary the process by catching a few flies from the air, eating some and carrying some to the nest."

Forbush (1927) gives the incubation period of the yellow-bellied sapsucker as "probably about 14 days."

A. Dawes DuBois furnishes the following note: "Yellow-bellied sapsuckers were observed feeding young in a nest, in Hennepin County, Minn., on July 5, 1937. The nest was about 25 feet above ground in a partially dead tree at edge of willow-and-alder thicket adjoining woods. Both parents were bringing food. The squeaky note of the young was repeated with such regularity (about four times a second) as to indicate that only one nestling was uttering it. When the nestling was being fed at the entrance, by the poking method, these notes went up to a higher pitch, and were sometimes choked off almost to inaudibility.

"Two days later, the parents were still feeding very frequently. The male, who on the first day had been seen to bring a bright red berry about the size of a pea, again brought a bit of small red fruit. On one occasion, when the parents were away, the nestling put its head out of the hole; but it did not do so when being fed. In general, alarm calls of the parents had little if any effect upon the squeaking of the nestling, though at one time, July 7, the squeaking seemed to cease for a short interval when the parent gave the alarm notes. For the most part the series of squeaky notes is continuous. It was by hearing these sounds that this nest was discovered."

Plumages.—[AUTHOR'S NOTE: The young sapsucker is hatched naked, as is the case with other woodpeckers, but the juvenal plumage is acquired before the young bird leaves the nest. The sexes are alike in the juvenal plumage. A young bird, not fully grown and probably not long out of the nest, taken June 25, has the black crown largely concealed by the long brownish tips of the feathers, "ochraceous-tawny" to "buckthorn brown"; each of the black feathers of the back has a large terminal spot of grayish white, or yellowish white, producing a boldly spotted pattern; the nape and sides of the neck have smaller spots of the same color; the wings and tail are as in the adult fall plumage; the chin and upper throat are dull white or pale buffy brownish; the lower throat and chest are pale brownish, broken by crescentic bars of dusky; and the center of the breast and the abdomen are pale yellow or yellowish white. Changes soon begin to take place, at irregular intervals, during which the sexes begin to differentiate. Young males may begin to show traces of red in the throat patch as early as July; and in August some may have the crown largely crimson; the black patch on the chest does not usually appear until much of the red has been assumed, but some birds show considerable of both red and black before the end of August. Other young males may not acquire much red before the end of September. Progress toward maturity continues all through fall, winter, and early spring by protracted partial molts; probably most individuals acquire the fully adult plumage by early spring, but I have seen birds that had not fully completed this prenuptial molt by the end of April.

Young females follow the same sequence of molts but are somewhat later in developing the red crown, which apparently is not acquired until October or later. The adult body plumage of both sexes is acquired during winter and early spring. Adults have a partial prenuptial molt about the head and throat early in spring and a complete molt late in summer and fall. In fresh fall plumage, the lighter markings are more or less suffused with yellowish or buffy tints, and the belly is deeper yellow.]

Food.—W. L. McAtee (1911) learned by stomach examinations that the yellow-bellied sapsucker consumed cambium and bast averaging 16.71 percent of its diet. He continues:

It must be noted also that cambium is a very delicate, perishable material, at certain times no more than a jelly, and thus never receives a percentage valuation in examinations of long-preserved stomachs corresponding to its bulk when first swallowed. Neither do we get any record of the sap consumed by these birds [the three species of sapsucker] and they are inordinate tipplers. Hence the value of the percentages cited lies not so much in their accuracy as to the quantity of cambium eaten as in the fact that they indicate a steady consumption of this important substance. There is no doubt that cambium, bast, and sap are depended upon by sapsuckers as stable diet.

We may get some idea of the amount of sap consumed by the bird from Frank Bolles' (1892) record of his three young captive sapsuckers. He says: "Ordinarily they disposed of eight teaspoonfuls [of diluted syrup] each during the twenty-four hours. Part of this evaporated, and part was probably secured by black ants which visited the cage by night."

Bolles (1891), describing the method of feeding of birds in the wild, says: "The dipping was done regularly and rather quickly, often two or three times in each hole. The sap glistened on the bill as it was withdrawn. I could sometimes see the tongue move. The bill was directed towards the lower, inner part of the drill, which, as I found by examination, was cut so as to hold the sap."

This is the common method of feeding, but sometimes, when two or more holes have coalesced into a vertical groove, the bird will run its bill upward along the edge of the wound, sipping the sap much as we might, with our finger, wipe off a drop running down from a pitcher's lip.

McAtee (1911) states that "about four-fifths of the insect food of the three species of sapsuckers consists of ants, the eating of which may be reckoned slightly in the birds' favor. The remainder of the food is made up of beetles, wasps, and a great variety of other insects, including, however, practically no wood-boring larvae or other special enemies of trees. The birds' vegetable food can not be cited in their behalf, as it consists almost entirely of wild fruits, which are of no importance, and of cambium, the securing of which results in serious damage."

F. E. L. Beal (1895) mentions, as articles in the sapsucker's diet, the berries of dogwood, black alder, Virginia creeper, and wild black cherries. Winfrid A. Stearns (1883) says: "Nuts, berries, and other fruits vary its fare; and to procure these it may often be seen creeping and hanging in the strangest attitudes among the terminal twigs of trees, so slender that they bend with the weight of the bird." Audubon (1842), in his plate of the sapsucker, gives an animated picture of the bird thus engaged

Brewster (1876a) shows the bird as an expert flycatcher. "From an humble delver after worms and larvae, it rises to the proud independence of a Flycatcher, taking its prey on wing as unerringly as the best marksman of them all. From its perch on the spire of some tall stub it makes a succession of rapid sorties after its abundant victims and then flies off to its nest with bill and mouth crammed full of insects, principally large *Diptera*."

Behavior.—The sapsucker, a bird of wide distribution and in some parts of its range the commonest woodpecker, has come to be regarded with disfavor by man, who accuses it of harming the trees it drills to obtain its food. Man accuses the bird of weakening trees by drawing away their life-blood and of killing many by girdling them with multiple punctures, and he blames the bird for marring the beauty of trunk and limb by pitting and scarring them.

A study of the habits of the sapsucker shows that its work on the trees varies with the season and, on the Atlantic coast, is spread over a territory 3,000 miles long or more. During the migrations, northward and southward, when the birds are scattered and on the move, comparatively little harm is done. Here and there a limb may be killed—either girdled or opened so that infection enters—and rarely a tree may die, but the chief effect is an esthetic one, the scarring of the bark with pits, notably in orchards where it is a matter of common observation that most of the pitted trees are in perfect health. On their breeding ground and in their winter quarters, however, where the birds are concentrated and remain in one locality for a considerable time, the effect is more serious. In the Southern States especially, the lumber industry suffers material financial loss due to the fact that deep in the wood cut from trees on which sapsuckers have worked extensively, when the trees were small, the grain is distorted and made unsightly by the scars of the wounds inflicted by the birds years before.

From an exhaustive study of the economic status of the woodpeckers by W. L. McAtee (1911), the salient points in reference to the yellow-bellied sapsucker are quoted below:

The results of sapsucker attacks on trees are so uniform and characteristic as to be distinguished easily from the work of other woodpeckers. Sapsucker holes are drilled clear through the bark and cambium and often into the wood. They vary in outline from circular to squarish elliptical, in the latter case usually having the longer diameter across the limb or trunk. Generally they are arranged in rings or partial rings around the trunk, but they often fall into vertical series. Deeply-cut holes arranged with such regularity are made only by sapsuckers.

After the original pattern of holes is completed, the sapsuckers often continue their work, taking out the bark between holes until sometimes large areas are cleanly removed. This often occurs on small limbs or trunks, where long strips of bark up and down the tree are removed, leaving narrow strings between. This effect is also produced by continually enlarging single punctures by excavating at the upper end, * * * which is done to secure fresh inner bark and a constant supply of sap. Occasionally, after a tree has been checkered or grooved after the above-described systematic methods, it may be barked indiscriminately, leaving only ragged patches of bark. * * * Even in such cases, however, traces of the regularly arranged punctures are likely to remain, and there is no difficulty in recognizing the work as that of sapsuckers, for no other woodpecker makes anything like it on sound, living trees.

All holes, grooves, or irregular openings made by sapsuckers penetrate at least to the outermost layer of sapwood or nongrowing part of the tree. This results in the removal of the exterior rough bark, the delicate inner bark or bast, and the cambium. Since the elaborated sap (upon which the growth of trees depends) is conveyed and stored in these layers, it is evident that sapsuckers attack the trees in a vital part. Each ring of punctures severs at its particular level part of the sap-carrying vessels, another ring made above destroys others, and so the process continues until in extreme cases circulation of elaborated sap stops and the tree dies. When the injury to the vital tissues is not carried so far, only a limb here and there may die, or the tree may only have its vitality lowered for a few years. If the attacks cease, it may completely recover. * * *

Recovery, however, does not mean that the tree has escaped permanent injury. Patches of cambium of varying size may be killed. Growth ceases at these points and the dead and discolored areas are finally covered by wood and bark. Until this process is completed, the tree is disfigured by pits with dead bark and wood at the bottom, and even when completely healed, the spot remains a source of weakness. In fact, all sapsucker pecking is followed by more or less rotting and consequent weakening of the wood, and renders trees more liable to be broken by the wind or other causes.

Sapsucker injuries usually stimulate growth of the wood layers at the points attacked, so that they become much thicker than usual. This results in a slight swelling of the bark, and when the birds reopen the old wounds year after year, as they habitually do, succeeding wood layers make excess growth and in time shelflike girdles develop.

McAtee (1911) gives a long list of trees attacked by the bird. Summarizing, he says: "Condensing the information contained in the foregoing lists, we find that the yellow-bellied sapsucker attacks no fewer than 246 species of native trees and 6 vines, besides 31 kinds of introduced trees. Twenty-nine of these trees and 1 vine are known to be sometimes killed and 28 others are much disfigured or seriously reduced in vitality."

Of "the effects of sapsucker work on lumber and finished wood products" he says:

Those relations of sapsuckers to trees which are detrimental to man's interest are by no means confined to the external disfiguration, the weakening, or killing of trees. Indeed in the aggregate sapsuckers inflict much greater financial loss by rendering defective the wood of the far larger number of trees which they work upon moderately but do not kill. Blemishes, reducing the value, appear in the lumber from such trees and in the various articles into which it is manufactured.

These defects consist of distortion of the grain, formation of knotty growths and cavities in the wood, extensive staining, fat streaks, resin deposits, and other blemishes. All of them result from injuries to the cambium, their variety being due to the differences in the healing. Besides blemishes, ornamental effects are sometimes produced during the healing of sapsucker wounds, such as small sound stains, curly grain, and a form of bird's-eye.

McAtee (1911) estimates that "the annual loss for the whole United States [from the impairment of lumber] is more than a million and a quarter dollars." He continues: "Sapsuckers do not prey upon any especially destructive insects and do comparatively little to offset the damage they inflict. Hence the yellow-bellied sapsucker * * * must be included in the class of injurious species."

The situation is quite different on the breeding ground. Here the birds resort to a group of trees, and confine their feeding activities almost exclusively to them. Frank Bolles (1891), in his study of the bird in the region about Mount Chocorua, N. H., terms these stations "orchards." He describes one of them as consisting "of about a dozen canoe birches and red maples, most of which were dead, some decayed and fallen. The tree most recently tapped was a red maple about forty feet high and two feet through at the butt." Of another "orchard," half a mile away, he says: "The tree in use last year was nearly dead. Two neighboring birches showing scars of earlier years were quite dead. All stood on the crest of a kame. About three rods along the ridge to the eastward a red oak and two or three canoe birches were in use by the birds." This report shows that sapsuckers undoubtedly cause the death of many trees as they return to their "orchards" year after year, but most of these trees are of small value, especially in the heavily forested regions where the birds commonly breed.

Bolles (1891) also notes the association of the sapsuckers with the ruby-throated hummingbirds, which were attracted to the pits by the running sap. In the main, hosts and guests got along well enough together, although attacks occurred on both sides from time to time. He says: "My notes refer again and again to the spiteful treatment of the Hummers at Orchard No. 1. On the other hand at Orchard No. 2 they say 'Male and young one dipping. Hummer comes in and dips several times *between them* and they offer no objection.'"

Major Bendire (1895), half in jest, we may presume, brings an accusation of inebriety against the sapsucker in these words:

That it should be fond of the sweet sap of trees does not surprise me, as this contains considerable nourishment, and likewise attracts a good many insects, which the birds eat; but it is not so easy to account for its especial predilection for the sap of the mountain ash, which has a decidedly bitter taste, and I believe possesses intoxicating properties, unless it be taken for the latter purpose; and the fact that after drinking freely of the sap of this tree it may often be seen clinging to the trunk for hours at a time, as if stupefied, seems to confirm this view. It is well known that some of our birds indulge in such disreputable practices, and possibly this species must be included in the number, as there are sots among birds as well as among the genus *Homo*.

Voice.—Just as the sapsucker in its behavior is conspicuous, almost boisterous, at one season of the year and retiring and unobtrusive at another, in the same way it is very noisy in spring and the early part of the nesting period and comparatively silent afterward.

Dr. C. Hart Merriam (1879) speaks of the bird thus: "In few species can the date of arrival, in spring, be ascertained with such precision as in the bird now under consideration; for, no sooner are they here, and recovered from the fatigue of their northward journey, than the country fairly resounds with their cries and drumming. * * * Noisy, rollicking fellows, they are always chasing one another among the trees, screaming meanwhile at the top of their voices, and when three or four vociferous males alight on the same tree, as often happens, their boisterous cries are truly astonishing."

William Brewster (1876a) mentions a "peculiar snarling cry" used as an alarm note, and of a pair at the nest he says:

Watching once a nest for an hour or two, I remarked that the birds relieved each other in the labors of incubation at intervals averaging about half an hour each. The one that had been absent would alight just below the hole, and, uttering a low *yew-ick, yew-ick*, its mate would appear from within, when, after the interchange of a few notes of endearment, the sitting bird would fly off and the other instantly enter the hole. * * *

Both young and old utter most frequently a low snarling cry that bears no very distant resemblance to the *mew* of the Catbird. The adults have also two other notes—one, already spoken of, when the opposite sexes meet; the other a clear, ringing *cleur*, repeated five or six times in succession, and heard, I think, only in the spring.

Of the voice of the sapsucker, Bendire (1895) says: "Its ordinary call note is a whining 'whäee,' and it utters a number of other sounds, some of these resembling the calls of the Blue Jay, and others those of the Red-shouldered Hawk. During the mating season, when the sexes are chasing each other, a series of notes like 'hoih-hoih,' a number of times repeated, are frequently heard. Although generally disposed to be more or less noisy, while clinging to their food trees they are always silent as far as my observations go."

The note mentioned above does resemble the cry of the blue jay somewhat in form, but the notes of the two birds need never be confused. The sapsucker's may be as long as the blue jay's, or the *caw* of a crow; again it may be given as a very short syllable. The note commonly is not nearly so loud as the blue jay's and the tone of voice is different; it is a complaining whine rather than a boisterous shout.

Another note, a minor note heard only when one is near the bird, is very like the explosive *hit* of the red-breasted nuthatch—the little conversational note that the nuthatches use as they scramble over the bark, not the nasal *toot*.

The most remarkable of the sapsucker's utterances, in that it does not resemble a bird note at all, is a single syllable sounded regularly over and over again—a low-toned *tuck*, like slow, sharp strokes on a nonresonant branch. This note might sometimes be mistaken for a chipmunk's pluck, except that it lacks completely any ringing quality of tone.

Field marks.—The colored plates in the illustrated books on ornithology lead one to expect to find the yellow-bellied sapsucker rather a brilliantly colored, conspicuous bird. However, when we meet it in the field, the colors, so bright and sharply outlined in the picture of the bird, are often dimmed by the shadows of limbs and leaves, and as the chief color is of a neutral tint, not unlike the bark of many trees, we may sometimes pass the bird by, unnoticed. Our first impression of the bird, when we catch a glimpse of it, is of a medium-sized woodpecker, dull old-gold in color, and almost without markings. A glass, however, brings out a thin line of white along the length of the closed wing, a red or reddish forehead and fore part of the crown, a black mark across the upper breast, and, if we look very carefully, a yellowish belly.

W. L. McAtee (1911) points out the black mark is characteristic of nearly all sapsuckers, and he links it up pretty successfully with a red forehead. For example, The red-breasted sapsucker lacks the black mark, but has a red head; the flicker, not a sapsucker, has a "black spot on breast, but top of head from bill is not red"; the pileated woodpecker "not a sapsucker. Entire lower parts black." He continues: "All sapsuckers have yellow bellies, few other woodpeckers have; all sapsuckers have a conspicuous white patch on the upper part of the wing, as seen from the side when clinging to a tree; white wing patches in other woodpeckers are on the middle or lower part of the wings. The yellow-bellied sapsucker of transcontinental range is the only woodpecker having the front of the head (i. e., from bill to crown) red in combination with a black patch on the breast."

Fall.—Generally when we see the yellow-bellied sapsucker in autumn, during its slow journey toward the Southern States, it is alone. A single bird may settle for two or three days in our dooryard, if there be a tree there to its liking, perching well up in it and rarely moving away. Here it is inconspicuous: its brownish color matches the bark closely; it moves deliberately, as if to avoid notice; by hopping behind a branch it keeps out of sight most of the time; and commonly it is perfectly silent. On occasion it makes use of its whining cry, and if two birds meet they may utter the red-breasted-nuthatch note, but as a rule this woodpecker is one of the quietest of migrants.

If we watch a bird for a time, we see that it is picking at the bark, dislodging bits of it in searching for concealed food. It hops forward, backward, and around the limbs, moving easily, taking rather long, rapid hops, seeming careless of a fall. When investigating crevices and peering under flakes of bark it cranes its neck, turning its head from side to side. The neck then appears constricted, like a pileated woodpecker in miniature.

At other times it may drill holes—even the young birds of the year, which can have had little experience in this kind of work. They drill with a sideways stroke, to one side, then the other, then, perhaps, a stroke straight at the branch. In this manner, before very long, a small area is denuded of bark, the sideways strokes giving it an oval shape with the long axis parallel to the ground. However, at this season, mid-October, in the latitude of Boston, little sap rewards their efforts.

Winter.—Sapsuckers spend the winter mainly in the Southern States, Central America, and on the islands south of North America, but there are a few records indicating that a bird rarely may remain nearly or quite as far north as the southern limit of the breeding range. For example, Fred. H. Kennard (1895) reports finding one in Brookline, Mass., on February 6, 1895. Collected, "he proved to be in fine, fat condition"; and Harriet A. Nye (1918) watched, in Fairfield Center, Maine, a bird throughout the winter of 1911, in which the temperature fell to 32° below zero. Apples formed a considerable part of this bird's diet, although he often hunted over the branches and trunks of trees. He was last seen April 5 "as sprightly as ever."

DISTRIBUTION

Range.—North and Central America and the West Indies, casual in Bermuda and Greenland.

Breeding range.—This species breeds **north** to southeastern Alaska (probably Skagway) ; southern Mackenzie (Nahanni Mountain, Fort Providence, and Fort Resolution) ; northern Manitoba (Cochrane River and probably Fort Churchill) ; Ontario (Lac Seul and probably Moose Factory) ; Quebec (Montreal, Quebec City, Godbout, Ellis Bay, and probably Eskimo Point) ; and Newfoundland (Fox Island and Nicholsville). **East** to Newfoundland (Nicholsville, Deer Lake, and Harrys River) ; Nova Scotia (Sydney and Halifax) ; Maine (Bucksport and Livermore Falls) ; southeastern New Hampshire (Ossipee and Monadnock Mountain) ; western Massachusetts (Chesterfield) ; New Jersey (Midvale) ; and western Virginia (Sounding Knob, Cold Mountain, and White Top Mountain). **South** to southwestern Virginia (White Top Mountain) ; northwestern Indiana (Kouts) ; central Illinois (Peoria) ; eastern Missouri (St. Louis) ; Iowa (Keokuk, Grinnell, and Ogden) ; southeastern South Dakota (Sioux Falls and probably Vermillion) ; New Mexico (Pot Creek and Diamond Peak) ; Arizona (Buffalo Creek and Kaibab Plateau) ; and southern California (San Bernardino Mountains, San Jacinto Mountains, and Mount Pinos). **West** to California (Mount Pinos, Big Creek, Cisco, Carlotta, and Mount Shasta) ; western Oregon (Prospect, Elkton, Salem, and Tillamook) ; Washington

(Tacoma and Seattle); British Columbia (Beaver Creek, Alta Lake, and Masset); and southeastern Alaska (Craig, Wrangell, and prob- ably Skagway).

Winter range.—The winter range extends **north** to southwestern British Columbia (Comox); northeastern Oregon (Haines); central Arizona (Oak Creek); southern New Mexico (Silver City); Kansas (Wichita, Topeka, and Bendena); Missouri (Lexington and Nelson); Illinois (Bernadotte and Mount Carmel); southern Indiana (Vin- cennes and probably Bloomington); southern Ohio (Hamilton and Hillsboro); northern Maryland (Hagerstown); southeastern Penn- sylvania (Edge Hill); and southern New Jersey (Newfield). From this point the species is found in winter **south** along the Atlantic coast to southern Florida (Miami, Royal Palm Hammock, and Key West); the Bahama Islands (Nassau, Watling Island, and Great Inagua); and the northern Lesser Antilles (St. Croix). **South** to the Lesser Antilles (St. Croix); rarely Haiti (Gonave Island); and rarely Costa Rica (Coli Blanco and Punta Arenas). From this southwestern point the winter range extends northward along the western coast of Central America (including Baja California) to California; Oregon; rarely Washington; and southwestern British Columbia (probably Barkley Sound and Comox). In the eastern part of the country the species is found irregularly **north** to southern Wisconsin (Madison); southern Michigan (Ann Arbor and Detroit); southern Ontario (London and Lindsay); southern Vermont (Ben- nington); and central Maine (Fairfield and Dover).

The range as above outlined covers the entire species, which has been separated into four subspecies or geographic races. The typical form, known as the yellow-bellied sapsucker (*S. v. varius*), is found during the breeding season over all the northern parts of the range east of Alaska and south to Missouri and the mountains of western Virginia. In winter it is found south to Central America and the West Indies. The red-naped sapsucker (*S. v. nuchalis*) is found chiefly in the Rocky Mountain region from central British Columbia south (in winter) to Baja California and central Mexico. The north- ern red-breasted sapsucker (*S. v. ruber*) breeds from southeastern Alaska south through the mountains to western Oregon and in winter to central California. The southern red-breasted sapsucker (*S. v. daggetti*) is confined to the mountains of California and northern Baja California.

Spring migration.—Early dates of spring arrival are: Quebec— Montreal, March 25; Westmount, March 30. New Brunswick—Scotch Lake, April 12; St. John, April 22. Nova Scotia—Wolfville, April 30. Northern Michigan—Blaney, April 2; Sault Ste. Marie, April 10; Houghton, April 24. Minnesota—Elk River, March 26; Minne- apolis, March 29. Nebraska—Omaha, April 14. South Dakota—

Faulkton, April 15. North Dakota—Fargo, April 15. Manitoba—Aweme, March 31; Margaret, April 17. Saskatchewan—Indian Head, April 4. Colorado—Estes Park, April 27. Wyoming—Yellowstone Park, May 12. Montana—Columbia Falls, April 13. Alberta—Stony Plain, April 1; Edmonton, May 2. Mackenzie—Fort Simpson, May 11. Alaska—Chilkat River, April 12; Admiralty Island, April 17; Forrester Island, May 6.

Fall migration.—Late dates of fall departure are: Alberta—Glenevis, September 24. Montana—Fortine, September 20; Kalispell, October 1. Wyoming—Yellowstone Park, October 2. Colorado—De Beque, October 1; Denver, October 8; Walden, October 16. Saskatchewan—Indian Head, September 25. Manitoba—Shoal Lake, September 30; Treesbank, October 14; Margaret, October 24. North Dakota—Rice Lake, October 1; Fargo, October 2. South Dakota—Yankton, October 5; Faulkton, October 20. Nebraska—Monroe Canyon, Sioux County, October 4. Minnesota—Elk River, October 15; Lanesboro, October 19. Northern Michigan—Blaney, October 1; Houghton, October 2; Sault Ste. Marie, October 22. Nova Scotia—Sable Island, October 9. New Brunswick—Scotch Lake, November 4. Quebec—Montreal, October 1; Quebec City, October 2.

Casual records.—According to Reid (1884) several specimens of this species were taken in Bermuda during the period 1847-1850 when it bred in that area. He also noted it in 1875. A specimen was found dead at Julianshaab, Greenland, in July 1845; another was obtained in that general region about 1858; and an adult female was collected at Loup Bay, Labrador, on May 5, 1899.

Egg dates.—Alberta: 19 records, May 20 to June 18; 10 records, May 30 to June 11, indicating the height of the season.

California: 13 records, May 12 to June 21; 7 records, May 30 to June 9.

Colorado: 19 records, May 27 to June 15; 10 records, June 4 to 12.

Illinois: 5 records, April 20 to June 3.

Nova Scotia: 14 records, May 28 to June 15; 7 records, June 5 to 10.

Oregon: 24 records, May 12 to June 12; 12 records, May 25 to June 2.

SPHYRAPICUS VARIUS NUCHALIS Baird

RED-NAPED SAPSUCKER

HABITS

The western race of the eastern yellow-bellied sapsucker occupies an extensive range in the general region of the Rocky Mountains, chiefly east of the Sierra Nevada and Cascade Ranges, from central British Columbia and Alberta to western Texas and Arizona.

Ridgway (1914) gives a full description of this form, which is worth quoting in view of his remarks as to its status; he describes it as—

Similar to *S. v. varius,* but with much less white on back, this forming two definite but broken stripes, converging posteriorly; nape always with more or less of red, under parts less strongly tinged with yellow, and wing and tail averaging decidedly longer; adult male with red of throat more extended, both laterally and posteriorly, covering malar region (except anterior portion), where meeting white sub-auricular stripe; adult female with at least lower half of throat red (sometimes whole throat red, only the chin being white); young much darker above than corresponding stage of *S. v. varius,* the pileum dark sooty slate, white markings on back less brownish, and under parts much less yellowish, the chest and foreneck brownish gray or grayish brown (instead of buffy brown), and usually less distinctly barred or lunulated with dusky.

On account of the conspicuous difference in coloration of the young, definite difference in color pattern of back, head, and neck in adults, and comparative rarity of intermediate specimens (which are far less common, relatively, than in the case of *Colaptes*), I believe that it would be better to consider this form as specifically distinct from *S. varius.* It is true that specimens do occur that are intermediate between *S. nuchalis* and *S. varius,* as well as between the former and *S. ruber;* but they may be (and I believe they are) hybrids; certainly there is no more reason for not considering them as such than in the case of *Colaptes;* and if *S. nuchalis* is to be considered as merely a subspecies of *S. varius* then, most certainly, must *S. ruber* also.

Mr. Ridgway (1877) says of its haunts:

Throughout the country between the Sierra Nevada and the Rocky Mountains, the red-naped woodpecker is a common species in suitable localities. Its favorite summer-haunts are the groves of large aspens near the head of the upper cañons, high up in the mountains, and for this reason we found it more abundant in the Wahsatch and Uintah region than elsewhere; indeed, but a single individual was observed on the Sierra Nevada, and this one was obtained on the eastern slope of the range, near Carson City. It was very rare throughout western Nevada, but became abundant as we approached the higher mountains in the eastern portion of the State. Among the aspen groves in Parley's Park, as well as in similar places throughout that portion of the country, it was by far the most abundant of the Woodpeckers; and it seemed to be as strictly confined to the aspens as *S. thyroideus* was to the pines.

The Weydemeyers (1928) say that, in northwestern Montana, "it occurs most abundantly and typically in mixed broad-leaf and conifer associations along streams, where it nests regularly. It ranges less commonly into virgin forests of fir, larch, yellow pine, and hemlock (*Tsuga heterophylla*) in the valleys; and into arborvitae, lodgepole pine, and spruce woods of the foothills. Occasional birds are seen in alpine fir and spruce woods upward to the lower borders of the Hudsonian zone."

Courtship.—M. P. Skinner says in his notes: "On May 13, 1915, I saw a red-naped sapsucker drumming on a hollow, dead lodgepole pine; soon he flew to the top of another pine, where his mate was, and the two began bobbing and curtsying in true cake-walk fashion much like flickers, except that these sapsuckers were on a vertical stub. There was no movement of the feet, but the body was bent from side to side, and there was a constant 'juggling' motion. The head was tilted back and the bill pointed up at an angle of sixty degrees, with neck outstretched. The neck, head, and bill were in constant motion. That of the bill reminded me of a musical director's baton."

Nesting.—The Weydemeyers (1928) say of its nesting habits: "As elsewhere in the state, this bird in Lincoln County nests most commonly in live aspens. Our records for this area include four nests in live aspens, one in a live larch, and one in a dead Engelmann spruce. These nests were all in the Transition zone, near streams, Three of the nests in aspens were in a single tree, in successive years. Nest-hole preparation usually commences immediately upon the arrival of the birds in the spring, about April 20."

Major Bendire (1895) gives an attractive account of finding a nest of this woodpecker in a live aspen, in a small grove of these trees, near Camp Harney, Oregon, on June 12, 1877: "Their nesting site was directly over my head, about 20 feet from the ground. * * * The entrance to the excavation was exceedingly small, not over 1¼ inches in diameter, about 8 inches deep, and about 4 inches wide at the bottom. It contained three nearly fresh eggs, lying partly embedded in a layer of fine chips."

He quotes the following observations of Denis Gale:

My observations have been that this subspecies invariably selects for its nesting site a living aspen tree. I have never met with it in any other. This tree favors the mountain gulches and low, sheltered hillsides, at an altitude of from 7,000 to 10,000 feet. Above this point they do not attain sufficient size, and are mostly dwarfed and scrubby. Here in Colorado *Sphyrapicus varius nuchalis* is seldom found above 9,000 feet or much below 8,000 feet. The aspen tree is short lived, and ere much of a growth is attained, a cross section, in the majority of instances, will show a discolored center of incipient decay, involving half or two-thirds of its entire diameter, with a sound, white sap zone on the outer circumference, next to the bark. This sound, healthy zone nourishes the tree until the decayed core discovers itself in some withered limbs, and frequently the top of the tree manifests the canker.

Such trees the Red-naped Sapsucker selects for its nesting site, and with great perseverance chisels through this tough, sound zone, from 1 to 1½ inches in thickness, commencing with a very small hole and gradually extending its circumference with each stage of the deepening process, working from the lowest center out, till the exact circumference of the intended aperture of entrance is attained. In thus radiating in circles from the central point the minute chips are chiseled out with considerable ease. This mode of working is observed until the tough zone is worked through; what remains then is comparatively easy work; the soft, soggy, lifeless inside is worked into and downward with greater facility, and a roomy, gourd-shaped excavation quickly follows, the female doing the excavating from beginning to end, and, according to exigencies, completes it in from six to ten days. * * *

Sphyrapicus varius nuchalis usually insists upon a new excavation each year. The height of the nesting sites from the ground varies from 5 to 30 feet; the full set of eggs is four or five in number; sometimes a smaller number of eggs mark a full set, presumably the nest of one of last year's birds. Fresh eggs may be looked for in Colorado from June 1 to 15, and should the first set be taken, a second one may generally be found from ten to fifteen days later; and, as a rule, the second nesting site will not be greatly distant from the first one. Several nests of this species may be found within a short distance of each other in the same aspen grove.

Eggs.—Major Bendire (1895) says of the eggs: "The number of eggs to a set varies from three to six, usually four or five; these are mostly ovate in shape, a few are more elliptical ovate; they are pure white in color; the shell is fine grained and moderately glossy." The measurements of 40 eggs average 22.89 by 17.28 millimeters; the eggs showing the four extremes measure 24.38 by 16.76, 23.60 by 18.50, 20.83 by 16.76, and 21.34 by 16.26 millimeters.

Young.—Major Bendire (1895) says: "I believe that both sexes assist in the labor of excavating the nesting site, the female appearing to do the greater part of the work, however, which is frequently very laborious, and that the male also shares the duties of incubation, which lasts about fourteen days."

Food.—Again, he writes: "Its general habits are similar to those of the preceding species [yellow-bellied sapsucker], and in the fruit-growing sections within its range, in southern Utah, for instance, it is said to do considerable damage to the orchards in the early spring and again in the fall, tapping the peach and apple trees for sap in the same manner as *Sphyrapicus varius* does in the East. Its principal food consists of small beetles, spiders, grasshoppers, ants, and such larvæ as are to be found under the loose bark of trees, as well as wild berries of different kinds."

W. L. McAtee (1911) gives a long list of trees that are attacked by this species of sapsucker, among which this western race is charged with doing considerable damage to many western trees, such as various pines, spruces, hemlocks, firs, redwood, cedars, cypresses, junipers, cottonwoods, aspens, willows, bayberry, walnuts, hophornbeam, white alder, oaks, laurels, sycamores, mahoganies, pears, apples, cherries, mesquite, ironwood, maples, *Ceanothus*, *Fremontia*, western dogwood, madrona, buckthorn, ashes, and probably others.

Dr. Joseph Grinnell (1914) says, referring to the Colorado Valley, where this sapsucker was evidently wintering among the willow thickets: "Willows were the trees attacked by this woodpecker; but in one case a single large mesquite, and the only one of many in the vicinity, had been selected for bleeding, and its main trunk and larger branches were plentifully bored. I visited this tree many times during the space of three days, March 2 to 4, opposite The Needles, and invariably found a sapsucker working about the borings. I shot two of the birds at this mesquite, and there was still one there the last time I visited the tree, although I had never seen but one at a time there."

W. L. Dawson (1923) remarks: "In lieu of maple sap the western bird makes heavy requisition on the fresh-flowing pitch of pine and fir trees. As for cambium, that of the aspen (*Populus tremuloides*) has marked preference, and the summer range of the bird, so far as it goes, is practically controlled by the occurrence of the tree. Inasmuch as this tree is short-lived and of slight economic importance, the depredations of the bark-eaters are not seriously felt."

Mr. Skinner says, in his Yellowstone Park notes: "I have seen the red-naped sapsucker pick and hammer on dead aspens and on the trunks of lodgepole pine for insects. On June 28, 1917, I saw one make frequent flycatcher-like sallies from an aspen out into the open."

Behavior.—John H. Flanagan (1911) witnessed a rather remarkable performance by a red-naped sapsucker, such as I had not seen recorded elsewhere. He had chopped out a nest containing two fresh eggs and was intending to leave them for a possible addition to the set, as he had done successfully before, when one of the birds, "both of which remained in sight, flew to the tree, perched a moment upon the edge of the cut hole, then went in, and shortly reappeared with one of the eggs in its beak. It flew to a nearby stub, not more than forty feet from where" he "was sitting, calmly devoured the egg and dropped the empty shell."

Winter.—Apparently the fall migration of this woodpecker consists largely of a withdrawal from the high altitudes, in which it breeds, to winter resorts in the lowlands. Major Bendire (1895) says: "During the winter months, I have occasionally observed a red-naped sapsucker in the Harney Valley, in Oregon, busily engaged in hunting for food among the willow thickets found growing along the banks of the small streams in that sagebrush-covered region, often long distances away from timber of any size."

Dr. Grinnell (1914) noted it, as a winter visitant, among the willows and mesquites in the lower Colorado Valley. And M. French Gilman (1915), referring to the Arizona lowlands, says: "The red-naped sapsucker (*Sphyrapicus varius nuchalis*) is a winter visitant along the Gila River, and while not to be called abundant, is frequently noticed. I have seen individuals from October 6 to as late as April 17, and in all the months between these two dates. Once I saw three in one mesquite tree. Signs of their work are frequently present on cottonwood and willow trees and occasionally on an Arizona ash. If there are any almond trees in the country they are sure to be attacked, as they are favorites with these birds. Only once or twice have I seen mesquite trees attacked."

SPHYRAPICUS VARIUS DAGGETTI Grinnell

SOUTHERN RED-BREASTED SAPSUCKER

HABITS

The above name was applied to this sapsucker by Dr. Joseph Grinnell (1901) and was characterized by him as smaller and paler than the northern race and with a maximum extent of white markings. It is evidently a well-marked race. But whether the red-breasted sapsucker should be considered a subspecies of the yellow-bellied sapsucker seems to me to be a decidedly open question, on which authorities seem to have differed, or to have changed their minds. In support of his views, Dr. Grinnell (1901) says: "I have examined a number of skins of the *nuchalis* type, and others approaching *ruber* in almost every degree, and I am certain that there is a continuous intergradation geographically between the eastern *S. varius* and *ruber* of the Pacific Coast. The intermediates do not appear to be the result of 'hybridization' and the case does not seem to be at all parallel to that of *Colaptes auratus* and *C. cafer*. Therefore I see no reason why the Red-breasted Sapsucker is of more than subspecific rank."

It is interesting to note that Ridgway used the name *Sphyrapicus varius ruber* in 1872 and again in 1874 (Ridgway, 1914, in synonymy), but 40 years later (1914) he gave the red-breasted sapsucker full specific rank, apparently having changed his mind. And, in the same work, in a footnote under the red-naped sapsucker, referring to the intergrades mentioned by Dr. Grinnell, he says: "But they may be (and I believe are) hybrids; certainly there is no more reason for not considering them as such than in the case of *Colaptes*."

Certainly the red-breasted sapsucker and the yellow-bellied sapsucker are as much unlike in appearance as the two flickers; and the hybrid flickers certainly show "every degree" of intergradation. In the large series of sapsuckers that I have examined, containing 87 typical *ruber* and 86 typical *nuchalis*, I was able to find only 8 specimens that could, by any stretch of the imagination, be considered as intermediates; I believe that these intergrading sapsuckers will prove to be relatively less common than are the hybrids between the two flickers.

It is interesting, too, to note that the first three editions of the A. O. U. Check-List, 1886, 1895, and 1910, all gave the red-breasted sapsucker full specific rank, in spite of the fact that Ridgway had called it a subspecies of the yellow-bellied in 1872, and Grinnell had done the same in 1901. But the fourth edition, 1931, adopts the subspecies theory, in spite of Ridgway's latest decision.

The southern race of the red-breasted sapsucker breeds in the Canadian and Transition Zones in the mountains of California, from the Trinity and Warner Mountains southward to the San Jacinto Mountains. Grinnell and Storer (1924) say that it "is found in the main forest belt during the spring, summer, and fall, but regularly performs an altitudinal migration which carries it down into the tree growths of the western foothills and valleys for the winter months."

Nesting.—Very little seems to have been published on the nesting habits of this sapsucker, which probably do not differ materially from those of its northern relative, about which more seems to be known. Wright M. Pierce (1916) located one of its nests in the San Bernardino Mountains, on June 26, of which he says: "The cavity was in the dead top of a large live silver fir about forty-five feet up. The cavity had a small opening and was only 5 or 6 inches deep; diameter, inside, 1½ or 2 inches. The nest held two large young and one smaller dead one. It was hard to see how more than one bird could survive in such a small space, so it was not surprising that the probably weaker bird had apparently been suffocated."

Eggs.—The red-breasted sapsucker lays usually four or five eggs, sometimes as many as six. Like all woodpeckers' eggs, they are pure white, usually with very little or no gloss, and they vary from ovate to rounded-ovate. The measurements of 13 eggs average 23.79 by 17.25 millimeters; the eggs showing the four extremes measure 24.6 by 17.0, 23.81 by **17.86, 22.5** by 17.5, and 24.5 by **16.6** millimeters.

Young.—Incubation is said to last about 14 days; this duty and the care of the young is shared by both parents. Mrs. Irene G. Wheelock (1904) says of a nest that she watched: "Incubation began May 30, and lasted fifteen days. The young were fed by regurgitation for the first two weeks. * * *

"The young sapsuckers left the nest on the seventh of July, and clung to the nest tree for three days. Here they were initiated by both parents into the mysteries of sap-sucking. A hole having been bored in front of each, with grotesque earnestness the mother watched the attempt to drink the sweet syrup. During this time both insects and berries were brought to them by the adults, in one hour one youngster devouring twelve insects that looked like dragonflies."

Mrs. Florence M. Bailey (1902) writes:

The last week in July at Donner Lake we found a family of dull colored young going about with their mother, a handsome old bird with dark red head and breast. They flew around in a poplar grove for a while, and then gathered in a clump of willows, where four young clung to the branches and devoted themselves to eating sap. The old bird flew about among them and seemingly cut and scraped off the bark for them, at the same time apparently trying to teach them to eat the sap for themselves; for though she would feed them at other times she refused to feed them there, and apparently watched carefully to see if they knew enough to drink the sap. When the meal was finally over and the birds had flown, we examined the branch and found that lengthwise strips of bark had been cut off, leaving narrow strips like fiddle-strings between. At the freshly cut places the sap exuded as sweet as sugar, ready for the birds to suck.

Plumages.—Like other young sapsuckers, the young of this species are hatched naked, but the juvenal plumage is acquired before they leave the nest. In the juvenal plumage, in which the sexes are alike, the wings and tail are essentially as in the adult; the head and neck, except for the white stripe below the eye, are dark grayish sooty, though the forehead and crown are usually more or less tinged with dull red; the sides and flanks are more or less barred with dull gray and white; and the abdomen is dull yellowish white.

By the last of July, or first of August, the molt into the first winter plumage begins, with an increasing amount of red coming in on the crown, throat, and breast; at the same time the yellow of the abdomen becomes brighter. This molt continues through fall and is often not complete until November or later. The young bird is now much like the adult. In fall birds, both adult and young, the red of the head and breast is much duller than in spring, "Brazil red" to "dragon's blood red" in the fall, and "scarlet red" or bright "scarlet" in the late winter and spring; this is due, of course, to the wearing away of the tips of the feathers; in early summer, just before molting, the red is decidedly brilliant.

Adults have a complete annual molt, beginning sometimes in July and lasting through August or later.

Food.—The food of the red-breasted sapsucker is much like that of its close relatives in the *varius* group. M. P. Skinner writes to me: "I have found red-breasted sapsuckers drilling on cottonwoods, willows, yellow pines, and lodgepole pines; but all the actual feeding I have seen was on willows. Mr. Michael tells me that these birds work largely on the apple trees that have been planted in various parts of the Yosemite Valley. When a sapsucker is at its wells, it takes a sip now and then, but considerable time is used in watchful guarding, or in driving away intruders or would-be robbers. In the case of such wells as I found on willow stems, I could see no established regularity in arrangement. They looked as if the bark had been irregularly scaled off. In fact, such work may be necessary to secure the inner bark; yet the birds actually took sap at such wells. One had a dozen willow stems on which it drilled and sipped in succession; each one was only a few inches from the next; and the bark of each, both above and below the wells, was worn smooth. This bird went from well to well in regular order, then back to the first well to begin again. Although sap formed the bulk of their food in August, I have seen them also searching the bark for insects during that same month."

McAtee (1911) lists the following trees that are attacked by the red-breasted sapsucker: Cottonwoods, willows, walnuts, birches, oaks, barberry, sycamore, mountain-ash, pears, apples, peaches, plums, apricot, orange, pepper, and blue gum (*Eucalyptus*). Emanuel

Fritz (1937) has, on several occasions, found this sapsucker attacking redwood trees. "In each instance the individual tree was 'peppered' with holes in horizontal rows, from the base to the top. In virgin timber, it is only an occasional tree that is attacked, and one searches in vain for another victim in the general vicinity. * * *

"During the present year, the writer came upon his first example of sapsucker work on so-called second-growth redwood. * * * The sapsuckers attacked every tree in two groups, or families, of sprouts."

W. L. Dawson (1923) writes:

The red-breasted sapsucker does puncture trees and drink sap both in summer and winter. In summer it attacks in this fashion not only pine, fir, aspen, alder, cottonwood and willow trees, but such orchard trees as apple, pear, prune and the like, as may lie within Transition areas. In winter at lower levels it gives attention to evergreen trees, white birch, mountain ash, peach, plum, apricot, English walnut, elder, and pepper trees. * * * Instead of gleaning at random, as we might expect, the Sapsucker makes careful selection, like a prudent forester, of a single tree, and confines his attentions henceforth, even though it be through succeeding seasons, to that one tree. Starting well toward the top of an evergreen, or well up on the major branches of an orchard tree, the bird works successively downward in perpendicular rows, whose borings are sometimes confluent. In this way the bird secures an ever-fresh flow of sap, from below. If carried on too extensively, or persisted in for successive seasons, these operations will sometimes cause a tree to bleed fatally, or at least to fall easy victim to insect pests. I have myself seen limbs of mountain ash trees, pear trees, and English walnut, done to death in this fashion. Yet it is only fair to say that but one or two trees in an orchard may be attacked, and there is scarcely more danger of the trouble spreading than there would be from successive strokes of lightning. * * *

For the rest, *Sphyrapicus ruber* is a large consumer of ants, and does some good in the destruction of leaf-eating beetles. Berries of the pepper trees (*Schinus molle*) are eaten to some extent, in winter, as are also, regrettably, seeds of the poison oak.

W. Otto Emerson (1893) says: "One I watched every morning from my tent fly to the top of a tall burnt tree and rap its roll-call as a kind of warning may be to the flying insects. It would then sail out like a flycatcher, catch an insect, and return to the burnt tree-top. Its movements were very graceful and regular. As it dipped or circled around for this or that insect the sunlight catching on the red breast lit it up like a patch of flame." He says elsewhere (1899): "One I found in a willow tree trying to get the best of a yellow jacket's nest, dodging back and forth either to get a mouthful of their stored sweets or the jackets themselves."

Junius Henderson (1927) gives, in his table, the percentages of animal and vegetable food, exclusive of sap, taken by this sapsucker. Based on a study of 34 stomachs the total animal food made up 69 percent and the total vegetable food 31 percent of the whole; 42

percent consisted of ants and 12 percent of fruits, mostly wild; insects accounted for 11 percent and seeds for 5 percent.

Behavior.—Grinnell and Storer (1924) write:

The Sierra red-breasted sapsucker is in our experience well-nigh voiceless and its work is done in such a quiet manner that it does not ordinarily attract attention, as do the woodpeckers that are wont to pound noisily. The most vigorous drilling of the sapsucker will scarcely be heard more than a hundred feet away. The bird moves its head through a short arc, an inch or two at the most, giving but slight momentum to the blows. The chips cut away are correspondingly small, mere sawdust as compared with the splinters or slabs chiseled off by other woodpeckers. The strokes are delivered in intermittent series, four or five within a second, then a pause of equal duration, then another short series, and so on. From time to time a longer pause ensues, when the sapsucker withdraws its bill and gazes monocularly at the work.

Mr. Skinner says, in his notes: "Although methodical, these birds seem quite nervous, moving from stem to stem. Generally they perch lengthwise of a limb when working or feeding but are apt to perch crosswise when hopping from limb to limb. After a sapsucker has its wells established, it finds it necessary to stay near to guard them from other birds attracted by the sap, or by the insects drawn there. Preening is often done while guarding the wells. The hairy woodpeckers chase these sapsuckers from tree to tree. The Audubon and lutescent warblers literally swarm to the sap-wells in the willows whenever the sapsuckers cease to guard them, but I do not know that there is active antagonism between the species. On one occasion, I saw a young sapsucker chase off a chipmunk that came too near."

Voice.—Ralph Hoffmann (1927) says that "the ordinary cry is a nasal squeal, *chée-arr*, somewhat suggesting the note of a red-bellied hawk." But it is apparently not a noisy bird, as Grinnell and Storer (1924) say that it is "well-nigh voiceless".

Field marks.—The red head and breast of the adult are unmistakable and very conspicuous. The young bird might be mistaken for the young of the red-naped sapsucker, as they are much alike, but the head of the red-breasted sapsucker is darker and often shows dull red. The broad, white band in the wing is conspicuous while the bird is perched or when flying; this is common to both adults and young, but the red-naped sapsucker has a very similar white band.

Winter.—Mr. Dawson (1923) writes: "Sapsuckers are more extensively migratory than any other woodpeckers, save *Colaptes*, but *ruber's* migrations are chiefly altitudinal. Retirement from the untenable heights is quite irregular, and dependent upon weather conditions. The winter distribution, also, appears somewhat irregular and haphazard. The bird is very quiet and rather stolid in winter, as becomes a bird of high feather. It is, however, quite as likely to be seen in a city park or on a shaded avenue as in a foothill forest."

SPHYRAPICUS VARIUS RUBER (Gmelin)

NORTHERN RED-BREASTED SAPSUCKER

HABITS

The northern race of the red-breasted sapsucker breeds from Alaska southward to western Oregon, chiefly in the Canadian Zone. Ridgway (1914) says that it is "similar to" the southern race, "but slightly larger and with coloration darker and brighter; the red of the head, neck, and chest averaging brighter, and whitish spots on back usually smaller (sometimes obsolete)."

Bendire (1895) says of its haunts:

Throughout its range I think this species breeds frequently at lower altitudes than *Sphyrapicus varius nuchalis*. Fort Klamath, however, although but 4,200 feet above sea level, has a very cool summer climate, frosts occurring in almost every month in the year. The surrounding country is very beautiful at that time. Heavy, open forests of stately pines and firs, among these the graceful and beautiful sugar pine, are found on the mountain sides and reaching well down into the green, park-like valleys. Interspersed here and there are aspen groves of various extent, their silvery trunks and light-green foliage blending artistically with the somber green of the pines. These aspen groves are the summer home of the Red-breasted Sapsucker.

Spring.—In the vicinity of Fort Klamath, Oreg., Bendire (1895) found this sapsucker to be "an abundant summer resident" and says:

They are among the earliest birds to arrive in the spring. The first bird of this species shot by me, in the spring of 1883, was obtained on March 13, and I have seen a few as late as November. On one of my collecting trips, the morning of April 4, 1883, while riding through a patch of pine timber, near Wood River, the principal stream running through the center of Klamath Valley, I noticed a flock of these birds, at least twenty in number. They were very noisy, apparently glad to get back to their summer homes, and seemed to have an excellent time generally, flying from tree to tree and calling to each other.

As I wanted a couple of specimens, I was compelled to disturb their jollification; those procured were both males, and presumably the entire flock belonged to this sex. By April 20 they had become very common, and some pairs at least were mated and had already selected their future domiciles, in every case a good-sized live aspen tree. The males might at that time be heard in almost all directions drumming on some dry limb, generally the dead top of one of these trees. They scarcely seemed to do anything else.

Nesting.—He says of the nesting habits in the Klamath Valley:

As far as my own observations go, healthy, smooth-barked aspens are always selected as suitable nesting sites by these birds. The trees used vary from 12 to 18 inches in diameter near the ground, and taper very gradually. The cavity is usually excavated below the first limb of the tree, say from 15 to 25 feet from the ground. The entrance hole seems to be ridiculously small for the size of the bird—perfectly circular, from 1¼ to 1½ inches in diameter only—so small, indeed, that it seems as if it took considerable effort for the bird to squeeze himself in and wriggle out of the hole.

The gourd-shaped excavation varies in depth from 6 to 10 inches, and it is from 3 inches near the top to 4 or 5 inches wide at the bottom. The finer chips are allowed to remain in the bottom, forming the nest proper, on which the eggs are deposited. Frequently they are more than half covered by these chips. The interior of the entire excavation is most carefully smoothed off, which must consume considerable time, considering the tough, stringy, and elastic nature of the wood when filled with sap, making it even more difficult to work when partly decayed, which seems to be the case with nearly all the aspens of any size. Probably eight or ten days are consumed in excavating a satisfactory nesting site. All the larger and coarser chips are dropped out of the hole and scattered about the base of the tree.

Johnson A. Neff (1928) says: "The nests of these birds are placed in whatever trees are abundant in their vicinity. In Klamath County, in the foothills and in the lower valleys, alders, cottonwoods and aspens were utilized; in the higher altitudes, firs were the common site, with the alder and willow along the small streams. In the Willamette Valley the firs, cottonwoods, willows, alders, and others, are used indiscriminately."

Near Blaine, Wash., Mr. Dawson (Dawson and Bowles, 1909) found an almost inaccessible nest of this sapsucker 50 feet from the ground in a big fir stub, "sixteen feet around at the base, above the root bulge, and perfectly desolate of limbs." He managed to reach the nest with the help of a rope and cleats nailed on the barkless trunk. He says:

"By the time I had a hole large enough to thrust in the hand, the eggs were quite buried in chips and rotten wood. But when they were uncovered, they were seen to lie, seven of them, in two regular lines, four in the front rank with sides touching evenly, and three in the rear with points dove-tailed between."

Harry S. Swarth (1924) also found some lofty nests in the Skeena River region of northern British Columbia; he writes: "During May and June a number of nests were found, mostly through seeing the old birds carrying food to the young. One was drilled in a live poplar, the tree a straight column with no branching limb save at the very top, the nest some seventy feet from the ground. Another was in a dead birch, sixty feet up. Many others were noted, all in birch or poplar, mostly dead trees, and no nest was less than fifty feet above the ground. One male bird collected had the abdomen bare of feathers. It obviously had been incubating eggs."

Eggs.—The red-breasted sapsucker lays four to seven eggs, usually five or six. Bendire (1895) describes them, as follows: "The eggs, when fresh and before blowing, like those of all Woodpeckers, show the yolk through the translucent shell, giving them a beautiful pinkish appearance, as well as a series of straight lines or streaks, of a more pronounced white than the rest of the shell, running toward and converging at the smaller axis of the egg. After blowing, the pink tint will be found to have disappeared and the egg changed to a pure, delicate white, the shell showing a moderate amount of luster. There is considerable variation in their shape, running as they do through all the different ovates to an elongated ovate."

The measurements of 54 eggs average 23.61 by 17.51 millimeters; the eggs showing the four extremes measure 25.40 by 17.78, 24.13 by 18.54, 21.84 by 17.27, and 23.11 by 16.26 millimeters.

Food.—Mr. Neff (1928) lists 67 species of fruit, forest, and ornamental trees and shrubs that are known to have been tapped by the red-breasted sapsucker, showing that this species is not at all particular as to what kind of sap it drinks. A total of 64 stomachs were examined, representing every month in the year. "The stomach analyses revealed 40.7 percent of vegetable food, and 52.53 percent insect food." Ants formed the bulk of the insect food, running as high as 80 percent in July; other items were boring beetles and their larvae, other beetles, weevils, caddiceflies, aphids, various flies, mites, and spiders. Fruit averaged less than 4 percent of the food and included elderberries, wild cherries, haw and dogwood berries. "No cultivated fruits were taken and seeds were almost a minus quantity. True cambium or soft inner bark averaged 31.35 percent; most of this was taken between October and April. Other bark, fibre, and miscellaneous vegetable matter averaged 5.14 percent."

Bendire (1895) says: "Their food consists principally of grubs, larvæ of insects, ants, various species of lepidoptera, which they catch on the wing, like Flycatchers, and berries. * * * They seem to be especially fond of wild strawberries."

Behavior.—Charles A. Allen, of Nicasio, Calif., wrote to Major Bendire (1895): "These Woodpeckers are very fond of hanging to telegraph poles, and may be found drumming along the line of the Central Pacific Railroad through the Sierra Nevadas, where you can hear them beating a tattoo for hours at a time. If you try to approach one, as soon as a certain distance is reached the bird will sidle to the opposite side of the pole, and then keep peeping around the corner at whatever has excited his suspicions, and as soon as it thinks it has a good opportunity to escape it will fly away with a shrill cry, and keep the pole in line between it and yourself for protection. Here they are very shy, and remain very quiet if discovered."

According to Bendire's own experience—

These birds are not at all shy during the breeding season, allowing you to approach them closely; but they have an extraordinarily keen sense of hearing. I frequently tried to sneak up to a tree close to my house which I knew had been selected by a pair of these birds, to watch them at work, but I was invariably detected by the bird, no matter how carefully I tried to creep up, before I was able to get within 30 yards, even when she was at work on the inside of the cavity and could not possibly see me. The bird would cease working at once, her head would pop out of the hole for an instant, and the surroundings

would be surveyed carefully. If I kept out of sight and perfectly still, she
would probably begin working again a few minutes afterward, but if I moved
ever so little, without even making the least noise, in my own estimation, she
would notice it and stop working again at once. If the tree were approached
too closely, she would fly off, uttering at the same time a note resembling the
word 'jay,' or 'chäe,' several times repeated, which would invariably bring the
male around also, who had in the meantime kept himself busy in some other
tree, either drumming or hunting for food. While the female was at work
on the inside of the excavation the male would fly to the entrance, from time
to time, and look in; * * * and at other times he would hang, for five or
ten minutes even, just below the entrance to the burrow, in a dreamy sort of
study, perfectly motionless and seemingly dazed."

Mr. Neff (1928) writes:

They have not been found to be particularly quiet excepting during the
hotter summer months. At other times they have been neither noticeably noisy
nor silent. The outstanding features of their behavior have proven to be pug-
nacity and noise during the mating season and while incubating and feeding the
young, and an extreme curiosity at other times. In many instances the writer
has located them by utilizing this curiosity; sitting motionless on a log or rock
after failing to find them, any sapsucker in the community would soon make
its presence known by a characteristic interrogative call, at first from a distance, gradually drawing nearer.

In winter they seem to be quite belligerent, for on several occasions one has
been located by the angry noise as if of a pitched battle; on closer investigation
it would be found that the sapsucker was attempting to drive some other woodpecker, generally the Gairdner, from some favorite tree.

Voice.—Bendire (1895) says: "While the nest was being rifled of
its contents both parents flew about the upper limbs of the tree,
uttering a number of different sounding, plaintive sounds, like
'peeye,' 'pinck,' and 'peurr,' some of these resembling somewhat the
purring of a cat when pleased and rubbing against your leg. I used
to note the different sounds in a small notebook at the very time, but
scarcely ever put them down alike; each time they appeared a trifle
different to the ear, and it is a hard matter to express them exactly
on paper."

Mr. Dawson (Dawson and Bowles, 1909) says that while he was
chopping out the nest the birds "made frequent approaches from a
neighboring tree, crying *kee-a*, *kee-aa*, in helpless bewilderment.
* * * When all was over, they raised a high, strong *qué-oo*,—
qué-oo, never before heard, and reminding one generically of the
Red-headed Woodpecker of boyhood days."

SPHYRAPICUS THYROIDEUS THYROIDEUS (Cassin)

WILLIAMSON'S SAPSUCKER

HABITS

Williamson's sapsucker is not only one of our most unique woodpeckers in its striking coloration, but it has an interesting history.
Owing to the radical difference in appearance between the two sexes,

they were for some time regarded as two distinct species. The female was the first to be described by John Cassin (1852, p. 349), based on a specimen collected by John G. Bell in Eldorado County, Calif. Under the name black-breasted woodpecker (*Melanerpes thyroideus*), Cassin describes and figures (1854) the adult female as the male of the species and says of the female: "Similar to the male, but with the colors more obscure, and the black of the breast of less extent and not so deep in shade," which is a very fair description of the immature female. The male was discovered and described and figured by Dr. Newberry (1857, p. 89, pl. 34) under the name *Picus williamsonii*, based on a specimen collected by him on August 23, 1855, on the shores of Klamath Lake, Oreg. Baird, Cassin, and Lawrence (1860) give a very good description of an adult male, as the male of the species, but say "female with the chin white instead of red," which, of course, is the immature male. Thus we have the adult of each sex regarded as the male of a species, and the young bird of each sex regarded as the female of a species. With careless, or improper, sexing of specimens, such an error might easily occur, but it is remarkable that it remained so long undiscovered. Baird, Cassin, and Lawrence (1860) describe the male as *Sphyrapicus williamsonii* Baird, Williamson's woodpecker, and the female as *Sphyrapicus thyroideus* Baird, brown-headed woodpecker. J. G. Cooper (1870), in the Geological Survey of California, edited by Baird, follows the same error but calls the female the round-headed woodpecker. Even Baird, Brewer, and Ridgway, in their history of North American Birds, had not discovered the error, for they use substantially the same nomenclature.

It remained for Henry W. Henshaw (1875) to discover the true relationship of the two supposed species and clear up the previous misunderstanding. He writes: "While near Fort Garland, I obtained abundant proof of the specific identity of the two birds in question; *williamsonii* being the male of *thyroideus*. Though led to suspect this, from finding the two birds in suspicious proximity, it was some time before I could procure a pair actually mated. A nest was at length discovered, excavated in the trunk of a live aspen, and both the parent birds were secured as they flew from the hole, having just entered with food for the newly hatched young."

Mr. Ridgway (1877) comments on the discovery as follows:

A suspicion that the two might eventually prove to be different plumages of one species several times arose in our mind during the course of our field-work, the chief occasion for which was the very suggestive circumstance that both were invariably found in the same woods, and had identical manners and notes, while they also agreed strictly in all the details of form and proportions, as well as in the bright gamboge-yellow color of the belly. Our theory that *thyroideus* was perhaps the *young*, and *williamsoni* the *adult*, proved erroneous, however; and it never occurred to us that the differences might be sexual, an oversight caused chiefly by the circumstance of our having seen in collections many specimens of *thyroideus* with a red streak on the throat and marked as males, while the type specimen of *williamsoni* had a white streak on the throat and was said to be a female. We were thus entirely misled by the erroneous identification of the sex in these specimens. We gave the matter up, however, only after shooting a very young specimen of what was undoubtedly *williamsoni*, and another of *thyroideus*, both of which very closely resembled the adults of the same forms, a circumstance which at once convinced us that the differences could not depend on age; so we finally concluded that the two must be distinct.

All observers seem to agree that this woodpecker is confined to the higher elevations in the mountains among the pines, in sharp contrast to the haunts of the red-breasted sapsucker at lower levels among the deciduous trees.

Joseph Grinnell (1908), referring to the San Bernardino Mountains, in southern California, says: "This Williamson sapsucker appeared to be restricted to the Canadian zone and upper edge of Transition. We found it only among the tamarack pines on the slopes and ridges of San Gorgonio peak, and among the silver firs, tamarack and yellow pines around Bluff lake. In the former locality the species was common for a woodpecker, especially around Dry Lake, 9,000 feet altitude, where several nests were found."

Courtship.—Charles W. Michael (1935) noted the mating behavior of a male Williamson's sapsucker, which had just left a fresh nest-hole, as follows:

He sounded his harsh call several times. Seemingly in answer to his call the female appeared. This was the first we had seen of the female. The female examined the nest hole, flew up on a branch and uttered a series of low notes. The male joined her, alighting a foot away and uttering a series of low chuckling notes. While giving these notes he strutted along the limb with wing-tips and tail jerking rapidly. As he approached his mate she crouched low on the limb and the mating act was accomplished. The act lasted several seconds before the birds separated to perch side by side on a limb. After a minute or so the female flew off through the woods and the male went into the nest hole. In about five minutes the female came to the nest hole and again uttered her soft coaxing notes. The male came out of the hole and both birds flew to a limb where again the mating act was consummated. The male returned to the nest. In our two-hour watch the female only went to the nest hole to call the mate out.

Nesting.—Dr. Grinnell (1908) says of its nesting in the San Bernardino Mountains:

Tamarack pines were selected as nest trees, usually old ones with the core dead and rotten but with a live shell on the outside. In one found June 22, 1905, there were four holes drilled one above the other about eighteen inches apart, and one of these holes contained three small young and two infertile eggs. * * * Later on in the same day another nest was found similarly located containing four half-fledged young. A nest with half-grown young was found in the same locality, June 14, 1906; and on June 26 of the same year a nest twenty feet up in a half-dead tamarack held five two-thirds-grown young and one rotten egg. So that a full set of eggs probably varies from four to six in number. On June 18, 1907, a nest with small young was located ten feet up in an exceptionally large nearly dead tamarack pine. This was one of the lowest of a series of forty-seven well-formed holes of similar external appearance, which penetrated this one tree trunk on all sides up to an estimated height of thirty-five feet.

W. L. Dawson (1923) writes: "One soon comes to recognize the rigid requirements of the Williamson Sapsucker in the matter of nesting sites. Given a pine which is beginning to die at the top, usually in a fairly sheltered situation, and a pair of birds will adopt it for a permanent home. They will occupy it from year to year, or perhaps the year around, nesting twice in a season; and a long occupation is evinced by a trunk riddled with holes at all levels. One such 'family tree,' closely examined, had 38 holes, apparently complete and fit for habitation or incubation. At the time of our visit, on June 19th, the male was industriously drilling a new excavation at a height of 45 feet."

Major Bendire (1895) says:

I obtained my first set of eggs of this species on June 3, 1883, about 9 miles north of Fort Klamath, in the open pine forest on the road to Crater Lake. It consisted of five eggs, slightly incubated. The nesting site was excavated in a partly decayed pine whose entire top for some 20 feet was dead; the height of the excavation from the ground was about 50 feet. The man climbing the tree reported it to be about 8 inches deep and about 5 inches wide at the bottom, and freshly made. A second set, of six fresh eggs, was taken June 12 of the same year, about 12 miles north of the Post, at a still higher altitude than the first one. It came also out of a pine about 40 feet from the ground. A third nest, found a week later, near the same place, contained five young, just hatched. This nest was in a dead aspen, about 20 feet from the ground. Only one brood is raised, and, like the other two species, it is only a summer resident in the vicinity of Fort Klamath.

Other observers have found nests in lodgepole pines, red firs, and larches at various heights from 5 to 60 feet above ground but always in conifer associations.

Eggs.—Bendire (1895) says: "The number of eggs laid to a set varies from three to seven, sets of five or six being most often found. These, like all woodpecker's eggs, are pure china-white in color; the shell is close grained, rather thin, and only slightly glossy. In shape they vary from ovate to elongate ovate, and a few approach an ovate pyriform, a shape apparently not found in the eggs of other species of this genus." The measurements of 30 eggs average 23.54 by 17.23 millimeters; the eggs showing the four extremes measure 25.91 by 17.27, 24.1 by 18.3, and 20.1 by 15.4 millimeters.

Young.—Both parents assist in the duties of incubation, but the length of time required for this function does not seem to be definitely known; both sexes also help in feeding the young. Dr. J. C. Merrill (1888) says, of two nests that he watched for some time: "The males brought food about twice as often as did the females, and frequently removed the excrement of the young on leaving the nest, alighting on the nearest tree for a moment to drop it and to clean their bills; I did not see either of the females remove any excreta. About four feet above one of the holes was another occupied by a pair of pigmy nuthatches, but neither species paid any attention to the other when they happened to arrive with food at the same time."

Dr. Grinnell (1908) writes: "We usually located the nests by watching the movements of the parent birds, which flew from their foraging places, often far distant, direct to the nest tree. The young uttered a whinnying chorus of cries when fed, and the adults, though generally very quiet, had a not loud explosive cry, more like the distant squall of a red-tailed hawk. The bill and throat of an adult male, shot as it was approaching a nest, was crammed with large wood ants, not the kind, however, that are common at lower altitudes and smell so foully."

Charles W. Michael (1935) watched a nest containing young, in the Yosemite region, of which he says:

When we arrived, about ten o'clock, both parent birds were bringing food. We watched the birds for an hour and a half and in this period of time the male made nine trips to the nest hole and the female made seven trips. The young were small, as the parent birds went completely into the nest hole. The birds, male and female, always came onto the tree trunk above the nest hole and hitched jerkily downward until on a level with the hole. They landed anywhere between five and fifteen feet above the hole; the female was likely to land nearest to the hole. * * * About every other trip excrement was carried from the nest. When the male cleaned nest he carried the feces away and dropped them some distance from the nest. When the female cleaned nest she came to the entrance from within, looked about and then dropped the refuse before leaving the nest hole.

Plumages.—The most remarkable characteristic of this woodpecker is the striking difference in the plumages of the two sexes at all ages, from the first plumage of the young bird to its maturity; in most birds the sexes are much alike in the juvenal plumage; but the young male Williamson's sapsucker is much like the adult male, and the young female is much like the adult female; the principal character common to both sexes at all ages is the white rump.

These young sapsuckers are fully fledged before they leave the nest.

The young male, in juvenal plumage in summer, differs from the adult male in having a smaller and weaker bill and softer, more blended plumage; the black areas, except the wings and tail, which are like those of the adult, are dull brownish black, instead of clear glossy black; there are usually numerous elongated white spots or streaks, more or less concealed, on the scapulars and upper back, and often a few small whitish spots on the crown; the chin and upper throat are white, instead of scarlet; the center of the breast and abdomen is dull yellowish white, instead of bright "lemon-chrome"; the sides and flanks are barred, instead of striped or spotted, with dusky.

The young female differs from the adult female in having a smaller and weaker bill and softer plumage; the black breast patch is entirely lacking; the breast, sides, and flanks are barred with dusky, but less distinctly than in the adult; and the yellow of the central breast and abdomen is much paler.

These two juvenal plumages are worn for only a short time in summer. I have seen young males molting into their first winter plumage, which is practically adult, as early as August 9; and young females begin to show the increasing black breast patch as early as August 6; but this molt is slow, or variable, and is sometimes not completed until November or December.

Adults apparently have their complete annual molt mainly in August and September.

Food.—Mrs. Florence M. Bailey (1928) says: "In 17 stomachs examined, 87 percent was animal matter and 13 percent vegetable. Of the animal contents, 86 percent was ants, and cambium made up 12.55 percent of the total food."

Grinnell and Storer (1924) write:

In the Yosemite region the Williamson Sapsucker is closely associated with the lodgepole pine. While this tree seems to furnish the bird's preferred source of forage, practically all other species of trees within its local range are also utilized. We saw workings attributable to this sapsucker on the alpine hemlock, red and white firs, Jeffrey pine, and quaking aspen.

The amount of work which this sapsucker will do upon a single tree was impressed upon us while we were at Porcupine Flat in early July, 1915. In that locality there was a lodgepole pine (*Pinus murrayana*) about 60 feet high, which showed no marks of sapsucker work previous to the current year. The tree was in full leafy vigor and measured 8 feet 3¼ inches in girth at 3 feet above the ground. There were numerous live branches down to within 6 feet of the ground. Twenty-six irregularly horizontal rows of fresh punctures were counted on one side of the trunk, the lowest being only 18½ inches above the ground, and the highest about 40 feet. * * *

During the winter months when sap is practically at a standstill in the coniferous trees at high altitudes, the Williamson Sapsucker must needs seek other fare. A few of our own observations added to those of other naturalists suggest that during the winter season the birds may forage in a large part on dormant insects or on insect larvae hidden in crevices in the bark. If such is the case, whatever the damage done by these birds to the forest as a whole during the summer months, it is partially offset by their wintertime activity. In any event, the attacks of the Williamson Sapsucker on the lodgepole pines of the central Sierra Nevada cannot be considered as of great economic importance, for these trees are there used little if at all for lumber or for any other commercial purpose.

Behavior.—Dr. J. C. Merrill (1888), at Fort Klamath, Oreg., found this sapsucker "shy and very suspicious. A noticeable habit here is the frequency with which it works down as well as up a trunk, and when one dodges around a tree, in which, by the way, it is unpleasantly expert, it is as apt to reappear twenty feet below where it was last seen, as above. In searching for food it will often work up and down a favorite tree repeatedly. In all its movements it is quick and active, and gives one the impression of being thoroughly wide awake, which impression the would-be collector is speedily convinced is correct."

Voice.—Mr. Michael (1935) says: "When the sapsuckers met at the nest site they exchanged greetings in a 'rubber doll' tone of voice. The nasal quaver of notes was remindful of a call often sounded by the red-breasted sapsucker. Another call that was occasionally shouted from the tree-tops was shrill and like that of a red-tailed hawk."

Dr. Elliott Coues (1874) says: "It has an abrupt, explosive outcry, much like that of other species of Woodpeckers, and also an entirely different call note. This sounds to me like a number of rolling *r*'s, beginning with a guttural *k—k'-r-r-r*—each set of *r*'s making a long syllable. This note is leisurely given, and indefinitely repeated, in a very low key."

Grinnell and Storer (1924) describe the voice as "a weak wheezy *whang* or *whether.*"

Field marks.—Such a conspicuously and uniquely colored woodpecker as the male Williamson's sapsucker should be easily recognized; its general appearance is largely black, with a large white patch in the fore part of the wing, and another on the rump and upper tail coverts; the yellow on the under parts is not so easily seen; neither is the red throat. The female appears mainly pale brown, with a white rump, brown head, and barred back and wings.

DISTRIBUTION

Range.—Mountainous regions of the Western United States and southwestern Canada south to west-central Mexico.

Breeding range.—Williamson's sapsucker breeds **north** to central Washington (Bumping Lake and probably Dayton); and southwestern Montana (Missoula, Pipestone Creek, Bridger Creek, and Red Lodge). **East** to Montana (Red Lodge); Wyoming (Yellowstone National Park and Laramie Peak); Colorado (Estes Park, Idaho Springs, Breckenridge, El Paso County, and Fort Garland); and New Mexico (Carson Forest, Santa Fe Canyon, Las Vegas, and Hermosa). **South** to southern New Mexico (Hermosa); Arizona (Tucson, Mogollon Mountains, and Fort Whipple); and southern California (San Jacinto). **West** to eastern California (San Jacinto, San Bernardino Mountains, Pyramid Peak, Tuolumne County, Echo

Lake, Lake Tahoe, Lassen Peak, and Eagle Peak); western Oregon (Rogue River Valley and Foley Springs); and west-central Washington (Bumping Lake).

Winter range.—In winter the species is regularly found **north** to central California (Yosemite Valley); central Arizona (Pine Springs, Oak Creek, and Mogollon Mountains); southwestern New Mexico (Black Range); and central Texas (San Angelo). **East** to Texas (San Angelo and probably Kerrville); eastern Chihuahua (Apache); and Jalisco (Bolanos and Guadalajara). **South** to southern Jalisco (Guadalajara). **West** to Jalisco (Guadalajara); northwestern Durango; western Chihuahua (Refugio, Casa Colorado, Bavispee River, and Colonia Garcia); northern Baja California (San Pedro Martir, Ville de la Trinidad, and Hanson Lagoon); and California (Pasadena and Yosemite Valley).

As outlined, the range applies to the entire species, which has been separated into two subspecies. True Williamson's sapsucker (*S. t. thyroideus*) is found in the Pacific coast region from British Columbia south to Baja California, while Natalie's sapsucker (*S. t. nataliae*) inhabits the Rocky Mountain region from Montana south to Jalisco.

Spring migration.—Although the species appears to be resident throughout considerable portions of its range, and but little is known of its migratory movements, the following early dates of arrival have been noted: Colorado—Boulder County, April 5; Colorado Springs, April 5; Evergreen, April 8; Denver, April 15. Wyoming—Yellowstone Park, April 29. Montana—Charcoal Gulch, April 23. Nevada—Carson City, March 10. Washington—Pullman, April 26. A late date of departure from the southern part of the winter range is Chihuahua, Palomas Lakes, April 7.

Fall migration.—Available late dates of fall departure are: Washington—Copper River, September 3. Oregon—Rustler Peak, November 6. Nevada—Lee Canyon, October 7; Carson City, November 27. Montana—Fort Custer, September 9. Wyoming—Yellowstone Park, September 22; Wheatland, October 4. Colorado—Del Norte, September 5; Rio Blanco, September 9; Boulder County, November 6. It has been noted to reach Hanson Lagoon, Baja California, on October 11.

Casual records.—There are a few records in extreme southern British Columbia, where it may breed occasionally. A pair were collected on April 22, 1913, on Schoonover Mountain, near Okanagan Falls; one was taken at Similkameen in June 1882, while Swarth (1917) records three from Midway.

Egg dates.—California: 14 records, May 27 to June 26.

Colorado: 29 records, May 24 to June 24; 15 records, June 1 to 8, indicating the height of the season.

SPHYRAPICUS THYROIDEUS NATALIAE (Malherbe)

NATALIE'S SAPSUCKER

PLATE 29

HABITS

Harry S. Swarth (1917) is responsible for the recognition of this race, which seems to differ from the Williamson's sapsucker of the Pacific coast in the same way that the northern white-headed woodpecker differs from the southern race of that species; he says:

The differences are as worthy of recognition in one case as in the other. It is my suggestion here that the Rocky Mountain race of the Williamson Sapsucker be separately recognized on the basis of its lesser bill measurements as compared with those of *Sphyrapicus thyroideus thyroideus* of the Pacific Coast.

As regards a name for this form, there is already one that seems to be clearly available for use. A specimen from Mexico was designated by Malherbe (Journ. für Orn., 1854, p. 171) as *Picus nataliae*, and an example from any part of Mexico (save possibly from the mountains of northern Lower California) would assuredly be of the Rocky Mountain subspecies. Also in the measurements given by Malherbe, length of bill ("du bec, du front 20 millimeters") places his bird unequivocally with this race.

It is reasonably certain that in the Rocky Mountain region the species does not breed south of the Mogollon Divide, though it does occur as a common winter visitant in southern Arizona and over a large part of the Mexican plateau. These winter visitants, as shown by numerous specimens at hand, are migrants from the Rocky Mountain region to the northward, and not from the Pacific Coast region. So the name *nataliae*, as given by Malherbe to a Mexican specimen, can safely be used for the Rocky Mountain subspecies, which may therefore stand as *Sphyrapicus thyroideus nataliae* (Malherbe).

Mrs. Florence M. Bailey (1928), referring to the striking difference in plumage between the male and the female in this species, remarks:

The cause of this strongly contrasted sexual coloration unique among the woodpeckers of the United States is one of the unsolved problems of ornithology that stimulates speculation and so adds zest to the study. Is it, as Mr. Swarth suggests, that the female is still in a primitive stage of development? Correlating the brown coloration of the pasture-frequenting flickers with the ant-eating habits so marked in the Rocky Mountain sapsucker, it would seem that the color of the female might have been ancestrally adapted to a more open habitat than that in which the pair are found today; or has the ant-eating habit been diverted from ants that live on the ground in the open to those that live on tree trunks? The feeding habits of the anomalous pair should be carefully studied in the field.

Dr. Edgar A. Mearns (1890b) says that in Arizona it "breeds very commonly at the highest altitudes, frequenting the spruce and fir woods. It seldom descends far into the pine belt during the breeding season, although it is found in the pines in winter, occasionally descending even to the cedars in severe weather; and after the nesting season it frequently roves down to the pine woods with its young. When shot, it usually fastened its claws into the balsam bark and remained hanging there after life was extinct."

Milton P. Skinner says in his Yellowstone Park notes: "In this Park, the Williamson sapsucker lives below 7,000 feet and prefers mixed forests of aspen and fir, but it is not particular whether in dense forest or in the borderland between forest and open."

Spring.—Mr. Swarth (1904) witnessed a well-marked spring migration in the Huachuca Mountains, Ariz., of which he says:

On April 6, 1902, I saw about a dozen Williamson Sapsuckers near the summit of the mountains at an altitude of about 9,000 feet. Though not at all in a compact flock they seemed to keep rather close together, and when one flew any distance away, the others soon followed. The bulk of them were females, and but one or two males were seen, one of which was, with great difficulty secured, for they were very wild. On April 9 several more were seen and a female secured at this same place; and a male was taken a mile or two from this place, at an altitude of nearly 10,000 feet. These were the last I saw in the spring, though they do occur later as I have a female that was taken in the Huachucas by H. Kimball on April 20, 1895.

Nesting.—The nesting habits of this woodpecker do not seem to differ materially from those of the species elsewhere. Bendire (1895) quotes W. G. Smith, as follows: "Williamson's Sapsucker is a common summer resident in Estes Park, Colorado, where it nests mostly in dead pines, often within a few feet of the ground, and again as high as 70 feet up. Full sets of fresh eggs are usually found here during the first week in June. The male appears to me to do most of the incubating, and hereabouts it is most often found at altitudes between 7,000 and 8,000 feet, but I have also taken it at much higher ones, where it nests somewhat later."

Mr. Skinner says in his notes: "On June 14, 1914, I discovered the nest of a pair of Williamson sapsuckers in the gulch beside the trail to Snow Pass at the beginning of the last ascent. The nest was in an aspen trunk about 6 inches in diameter. The opening to the nest was 1½ inches in diameter and located 5 feet above ground. On June 30, 1915, the nest was in the same tree, but 2 feet above the 1914 nest and in a fresh opening."

Eggs.—The eggs of Natalie's sapsucker do not differ materially from those of the other race of the species. The measurements of 51 eggs average 23.60 by 17.41 millimeters; the eggs showing the four extremes measure 26.2 by 17.9, 24.2 by 19.4, 21.5 by 17.0, and 22.0 by 16.0 millimeters.

Young.—Mr. Skinner says in his notes that the young "seem to arrive irregularly between June 10 and July 1. I have seen young Williamson's sapsuckers hunting by themselves before August 10. In the nest recorded above there were five young on June 14, 1914, and both parents were kept constantly busy bringing food, and frequently came so fast that one parent had to wait for the other to leave the nest. In feeding the young the adults disappeared completely into the nest cavity and came out head first. In 1915 there were five more young on June 30 and they were still there on July 10. When I visited them on June 30, the male was in the nest, and it required about five raps on the tree trunk to dislodge him, although he came to the opening and looked out at each rap."

Food.—The feeding habits of Natalie's sapsucker are apparently similar to those of the species elsewhere, but Mr. Skinner tells me he has "seen it drumming on firs for insects, picking insects from a crotch of a lodgepole pine and catching spruce-budworm moths from fir foliage."

Behavior.—The feeding and other habits of Natalie's sapsucker seems to be similar to those of the other subspecies, but Bendire (1895) quotes the following notes from Denis Gale, about its behavior around the nest, which are worth repeating here:

A marked peculiarity I have noted with *Sphyrapicus thyroideus* is that the male takes a lookout station upon some suitable tree, where, at the approach of any possible danger, he gives the alarm by striking a short dry limb with his bill, by which a peculiar vibrating sound is given out, which the female, not very distant, fully understands, and is at once on the alert. If either excavating, guarding, or covering her eggs, she will immediately look out of her burrow, and, should the intruder's path lie in the direction of her nest, she will silently slip away and alight in a tree some distance off, but in view of both her nest and the intruder. The first or second blow of a hatchet upon the tree trunk in which the nest is excavated will mark her movement again by a short flight, so managed as not to increase the distance—in fact oftener coming nearer. When satisfied that her treasures have been discovered, she utters a peculiar, low, grating sound, not unlike the purring of a cat. The male then comes to the fore and braving the danger, is very courageous, and, should the eggs be far advanced in incubation, he will even enter the nest when you are almost within reach of it. When the latter are rifled, he is always the first to go in and discover the fact, often passing in and out several times in a surprised sort of manner.

CEOPHLOEUS PILEATUS PILEATUS (Linnaeus)

SOUTHERN PILEATED WOODPECKER

HABITS

The above name is now restricted to the pileated woodpeckers of the Lower Austral forests of the Southern United States, except southern Florida, east of the Rocky Mountains. When Outram Bangs (1898) applied the name *abieticola*, to the northern race, he said: "Linnaeus based his *Picus pileatus* on Catesby and Kalm. Taking Catesby as the best authority, southern South Carolina must be considered the type locality of the species, and birds from this region are as extreme of the southern race as those from Florida."

The southern pileated woodpecker is decidedly smaller than the northern bird and somewhat darker in coloration. Ridgway (1914) says of this race, in a footnote: "Some of the more northern examples are quite as slaty as the extreme northern form (*P. p. abieticola*) but they are distinctly smaller. In other words, I have restricted the name *pileatus* to an intermediate form, characterized by the small size of *P. p. floridanus* combined with an appreciably lighter (more slaty or sooty) coloration, often approaching closely the lightness of hue of *P. p. abieticola*."

Arthur T. Wayne (1910) says that in South Carolina "this fine species is abundant wherever the forest is of a primeval nature, but where the heavy growth has been cut away it is seldom met with." Wright and Harper (1913), writing of its haunts in southern Georgia, say: "With the exception of the red-bellied woodpecker, this is the most abundant member of its family in the Okefinokee. In fact, we saw as many as four Pileated Woodpeckers in a single tree. In every part of the swamp—especially the cypress bays, but also the hammocks. and the piny woods on the islands, and even the 'heads' on the prairies— these magnificent birds are at home."

George Finlay Simmons (1925) says that in the Austin region of Texas this woodpecker lives in the "wilder country only; cypress swamps, and the most heavily timbered bottomlands, generally in very thinly settled sections; post oak woods on gravelly river terraces; edges of woodland meadows; along margins of both large and small streams; Austroriparian forests; in or near edges of timber, venturing out onto fields to feed."

Charles R. Stockard (1904) says of his experience with this species in Mississippi:

During three seasons seventeen nests were watched in Adams County. In the vicinity where observations were made every small woods had its pair of these large woodpeckers. The individuals of this species seemed to occupy very small feeding areas. Of the seven nests that were found in 1902 five pairs of the birds were located in their respective woods during the previous December and January. Whenever a pair was once seen feeding in a wood during the winter the same pair could always be found very close to that place. At the beginning of the nesting season they would invariably make their burrow in some dead but sound tree near the edge of the brake. From continued observation it appeared certain that whenever a pair were found in a small wood during the winter they were sure to nest there the following spring. * * *

In four instances, all of which had lost their eggs the year before, the birds built their new burrows in their several woods within a distance of about one quarter of a mile from the previous nest site. These four are the only cases which were watched with special care.

Nesting.—The only nests of this race that I have seen were shown to me by A. T. Wayne, on May 19, 1915, near Mount Pleasant, S. C. They were in tall, dead pine trees (*Pinus taeda*) in a heavily forested region of open, mixed woods. One was 43 feet from the ground; he had taken three fresh eggs from this nest on April 24, 1915. The other I estimated as over 60 feet up, but he said it was 80 feet from the ground; it probably held young at that time, as both birds were much in evidence and very noisy.   Mr. Wayne told me that these two pairs of birds had nested in this tract of timber for many years. He writes (1910) regarding their nesting habits:

If the season is a forward one the birds mate early in February and towards the latter part of the month begin to excavate their hole, which requires exactly a month for completion.   During the month of March, 1904, I made observations on a pair which excavated their hole in a dead pine.   On March 21, the opening was commenced by the female, who drilled a small hole, and by degrees enlarged it to the size of a silver dollar.   The male assisted in the excavation, but the female did by far the larger part of the work.   The size of the aperture was not increased until necessary to admit the shoulders of the bird.   I visited these birds every day in order to note the progress of their work, and, being so accustomed to seeing me, they were utterly fearless and I could, at any time, approach within twenty feet without hindering the work, although the hole was only about thirty feet from the ground.   This hole was completed on April 21, and the first egg was laid the following morning.   * * * In this case the excavation was made under a dead limb, and was about eighteen inches deep, being hollowed out more on one side than the other.   This woodpecker is so attached to the tree in which it has first made its nest that it continues to cling to it as long as it can find a suitable spot at which to excavate a new hole.   It never uses the same hole a second time.   I know of a pair of these birds which resorted to the same tree for four consecutive years, and each year they excavated a new hole.   * * * If this bird is deprived of its first set of eggs, it at once excavates a new hole, and the length of time consumed in its construction is about twenty-five days.   A curious habit is that even when it is incubating or brooding its young, this bird frequently taps in its hole as if excavating.

Vernon Sharpe, Jr. (1932), says that in Tennessee "for a nesting site a dead tree is invariably selected and preferably one of large size, from which the branches have fallen.   The cavity is situated from 20 to 85 feet above the ground, with a depth ranging from 20 to 26 inches.   Generally the four-inch opening is broader at the base and angular at the top, forming somewhat of a triangular shape.   While incubating, this species will continue to enlarge the nest cavity, as was proved by personal experience."

M. G. Vaiden writes to me that the pileated woodpecker is fairly common in certain localities near Rosedale, Miss.   He has located seven nests in cypress, sycamore, hackberry, or sweetgum trees, at estimated heights ranging from 60 to 75 feet.   His nesting dates range from April 14 to April 29.

Of the nest location, in Texas, Mr. Simmons (1925) says: "Cavity in upper part, usually 30 to 60 feet from ground, in solid trunk of live, sound tree, less commonly in dead or partly dead limbs or trunks, generally tall cottonwood, cypress, elm, or oak, on the edge of woods or in marginal timber skirting stream, and usually easily located by the half-bushel of big fresh chips scattered about on the ground below; tree 10 or more inches in diameter at cavity."

Mr. Stockard (1904) says, of the 17 pairs that he watched in Mississippi, that the birds do not lay a second set after the nest has been robbed, but they remain in the same woods during the remainder of the season. He says of the nests:

The burrow is very large and requires in most cases about one month for construction, being commenced in this locality about the latter part of February. But it was very difficult to note the exact length of time consumed in burrowing, as the birds try so many parts of the same tree before striking one to suit their taste. The nest tree and other dead trees close at hand were often scarred from top to bottom. In two cases they began a nest, then seemed to start one in another place, and then returned to the former and completed it. * * *

The first nest, a burrow twenty-five feet from the ground in an old sycamore stump, contained one egg on March 22; March 26 it contained three, and on April 1, when the set was removed, it consisted of four slightly incubated eggs. * * *

Only one pair was observed that had their nest in a dead tree which stood in an open field at least sixty or seventy yards from the wood. The female in this case flew about the nest tree and lit once on the upper part and again just over the nest hole while a person was in the act of climbing the tree. This was by far the most daring bird seen and, as mentioned above, because of the isolation of the tree, her burrow was unusually exposed for this species.

Eggs.—The pileated woodpecker lays ordinarily from three to five eggs; Audubon (1842) claims to have found six. The eggs vary from ovate, the commonest shape, to elliptical-ovate; some are even quite pointed. They are a brilliant china-white and usually decidedly glossy. The measurements of 52 eggs average 32.90 by 24.72 millimeters; the eggs showing the four extremes measure **35.70 by 27.00, 30.22 by 22.35,** and 29.30 by **22.00** millimeters.

Young.—Bendire (1895) says that "an egg is deposited daily, and incubation begins occasionally before the set is completed, and lasts about eighteen days, both sexes assisting in this duty, as well as in caring for the young. Like all Woodpeckers, the Pileated are very devoted parents, and the young follow them for some weeks after leaving the nest, until fully capable of caring for themselves. Only one brood is raised in a season."

Plumages.—I have seen no small nestlings of this species, but they are probably hatched naked and blind, like all other woodpeckers; the juvenal plumage is evidently acquired before the young bird leaves the nest.

The young male, in juvenal plumage, is much like the adult male in general appearance, but the body plumage is softer, less firm, and rather lighter and more sooty in color; the tips of the primaries have dull-white narrow margins, which soon wear away; the red of the head is duller, paler, and more restricted; on the fore half of the crown and the malar region, the feathers are basally grayish brown, the red showing only on the tips of most of the feathers, producing a mixed color effect. The young female is similar to the young male but with even less red in the head; the forehead and most of the crown are grayish brown, which invades the red posterior portion of the crown; and there is no red in the malar region. Audubon (1842) says that the bill of the young bird is considerably longer than that of the adult.

The juvenal plumage is apparently worn for only a short time, during the summer and early fall; I have not been able to detect it beyond August; this is followed by a prolonged molt into a first winter plumage, which is scarcely distinguishable from that of the adult. Adults have a complete molt between June and September.

Food.—The food of the southern pileated woodpecker is not essentially different from that of the other races of the species, with due allowance for the difference in environment. Prof. F. E. L. Beal (1895) says: "Six stomachs, collected by Dr. B. H. Warren on the St. Johns River in Florida, contained numerous palmetto ants (*Camponotus escuriens*), and remains of other ants, several larvae of a Prionid beetle (*Orthosoma brunnea*), numerous builder ants (*Cremastogaster lineolata*), one larva of *Xylotrechus*, and one pupa of the white ant (*Termes*)."

George Finlay Simmons (1925) says that in Texas it "feeds on ants, particularly about decayed stumps; the eggs, larvae, and adults of wood-boring insects, particularly beetles; and on berries, acorns, nuts, and wild grapes. When digging for insects beneath the bark or in the wood of dead limbs or trunks of trees, it pounds steadily away, head swinging back in an impossible arc and driving straight down with the force of a blacksmith's sledge, chips flying every stroke or two; by employing a wrenching stroke with its chisel-bill, it knocks three-inch, four-inch, or even six-inch chips from the tree and causes them to fly for some distance."

Arthur H. Howell (1924) says that in Alabama its food "consists mainly of ants, beetles, and wild fruits and berries, including sour gum, tupelo gum, dogwood, persimmon, frost grape, holly, poison ivy, sumac, and hackberry."

Behavior.—The pileated woodpecker is ordinarily a wild, shy bird of the wilderness forests, though in some places it is said to be quite unsuspicious, where perhaps it has not yet learned to fear man, or where familiarity has taught it to trust him. Its flight is rather slow, but vigorous and usually direct, after the manner of a crow; at times, however, in short swings, it adopts the bounding flight, so common to many woodpeckers. It is an adept at keeping out of sight behind a tree trunk and will lead a hunter a long chase by flying from tree to tree well in advance of him. When shot dead, it may cling for some time to the branch or trunk, until its muscles relax and allow it to fall. If wounded, it keeps up a constant chatter while falling and will not become quiet while life remains; a wounded bird should be handled carefully, for it can inflict a painful wound with its powerful beak.

Audubon (1842) relates the following story, as told to him by the Rev. John Bachman: "A pair of pileated woodpeckers had a nest in an old elm tree, in a swamp, which they occupied that year; the next spring early, two blue-birds took possession of it, and there had young. Before these were half grown, the woodpeckers returned to the place, and, despite of the cries and reiterated attacks of the blue-birds, the others took the young, not very gently, as you may imagine, and carried them away to some distance. Next the nest itself was disposed of, the hole cleaned and enlarged, and there they raised a brood. The nest, it is true, was originally their own."

Robert P. Allen has sent me the following note: "When in one of the Carolina river swamps with Herbert L. Stoddard, early in December 1936, we were interested in the actions of pileated woodpeckers that we called to us by tapping on the side of our cypress dug-out in imitation of the birds. We paddled our canoe close against the buttress of a large cypress tree, so that we were partially concealed by the trunk itself and by a dense growth of intertwining branches overhead. As many as four pileateds at one time responded to our efforts, and all these appeared to be males. As they swooped low, to get a look at this stranger in their midst, each bird made what we took to be an *intimidating* noise with its wings.

"From the immediate and pugnacious interest that these male (?) pileateds showed in our presence, it would seem as if they had previously cataloged the pileated population of that area and had, therefore, rushed over to investigate the presence of a bird that could not be accounted for, except as a stranger and a trespasser. Their efforts at intimidation were evidently designed to drive us out of the region."

Voice.—The most familiar note of the pileated woodpecker is the loud, ringing call, suggesting the "yucker" call of the flicker, but louder and stronger, less rapid, more prolonged, and on a lower key.

Mr. Simmons (1925) has summed up the notes of this woodpecker very well, as follows: "A loud *cac, cac, cac* as it flies. A sonorous *cow-cow-cow*, repeated many times; a clear *wichew*, when two birds are together. A loud cackle, like loud, ringing, derisive laughter, *chuck-chuck; chuck, chuck-ah, chuck, chuck-ah, chuck, chuck, chuck, chuck;* or *chuck, chuck, chuck, chuck, chuck, chuck, chuck.*"

Field marks.—The pileated woodpecker has the appearance of a large, black bird, nearly as large as a crow and somewhat like it in flight, but the large, white patches in the wings are distinctive, as well as the flaming red crest. As it bounds through the woods in long swinging flights from tree to tree, it is unmistakable. While hammering on a tree trunk, its long neck and heavy head and beak are conspicuous and distinctive.

Winter.—Throughout most of its range the southern pileated woodpecker is a permanent resident; in fact, there is very little southward movement for the species, even in the more northern portions of its range, except for winter wanderings in search of a suitable food supply.

Vernon Sharpe, Jr. (1932), writing from Tennessee, says: "The winter roosting place of this bird is rather interesting. A live hollow tree is selected, and there two or more holes are dug, presumably with the thought of using one for escape should any attack by some night marauder take place. These roosting places are used year after year; in fact, there is one site in the Overton Hills, south of Nashville, that has been used for so many seasons it has become essential for the woodpecker to cut away a portion of the tree that is trying to heal over the cavity."

DISTRIBUTION

Range.—North America; chiefly timbered regions east of the Great Plains and from southern Mackenzie to western Montana and California.

The range of the pileated woodpecker extends **north** to northern British Columbia (Buckley Lake and Thutade Lake); southern Mackenzie (Fort Liard and Fort Smith); northern Saskatchewan (Poplar Point); northeastern Ontario (Moose Factory); and southeastern Quebec (Godbout and Mont Louis Lake). **East** through the wooded areas along the Atlantic coast to southeastern Florida (Everglades, Royal Palm Hammock, and Key West). **South** along the Gulf coasts of Florida, Mississippi, and Louisiana, to southeastern Texas (San Point). The species is not known through the southern Rocky Mountain and Great Basin regions, appearing next in central California (Yosemite Valley and Napa County). From the latter point it occurs north along the Pacific coast through Oregon and Washington, to northwestern British Columbia (Hazelton and Buckley Lake).

The range above outlined is for the entire species, which has, however, been separated into four subspecies. The southern pileated woodpecker (*C. p. pileatus*) is found in the Eastern United States from central Texas and northern Florida north to Oklahoma, southern Illinois, southern Indiana, southern Pennsylvania, and Maryland; the northern pileated woodpecker (*C. p. abieticola*), occupies the balance of the range in Eastern North America, except for the peninsula of Florida to which the Florida pileated woodpecker (*C. p. floridanus*) is restricted. The western pileated woodpecker (*C. p. picinus*) is found chiefly in the humid areas of the Northwest coast district but also south to central California and east to western Montana and Idaho.

Casual records.—Two specimens have been taken in North Dakota, one at Grafton on May 30, 1905, and the other at Fargo on October 16, 1915. It may occur rarely in Wyoming, although no specimen is at present known. The Colorado and New Mexico records are not considered satisfactory.

Egg dates.—Alberta: 18 records, May 10 to June 22; 9 records, May 15 to 30, indicating the height of the season.

Arkansas: 18 records, April 5 to May 15; 9 records, April 15 to 30.

Florida: 32 records, March 22 to May 25; 16 records, April 10 to 23.

New Hampshire: 6 records, May 6 to 25.

Pennsylvania: 7 records, April 23 to May 21.

Texas: 8 records, March 4 to May 16.

CEOPHLOEUS PILEATUS ABIETICOLA Bangs

NORTHERN PILEATED WOODPECKER

PLATES 20–24

HABITS

CONTRIBUTED BY BAYARD HENDERSON CHRISTY

This, the largest race of *Ceophloeus pileatus*, inhabits the forests of the Transition and Canadian Zones, from the Atlantic coast to the Rocky Mountains. In the South it is replaced by *C. p. pileatus* and in the West by *C. p. picinus.* The southern limit of its range lies across southern Pennsylvania, West Virginia, central Ohio, southern Indiana, southern Illinois, and Missouri. The most northerly record of its occurrence is that of John Reid, noted by Bendire (1895). He took a specimen on Big Island, in Great Slave Lake (lat. 61° N.). Bangs (1898), who described the northern form and named it *C. p. abieticola,* believed that in the mountains of Virginia and West Virginia lay the line of transition from the southern to the northern form; but later investigators have determined that the line lies, as first noted above, somewhat northward of Bangs' location.

The characteristics that distinguish the northern from the southern form are greater size, longer bill, slatiness rather than sootiness of the black of the plumage, and greater extent of the white areas.

Catesby (1731) depicted the bird (in its southern form) and called it "the large red-crested woodpecker"; and Linnaeus (1758), citing Catesby as his source, named it, for his purposes, *pileatus* (= crested). Following Linnaeus, the English naturalist Latham (1783) began in 1781 to publish his General Synopsis; and he, lacking knowledge of the bird in its haunts, and finding Catesby's circumlocution unwieldy, took from Linnaeus's Latin, as a name for common usage, "pileated woodpecker." The indications are that Latham coined the name; certainly he gave it currency.

The bird already possessed a common name; and it is a pity that Latham did not know it. In its native land it was, and still is, commonly called, the log-cock. That is a good name—apt, picturesque, and widely used. Wilson (1811) knew it well enough, and so did Audubon (1842) ; and they would have done well, had they given it place as the established vernacular name. But Wilson, under Bartram's tutelage, followed Latham, and Audubon followed Wilson. They, in their prestige, have settled the matter. Nuttall (1832) tried to make a stand for log-cock, and others since have tried, but in vain. And now upon this splendid creature a dull piece of pedantry remains hopelessly fixed.

Another homespun name in extensive use is *Cock-of-the-woods;* yet another is *Wood-cock.* This last is suitable enough, but it leads obviously to confusion. Accordingly, within the range of the true woodcock (*Philohela minor*), the woodpecker is commonly distinguished as the "black woodcock." Other appellatives that have been picked up here and there and gathered in the books are "black woodpecker," "English woodpecker," "black log," "king-of-the-woods," "stump breaker"; and, because of its cackling cry, "wood-hen," "Indian-hen," "laughing woodpecker," "johnny-cock," "woodchuck," and "cluck-cock." (The last, given by Scoville, 1920, as current in Juniata County, Pa., is, perhaps, an assimilation from the Pennsylvania Dutch.)

The subspecific name *abieticola* (=dweller amid fir trees) is in some degree misleading, for, in the Northeastern States at least, the bird is commonly found in forests of mingled conifers and hardwoods; it shows no partiality to firs, nor even to conifers generally; and it cuts its nesting cavities, in the large majority of cases, in the dead and standing trunks of deciduous trees. In the Rocky Mountains, however, according to the Weydemeyers (1928), it prefers growths of larch, yellow pine, and Douglas fir.

It is a denizen of extensive forests. It will adapt itself to second growth—particularly where the young trees have sprung up about some remnant of the old; but in any case it requires wide areas. As forests dwindle to woodlots, along with the wild turkey, the barred owl, and the raven, it disappears. From regions once forested but now devoted to agriculture it is gone; in the mountains, however, in the marginal areas, where wooded ridges extend out to the plains, and in forested swamp lands, it continues. In such territories, indeed, its numbers during the past 50 years have increased, and it has reappeared in localities once deserted. Reports of such recrudescence are many, and they come from widely scattered places, particularly in the States to eastward of the Mississippi River.

Roger T. Peterson (MS.) says: "The pileated woodpecker has greatly increased in the Northeast during the past few years. At one time it was nearly gone from many parts of New York State and southern New England, where it had occurred in fair numbers. The bird disappeared from northern New Jersey about 1880, and from southern New Jersey in 1908. About 1920 W. DeWitt Miller found it again at two or three points in northern New Jersey; and now it is fairly common in many places in the northern part of the State, and as far east as in Bergen County, within 15 miles of New York City. Within the past 5 years it has reappeared in the lower Hudson Valley. It is especially common in some portions of south-western New York State. In one recent year I found four nests near the city of Jamestown, N. Y. Similar increases have been noted by bird students in Massachusetts, Connecticut, Ohio, and Missouri"—and, he might have added, in Pennsylvania.

Ludlow Griscom (1929) wrote: "I incline to the view that the increase in this Woodpecker is not so much due to conservation, as to its adaptation to less primeval conditions. The generation that regarded this species as a game-bird died off in this Region [the Northeastern States] before it returned."

Granted that the species shows itself to be adaptable, it still is pertinent to note other ameliorations of circumstance. When lumbering operations have been carried through to completion, when the camps are gone from the woods, and when new growth has begun to spring up, it is generally true that animal life in its larger forms tends to reappear and to increase. Again, the development of more fertile lands in the West has had effect in the abandonment of poorer lands in the East. Extensive areas, in New England particularly, that a hundred years ago were farmed, have now long since returned to wilderness. The forests of second growth, as they approach maturity, may be supposed increasingly to afford the food resources proper to this denizen of the great forests. And, finally, protective laws have been more intelligently framed, more widely adopted, and more generally respected.

The birds range over plain and mountain side. They prefer "the edges of the balsam and cedar swamps, when surrounded with forests of hardwood and hemlocks" (Blackwelder, 1909, Iron County, Mich.). Their nesting places are ordinarily in lowlands, and near water. In the region where I have known them best—the Huron Mountains, in Marquette County, Mich.—I have found the birds to occur in pairs or families at intervals of two or three miles along the course of a river that flows through primeval forest land. This I take to be a fair indication of the saturation point in pileated woodpecker population.

Migration.—Generally speaking, the species is resident wherever found. Some of the earlier naturalists supposed that it retired in winter from the more northerly portions of its range; but none affords any evidence. George Miksch Sutton (1930), when ornithologist for the Game Commission of Pennsylvania, having reviewed the reports of the wardens, said that they tended to indicate a gradual movement of the birds in winter around the eastern end of Lake Erie and southward into Pennsylvania. Such may be the case. On the other hand, it is true that, after the nesting season has passed, and throughout fall and winter, the birds wander and appear in areas where at other seasons they are unknown; and it may be that Dr. Sutton's wardens were basing their reports upon such seasonal reappearances. More precise observations must be made before it can be asserted with confidence that there is migration in any sense other than that here recognized.

Courtship.—It is usual to find the birds associated in pairs, even after the nesting season has passed; and from this the inference has been drawn (Morrell, 1901; Knight, 1908) that they continue, year after year, constantly mated. Lewis O. Shelley, writing from East Westmoreland, N. H., says (MS.): "It is my belief that the pileated mates for life, for, seen almost daily, one pair is known to have shown no active spring display for the past few years, nor was a third bird (male) seen near." This inference may be sound; nevertheless, an element of conjecture here should not be overlooked, and further data should be sought.

In some cases, certainly, the birds engage in mating antics, and Edmund W. Arthur (1934) relates an example:

On April 14, 1933, while driving with a companion * * * from Slippery Rock [Pennsylvania] * * * to Grove City, I observed a Pileated Woodpecker * * * flying across the highway a short distance south of Barmore Run. Stopping our car, we got out and followed the bird with our eyes, until it alighted on a tall tree a thousand feet away in the swampy woodland. Presently another, and then a third, were seen. They were quite restless, though apparently fearless, as evidenced by their flying about, alighting in plain view of us upon trees not fifty yards distant. After several minutes one of them—a female we thought—alighted upon a grassy knoll in a pasture to the left of the road, where it walked about for a brief interval, until a second came to the knoll and approached within three or four feet of the first. Then began a curious movement, much resembling the dance of Flickers, wherein with bowing and scraping one bird, stepping sideways, made a circle about the other, who slowly turned, facing the performer. When the dance ceased there was a sudden jerky movement on the part of each, and thereupon they flew away. There are two houses at the intersection, and the people living in one of them told us that a pair of these birds had nested the year before in a maple just in the rear of their house.

Francis H. Allen has written a description of a formal dance at a season remote from mating time; and, since the description has not been published, and since it is pertinent to the question of permanence of mating, it is here given at length:

"On the side of Mount Monadnock, N. H., October 13, 1908, I watched two birds executing a sort of dance. When first seen they were clinging to the bole of a spruce, near the ground. They hopped up and down the trunk, frequently pecking at each other's bills simultaneously, now on one side of the tree, now on the other. When I got too near they flew a short distance to another tree, and I followed them about from tree to tree for about half an hour, often within 50 or 60 feet of them. They always lit at the base of the tree and worked up a few feet, seldom going more than 5 feet up, I think. They hopped backward and downward a great deal, and often they lifted and partly spread their wings. Their motions were limber and undulating, marked by a certain awkward grace, without the stiffness of the smaller woodpeckers. The crests were elevated occasionally. I noticed no difference in the markings, but I was then unacquainted with the sexual differences of the species, and I cannot say whether or not they were male and female. They occasionally uttered a faint *wahk, wahk, wahk,* in a soft, conversational tone; but it was for the most part a silent performance."

The bird drums a roll, as do other woodpeckers. The only other drumming of comparable intensity is that of the yellow-bellied sapsucker, but commonly the pileated woodpecker's performance is so heavy as to be unmistakable. Often the drumming consists not of a roll but of slow heavy beats. Dr. Sutton (1930) writes: "On May 19, 1925, * * * I heard a male drumming for over an hour * * * During the whole period there was a noticeable similarity of the performances * * * At least fifty or sixty times there was an introductory, rapidly given *roll;* then a pause, followed by three distinct blows, * * * giving much the impression of a queer rhythm beat upon an aboriginal drum." With this the description of the drumming of the sapsucker given by Dr. Harry C. Oberholser (1896b) may be compared.

Ernest Waters Vickers (1915) gives the following description of "the masterly roll of the great log-cock":

This roll is composed of twelve strokes or blows, forming an ascending and descending climax; increasing in rapidity and volume to the middle and dying in force and rapidity just as it began. While the bird may not give the complete roll, may break off anywhere, it is always, so far as I have heard, a part of the above * * * A mellow yet powerful cellular jar to which the whole wooded heart of the forest makes echoing response—a solemn and ancient sound. * * *

Thus * * * I heard one drumming far away on a sounding board of peculiar musical resonance and power to carry * * * I had often heard this roll a full mile and a half away; once or twice I had even heard it in the house with doors and windows closed! * * * This old sounding-board was the hollow limb or arm of a big tulip tree or "white wood" flung out at right angle from the trunk 60 or 70 feet from the ground, a mere shell as appeared * * * sound and hard and barkless. The spot where he hammered was white where the weathered gray fibers had been beaten off by constant use. * * *

That April day * * * he sat upright upon the limb grasping it firmly, * * * poising himself, making a motion or two as a neat penman about to begin writing starts with a preliminary flourish, struck the limb somewhat lightly at first and deliberately, accelerating both speed and power, diminishing to stop as he started. He then paused to listen to the effect, attend to the echoes, or wait for the response of his mate perhaps, which occasionally rolled back from somewhere away east in the woods. He would hop about a trifle, cock his head examining his neighborhood a little, dress his feathers or search for parasites;—but not for long did he forget what he was there for; then gather himself up for another reverberation. With such energy did he hammer that his whole body shook and his wings quivered. He fairly hurled himself wildly at it. The great loose hair-like scarlet crest flowed in the sun and his scarlet moustache added to his noble and savage appearance."

Nesting.—The birds are very tenacious of their nesting places, returning year after year to the same location and even to the same tree trunk. It is usual to find several nesting holes (and, perhaps, winter quarters too) within an area, say, 100 yards square. In such preference, held to even when the forest has been partially cut down, the reason probably lies why nests sometimes are found in open places. Commonly, however, the nesting stub stands in heavy forest and within the shadow of the leafy canopy. There are a few records of nests on mountain sides and ridges, but, typically, the nesting tree stands in valley or bottomland and near the margin of lake or stream or in a swamp. The boles of trees riddled and furrowed in the pursuit of food are in no case used for nesting. An ant-infested trunk may be supposed to be definitely not suitable for such use.

Data are at hand upon 33 nests, from points widely scattered throughout the range. Of these, one cavity was sunk in a large dead hemlock, one in a dead pitch pine, one in a telegraph pole (an oddity—Roberts, 1932), and 30 in the boles of deciduous trees. Three are reported as dug in living trees; four are more particularly reported as in the dead tops of living trees; the remaining 20-odd were, certainly most of them, and (for all that appears) all of them, in dead stubs. Of the 30, eight were in beech trees; six in poplar, and a seventh in tulip poplar. Three were in birches, three in oaks, three in hickories. Two were in sugar maples and one in a red maple. One was in an ash, one in an elm, and one in a basswood. One was as low as 15 feet from the ground; three as high as 70 feet. The average height was about 45 feet.

The trunk at the point where the hole is drilled will ordinarily be from 15 to 20 inches in diameter. The hole commonly, though not invariably, faces the east or the south. Such is the preferred position, but, as may be supposed, the slope of the surface of the tree trunk and the quality of the wood are factors in the choice; and holes sometimes are found drilled in west and north faces of the trunks. The hole may be drilled through bark; more frequently it is through the bleached and bonelike surface of a stub from which the bark has long been stripped away. Though sometimes quite circular, the hole tends to be of triangular outline, peaked above and leveled below. The lower margin of the hole is outwardly and downwardly beveled and very nicely finished. The orifice varies from $3\frac{1}{4}$ to $4\frac{1}{2}$ inches in diameter, and typically may be $3\frac{1}{4}$ inches in width and $3\frac{1}{2}$ in vertical extent. The only other notable item in external appearance is that, if the tree be bare of bark and smooth surfaced (as is usual), an area of surface a few inches below the hole will be seen to have become polished by the rubbing of the tail feathers of the parent birds. And this spot, perhaps in consequence of difference in the absorption of moisture and fungus growth, may persist and be still plainly discernible in later years.

A nesting tree that may be regarded as typical stood in a dense forest, entirely of hardwood—maples, elms, and yellow birches—on the plain of a high and ancient beach of Lake Superior, cut through by a mountain stream, and about a hundred yards from the water. It was the smooth and barkless stub of a dead elm, about 45 feet high and having a girth, breast-high, of 76 inches. The bole was smooth and white, and the wood was still firm. The stub stood well shaded beneath the living trees. A few flecks of morning sunlight fell upon its eastern face; but throughout the greater part of the day it remained in shadow. It had been the woodpeckers' nesting place certainly for four years. The highest hole seemed to be the oldest—in the south face and near the top. The uppermost 6 feet of the stub had since become weathered and checked and manifestly unsuitable. Next, on the north face, there was an old and black-looking hole about 36 feet up. The third and lowest hole was in the east face and about 25 feet up; and, lastly, there was the hole of the year, 34 feet up and also in the east face.

The chamber within is capacious and is ordinarily of conical form, tapering slightly from a low domed roof downward to a bowllike bottom. There may be a slight bulging of the walls below a narrowed median portion. The depth may vary from 10 to 24 inches (extreme figures of 6 and 26 have been recorded). The average of 15 measurements is 19 inches. The entrance hole leads to the upper widest portion, and there the chamber is 7 or 8 inches across. The distance from the outer surface of the bole of the tree to the remote wall of the chamber is about 11 inches. The entrance passageway about 2 inches inward is ridged across, and from this median ridge the floor of the passageway slopes downward, both inwardly and outwardly, and this outward slope forms the bevel already mentioned. The bowl at the bottom is 6 or 6½ inches across. In a specimen before me as I write, the wall of the chamber below the entrance hole is 4 inches thick. The ridge across the floor of the entrance passageway is rounded. Its crest is 2¼ inches inward from the outer surface of the tree trunk, and the vertical depth of the outward bevel is 2 inches. All the surfaces of the cavity are neatly and uniformly chiseled. Along the sides of the entrance passageway extend in parallel curves the tool marks of the bird's beak. No nesting materials are brought in. A feather or two will be the only trace of occupancy remaining after the young are flown. In some though not in all cases it is possible for a man to thrust in his arm and reach the bottom of the chamber.

As a general rule, certainly, a new cavity is drilled for every brood. Such exceptions as have been recorded have explanation in human interference. Samuel Scoville, Jr. (1920), quotes Richard C. Harlow to the effect that but once in his experience had a second use of a nesting cavity occurred. Afterward Mr. Harlow said to me in conversation that even in that instance the cavity had been deepened before it was used for a second time. The only other instance that has come to my attention is one recorded by Morrell (1901) in which a single cavity was used three times—in 1895, in 1897, and in 1898. In preparation for the third nesting the cavity had been deepened by three inches. This nesting was in "a small patch of good sized trees * * * separated [from] the main growth by cutting," and it may be supposed that the woodpeckers had been unduly limited in the choice of nesting sites. In both cases the birds were subject to the disturbance of persistent egg-collecting. It stands to reason that, in avoidance of parasites, the practice should have evolved of drilling a fresh cavity for each brood.

Mr. Harlow (1914) found that in one instance the drilling of the nesting cavity was in progress in March and was continued "all during March and April." The female worked alone, and the male continued near by. This nest, an unusually early one, contained, on April 30, three eggs. In the Northern States the eggs commonly are laid early in May. Incubation continues, according to Burns (1915), for 18 days. The young leave the nest about the middle of June.

The range of date in nesting is illustrated by two records that come from Centre County, Pa. (Scoville, 1920; Burleigh, 1931). One is of a set of eggs that hatched on May 11. These eggs must have been laid before April 23. The other record is of a set collected May 11 and found to be practically fresh. The interval at which these two cases stand apart is about 25 days. Scoville (1920) quotes Harlow, a collector whose experience was chiefly in Centre County, to the effect that "May 10 is the standard date for a full clutch of eggs."

Records of nests are at hand from Maine, New Hampshire, New York, Pennsylvania, Ohio, and Wisconsin. The total body of data, however, is small; and it is not possible to discover what the difference may be in mean nesting date from south to north within the region covered. There is a record from Maine, for instance (Morrell, 1901), of a set of eggs found to be heavily incubated as early as May 13.

Eggs.—The eggs are white, with a gleaming smoothness and translucence of shell. They rest at the bottom of the cavity, on the bare bed of finely splintered wood. Three eggs often complete the set, but more commonly four. Of 17 recorded sets, 4 are sets of three, and 13 are sets of four. Some of the earlier writers (Wilson, for instance, 1811) said the number of eggs might be five or even six; but no specific record of so large a number has been found. The eggs are of ovate outline.

The measurements of 51 eggs average 33.16 by 25.21 millimeters; the eggs showing the four extremes measure **38.2** by **27.1, 30.2** by 25.2, and **33.05** by **23.75** millimeters.

There are cases on record in which a pair of these birds, robbed of their eggs, have laid again (and in the same cavity); with this qualification, there is but a single brood in a season.

Young.—In a particular instance, which I take to be typical, of a nesting (in northern Fulton County, Pa.) I found the male to be no less attentive than the female to the duties of incubation and nurture. In one respect, indeed, the male seemed to be the more attentive, for on both of the two occasions when I had opportunity to observe—once shortly before, the other shortly after the hatching of the eggs—it was the male bird who at sunset retired within the hole and who at sunrise the following morning appeared from within. And I mention this the more confidently since I find chance confirmation in the narrative of another observer, Morrell (1901), and since like observations have been made upon other species of woodpeckers—upon the flicker, for instance, and upon the ivory-billed woodpecker (Allen, 1937).

When incubation was in progress I found the parent birds to be relieving one another at intervals of about two hours; and a week later, when the young were still small, they were coming in with food and replacing one another at intervals of approximately one hour. It may have been accidental, and yet it seemed to me noteworthy, that the routine of hourly visits was broken when the female returned after an absence of 10 minutes to afford the male freedom for 40 minutes before he returned to retire within the cavity for the night.

At the time when hatching was near, and afterward when the young were newly hatched, one or the other of the parent birds was constantly present in the nesting chamber and, the weather being warm, was much of the time perched immediately within the hole. And I then realized the value of the larger dimensions of the upper portion of the chamber. The waiting bird was constantly moving about, thrusting its head out and withdrawing it again, turning about within the chamber so that it had free view outward, preening, reaching upward with its foot and scratching its head. And all this movement was free because the space was wide.

Each of the parents seemed to have its own path of approach to the nest. One of them came almost invariably to a particular position on the trunk, about 6 feet below and to the right, and hopped up thence to the entrance, but the other bird followed a different course.

I was impressed, too, with the comparative silence of the birds at their nesting tree. Such small converse as took place there (a flicker-like *wuck-a-wuck*—and it occurred irregularly) was so soft as to be scarcely audible to human ears at a distance of fifty yards.

The feeding of the young is by regurgitation; and, while the young are still small and remain at the bottom of the nesting cavity, the parents may be seen to follow an interesting routine. The incoming bird hops to the hole, perches on the ridge of the entrance passageway, and then swings inward and downward, at the same time elevating the posterior part of its body until the tail presses upon the outer upper rim of the hole. In this position, evidently, the parent's bill meets those of the nestlings. This attitude is maintained often for as much as a minute, and while it is maintained the body of the bird may be seen to shake convulsively— plainly indicating that regurgitation is in progress.

When the young are small, the parent, after feeding, does not immediately leave the nest but awaits the incoming of its mate. It then glides away on wide-spread wings; and, while I suspected that the excrement of the young is carried in the bill and dropped, I was unable to detect this. Quite possibly, in this early stage at least, the excrement is swallowed by the parent.

Charles W. Townsend (1925) gave account of a family observed in Worcester County, Mass., when the young were well developed and nearly ready to leave the nest:

On June 11, 1924, I spent five hours within twenty-five feet of the base of the stub, unconcealed, and on June 14, six hours, but after the first hour I took up a position about fifty yards away, partially concealed by bushes.

My observations may be summarized as follows: the young were fed eleven times at the first visit, four times at the second when the adults acted in a very shy manner. As a rule the female fed the young, but on three occasions the male was identified at the hole. * * *

As a rule the adult appeared suddenly at the hole, flying noiselessly through the forest. Occasionally it alighted below the hole and rapidly ascended by hops, or it alighted on some neighboring tree, and often calling like a Flicker, glided on motionless outstretched wings in a graceful curve to its young. The flight away from the hole was always direct after a preliminary downward glide and lacked the usual woodpecker undulations. * * *

The three young crowded to the hole as soon as a parent appeared anywhere in the neighborhood and eagerly stretched forth their heads and necks. * * * They were always hungry and screamed with rasping voices for food, once or twice they uttered low whinnies. The adult inserted its bill to its full length into the throats of the young and vigorously regurgitated and pumped in the nourishment. * * * After feeding the young, the female on several occasions, the male on one, entered the nest, to emerge after a minute or two and glide away. Once I detected a white piece in the bill, once, something dark, but the other times nothing at all.

Herbert L. Stoddard (1917) has noted the "hissing" noise of the young within the nesting cavity when the trunk is jarred, "similar to young flickers, but a great deal louder."

When the young have flown from the nest, the cavity is not utterly abandoned. I once saw one of the parent birds reenter at midday a cavity from which the young had recently flown and remain within for 40 minutes. Why, I know not. The mate accompanied this returning bird and waited near by. Maurice Brooks writes (MS.): "Nest cavities are sometimes used as roosting places after the nesting season. On the evening of August 2, 1937, at Jacksons Mill [Lewis County, W. Va.], I saw six birds (two adults and four young) enter a cavity that had held a nest earlier in the season. This was probably the brood of the year, with the parents."

Food.—The pileated woodpecker lives upon insects that infest standing and fallen timber and supplements this diet with wild berries and acorns.

Ants are the chief item of food. It is in pursuit of ants that the woodpecker cuts its great furrows in the boles of standing trees, living and dead. On examination the heart wood exposed by the woodpecker's operations will be found to have been penetrated by the labyrinthine passageways of the great carpenter ants, *Camponotus herculeanus* (Linnaeus).

All the observations of others that have come to my attention upon the woodpecker when actually engaged in cutting these great trunk-penetrating chasms have been made in winter and early in spring, and with them my own are in agreement. It is a natural surmise that only in winter is such heavy work done, since in summer proper food is more easily available. Another surmise along the same lines is that the disappearance of the bird from particular areas, followed after an interval of years by reappearance, may perhaps have occurred in correspondence with precisely such a fluctuation in its essential, wintertime food supply: it must find, when the ground is snow-covered, ant-infested trunks of large trees.

In September I once made leisurely observation upon a bird at work upon a dead but standing hemlock tree. With swinging, obliquely directed blows it was splitting off the outer leaves of the scalelike bark and pausing intermittently with head turned to the trunk, licking up, as I supposed, the insect life thus exposed. Again, in September, I came upon a pair feeding together upon the ground. They had been tearing up a carpet of moss that spread over damp surfaces both of wood and of rock, and I thought that their prey must be insect life that they were finding in the moss itself.

And yet again, on September 21, I watched for many minutes an adult female feeding on a charred and decayed stump that remained in a young forest of jack pines. She was perched about a foot from the ground. Her method was by deliberate and swinging blows to break away platelike fragments of still firm wood, and then to intrude her bill and search with her tongue (as was evident) the opened cavity. This licking was always, or nearly always, upward, and often the head was turned, crown inward, throat outward. A jay might call or some other forest sound be heard, and the bird would pause, listen for an instant, and then resume her work. A day or two later I visited the stump and with my knife made an incision in it, and I found it to be the home of a colony of ants—not of the large *Camponotus* but of a smaller, wine-black species about a quarter of an inch long. The body of the stump was honeycombed with their galleries.

Of the major wintertime operations Vickers (1910) has written:

Like the flicker, the [pileated woodpecker] is a great lover of ants, which accordingly occupy a large place in his bill-of-fare. So, to dine on the big black timber ants, which are his special delight, he drives holes to the very heart of growing forest trees, tapping the central chamber of the colony, where, in winter, he finds the dormant swarm unable to move and feasts upon them at leisure . . . And the Log-cock makes no mistakes, though man might find no outward sign of an ant-tree. Doubtless that strong formic smell, coupled with his experience in sounding tree trunks,—as a man tells a ripe watermelon by the *plunk* of it,—enables him not only to find the tree, but, what is more remarkable, to drive his hole with such precision that he taps the heart of the community.

O. M. Bryens (1926) wrote from St. Joseph County, Mich.:

On February 16, 1925, I was able to approach within twelve feet of one of these Woodpeckers busily engaged in digging in a maple stub, two feet in diameter and about twelve feet high. He was after insects whose borings I found later upon examining the wood. I watched him for about an hour.

He seldom gave more than three or four pecks at a time, and would then swing his head round to one side or the other, sometimes raising his scarlet crest. He seldom threw back his head without tossing a chip back of him, and when I examined his work after he had left, later in the day, I found some chips near the stub, which were three inches long and one inch wide. Others half this size had been thrown out on the snow a distance of four feet. The hole was on the west side and measured six inches across and ten inches long, and extended to a depth of six inches toward the heart of the stub. There was another hole six inches square on the south side. The bird seemed to chisel out a section three inches wide across the hole and then move down and cut out another section. The two holes were dug in about two hours.

Of summertime feeding Ora W. Knight (1908) says: "Except the Flicker this is the only species of Woodpecker I have observed feeding on the ground, but this species likes to tear open the ant hills found in open places in the woods and feed on the ants and their larvæ." He also says that in the fall these birds eat "dogwood berries, choke and black cherries and other wild fruits and berries, also beechnuts and acorns for which it has a decided fondness."

Dr. Sutton (1930) says:

The food of this species in Pennsylvania, according to official examination of four stomachs, is largely of ants. The stomach and crop of a male specimen weighing nine ounces, collected at Northumberland, Northumberland County, on November 10, 1928, contained 469 carpenter ants (*Camponotus herculaneus*), most of them so recently swallowed as to permit of counting them easily. The stomach of a female taken at Aitch, Huntingdon County, on November 30, 1928, contained the remains of at least 153 carpenter ants, one small carabid beetle, the legs of a small bug (apparently a squash-bug), and 17 wild grapes, swallowed whole.

F. E. L. Beal (1911) gave the results of examination of the contents of 80 stomachs collected far and wide throughout the range of the species. Animal food amounted to 72.88 percent; vegetable, 27.12 percent. Beetles made up 22.01 percent of the total, and ants 39.91 percent. As many as 2,600 ants were counted in a single stomach. The ants were "mostly of the larger species that live in decaying timber." Ants and beetles together made up the bulk of the animal food (61.92 percent).

The Biological Survey (A. L. Nelson) has kindly made reply to my inquiry concerning stomach examinations of the subspecies *abieticola* alone. Data were available from 23 specimens, three collected in January, two in June, two in July, six in October, eight in November, and two in December. They were collected, two in Canada, two in New Brunswick, four in New York, four in Pennsylvania, six in Michigan, two in Illinois, two in Minnesota, and one in Iowa.

Animal food amounted to 83 percent of the whole; vegetable, 17 percent, with but a trace of gravel (one stomach only). The chief item was ants, principally large black ants, such as *Camponotus* and *Crematogaster;* this item alone constituted 60 percent of the whole. The animal food otherwise consisted of a variety of beetles and of a very few (2 percent) caterpillars. The vegetable food was made up of wild berries (*Ilex, Cassine, Vitis cordifolia, Nyssa sylvatica,* and *Viburnum nudum*—in all, 11 percent of the whole), mast (2 percent), and rotten wood (4 percent).

Catesby's (1731) assertion, repeated time and again by the earlier writers, that the pileated woodpecker sometimes pierces the husks of maize standing in the field, was almost certainly based on faulty observation. No modern confirmation is to be found of this or of any other predatory practice. To the contrary, the finding after careful investigation (Beal, 1911) is: "The food of the pileated woodpecker does not interest the farmer or horticulturist, for it is obtained entirely from the forest or the wild copses on its edge. This bird does not visit either the orchard or the grain field, and all its work in the forest helps to conserve the timber * * *. Its killing should be strictly prohibited at all times."

Behavior.—The bird is but little known—surprisingly little, considering how large a bird it is. It is a forest dweller; it lives almost wholly within the canopy of the treetops; it is alert, furtive (almost) as a bear, rather silent in midsummer (the season when city dwellers ordinarily visit the northern forests); and it easily eludes observation. It is not strange then that, its gigantic operations remaining in evidence, the bird itself should in common thought have become a somewhat fabulous creature. Thoreau (1906) never saw it; and this is what he wrote of it in the Moosehead Lake journal under date of July 25, 1857: "Our path up the bank here led by a large dead white pine, in whose trunk near the ground were great square-cornered holes made by the woodpeckers. * * * They were seven or eight inches long by four wide and reached to the heart of the tree through an inch or more of sound wood, and looked like great mortise-holes whose corners had been somewhat worn and rounded by a loose tenon. The tree for some distance was quite honeycombed by them. It suggested woodpeckers on a larger scale than ours, as were the trees and the forest."

To one who visits its haunts the presence of the pileated woodpecker is immediately made manifest by operations such in magnitude as to have astonished Thoreau. Dead Norway pines may be found, gaunt and bare, their bark split away in plates and lying heaped at the base, and living white pines—young trees, particularly—pierced to the core with deep pyramidal incisions. The freshly cut wood gleams clean, and turpentine in pellucid globules rims the cut and drips downward. Great boles of maples and basswoods stand, furrowed from broken top to base, the ground below littered with splinters, often half a hand's breadth in extent. The cuts are roughly rectangular in outline. They may be 4, 5, or even 6 or 8 inches wide and are sunk deep into the heart of the tree. They may extend vertically for a few inches or for a foot or more. They may be aligned in vertical rows, and may run together in furrows of several feet in length. Crumbling stumps and moss-covered logs lying on the forest floor will often be found ripped and torn by the woodpecker's beak.

It is, as has been said, a wary creature, and is not easily stalked. On one occasion, when I had successfully approached a male that was idling in the top of a gaunt chestnut near the nesting tree, I paused, before shifting from an uncomfortable position, until the bird should sidle around the limb. Even so, he was quicker than I; for, before I had completed my movement, he was peering from the opposite side, and, detecting me, was off. Again I came upon a bird—a male—suddenly, in open forest. He did not immediately take wing, but, hitching downward upon the tree trunk, he reached the ground, hopped off, and then flitted away through the undergrowth, so that I scarcely saw him go. And when I came upon him again he repeated the maneuver.

With all their alertness, the birds have a large store of curiosity. Dr. Sutton (1930) has remarked that some individuals will "fly up hastily and boldly upon hearing a commotion in the woods." They may sometimes be called up by imitating their cry, by clapping together the cupped palms of one's hands, or by pounding with a billet of wood upon a tree trunk. I was following one morning a forest trail, where I knew a pair of the woodpeckers to be in residence, and had a glimpse, as I walked, of a large bird flying away. There stood against the sky, in the direction of the retreat, the stub of a great treetop. Pausing in my tracks, I waited until, after a few minutes, the suspected woodpecker came leaping up the stub— to have a look at me, as I supposed. In such case, the square shoulders of the bird, the slender white-striped neck, and the hammer head with its pointed scarlet crest are very conspicuous.

Maurice Brooks (1934) has remarked upon the playfulness of the birds when at ease.

For all their alertness, it remains still to be said that on occasion, when the birds are feeding, or when tending a nestful of young, it is possible to approach quietly and to remain watching, while they, unheeding, continue their activities.

It is common to find hairy and downy woodpeckers associated with the pileated, both on nesting grounds and when feeding. There is here, I believe, some measure of commensalism. I have in mind an observation upon a downy on the same dead hemlock tree with a pileated woodpecker. The larger bird was scaling off the bark and feeding; the smaller seemed to be gleaning over areas the pileated had left.

Tucked in the niche formed by a great furrowlike incision in the bole of a basswood tree, and about 10 feet from the ground, I once found a nest of the olive-backed thrush.

When I cut down the stub of which I have spoken, and which contained four old nesting cavities of the pileated woodpecker, I found the lowest, 25 feet from the ground, to be occupied by a family of white-footed mice (*Peromyscus maniculatus*), and I have no doubt that these cavities, after their abandonment by the woodpeckers, are commonly used by flying squirrels, by owls, and by tree-nesting ducks.

Prof. Brooks (1934) has most engagingly described the enticement of pileated woodpeckers to come to feeding trays, and, incidentally, has adduced evidence of their traits of caution and of curiosity. To this he adds (MS.): "I have indicated, in an article in Bird-Lore, that we have found Pileated Woodpeckers something of clowns. The gourd experience described in the above-mentioned article seemed to be in a spirit of play. The evident curiosity displayed by many birds observed is noteworthy; under its urge they apparently lose much of their fear. Around our blinds they have used a slow and cautious approach, but once at the feeding shelves, they have not been particularly nervous or excitable. At times I have found them surprisingly tame in the open woods."

The pileated woodpecker lives, as has been said, almost entirely within the forest cover. Its flight is commonly a matter of gliding and of slow-measured flapping through the trees. Its appearance then is unmistakable—large and black, with a flashing pattern of white beneath the wings, and a gleaming scarlet crest.

At times it rises above the treetops and moves over greater distances, and then its manner of flight bears greater likeness to the typical bounding or galloping flight of the generality of woodpeckers. Its outline against the sky is not unlike a kingfisher's. Dr. Sutton (1930) describes an encounter in the Pennsylvania mountains with a bird that "cackled for about fifteen minutes, pounding intermittently on a tree trunk. It then rose in air, mounted to a plane above the tree-tops, and flew in direct course down the valley, uttering a single, loud, even-toned *puck* about every two seconds, as far as we could hear it. The bird was still flying high when it faded from view."

Cornelius Weygandt (1912) described from Monroe County, Pa., the appearance of "the Logcock that in late July and early August made the sunset hour more memorable by its passing":

It was on the evening of July 26 that we first saw him * * * we noticed a large bird flying heron-like toward us. He passed us and made his way onward toward a tall broken-topped gum tree that stood out black against the sunset. He "landed" on its side near the top, woodpecker fashion, and bobbed downtrunk backwards for several yards. The sky was mauve and gold and crimson, and the great bird loomed blacker and bigger than he really was, limned sharply against it. He had not dropped along like the smaller woodpeckers, but had kept on more steadily, very like a heron, with only slight risings and fallings. After a rest on the gum tree of some three minutes he flung himself into the air and dove down into the Buck Hill Gorge.

Vickers (1915) characterizes the bird's flight as "powerful and straight-forward, his head and neck carrying his powerful beak like a spear * * * [the bird] large as a crow and with a certain short, sturdy, kingfisherlike aspect."

In general conclusion it may be said that the pileated woodpecker has the habit and manner of a giant, forest-loving flicker.

Voice.—Throughout the greater part of the year the pileated woodpecker is a relatively silent bird, but during the nesting season drumming and calling are frequent. The usual call is a cackle, resembling that of the flicker, though louder and of more sonorous quality. The "song" of the white-breasted nuthatch so far resembles it in pitch and tempo that a nuthatch near at hand may, for an instant, suggest the woodpecker far away. The *ka, ka, ka* of the woodpecker's cackle is variable in quality, in speed of iteration, and in continuity, and seems to be expressive, sometimes of alarm, sometimes of companionship, sometimes of contentment. Aretas A. Saunders (1935) has noted that often there is rise in pitch at the beginning of a rendition and a slight fall at the end; and Samuel Scoville, Jr. (1920), distinguishing this from the flicker's similar call, has remarked on "a queer little quirk at the end." When a pair of birds cackle in alternation, as commonly they do, a difference in pitch will be noted; but whether that be a constant sexual difference, or a matter of individuality merely, I cannot say.

In the nesting season the mated birds have another flickerlike *wuck-a-wuck* call that seems to be peculiarly associated with their conjugal relationship. They use it in courtship and when they relieve one another in attendance at the nest.

Dr. Sutton (1930) mentions yet another call and describes it as "whining notes, suggesting the *mew* of the yellow-bellied sapsucker." But it is more than that. It is a loud cry, that resembles the scream of a hawk. It is commonly reiterated slowly in five or six repetitions. Unless one were to follow the sound and discover its source, he would hardly impute it to this bird. It too, I believe, is a call peculiar to the nesting season.

When the bird is in flight a slowly uttered *puck, puck* may sometimes be heard, and sometimes what for lack of a better term may be called a creaking of the moving wings.

Besides these there is a high-pitched scream—"a bugle call," says Florence Merriam Bailey (1902), with which the bird greets the rising sun. Horace W. Wright (1912) has noted that in June the bird is first heard within a few minutes after sunrise and has described the awakening thus: "There are eight records, when a bird has been heard loudly rapping in the distance with slow and measured blows or has called lustily and long, sometimes answered by another."

Enemies.—The number of eggs laid suggests that there must be some wastage: that somewhere in the round of life the bird must be peculiarly exposed to destruction; and to this point Dr. Sutton (1930) speaks:

The Duck Hawk (*Rhynchodon peregrinus anatum*) appears to be the chief, indeed perhaps the only, natural enemy of this woodpecker in this State [Pennsylvania]. At Spruce Creek, Huntingdon County, where these falcons have nested for years, I found, on March 21, 1921, the head and plumage of a male woodpecker which had not been dead long. Near Palmerton, Carbon County, I saw a Duck Hawk pursue and with ease strike down a pileated woodpecker that had started to fly across the river. The hawk flew so fast that the woodpecker seemed to have been unaware of the pursuit. A cloud of feathers burst from the body of the victim as it collapsed. The duck hawk apparently winters regularly along some of our streams, and takes whatever comes along, with a preference, perhaps, for the somewhat larger birds; and to it the comparatively clumsy log cock falls easy prey. So far as I know, neither the great horned owl nor the Cooper's hawk ever captures the bird, and our stomach examinations of several hundred Goshawks revealed none of its bones or plumage, though this savage predator no doubt occasionally captures such birds as are to be found throughout the winter.

R. B. Simpson (1910) wrote: "I once shot a Sharp-shinned Hawk that was making a desperate attempt to catch a pileated * * *. A year or two ago in summer along a trout stream in virgin forest back in the mountains [of northern Pennsylvania], I came to a mossy spot where a pileated had been wrecked and a close inspection showed the tracks of a huge wildcat who had no doubt caught the big woodpecker on the ground or on a log." See also Bendire (1895).

In addition to man's disturbance of habitat with which this paper has had largely to do, the following matters are noteworthy:

Pennant (1785) wrote that the Indians made a practice of decking their calumets with the crests of these birds. And see Bendire (1895).

Audubon (1842) said of the pileated woodpecker: "Its flesh is tough, of a bluish tint, and smells so strongly of the worms and insects on which it generally feeds, as to be extremely unpalatable." Sutton (1930), however, was able to show, both by the testimony of living witnesses and by written record as well, that these birds, along with other smaller birds, were once commonly exposed for sale as food in city markets.

Major Bendire (1895) wrote:

I have occasionally seen bunches of these birds, numbering from four to twelve, exposed for sale in the markets of Washington, D. C. * * * I tried to eat one, when short of meat, while traveling through the Blue Mountains of Oregon, but I certainly can not recommend it. It feeds to a great extent on the large black wood ants, which impart to it a very peculiar, and to me an extremely unpleasant flavor, a kind of sweet-sour taste, which any amount of seasoning and cooking does not disguise, and I consider it as a very unpalatable substitute for game of any kind.

Winter.—As is true of other members of the family, the pileated woodpecker may in fall be found digging for himself a cavity for winter occupancy. Few birds other than the woodpeckers make what may be called habitations, except as part of or incident to the activities of reproduction. And in the case of the woodpeckers, while I know that in particular instances these winter retreats are not so used, I am unable to say that they never are subsequently used as nesting cavities.

Hoyes Lloyd (1932) wrote:

One of the most delightful bird adventures we have had at Rockcliffe Park [near the City of Ottawa] was the visit to us of a pileated woodpecker. It first came at 4:30 p. m., on October 12, 1928, and excavated a hole in a hollow basswood for sleeping quarters * * *. The chips, from live wood, were up to three inches by two inches in area, and an eighth of an inch thick. Each chip had two or three gouge-like beak marks across its surface. At 4:50 p. m. on the next day the pileated came home, and although we were all outdoors, it went directly to its own tree and after a brief survey of affairs in the vicinity, retired. The approach was silent except, possibly for a single Flicker-like note in the distance. About 9 a. m., on the 14th, our bird woke me up with a loud *kuk-kuk-kuk* call and it looked very large as it climbed up the home basswood. Promptly at quarter to five it came home, undoubtedly after a day among the big hardwoods of the neighborhood. We were all impressed by its great length of neck, as it swung its head with a curious bobbing motion, that was used, without doubt, to give a view on each side of the home tree, before going into the hole for the night. A pileated, thought to be the same bird, came back on March 22, 1929, possibly, or certainly on the 23rd, and slept in its winter home.

Prof. Brooks writes (MS.): "At French Creek [Upshur County, W. Va.], two birds used a nesting cavity as a roosting place during the following winter."

CEOPHLOEUS PILEATUS FLORIDANUS (Ridgway)

FLORIDA PILEATED WOODPECKER

HABITS

This is the race that is supposed to inhabit central and southern Florida, as far north as Orange County, but there seems to be some doubt as to the desirability of naming it. Ridgway (1914) describes it as "similar to *P. p. pileatus,* but decidedly blacker (that is, the general black color less slaty or sooty), and average size less, with bill usually relatively shorter and broader." But he admits his doubt, in a footnote, saying:

I have found it very difficult to decide as to the propriety of separating a form of this species from central and southern Florida, but after having several times laid out and carefully compared the entire series of specimens from more southern localities, have come to the conclusion that to do so will, apparently, best express the facts of the case. Going by size alone, there is little difference between specimens from southern and central Florida and those from localities as far northward as Maryland (lowlands), southern Illinois, and Missouri; in fact some of these more northern specimens are quite as small as Florida ones. But the series from central and southern Florida are uniformly decidedly blacker than the rest. * * * I have restricted the name *pileatus* to an intermediate form, characterized by the small size of *P. p. floridanus* combined with an appreciably lighter (more slaty or sooty) coloration, often approaching closely the lightness of hue of *P. p. abieticola.*

Bangs (1898), in separating the northern race from the southern, says that "southern South Carolina must be considered the type locality of the species, and birds from this region are as extreme of the southern race as those from Florida." Furthermore, Arthur H. Howell (1932) observes that "careful study of a large series from Florida in comparison with a series of typical *pileatus* from the Middle States shows no constant difference in color, as claimed by Ridgway for the subspecies '*floridanus*'; evidently specimens kept for some years become more brownish (less sooty), which fact probably explains Ridgway's mistake, he having compared fresh Florida skins with older skins from the Middle States." Probably, also, if specimens from the two regions in similar seasonal plumage were compared, there would not be so much difference in coloration as Ridgway claims. Even if Ridgway is correct in his diagnosis, it would seem unwise, in the author's opinion, to recognize the Florida race and thus establish an intermediate race, where the gradation in both size and color warrants the naming of only the two extremes.

Mr. Howell (1932) says of its haunts: "The pileated woodpecker in Florida inhabits several different types of country—pine woods, cypress swamps, hardwood swamps, and hammocks of cabbage palmetto and other trees. The birds are perhaps most numerous in hammocks or swamps, where there is an abundance of decaying trees."

Nesting.—Mr. Howell (1932) writes: "We found a number of pairs breeding in cypress trees along the borders of Lake Istokpoga. The nests are excavated either in living trees or in rotten stubs, from 12 to 75 feet from the ground. The trees commonly used for nesting sites are cypress, pine, black gum, oak, and cabbage palmetto." While collecting in the Florida Keys in 1908, I found a pair of pileated woodpeckers nesting on Murrays Key on April 3 and surprised one of the birds working in its nesting hole; the excavation was about 12 feet from the ground in the main trunk of a live black mangrove, which stood in the inner fringe of mangroves around the borders of the island. I climbed up to it and reached into the cavity but could not touch the bottom of it; we were unable to visit the island again.

Major Bendire (1895) writes:

In southern Florida the mating season commences early in March, and farther north correspondingly later. A suitable tree having been selected, generally a dead one in large and extensive woods, both birds work alternately on the nesting site. This is usually excavated in the main trunk, from 12 to 75 feet from the ground, and it takes from seven to twelve days to complete it. The entrance measures from 3 to 3½ inches in diameter, and it often goes 5 inches straight into the trunk before it is worked downward. The cavity varies from 7 to 30 inches in depth, and is gradually enlarged toward the bottom, where it is about 6 inches wide. A layer of chips is left at the bottom, on which the eggs are deposited. Occasionally the entrance hole, instead of being circular, is oval in shape, like that of the Ivory-billed Woodpecker. The inside of the cavity is quite smooth, the edges of the entrance are nicely beveled, and, taken as a whole, it is quite an artistic piece of work.

Dr. William L. Ralph told Bendire of a clever trick practiced by this woodpecker; he found a nest "in the second week in April, about the time nidification is at its height there. On rapping on the trunk of the tree the bird, which was at home, stuck his head out of the hole and dropped some chips, naturally causing the Doctor to believe that the nesting site was still unfinished. The same performance was repeated on several subsequent visits, and finally he concluded to examine the nest anyhow, when he found nearly full-grown young. This pair of birds must have had eggs at the time he first discovered the nest, and the chips were simply thrown out as a ruse to deceive him."

Eggs.—This woodpecker lays, ordinarily, three or four eggs, rarely five. These are indistinguishable from those of the species from other southern States. The measurements of 22 eggs average 33.61 by 24.75 millimeters; the eggs showing the four extremes measure **36.2** by 24.5, 35.70 by **26.19, 31.5** by 24.0, and 34.2 by **22.8** millimeters.

Food.—Mr. Howell (1932) states that "this large woodpecker is a decidedly useful species. It never injures farm crops, but feeds entirely in the forests, rendering good service there in the destruction of wood-boring beetles. It eats, also, ants and wild fruits and berries, including the fruit of the sour gum, tupelo gum, dogwood, persimmon, frost grape, holly, poison ivy, sumac, and hackberry." C. J. Maynard (1896) says that they "are partial to the berries of the palmetto, feeding, in Florida, upon little else when these are in season."

CEOPHLOEUS PILEATUS PICINUS (Bangs)

WESTERN PILEATED WOODPECKER

HABITS

In describing and naming this large, dark-colored race from the Northwest coast region, Outram Bangs (1910) says that it is "as large as, or even larger than, *P. pileatus abieticola* (Bangs), but color sooty black as in *P. pileatus pileatus* (Linn.), the throat usually much marked with sooty, and the sides and flanks but slightly marked with grayish."

Major Bendire (1895) writes of its haunts: "In the mountains of Oregon, and presumably in other localities, the pileated woodpecker is most frequently met with in the extensive burnt tracts, the so-called 'deadenings,' where forest fires have swept through miles of fine timber and killed everything in its path. Such localities afford this species an abundant food supply in the slowly decaying trees, and are sure to atract them."

Grinnell, Dixon, and Linsdale (1930) say that in the Lassen Peak region in California "individuals of this woodpecker were found in or among white firs, red firs, incense cedars, and yellow pines. Foraging birds were often working on rotting stumps or logs close to the ground. Almost invariably, even when in the tops of tall trees, the birds were on dead or softened wood."

Nesting.—J. A. Munro (1923) says: "In southern British Columbia nesting begins early in May. The nest is a chiselled hole in a tree, fourteen to eighteen inches deep, cut occasionally in a green cottonwood or poplar, more often in a dead pine or fir, and rarely in any but the tallest trees and at a considerable distance above the ground. On a cushion of fine chips three or four rose-white eggs are laid."

Carriger and Wells (1919) give an interesting account of the nesting of the western pileated woodpecker in Placer County, Calif. The first nest, containing young birds, was found early in June 1915. "The tree stood about fifteen feet from the shore of the lake and in about five feet of water. At its base the diameter was about eighteen inches, at the nest entrance about ten. The tree was a live aspen. * * *

"The nest cavity was eighteen inches deep and six inches in diameter, while the entrance was three inches in width. The entire excavation had been made in live wood although there were plenty of large dead trees near by."

On May 16, 1916, they returned to this locality and found the birds nesting in the same tree in a new hole "located three feet higher up and on the opposite side of the tree." The nest contained three newly hatched young and one unhatched egg. Another visit was made the following year, on May 5, but the woodpeckers "had abandoned the lake and were making their home in a tree located in the channel of a small stream which flowed into the lake and about three hundred yards from their former site. The nest was found to be about half completed. Visits were made to it on several occasions until May 26, but the birds were not seen again."

In 1918 they were more successful. There was practically no water in the lake; and, on May 2, a search was "made through the aspen grove which in former years had stood in its entirety in from two to seven or eight feet of water, with the result that Mr. Flickinger discovered a fresh hole forty feet up in a live aspen growing close to the lake shore." The nest had been completed, but no eggs had been laid. Returning on May 12, they collected a set of four fresh eggs. They say:

The nest cavity was eighteen inches deep by about six in diameter, while the entrance was nearly four inches across.

The nest was visited again on June 1 by both of us, and to our surprise we found that the birds had used the same cavity for a second set of eggs, four in number, which were three-quarters incubated. The short time intervening between the two sets shows that the birds did not lose any time after their first set was lost to them. The locality was again visited on June 30 and we found that the birds had finished another cavity about two hundred feet from the first tree and apparently the female was brooding a third set. We did not disturb the bird and hope that she successfully raised her brood.

Inasmuch as the lake contained no water at this point we made a careful search of the upper end of the basin with the result that twenty cavities in all were located in various trees in what is usually the lake or very close to its shores. Most of these cavities were in live aspens. Apparently this pair of birds has nested here for a great many years, for although we have carefully worked the surrounding country for miles in every direction we have never discovered other birds or their cavities.

Eggs.—The western pileated woodpecker apparently lays either three or four eggs; I have no record of five. The eggs are indistinguishable from those of the northern pileated woodpecker. The measurements of two eggs in the P. B. Philipp collection are 30.9 by 23 and 29.6 by 22.9 millimeters. W. L. Dawson (1923) gives the average measurement as 32.5 by 24.1 millimeters.

Young.—Mrs. Irene G. Wheelock (1904) gives the following interesting account of the young:

The parents are very devoted to their treasures whether they be eggs or infant woodpeckers, and the male rarely fails to stand on guard on a high perch ready to warn and defend should possible danger threaten. The method of feeding is like that of the flickers, by regurgitation for the first two weeks or longer. The adult comes with gular pouch full of food and alights at one side of the nest hole to rest a moment. Though he may have come noiselessly and from the other side of the tree, yet his approach is always heralded by a mowing-machine chorus from the young, plainly heard some yards away. If old enough, the queer-looking little heads are thrust out of the doorway, and the parent, inserting his long bill into the open mouth of a youngling, shakes it vigorously, thereby emptying the food from his throat into that of his offspring. Each in turn is fed in this odd fashion. * * *

For a week or two after the young have left the nest, they follow their parents begging for food with ludicrous eagerness; at this time the provender brought them consists of nuts, berries, ants, and the larvae of beetles. These, especially the nuts, are often placed in a crevice of the bark, and the youngster is compelled to pick them out. After a few trials he learns to hammer right merrily and is ready to forage for himself.

Food.—The western pileated woodpecker lives on much the same kind of food as its eastern relative, but naturally on different species of insects and berries. Dr. Harold C. Bryant (1916) examined the stomach of one, taken in Lake County, Calif., on November 5, 1915, and says: "The stomach contained more than fifty carpenter ants (*Camponotus herculaneus* subsp.) and 131 seeds of poison oak (*Rhus diversiloba*). As the seeds of poison oak are hard and without a noticeable covering of softer material it is difficult to understand what there is about them that is attractive to birds. Certain it is that the seeds are incapable of complete digestion by woodpeckers." And he adds: "The stomachs of two pileated woodpeckers taken in or near Yosemite National Park * * * were filled with carpenter ants (*Camponotus herculaneus modoc* Wheeler), many of them winged. Each stomach contained more than a hundred of these ants. In addition one stomach contained a whole fruit of manzanita (*Arctostaphylos nevadensis* Gray) and the other, four large beetle larvae (*Cerambycidae*), unidentifiable as to genus or species, which had evidently been dug out of some dead tree, as the stomach contained slivers of dead wood."

J. A. Munro (1930) writes: "On December 2, 1926, a pileated woodpecker was seen scrambling among the thick entwined branches of Virginia creeper that partly covered the walls of a house situated on the shore of Okanagan Lake. Here it remained for twenty minutes, busily picking off the fruit. Subsequently, during the month of December, it often was observed eating these berries at the same place and likewise at a vine-covered house half a mile distant. Sometimes it appeared at both houses on the same day, but more often only one house was visited."

Charles W. Michael (1928) gives the following interesting account:

Beside the road, with branches overhanging it, stands a group of mountain dogwoods (*Cornus nuttalli*). These trees bore this year a heavy crop of fruit. At the end of each flower stalk was a bunched cluster of ripe berries. The Pileated Woodpecker was here today [September 19] to collect his toll of fruit. The fruit being at the ends of slender branches we thought the heavy-bodied bird would be out of luck. How could the big fellow reach the fruit? He was apparently not just sure himself. At first he tried walking out the heavier branches; but always as he approached the tip-ends they bent under his weight and threw the berries beyond reach. By working out on a cedar branch that intermingled with the dogwood branches he did manage to get a taste of fruit, just enough to tease his appetite. He was not to be cheated, however; for his next move was to flutter clumsily up to a branch containing berries, clutch the branch firmly with his strong feet, and then drop to swing like a great pendulum. He now had the system. Swinging head down he would pick the berries one by one, loosen his hold, swing into flight and then repeat the performance on another branch.

MELANERPES ERYTHROCEPHALUS (Linnaeus)

RED-HEADED WOODPECKER

PLATES 25–27

HABITS

This handsome and conspicuously colored woodpecker enjoys a wide distribution over much of North America, from southern Canada to the Gulf coast, east of the Rocky Mountains, and west of New England and eastern Canada. It is recorded from British Columbia, and is rare in New England. The only one I have seen in southeastern Massachusetts, in 50 years of field work, was chased across the line from Rhode Island before I shot it. Throughout the northern portion of its range, it is a summer resident only, though in mild winters, when food is abundant, it may remain all through winter.

The red-headed woodpecker is essentially a bird of the open country and not in any sense a forest dweller. I first met this woodpecker in northern New York while on a fishing trip on the St. Lawrence River; here it was fairly common in open groves of large trees or in groups of scattered trees in open fields, where its brilliant color pattern made it very conspicuous; it was frequently seen sitting on telegraph poles, fence posts, the dead tops of tall trees, or on dead stubs. Dr. Elon H. Eaton (1914) says of its haunts in that State: "The preferred home of this woodpecker is in open groves and 'slashings' and 'old burns' and tracts of half-dead forest where the live trees are scattered and dead stubs are in abundance."

Spencer Trotter (1903) writes: "I first saw the bird on a certain hill-side in Maryland that was grown up with tall white-oaks, not thickly, but open enough for a sheep-pasture, with vistas of close-cropped grass among the gray tree-trunks. In this setting a Woodpecker winged before me from tree to tree with its strongly contrasted blotches of black, white, and crimson flashing in the sunlight."

In Florida I have found it most commonly in the large burned-over areas in the pine woods, where numerous dead trees and stubs are left standing; these offer attractive nesting sites and some food supply. But Arthur H. Howell (1932) says: "The red-head is the most domestic of our woodpeckers, living frequently in the heart of populous towns and nesting in telephone poles on village streets. The birds are especially attracted to newly cleared lands, where many dead or girdled trees are left standing. They are common, also, in open pine forests in certain sections, but in other seemingly suitable localities are not to be found."

Nesting.—As my experience with the nesting habits of the red-headed woodpecker is almost nothing, I shall have to draw on the

observations of others.   Major Bendire (1895) makes the following
general statement:

Some of its nesting sites are exceedingly neat pieces of work; the edges of
the entrance hole are beautifully beveled off, and the inside is as smooth as if
finished with a fine rasp.   The entrance is about 1¾ inches in diameter and
the inner cavity varies from 8 to 24 inches in depth; the eggs are deposited
on a layer of fine chips.   It usually nests in the dead tops or limbs of deciduous trees, or in old stumps of oak, ash, butternut, maple, elm, sycamore, cottonwood, willow, and other species, more rarely in coniferous and fruit trees, at
heights varying from 8 to 80 feet from the ground, and also not infrequently
in natural cavities.   On the treeless prairies it has to resort mainly to telegraph poles and fence posts, and here it also nests under the roofs of houses
or in any dark corner it can find.

John Helton, Jr., tells me that in Alabama the favorite nesting
site is in a rotten stump from which the bark has peeled off; he very
seldom finds a nest in a tree with bark on it.   M. G. Vaiden sends
me a note on a nest that was only 5 feet from the ground in a limb
of a dead oak near Rosedale, Miss.   The nests are often placed near
houses or in trees on town or village streets.   Two broods are often
raised in a season and sometimes in the same cavity; A. D. DuBois
tells, in his notes, of such a Minnesota nest; the earlier brood had been
raised in a newly excavated cavity that was 14 inches deep; the
second set of eggs was laid at a depth of only 9 inches, the bed for the
eggs having been raised 5 inches by chiseling fresh chips from the
inner walls of the cavity.   Dr. H. C. Oberholser (1896b) gives the
average measurements of four Ohio nests as follows: Total depth
10.75; diameter of entrance 2.06 by 1.66; diameter at entrance 3.81
by 2.69; diameter at middle 4.50 by 3.88; and diameter at bottom
4.41 by 3.35 inches.

In the prairie regions and in other places, where trees are scarce
and these woodpeckers are common, some unusual and odd nesting
sites have been noted.   Kumlien and Hollister (1903) write: "Among
some of the odd nesting sites we have noted are the following: Between two flat rails on an old style rail fence; the hub of a broken
wagon wheel, leaning against a fence; the box of a grain drill left
standing in a field; a hole excavated in the hollow cylinder of an
ordinary pump; common fence posts and telegraph poles.   These
were usually in prairie regions where there were few, if any, suitable
trees."

G. S. Agersborg (1881) mentions a nest that "was in the angle
formed by the shares of an upturned plow" in South Dakota.   And
E. A. Stoner (1915) flushed a red-headed woodpecker from a blue
jay's nest in Iowa.   "The nest was eight feet up in an oak sapling
and was a typical Blue Jay's but was found to contain three pure
white and unmistakably Woodpecker eggs."

Eggs.—Major Bendire (1895) writes: "The number of eggs to a set varies from four to seven, sets of five being most frequently found, while occasionally as many as eight eggs have been taken from a nest. Mr. R. C. McGregor records taking a set of ten eggs of the red-head, varying in size from ordinary down to that of the song sparrow. Incubation varied from fresh in the smallest egg to advanced in the larger (Oologist, vol. 5, p. 44, 1888)."

If the first set of eggs is taken, another set will be completed within the next 10 or 12 days, usually in the same hole. Like the flicker, this woodpecker is very persistent in its attempt to raise a brood and will keep on laying, if repeatedly robbed. C. C. Bacon (1891), of Bell, Ky., reports taking six sets of eggs, 28 eggs in all, from the same nest in a single season, after which the birds drilled a new hole in the same tree and raised a brood of four young; this persevering pair drilled two holes and laid 32 eggs before they succeeded in raising a brood.

The eggs vary in shape from short ovate to rounded ovate, are pure white in color, and somewhat glossy when incubated. The measurements of 54 eggs average 25.14 by 19.17 millimeters; the eggs showing the four extremes measure **27.18** by 19.30, 26.16 by **20.57, 23** by 18.20, and 23.11 by **17.78** millimeters.

Young.—Incubation is said to last for about 14 days. Both sexes assist in this duty, as well as in the care of the young. As an egg is laid each day, and, as incubation often begins before the set is complete, the young may hatch on different days.

Mr. DuBois writes to me that one nest that he watched held newly hatched young on June 11; they were in the nest on July 7 but had left before 2 p. m. on the 9th, making the period in the nest approximately 27 days. He says: "The newly hatched, naked young have extremely long necks, longer in fact than their bodies. The four young all faced inward, each toward a point to the right of the center of the nest; and when in repose, each neck crossed the necks of the two others at right angles to its own—like woof and warp in a loom. A little noise on my part made all four of them stretch their necks straight upward; but when they collapsed, their necks became again interwoven. Each lowered its head to its own right side of the one opposite it. There were egg shells still in the nest."

Julian K. Potter (1912) says of a nest that he watched at Camden, N. J.:

The old birds fed the young at varying intervals, sometimes going to the nest once in every three or four minutes for a half hour, then not appearing again for fifteen or twenty minutes. * * *

The young birds left the nest about June 25. On that day I saw them out in the open, quite able to take care of themselves, although the parents fed them occasionally. [This pair raised a second brood that season, and had young on July 30.] Meanwhile the young of the first brood were being very much misused by their parents, and were driven away whenever they came in sight;

in fact they were persecuted to such an extent that they must have been driven from the locality, for I was unable to find them after July 30.

Some writers have said that only one brood is raised in a season, and others that two broods are raised only in the southern part of the breeding range. But Mr. DuBois reports two broods in Minnesota; and Mr. Potter one brood one season and two broods the next season for his pair in New Jersey.

Plumages.—The young are hatched naked and blind, but they acquire the juvenal plumage before they leave the nest. The sexes are alike in all plumages, and the juvenal plumage is quite unlike that of the adult. In the juvenal plumage, the head, neck, and upper chest are brownish gray, spotted above and streaked below with dusky; the back is black but not glossy as in the adult; the wings are as in the adult, except that the secondaries and tertials are white but more or less patterned or barred with black, chiefly near the tips, and the primaries are edged with buffy white on the outer webs; the under parts below the chest are dull white, clouded with brownish gray and more or less streaked with dusky, chiefly on the sides and flanks. This plumage is usually worn in its purity through July and August and sometimes into October, though sometimes a few red feathers are seen in the head; I have seen two or three red feathers in the head as early as June 29 and a bird not much farther advanced on December 1. But usually the complete molt into the adult plumage begins in September and lasts through winter; the change begins on the head and back in fall, but the wings are not usually molted until April, and even then some of the juvenal secondaries may be retained. Most young birds are in practically adult plumage before May.

Adults have a complete postnuptial molt in August and September; they may have a partial molt in spring, but I have not seen it. Some highly plumaged birds, probably old birds and mostly from western localities, have the abdomen tinged with red.

Food.—Much has been written on the food habits of the red-headed woodpecker, a most resourceful feeder on a greatly varied diet. Prof. F. E. L. Beal (1895) makes the following report on the contents of 101 stomachs, collected throughout the year in various parts of the country:

Animal matter, 50 percent; vegetable matter, 47 percent; mineral matter, 3 percent. * * * The insects consist of ants, wasps, beetles, bugs, grasshoppers, crickets, moths, and caterpillars. Spiders and myriapods also were found. Ants amounted to about 11 percent of the whole food. * * * Beetle remains formed nearly one-third of all food. * * * The families represented were those of the common May beetle (*Lachnosterna*), which was found in several stomachs, the predaceous ground beetles, tiger beetles, weevils, and a few others. * * * Weevils were found in 15 stomachs, and in several cases as many as 10 were present. Remains of Carabid beetles were found in 44 stomachs to an average amount of 24 percent of the contents of those that contained them, or 10 percent of all. The fact that 43 percent of all the birds taken had eaten these beetles, some of them to the extent of 16 individuals, shows a decided fondness for these insects, and taken with the fact that 5 stomachs contained Cicindelids or tiger beetles forms a rather strong indictment against the bird.

The vegetable food includes corn, dogwood berries, huckleberries, strawberries, blackberries, raspberries, mulberries, elderberries, wild black cherries, choke cherries, cultivated cherries, wild grapes, apples, pears, various seeds, acorns, and beechnuts. Prof. Beal (1895) reports that—

corn was found in 17 stomachs, collected from May to September, inclusive, and amounted to more than 7 percent of all the food. While it seems to be eaten in any condition, that taken in the late summer was in the milk, and evidently picked from standing ears. This * * * corroborates some of the testimony received, and indicates that the Redhead, if sufficiently abundant, might do considerable damage to the growing crop, particularly if other food was not at hand. While the fruit list is not so long as in the case of the Flicker, it includes more kinds that are, or may be, cultivated; and the quantity found in the stomachs, a little more than 33 percent of all the food, is greater than in any of the others. Strawberries were found in 1 stomach, blackberries or raspberries in 15, cultivated cherries in 2, apples in 4, and pears in 6. Fruit pulp was found in 33 stomachs, and it is almost certain that a large part of this was obtained from some of the larger cultivated varieties. Seeds were found in but few stomachs, and only a small number in each.

Audubon (1842) gives this woodpecker a rather bad name, saying:

I would not recommend to anyone to trust their fruit to the red-heads; for they not only feed on all kinds as they ripen, but destroy an immense quantity besides. No sooner are the cherries seen to redden, than these birds attack them. * * * Trees of this kind are stripped clean by them. * * * I may safely assert that a hundred have been shot upon a single cherry-tree in one day. * * * They have another bad habit, which is that of sucking the eggs of small birds. For this purpose, they frequently try to enter the boxes of the Martins or Bluebirds, as well as the pigeon-houses, and are often successful. The corn, as it ripens, is laid bare by their bill, when they feed on the top parts of the ear, and leave the rest either to the Grakles or the Squirrels, or still worse, to decay, after a shower has fallen upon it.

Bendire (1895) adds to the evidence against this gay villain. He personally saw a red-headed woodpecker rifle a nest of a red-shafted flicker and carry off an egg. He quotes from one observer who had seen one of these woodpeckers clean out a nest of young of the tufted titmouse, and from another who had seen one carrying off a freshly killed young robin. W. G. Smith wrote to him from Colorado: "The red-headed woodpecker is a common summer resident in the lower foothills along the eastern slopes of the Rocky Mountains in this State, and I consider it a veritable butcher among our nuthatches and chickadees, driving every one away from its nesting sites, and woe to the bird that this villain can reach. It destroys both eggs and young, dragging the latter out of their nests and frequently leaving them dead at the entrance of their holes."

He also relates the following personal experience:

We noticed a red-headed woodpecker take something, apparently a bunch of moss, from a crotch of a maple and carry it to a fence post of an adjacent field. After worrying some time in trying to swallow something rather too large for his gullet, he finally succeeded, after an effort, and then worked some little time, evidently trying to secrete the remainder. Both of us had our field glasses and were watching the bird's actions closely. After some little time he flew back to the tree he had started from, while we proceeded to the fence post to investigate, and, much to our disgust and surprise, we found the freshly killed and partly eaten body of a young bird, almost denuded of feathers, securely tucked away behind the loose bark of the post. His victim was too much mutilated to identify positively, but looked like a half-grown bluebird, whose head had been crushed in, the brain abstracted, and the entire rump and entrails torn out; the only parts left intact were the breast, upper part of the back, and the lower portion of the head. The missing parts had evidently just been eaten by the rascal while clinging to the top of the post, and the remnant was then hidden for future use.

Howard Jones (1883), of Circleville, Ohio, reports the following incident:

Under the eaves of a large barn near Mt. Sterling, O., a colony of Cliff Swallows have built for some years. Last year they were nearly exterminated by several woodpeckers. The redheads would alight at the doors of the mud huts and extract the eggs from the nests with their bills. In some nests the necks or entrance-ways were so long that the woodpeckers could not reach the eggs by this means, but not willing to be cheated of such choice food they would climb around to the side, and with a few well directed blows of their bills make openings large enough to enable them to procure the eggs. Of the dozens of nests built not a single brood was reared in any. One woodpecker bolder than the rest began eating hen's eggs wherever they could be found.

Mr. DuBois says in his notes: "A redhead, seeing a young lark sparrow flutter in the grass, attacked it and might have killed it, had I not intervened. He had struck the young bird at one of his lores and had brought blood. I have also seen this woodpecker attack a young bluebird, on the ground, just after it had left the nest."

But not all red-headed woodpeckers are cannibals or murderers; perhaps many individuals never indulge in such practices; and all of them have some harmless and useful feeding habits. Their insect-eating habits are impressive. They are very fond of grasshoppers and destroy them in large numbers. H. B. Bailey (1878) quotes the following from a letter from G. S. Agersborg, of Vermillion, S. Dak.:

Last spring in opening a good many birds of this species with the object of ascertaining their principal food, I found in their stomachs nothing but young grasshoppers. One of them, which had its headquarters near my house, was observed making frequent visits to an old oak post, and on examining it I found a large crack where the Woodpecker had inserted about one hundred grasshoppers of all sizes (for future use, as later observations proved), which were put in without killing them, but they were so firmly wedged in the crack that they in vain tried to get free. I told this to a couple of farmers, and found that they had also seen the same thing, and showed me the posts which were used for the same purpose. Later in the season the Woodpecker, whose station was near my house, commenced to use his stores, and to-day (February 10) there are only a few shrivelled-up grasshoppers left.

Milton P. Skinner (1928), referring to the feeding habits of this woodpecker in North Carolina, writes:

Flying insects are an important source of food supply all through the winter, but with the increase of the number of insects in March this activity greatly increases. The observation post for fly-catching is usually the one in which the nest hole is situated. But I noted at least one bird that used four tall trees in succession for this purpose. On February 1, 1927, a red-headed woodpecker was seen clinging to the side of a telephone pole. Twice it left the pole, flew out twenty feet, caught an insect each time, and returned to the pole to eat it. Two weeks later another bird was seen to make six trips similarly out and back during six minutes, sometimes going more than a hundred feet from its perch. As the bird went direct to the insect, caught it and returned immediately to its perch, it seemed likely that the insect was seen each time before the bird started, indicating wonderful eyesight. While not engaged in thus hawking, this bird hunted the limbs for prey. Ten days later I found this bird watching for insects and making ten fly-catching sallies in minute and a half. Its flights were from ten to one hundred and fifty feet in length, and all the insects were from forty to sixty feet above the ground. One of the redheads seen fly-catching in December, returned to its dead stub where it drilled for grubs and borers in the usual woodpecker fashion, except that its strokes were heavy and deliberate. On another occasion, I saw one of these birds fly down into the road to catch and eat an earthworm.

E. D. Nauman (1930), in Iowa, watched a red-headed woodpecker feeding a young bird in the top of a tall tree. "The adult bird was at work, darting off every few moments into the air in pursuit of insects and returning after each flight to the young bird on the tree with its prey. I watched and timed it carefully for an hour. It made from five to seven trips per minute, always at an elevation of 50 to 100 feet, and caught at each trip from one to three or more insects. * * *

"A computation based upon careful observation showed that a single individual Redhead had destroyed over 600 insects in one hour. When I left, the bird was still at work, and I am, of course, unable to state how long it had been at work at this place before I came there."

A. V. Goodpasture (1909), of Nashville, Tenn., made some interesting observations on the feeding habits of this woodpecker. He watched one preparing insect food for its young on a stump, some 4 feet high, near its nest, and says:

When one of the woodpeckers came in, it did not go directly to the nest, but always alighted first on this stump, where it hammered away for a time, then proceeded to the nest with a shapeless mass in its beak. My glass having failed to disclose their object in thus lighting and hammering on the stump before feeding their young, I went down to reconnoiter. The place looked like a field hospital after a severe engagement. There were wings, and wing-covers, heads and legs strewn around the stump in great profusion. Then I understood it all. The stump was their meat-block, and they were preparing the food for their young by removing the hard and indigestible parts. They dispatched this work with much dexterity, without using their feet to confine the insect; they laid it on the stump, and, with the bill alone, succeeded in removing the undesirable parts.

The kinds of insects whose remains were found there was a study. They were almost as gaudy as the woodpecker himself. * * * Woodpeckers can undoubtedly distinguish between colors; they find the ruddiest apple and the rosiest peach in the orchard. In like manner, they seem to be attracted by bright-colored insects. They prefer beautiful butterflies, silky moths, and brilliant beetles. The favorite food of this pair was the June-bug; not the plain brown beetle of the northern states, but the beautiful green and gold June-bug of the South—associated in the mind with sultry summer days, and ripe blackberries, on which he feeds. * * *

I found not only the dismembered wing-covers of the June-bug around the Woodpecker's meat-block, but, in a pit on the splintered top of the stump, I found a live June-bug. And what a prison he was in! It was a thousand times worse than the Black Hole of Calcutta. They had turned him on his back and pounded him into a cavity that so exactly fitted him that he could move nothing but his legs, which were plying like weaver's shuttles in the empty air. I always found the June-bugs deposited on their backs, and always alive.

The red-headed woodpecker also shares with the California wood-pecker the provident habit of storing acorns and nuts. Fannie Hardy Eckstorm (1901) says:

Lately it has been discovered that they not only eat beechnuts all the fall, but store them up for winter use. This time the observation was made in Indiana. There, when the nuts were abundant, the red-heads were seen busily carrying them off. Their accumulations were found in all sorts of places; cavities in old tree-trunks contained nuts by the handful; knot-holes, cracks, crevices, seams in the barns were filled full of nuts. Nuts were tucked into the cracks in fence-posts; they were driven into railroad ties; they were pounded in between the shingles on the roofs; if a board was sprung out, the space behind it was filled with nuts, and bark or wood was often brought to cover over the gathered store.

Unlike the California woodpecker, it does not make holes for the reception of the nuts but uses what cavities it can find. Dr. Thomas S. Roberts (1932) says that, on the outskirts of St. Paul, "a red-head spent most of October putting acorns into cracks and climbing-iron holes in a telephone pole and under the shingles of a near-by house. One crack was closely plugged for a distance of twenty feet. When the nuts were too large for the cracks they were split and driven in in pieces."

George A. Dorsey (1926) tells of an amusing attempt of a young redhead to fill a hole in a telephone pole:

Finally he found a hole to his liking, and, chattering as he worked, he drove the acorn in   Imagine my surprise when I saw a couple of acorns fall out on the other side of the pole! The hole was bored straight through the pole, and the Woodpecker was wasting his time by pushing the acorns through. He seemed to know that something was wrong, but couldn't quite reason it out. He would chatter agitatedly and hitch around the pole to examine the other side of the pole, but would finally give it up and go off for another acorn. I watched him poke acorns in the hole several times, only to have some of the ones he had previously placed there fall out on the other side. On the ground under the pole was about a double handful of acorns that had fallen out.

E. D. Nauman (1932) saw a house mouse running across a paved street, but it had not gone very far when a red-headed woodpecker "darted down out of the grove and made an attack upon it. The woodpecker struck the mouse several hard and vicious blows with its stout bill, rolling and tossing it over and over. It appeared that a moment more of such treatment must have finished the mouse, had not a vehicle approached just at that instant, threatening to crush both the red-head and its prey. The bird darted away just in time to save itself, and the mouse, not having been struck by the wheels, hurriedly limped to the edge of the pavement, got over the curb with difficulty, and hid in the grass. The red-head flew back immediately to see what had become of its prospect for dinner, but the mouse was so well hidden that the bird had to give up the chase."

Mr. DuBois writes to me that "a red-headed woodpecker was observed hanging upside down from the small twigs at the end of a branch of a large oak, evidently gleaning insect life of some sort from the twigs. It flew to another tree and repeated this method of feeding."

Lewis O. Shelley tells me that he observed one "feeding on ants in a dry, harvested oat piece, obtaining the ants by thrusting the bill into an ant tunnel entrance and working the bill to form a cone-shaped opening, up through which the ants emerged at the disturbance, and were licked up without the bill being withdrawn from this foodhopper."

Behavior.—Audubon (1842) writes attractively of the behavior of this woodpecker:

With the exception of the mocking-bird, I know of no species so gay and frolicsome. Indeed, their whole life is one of pleasure. They find a super-abundance of food everywhere, as well as the best facilities for raising their broods. * * * They do not seem to be much afraid of man, although they have scarcely a more dangerous enemy. When alighted on a fence-stake by the road, or in a field, and one approaches them, they gradually move sidewise out of sight, peeping now and then to discover your intention; and when you are quite close and opposite, lie still until you are past, when they hop to the top of the stake, and rattle upon it with their bill, as if to congratulate themselves on the success of their cunning. Should you approach within arm's length, which may frequently be done, the woodpecker flies to the next stake or the second from you, bends his head to peep, and rattles again, as if to provoke you to a continuance of what seems to him excellent sport. * * *

They chase each other on wing in a very amicable manner, in long, beautifully curved sweeps, during which the remarkable variety of their plumage becomes conspicuous, and is highly pleasing to the eye. When passing from one tree to another, their flight resembles the motion of a great swing, and is performed by a single opening of the wings, descending at first, and rising towards the spot on which they are going to alight with ease, and in the most graceful manner. They move upwards, sidewise, or backwards, without apparent effort, but seldom with the head downwards. * * *

On the ground, this species is by no means awkward, as it hops there with ease, and secures beetles which it had espied whilst on the fence or a tree.

Red-headed woodpeckers are quite quarrelsome at times with other species; besides attacking various small birds, driving them away from their nests, or robbing them of their eggs or young, they contend with other hole-nesting birds, such as starlings and the smaller woodpeckers, for the possession of nesting holes. They are jealous of their food supply and will drive other birds away from their favorite feeding places or from any choice morsel of food. They are generally the winners in such encounters, even against such aggressive rivals as blue jays and starlings. But toward birds of their own species they are often solicitous, friendly, and helpful to birds in trouble. Mr. DuBois writes to me: "A wounded female, after several attempts to fly, fluttered to the ground; and while she was fluttering in the air, her mate flew to her and apparently tried to help her to a place of safety. After reaching the ground, the female lay still in the grass, although only winged; but her mate clung to a nearby tree, from which he flew down to her repeatedly, showing great distress."

H. M. Holland (1931) tells the following story:

A red-head was caught by one wing, and possibly a foot, in a crack formed at the tip of a tall, dead tree where the trunk had been broken off and left a splintered stub. Perhaps a dozen red-heads were present, all flying here and there, evidently much excited, and make a great ado, a veritable woodpecker hubbub.

First one and then another would alight just below and apparently peck at, or more often while in flight would strike or brush against the hapless victim, whose struggles were renewed at each encounter. The clamor became actually distressing. At times two or three were simultaneously fluttering close to the captive. These activities continued for several minutes when suddenly the bird was freed, to accomplish which it would seem that a concerted effort had been made. Quiet was restored almost at once and the participants dispersed.

Julian K. Potter (1912) noticed that sparrows bothered his woodpeckers considerably about their roosting holes and saw one of them fighting two starlings for the possession of a cavity, but all were eventually driven away and learned the lesson of "no trespass." He says: "On one occasion, when I watched the woodpeckers until dark, I found that one went to roost in the nesting-hole about dusk, and the other, probably the male, shortly after went into an old hole in the same dead tree higher up."

Mrs. John Franklin Kyler (1927) gives an interesting account of a red-headed woodpecker that she raised by hand from the nest, beginning before the young bird had opened its eyes; it developed into a very satisfactory pet, with marked affection for its foster mother; anyone who wants to try raising young birds could learn much by reading her story.

Voice.—Bendire (1895) writes: "Its ordinary call note is a loud 'tchur-tchur'; when chasing each other a shrill note like 'chärr-chärr' is frequently uttered, and alarm is expressed by a harsh, rattling note, as well as by one which, according to Mr. Otto Widmann, is indistinguishable from the note of the Tree-frog (*Hyla arborea*). He tells me that both bird and frog sometimes answer each other."

Describing their spring notes, W. L. Dawson (1903) says:

Then the woods and groves soon resound with their loud calls, *Quee-o— quee-o—queer*. These *queer* cries are not unpleasant, but the birds are a noisy lot at best. When one of them flies into a tree where others are gathered, all set up an outcry of *yarrow, yarrow, yarrow*, which does not subside until the newcomer has had time to shake hands all around at least twice. Besides these more familiar sounds the red-heads boast an unfathomed repertory of chirping, cackling, and raucous noises. The youngsters, especially,—awkward, saucy fellows that most of them are—sometimes get together and raise a fearful racket until some of the older ones, out-stentored, interpose.

Field marks.—The red-headed woodpecker is so conspicuously marked that it hardly could be mistaken for anything else. The large white areas in the wings and on the rump are much in evidence, in any plumage, especially in flight. The bright red of the entire head and neck and the plain white breast of the adult are also very conspicuous.

Enemies.—The red-headed woodpecker has some bad habits, which have at times caused considerable damage to property, arousing the enmity of those who have suffered from its depredations and resulting in the destruction of large numbers of these birds. Raids on cultivated fruits have given these woodpeckers a bad name and many have been killed by fruit growers. Audubon (1842) asserts that as many as "a hundred have been shot upon a single cherry tree in one day. Pears, peaches, apples, figs, mulberries, and even peas, are thus attacked."

They do considerable damage to pole lines by excavating their nests in them. An editorial in The Osprey (vol. 1, p. 147) quotes, as follows, from an article in the Kansas City Star:

The little red-headed woodpecker has become such a nuisance on the electric lines of the metropolitan street railway system, that it has become necessary to appoint an official woodpecker exterminator. The title has been conferred on Coffee Rice, an Independence young man, and yesterday he killed nineteen of the destructive birds on the Independence line. The woodpeckers attack the large poles which hold up the feed cables and dig holes into the center and downward to a depth of more than a foot. * * * The result is that in a season the water gets into the heart of the pole and it rots off and breaks, requiring a new pole to be set up; whereas, ordinarily, the life of the big pole is several years. A large number of the electric line poles have been ruined this way, and there was a threatened loss of many thousand dollars unless the pest was checked.

Red-headed woodpeckers seem to be oftener killed on highways by speeding automobiles than any other species, as attested by several observers. Dr. Dayton Stoner (1932) made some observations on this point on an automobile trip, on July 15, 1924, for a distance of 211 miles on well-graveled roads in Iowa. He says:

En route, 105 dead animals representing fifteen species were counted; of these, thirty-nine were red-headed woodpeckers. The mortality in this species was higher than for any other species of vertebrate animal noted and I believe that several contributory factors are responsible for it. First, these birds have a propensity for feeding upon insects and waste grain in and along the roads; second, they delay taking wing before the approaching car, in all probability being poor judges of its speed; and third, they have a slow "get-away," that is, they can not quickly gain sufficient speed to escape the oncoming car. However, I feel certain that a speed as high as thirty-five to forty miles an hour is necessary in order to overtake these birds.

Alexander Wilson (1832) writes:

Notwithstanding the care which this bird, in common with the rest of its genus, takes to place its young beyond the reach of enemies, within the hollows of trees, yet there is one deadly foe, against whose depredations neither the height of the tree nor the depth of the cavity, is the least security. This is the black snake (*Coluber constrictor*), who frequently glides up the trunk of the tree, and, like a skulking savage, enters the woodpecker's peaceful apartment, devours the eggs or helpless young, in spite of the cries and fluttering of the parents; and, if the place be large enough, coils himself up in the spot they occupied, where he will sometimes remain for several days.

Fall.—The fall migration is often well marked. A. H. Helme (1882), writing from Millers Place, Long Island, N. Y., where the bird occurs mainly as a migrant, says:

The first one observed this season was on the 10th of September. On the 12th I saw three, and on the 20th I saw one. Early on the morning of the 24th of September they began to pass over in large numbers, and continued to pass until about 10 o'clock, after which very few were seen, except straggling groups of three or four, and occasionally a single one was seen to pass over during the day. The flight must have consisted of several hundred, principally young birds. They came from the east and were flying west. Many of them in their flight would alight for a few minutes in the orchards and corn fields to feed on the half-ripened corn, or search among the apple trees for the larva or eggs of insects but would soon continue on their journey, and their places would be supplied by others. I noticed one or two to dart out and seize an insect in the manner of a flycatcher. The following day but two or three were seen. A few stragglers, however, were occasionally met with up to the 10th of October, and one was seen as late as the 23rd of November.

John B. Semple (1930) writes:

On September 16, 1929, a flight of red-headed woodpeckers (*Melanerpes erythrocephalus*) was observed passing over the marshes at the head of Sandusky Bay, Ohio. The birds were flying in little groups of two to five against a stiff south-west wind heading nearly south and at an elevation of sixty to eighty yards. Rather more than half of them were immature birds but the old and young were not segregated. I was hunting ducks at the time and counted forty-eight wood-peckers passing in a little more than two hours. They apparently came from Ontario and probably crossed Lake Erie by way of Point Pelee and Bass Island which would make the flight over water only about nine miles. It was interesting to note that each successive group of birds followed exactly the same route over the marshes although those that had gone before were well out of sight.

Winter.—The red-headed woodpecker is generally considered to be a migratory species throughout the northern portion of its breeding range, but its movements seem to depend almost entirely on the abundance or scarcity of its winter food supply, mainly acorns and beechnuts; when these nuts are available in considerable quantities, this woodpecker is to be found in reasonable numbers within its sum-mer range in the northern States. When Dr. C. Hart Merriam (1878) referred to it as remaining occasionally in northern New York, Lewis County, in winter, some of his ornithological friends were skeptical. He says:

I therefore wrote to my friend, Mr. C. L. Bagg, asking him to send me a lot of red-headed woodpeckers as soon as possible, and in a week's time received a box containing over twenty specimens,—all killed in Lewis County and when the snow was three feet deep! This was proof positive. Notes kept by Mr. Bagg and myself during the past six years show that they were abundant here during the winters 1871–72, 1873–74, 1875–76, and 1877–78; while they were rare or did not occur at all during the winters of 1872–73 and 1876–77. Their absence was in no way governed by the severity of the winters, but entirely dependent upon the absence of the usual supply of beechnuts. While the greater portion of nuts fall to the ground and are buried beneath the snow far beyond the reach of the woodpeckers, yet enough remain on the trees all winter to furnish abundant subsistence for those species which feed on them. * * *

During the autumn the scattered pairs for several miles around usually con-gregate in some suitable wood, containing a plenty of beech-trees, and here spend the long cold winter in company, chattering and chasing one another about among the trees to keep warm, and to help while away the time. "Coe's woods," in this immediate vicinity, has long been famous as the great winter resort for the red-headed woodpeckers of the neighborhood, and it is certainly the most suitable place for their purposes to be found for many miles around. This piece of woods, not over an eighth of a mile in extent, contains, besides hundreds of beeches (*Fagus ferruginea*), a large number of elms (*Ulmus americana*), and white ash-trees (*Fraxinus americana*) of great size, most of the tops of which are now dead. What more favorable location than this woods could a woodpecker desire? Here they have beechnuts in abundance and a bountiful supply of dead limbs and tree-tops far above the reach of the small charges commonly used by bird-collectors.

James B. Purdy (1900) says that "the presence of the Red-headed Woodpecker (*Melanerpes erythrocephalus*) during the winter months in Michigan does not depend upon the temperature, but entirely upon the food supply, viz.: the crop of acorns and beechnuts which precedes the winter. If these nuts are plenty, the red-headed woodpeckers will always be found during the winter months, but in no great abundance. If there are no acorns or beechnuts, this bird will be entirely absent in our Michigan forests."

Robert Ridgway (1881) writes:

Ordinarily this species (*Melanerpes erythrocephalus*) is decidedly the most numerous of the Woodpeckers in Southeastern Illinois, while during the winter season it is often so excessively common in the sheltered bottom-lands as to outnumber all other species together, and, in fact, is voted a decided nuisance by the hunter, sportsman, or collector, on account of its well known habit of following any one carrying a gun, and annoying him by its continued chatter; at intervals sweeping before him and thus diverting attention. Being at this season always semi-gregarious, while they are of all woodpeckers the most restless and sportive, the annoyance which they thus cause is really no trifling matter.

Evidently, they do not always spend the winter even here, for he says: "In the early part of October, 1879, I paid my usual yearly visit to my old home, and scarcely had arrived at the house ere my father informed me, as a bit of news which he was well aware would both interest and surprise me, that the red-headed woodpeckers had all migrated; that for a number of nights preceding he had heard overhead their well-known notes as they winged their way to some more or less distant region; in short, that the woods that had been their home 'knew them now no more.'"

Even as far south as South Carolina, according to Arthur T. Wayne (1910): "The controlling influence upon the migration of this species in winter is the presence or absence of acorns of the live and water oaks. If the crop of acorns is large, this woodpecker is abundant during the winter months, but if there are no acorns, the bird is entirely absent, no matter whether the season is mild or severe."

DISTRIBUTION

Range.—Southern Canada and the United States east of the Rocky Mountains; irregularly migratory in the northern parts of its range.

Breeding range.—The breeding range of the red-headed woodpecker extends **north** to northern Montana (Strabane, Lewistown, Fairview, and Terry); northern North Dakota (Arnegard and Willow City); southern Manitoba (Lake St. Martin and Winnipeg); southern Ontario (Kenora, Cobden, and Ottawa); southern Quebec (Three Rivers and Hatley); and southern New Brunswick (St. John). The **eastern** limits of the range extend from New Brunswick (St. John) south along the Atlantic coast to Florida (Orlando and Fort Myers). **South** through the Gulf coastal regions of Florida, Mississippi, and Louisiana; central Texas (Waco); and central New Mexico (Fort Sumner and Albuquerque). **West** to New Mexico (Albuquerque and Santa Fe); central Colorado (Hotchkiss, Golden,

Estes Park, and Fort Collins); eastern Wyoming (Laramie and Careyhurst); and Montana (Kirby, Billings, Lewistown, and Strabane).

During the summer season the species also has been taken or observed north to southeastern Alberta (Medicine Hat, Big Stick, and Eastend); southern Saskatchewan (Oak Lake, Aweme, and Pilot mound); Quebec (Quebec City); and New Brunswick (Beaver Dam).

Winter range.—The normal winter range of the red-headed woodpecker appears to extend **north** to Oklahoma (Oklahoma City and Okmulgee); northeastern Iowa (National); Illinois (Ohio and Mount Carmel); Tennessee (Nashville and Knoxville); West Virginia (Charlestown and Clarksburg); and southeastern Pennsylvania (Philadelphia). At this season it is never common on the Atlantic coast north of South Carolina (Charleston), but is found from there **south** to southern Florida (Miami). From this point it winters westward along the Gulf coast to Louisiana and probably Texas. The **western** limits of the winter range appear to be central Texas (probably Somerset) and Oklahoma (Caddo and Oklahoma City).

In addition to the winter range above given, it also has been noted casually at this season in eastern Kansas and Nebraska, southeastern South Dakota (Yankton, January 2, 1929, and the winter of 1936–37); North Dakota (Grafton, specimen collected January 24, 1905); Minnesota (frequent in the southern part); Wisconsin (occasional north to Meriden and New London); southern Michigan (Grand Rapids, Lansing, and Detroit); southern Ontario (Coldstream, Toronto, and Kingston); southern Vermont (Bennington); and Massachusetts (Boston).

Migration.—The migrations of the red-headed woodpecker are imperfectly understood, and, as will be noted from the numerous casual winter records, individuals of this species sometimes winter north almost to the limits of the breeding range. This makes difficult the designation of early and late dates of migration. Nevertheless, the following dates may be considered representative of most seasons in that portion of the range where the species is normally migratory:

Spring migration.—Early dates of arrival are: New Jersey—Elizabeth, February 27; New Providence, March 13; Cape May, March 27. Northwestern Pennsylvania—Beaver, April 15. New York—Penn Yan, April 3; West Brighton, April 12; Syracuse, April 14. Connecticut—Fairfield, March 2; Meriden, March 28. Massachusetts—Bernardstown, April 4; Russell, April 21. Vermont—St. Johnsbury, April 19. Maine—Lewiston, May 8; Portland, May 15. Quebec—Montreal, May 7. Ohio—Wauseon, March 7. Michigan—Saginaw, March 9; Sault Ste. Marie, May 22. Ontario—London, March 13;

Hamilton, April 15; Toronto, April 26. Wisconsin—Ladysmith, April 23. Minnesota—Redwing, March 30; St. Cloud, April 1; Hutchinson, April 14. Kansas—Fort Hays, April 11; Bendena, April 13; Harper, April 25. Nebraska—Omaha, April 29; Neligh, May 3; Scribner, May 7. South Dakota—Yankton, April 13; Vermillion, April 29; Sioux Falls, May 4. North Dakota—Jamestown, April 21; Argusville, May 8; Fargo, May 9. Manitoba—East Kildonan, May 6; Aweme, May 19. New Mexico—Glenrio, April 26. Colorado (occasionally winters)—Burlington, May 7; Lamar, May 11; Denver, May 15. Wyoming—Laramie Peak, May 2; Careyhurst, May 15; Torrington, May 17. Montana—Albion, May 19; Fort Custer, May 20.

Fall migration.—Late dates of fall departure are: Montana—Sun River, September 5. Wyoming—Laramie, September 4; Wheatland, September 6; Panco, October 2. Colorado—Greeley, October 1; Denver, October 21; Boulder County, October 23. New Mexico—Koehler Junction, October 24. Manitoba—Margaret, September 20; Aweme, October 8. North Dakota—Medora, September 18; Wahpeton, September 29. South Dakota—Sioux Falls, September 20; Harrison, September 28; Yankton, October 7. Nebraska—Red Cloud, October 3; Blue Springs, October 4. Kansas—Harper, October 15; Lawrence, October 18; Fort Hays, October 29. Minnesota—Hutchinson, October 20; Minneapolis, October 26. Wisconsin—Prescott, October 10; Reedsburg, October 16; and La Crosse, October 29. Northern Michigan—Sault Ste. Marie, November 15. Ontario—Toronto, September 15; Ottawa, September 18; Point Pelee, October 14. Maine—Skowhegan, October 26. Vermont—Wells River, September 24; Rutland, October 14. Massachusetts—Springfield, October 9; Boston, October 15. Connecticut—Fairfield, October 8; Hartford, October 13. Northern New York—Watertown, October 16; Geneva, October 24; Rochester, November 11. Northwestern Pennsylvania—McKeesport, October 19; Berwyn, November 8; Erie, November 17. New Jersey—Passaic, October 21; Cape May, October 21; Morristown, November 2.

An examination of the banding files in the Biological Survey adds but little information to knowledge of the migrations of this bird. Although it has been banded in fair numbers (more than 1,700 previous to July 1, 1937) the farthest recovery record is only about 80 miles south of the point of banding. There are, however, several cases of return in subsequent seasons to the banding stations.

Casual records.—Records of this species outside its normal range are not numerous. A single specimen was taken in the Chiricahua Mountains, Ariz., in the spring of 1894; one was observed in Salt Lake City, Utah, in June 1874; and one was noted near Fortine, in northwestern Montana, on June 18, 1931.

Egg dates.—Alabama: 12 records, April 20 to July 15; 6 records, May 26 to June 17, indicating the height of the season.

Illinois: 19 records, May 9 to July 10; 10 records, May 19 to June 15.

Michigan: 16 records, May 9 to August 20; 8 records, May 15 to June 3.

New York: 15 records, May 21 to June 19; 8 records, May 26 to June 5.

South Carolina: 12 records, May 6 to July 2.

BALANOSPHYRA FORMICIVORA FORMICIVORA (Swainson)

ANT-EATING WOODPECKER

HABITS

The type race of the species is now restricted in its distribution to the region from south-central Texas (Kerr County and the Chisos Mountains) to eastern and southern Mexico. It differs from the other races in the width of the white frontal band, the amount of streaking on the breast and sides, and the amount of yellow in the throat patch, as well as in size. It differs from *bairdi* and *aculeata* in having the chest mostly streaked, at least on the median portion, instead of mostly uniform black. The white frontal patch is broader than in *angustifrons*, and the black band across the female crown is much wider. It is slightly larger than *aculeata*, and somewhat smaller than *bairdi* but decidedly larger than *angustifrons*. Its throat patch is paler yellow than in *bairdi* and *angustifrons*.

I cannot find anything of consequence in print relating to the habits of the race, which probably do not differ materially from the habits of the species elsewhere. There are two sets of eggs in the Thayer collection, one of six and one of five eggs, taken in Tamaulipas, Mexico, on April 18 and 22, 1908; in each case the nest is said to have been 20 feet from the ground in a pine. The measurements of these 11 eggs average 26.47 by 19.00 millimeters; the eggs showing the four extremes measure 28.1 by 19.0, 26.7 by 19.3, 25.9 by 18.9 millimeters.

DISTRIBUTION

Range.—Western United States, Central America, and northwestern South America; nonmigratory.

On the Pacific coast the ant-eating woodpecker ranges through the Coast and Sierra Nevada ranges **north** to southwestern Oregon (Cow Creek and Ashland). In the interior it is found **north** to northern Arizona (Hualapai Mountain, Williams, and Grand Canyon); northern New Mexico (Largo Canyon and the headwaters of the Gallina River); and southwestern Texas (Fort Davis and

Kerrville). From these regions the species is found **south** through both eastern and western Mexico (including Baja California) and other Central American countries, at least to central Colombia.

Several subspecies of this woodpecker are found only in Central and South America, but three varieties occur regularly in the United States, while two others are confined to Baja California. The true ant-eating woodpecker (*B. f. formicivora*), which ranges through eastern and southern Mexico, is found also in south-central Texas (Chisos Mountains and Kerrville). Mearns's woodpecker (*B. f. aculeata*) occupies the range in Arizona, New Mexico, and western Texas (Fort Davis) south through the Mexican States of Sonora, Chihuahua, and Durango. The California woodpecker (*B. f. bairdi*) is found in the Pacific coast region from Oregon south to northern Baja California. In this Mexican State the narrow-fronted woodpecker (*B. f. angustifrons*) is confined to the region of Cape San Lucas, while the San Pedro woodpecker (*B. f. martirensis*) is found in the northwestern part of the area nearly to the United States border.

Egg dates.—Arizona: 9 records, May 10 to June 10.

California: 66 records, April 2 to June 15; 33 records, April 20 to May 15, indicating the height of the season. Second and third broods have been found in September and October.

Baja California: 4 records, May 10 to June 3.

BALANOSPHYRA FORMICIVORA BAIRDI (Ridgway)

CALIFORNIA WOODPECKER

PLATE 28

HABITS

The above common name is well chosen, as this is one of the commonest and most conspicuous birds throughout its range in California. Anyone who spends much time afield in the valleys, foothills, and canyons of southern and western California is sure to see this strikingly colored and active woodpecker making itself conspicuous among the oaks and pines; and, where one is seen, there are almost sure to be others, for it is a sociable species.

Referring to the Lassen Peak region, Grinnell, Dixon, and Linsdale (1930) say:

Two environmental factors of seeming importance for the presence of this bird were an available supply of acorns and wood or bark of sorts into which the birds could bore storage holes. As to species of oak, out of the six or more present, our impression remains that no outstanding choice by the woodpeckers was shown. About as many of the birds were seen among the black oaks in the vicinity of Payne Creek P. O., as among the valley oaks around Cone's. However, tracks of black oaks recurred east of the main mountain mass in the section, as along the upper Susan River and near Eagle Lake, where no California woodpeckers were ever seen by us. To repeat, none of this species of woodpecker was seen by us east of about the western edge of the yellow pine belt (Transition life-zone). * * *

Situations where individuals of this woodpecker were observed are as follows: top of sycamore; dead sycamore stub; in cottonwood; about clumps of fruiting mistletoe; at tips of twigs of large valley oak; in black oak; in blue oak; on dead upper limb of living blue oak; in orchard tree; on isolated digger pine; in large yellow pine; at top of dead incense cedar; on ground at roadside; on fence post; on barn end; on telephone pole.

Courtship.—I first became acquainted with this handsome woodpecker in the Arroyo Seco, on the outskirts of Pasadena, during the winter and spring of 1929, where I often saw these birds busy with their courtship activities in the tops of the tall sycamores. They were flying about among the treetops, making a lot of noise, two males sometimes chasing a female and showing off their brilliant colors, the white spaces in their wings and the white rumps being especially conspicuous; doubtless the red crown and yellow throat, set off by black and white, played an important part in the display. They reminded me of flickers, as they danced on, or dodged around, the branches in playful, showy antics.

Nesting.—*Bendire* (1895) writes:

In the more southern portions of its range nidification commences sometimes as early as April, and somewhat later farther north. The nesting sites are mostly excavated in white-oak trees, both living and dead, but preferably one of the former is selected in which the core of the tree is decayed. It also nests occasionally in sycamores, cottonwoods, and large willow trees, and more rarely in telegraph poles. Both sexes assist in the excavation of the nesting site, as well as in incubation. The entrance hole is about 1⅜ inches in diameter, perfectly circular, and is sometimes chiseled through 2 or 3 inches of solid wood before the softer and decayed core is reached. The inner cavity is gradually enlarged as it descends, and varies from 8 to 24 inches in depth, usually being from 4 to 5 inches in diameter at the bottom, where a quantity of fine chips are allowed to remain, on which the eggs are deposited.

Milton P. Skinner writes to me: "On May 12, 1933, I found a nest in the main trunk of an almost dead black oak. The opening, 25 feet above the ground, seemed very small and was placed on the southeast side of the tree.

"In the Yosemite Valley, these birds nest in the trunks and large limbs of the Kellogg oaks, and their abandoned holes may be used by pygmy owls another year. As a rule, the California woodpeckers and the pygmy owls show little antagonism toward each other. In spite of this usual custom of nesting in the oaks, most of the birds I saw in the Yosemite were actually in the cottonwoods along the river. After some searching, I found at least one nest there in a short, dead stub of a cottonwood, on July 24, 1933. I saw one bird fly down and feed another that was inside, and then fly away. The hole was about 12 feet above the ground and on the north side of the stub, facing the river and away from the meadow behind it. All the trees in the vicinity were cottonwoods, but there was one oak 150 feet east of the nesting site. There were six other holes in the stub, all on the north side and from 6 to 18 feet above the ground."

Grinnell and Storer (1924) write:

The more intensive occupancy of the Yosemite Valley during recent years and the operations of the government employees in promptly removing dead but standing trees to be cut up for wood has operated to the detriment of the woodpeckers which seek such trees for nesting holes. So it was no surprise, in May, 1919, to find a number of telephone or electric power poles near Redwood Lane which had been prospected for nesting sites by woodpeckers—the California, to judge from the size of hole and general location. Dearth of suitable natural sites had forced the birds to at least investigate these newly established dead-tree substitutes. With no substitutes at all available, the only result to be logically looked for, as a result of man's interference with the natural order of affairs, would be the disappearance of woodpeckers. The question arises here as to the justification of the administratiton in so altering natural conditions in National Parks as to threaten the persistence there of any of its native denizens.

Eggs.—The California woodpecker lays ordinarily four or five eggs; six eggs are not very rare; and as many as ten have been found in a nest, probably the product of two females. The eggs vary from short-ovate to elliptical-ovate. They are pure white, with very little or no gloss. The measurements of 52 eggs average 25.98 by 19.78 millimeters; the eggs showing the four extremes measure **29.9** by 19.0, 27.9 by **22.6, 22.0** by 18.6, and 24.38 by **18.29** millimeters.

Young.—The period of incubation is said to be about 14 days, in which both parents assist. Both also help to feed the young. Harriet Williams Myers (1915) made some interesting observations on a late brood of young California woodpeckers, which she found in a hole in a telephone pole, on September 11, between Los Angeles and Pasadena. She says:

In an hour's watching the birds fed 28 times, the shortest interval being one-half minute, the longest eight. In nine minutes they fed eight times.

On the 15th of the month, when I believe the young must have been about ten days old, they were fed 24 times in 58 minutes. The food given them now was mostly acorns which the adults took from the nearby poles, sometimes digging them out in pieces, and sometimes taking them to the top of a flat pole where they pounded away for some minutes before coming to the nest with their bills stuffed full of the white bits. From this time until the young left the nest they were fed mostly on these acorns.

One of her most interesting observations was that an apparently young bird, presumably a fully grown member of an earlier brood, joined the two parents that were feeding the young in the nest. At one time, this immature bird entered the nest, while the parents were away, apparently for the purpose of being fed by them, and remained there for some time. Meanwhile—

when the adults came to feed they did not go inside but reached over, fed, and flew away. Three times one of them did this, but the fourth time, when the male came, he stood on one side of the hole and I heard him give low, guttural notes. * * * Presently, the truant young, for such he proved to be, appeared in the doorway and, with open mouth, begged for just one bite. * * * But the old bird was unrelenting and stayed in his position by the hole until the bird inside, which was undoubtedly a former nestling, came out and flew onto the wire above, when the adult male went within.

Just to prove that he was not all baby, the former nestling turned in and helped feed. Several times he went into the hole and came directly out, and I might have thought that he was in there in hopes of getting fed had I not distinctly seen a big fly in his bill as he entered. Each time as he bobbed into the hole several white bars showed plainly on the underside of the outer tail feathers. It was this marking of a young bird which convinced me that he was a former nestling. In every other respect he resembled a male California Woodpecker. Once more, during my watching, he slipped into the nest, staying eight minutes before they got him out. The first time it had been twenty minutes.

From the above, and from the observations of Frank A. Leach (1925), to be referred to later, it seems that the California woodpecker often, if not regularly, raises two or even three broods in a season.

Plumages.—The young are hatched naked and blind, but the juvenal plumage is acquired before the young bird leaves the nest. In this plumage the young male closely resembles the adult male and the young female is much like the adult female in general color pattern, but the red of the crown and nape is duller and more or less mixed with dusky or black; sometimes the crown is nearly all black mixed with some scarlet feathers; the colors everywhere are duller, lacking in gloss, and the plumage is softer, less firm; the yellow of the throat is less pronounced; the streaks on the breast are less sharply defined; the tertials and scapulars are tipped with white, and there are narrow white tips on the two outer tail feathers on each side, but these tips wear away during winter, or sooner; there are at least two white spots on each web of the outer tail feather, which are in evidence all through the first year; as the juvenal wings and tail are retained until the next summer molt, birds of the year may be thus recognized; the bill is smaller and weaker than that of the adult. The molt of the juvenal contour plumage begins in August or September.

Adults have a complete annual molt between July and September, mainly in August.

Food.—Some prominent California ornithologists have named this bird the "California acorn-storing woodpecker," a rather long but very appropriate name, for it designates one of its most characteristic habits and names the largest item in its food supply. W. L. Dawson (1923) has this to say on the subject:

From time immemorial this bird has riddled the bark of certain forest trees and stuffed the holes with acorns. Speculation is still rife as to the cause or occasion or necessity or purpose of this strange practice, but the fact is indisputable and the evidence of it widely diffused. * * *
What he accomplishes the photographs show well enough,—the close, methodical studding of bark or wood of any kind with acorns, chiefly those of live-oaks,

over immense areas. The cultures, once started, are wrought upon continuously year by year, as material avails or the colony flourishes. Live-oaks themselves are the commonest hosts, together with the white, or post, oak, and the black oak of the southern counties. After these come sycamore and yellow pine or, more rarely, eucalyptus. Telegraph and telephone poles, gables, cornices, and, in fact, any wooden structure where they are permitted to work, if near the source of acorn supply, may come in for ornamentation. On a small square-sawed telephone pole near Marysville I found sixty acorns (and pecans purloined from a neighboring orchard) imbedded in a space five inches wide and two feet long. At that rate the pole carried some 1500 of these tiny storehouses.

In Tecolote Canyon, west of Santa Barbara, there is a giant sycamore which I count one of the handsomest examples of Carpintero's workmanship—an unbroken shaft, at least forty feet high and three feet across the inlaid face, covered with a "solid" mass of acorns totalling, say, some 20,000. Strawberry Valley in the San Jacinto Mountains appears to be a paradise for the California Woodpecker. Here majestic oaks (*Quercus californica*) alternate with still more majestic pines (*Pinus ponderosa*), the former for sustenance and the latter for storage, and the doughty "California" is probably the most abundant bird in the valley. The boles of the most enormous pines are methodically riddled with their acorn-carrying niches, and in some of the trees the work is carried through from base to crown. In one such tree I estimated that there were imbedded no less than 50,000 acorns.

Dr. William E. Ritter has made an intensive study of this interesting habit of the California woodpecker and has published the results of his observations and theories in three extensive papers (1921, 1922, 1938). There is much food for thought in these scholarly papers, to which the reader is referred, but space here will permit only brief quotations from or references to them. As to whether the hole drilling is injurious to the trees, he says (1921): "Although I have examined many storage pines in widely separated localities, I have never seen anything even suggestive of harm to the trees from the holes. Never, so far as I have noticed, do the holes pierce through into the deeper living layers of the bark." He noticed that "almost without exception the nuts were inserted tip in and base out, most of them fitting the hole snugly," having been driven in good and hard, and flush with the surface of the bark, or even countersunken below it; and that "to a certain extent the store holes are made to fit the size of the acorns they are to receive"; this latter point was discovered when he noted that, in a region where the black oak (*Quercus kelloggii*) predominated, the holes were considerably larger than they were in the live-oak region, the acorns of the black oak being sharply larger than those of the live oak. In some cases the acorns were not driven in flush with the bark, the base being left protruding somewhat and thus leaving them vulnerable to pilfering by rodents and perhaps some birds; in this connection, he says: "Conclusive evidence that nut-eating rodents (squirrels, rats) prey upon the acorns stored by the woodpeckers was first obtained on the present visit. Two trees were found on which the bark immediately around acorn holes had been gnawed by rodents, as unmistakably proved by the tooth marks. The acorns were gone from some of these holes, but not from all, thus showing that the marauders had failed in some of their efforts."

Summarizing his first paper, he makes the following statements:

As to hole drilling: While the holes are made expressly for the reception of acorns, many holes are probably made which are never used, holes are made at seasons of the year when there are no acorns to store, and large numbers of perfectly serviceable holes seem to be abandoned even in localities where both birds and acorns are abundant, and new holes are being made.

As to the storing business itself: While this is of distinct service to the food necessities of the woodpeckers, the instinct sometimes goes wrong to the extent of storing pebbles instead of acorns, thus defeating entirely the purpose of the instinct. Again, large numbers of acorns are sometimes stored, the use of which is so long delayed that the acorns become wholly or largely unfit for food, and this in places where the bird population seems normal. Finally, acorns are sometimes stored in such fashion as to make them easy prey for marauding rodents, when with some definite foresight and a little more work such exposure could easily be largely avoided.

In his second paper (1922), after further observations, he states[1]:

My previous surmise that the birds are more interested in the grubs contained in the acorns than in the acorn meats has not been substantiated. What I could make out while in camp among them, by watching them gather and eat their breakfasts, was to the effect that good uninhabited acorns were chiefly used. Again and again birds were seen to pick nuts from the top-most branches of the black oak, fly with them in their beaks to some approximately horizontal surface of a large limb on a pine or another oak, make the surface aid them somehow (I never could see exactly how, as the "breakfast tables" were, of course, all on the upper surfaces of the limbs, and too high for my vision) in breaking and tearing open the nuts. Apparently cracks and chinks in the table top serve as holders for the acorns while they are being opened and eaten. This is indicated by the fact that dead and partly decayed trees or parts of trees were mostly used. I saw no indication of the feet being used in handling the nuts. The litter on the ground under the dining trees, consisting of shell fragments and lost bits of meat, indicated grubless nuts almost entirely. This result as to the use of mast is in agreement with Beal's examination of the stomach contents of our woodpecker.

Charles W. Michael (1926), in the Yosemite Valley, made the interesting discovery that the California woodpecker has been known to learn by experience and to show some intelligence in its acorn storing. For a number of years when acorns were abundant no extensive storing was done, yet the woodpeckers lived in the valley all winter. Then came a lean year, with no acorn crop, when no storing *could* be done; and that winter the woodpeckers were forced to leave the valley for lack of food. The following year there was a bountiful crop of acorns, and the woodpeckers, having learned by experience, were busy filling up their storehouses. "From the above observations," he

---

[1] Prof. Ritter's extensive book (1938) on the California woodpecker appeared while this bulletin was in press.—EDITOR.

says, "one might conclude that an abundance of acorns is not directly responsible for prodigious storing. In a land of plenty the necessity of laying aside stores for future consumption is obviated. It is the barren years that teach the value of thrift. Intelligence plus experience may well have been the cause of the excessive storing of this year. A few of the more intelligent woodpeckers that were forced last winter to abandon the valley for lack of food are now preparing against the next lean year."

Claude Gignoux (1921) reports finding almonds stored in the bark of an oak tree on a ranch near Marysville, Calif., as well as in the side of a barn.

Dawson (1923) says: "A regrettable taste for fruit is occasionally cultivated, but this has not reached economic proportions, save in the case of almonds. Almond orchards thrive best at a very considerable distance from oak groves."

Although acorns, almonds, walnuts, and pecans constitute nearly 53 percent of its food, and much more than that in fall and winter, the California woodpecker eats quite a variety of other food at different seasons. Prof. F. E. L. Beal (1910) examined the contents of 75 stomachs, which contained "22.43 percent of animal matter to 77.57 percent of vegetable." Bendire (1895) says: "During the spring and summer its food consists, to a great extent, of insects, including grasshoppers, ants, beetles, and different species of flies, varied occasionally with fruit, such as cherries, which are carried off whole, apples, figs, and also berries and green corn."

Mr. Skinner says in his notes: "At times this bird feeds very much like an eastern red-headed woodpecker. On May 9, 1933, one was seen on the trunk of an oak, only 4 feet above ground, making flycatcherlike sallies up under the foliage of the oak. And many times thereafter I saw the birds operating similarly within the foliage itself. In some instances I have seen these woodpeckers dart out from high up in tall yellow pines after passing insects, then gliding back on set wings. Sometimes they do this from tall electric poles, at times going out as much as 50 feet. Since there was every reason to suppose that the bird saw the insect before it started, this speaks well for its keenness of eyesight. At times, these woodpeckers glean insects from the bark of trees. In July, in the Yosemite Valley, hunting the twigs and bark for insects seemed the favorite method of getting food."

Dr. Joseph Grinnell (1908) saw one of these woodpeckers, in the San Bernardino Mountains, drive a sapsucker away from its borings in an alder and then go "the rounds of the borings" drinking from each. Dr. Harold C. Bryant (1921) saw a California woodpecker robbing a nest of a pair of western wood pewees; he was "calmly perched on the pewee's nest and eating one of the eggs. I could see the white and the yolk of the egg on the woodpecker's bill, as he raised his head. After watching for some time, I attempted to frighten the robber away, but experienced considerable difficulty in doing so. When he finally left the nest the pewees continued to dart at him, to drive him farther away. Soon one of the pewees, apparently the female, returned to the nest, picked up an eggshell and flew off with it. I was unable to see what she did with it. In half a minute she returned and began incubating the remaining eggs."

Behavior.—The California woodpecker flies in true woodpecker fashion, an undulating flight, interspersed with long dips during which the wings are partly closed and somewhat pressed against the sides of the body; during the rises the wings are flapped, displaying the black and white markings conspicuously; there is an upward sweep before alighting. Grinnell and Storer (1924) say: "When alighting on a tree trunk, these birds assume a vertical posture, head out, tail appressed to the bark. They move up by a hitching process—head in, tail out; up; tail in, head out. If a bird perches on a small horizontal branch, his position is more likely to be diagonal than directly crosswise. If a bird alights on the square top of a fence post, he seems ill at ease and soon backs over the edge into a more woodpecker-like posture."

Mr. Dawson (1923) writes: "A most characteristic flight-movement is an exaggerated fluttering wherein progress is at a minimum and exercise at a maximum. In this way, also, they ascend at acute angles, sometimes almost vertically. With this movement alternates much sailing with outspread wings, and certain tragic pauses wherein the wings are quite folded." A similar flight is thus described by Grinnell, Dixon, and Linsdale (1930) as follows: "Individual woodpeckers were often seen making a kind of flight the object of which we did not determine. A bird would fly in a nearly vertical direction from its perch for three meters or more and then commence an irregular swooping flight, finally coming back to the original perch."

M. P. Skinner says in his notes: "In many of their ways, motions, and mannerisms these birds strongly resemble the red-headed woodpeckers of Eastern United States. Often they are very quiet and remain motionless in one position for many minutes at a time. They are as apt to perch crosswise as lengthwise of a horizontal, or nearly horizontal, limb. At times, they hop along a limb, or the cross-arm of an electric pole, while their bodies are turned a little sideways. Although one exhibited the usual woodpecker habit of nervously jumping down backward, and swaying from side to side, so as to be seen first on one side of his dead stub and then on the other, he was really noticeably quiet and motionless most of the time. One was seen in the Yosemite Valley on the under side of a cottonwood twig, clinging there with his back down."

Bendire (1895), on the other hand, says: "It is one of the most restless Woodpeckers I know of, and never appears to be at a loss for amusement or work of some kind, and no other bird belonging to this family could possibly be more industrious." This was my impression of it, as well as the opinion of others.

Henry W. Henshaw (1921) evidently considered this woodpecker playful, for he writes: "In searching for the motives underlying the storing habit of the California Woodpecker we should not lose sight of the fact that the several acts in the process, the boring of the holes, the search for the acorns, the carrying them to the holes and the fitting them in, bear no semblance to work in the ordinary sense of the term, but is play. I have seen the birds storing acorns many times, and always when thus engaged they fill the air with their joyous cries and constantly play tag with each other as they fly back and forth. When thus engaged they might not inaptly be likened to a group of children at play."

California woodpeckers are well known to be sociable birds and to live more or less in communities or loose colonies, where food conditions are favorable. But a most remarkable story of apparently communal nesting is told by Frank A. Leach (1925). On February 2, 1922, he discovered these woodpeckers excavating a nest in a wooden trolley pole at Diablo, Calif. He estimated that they must have started work on this hole about the middle of January and thinks that it was some time near the latter part of April before it was finished. On March 1, he "saw two go in one after the other. Both appeared to be working on the inside. Two other birds on the pole showed interest in the work by remaining there and taking an occasional peep into the hole." On April 3, there were "from four to six woodpeckers about the place all day. On one occasion saw three go into the hole. Heard digging while they were inside." On April 17, he saw "three birds go into the cavity and soon after heard two of them working. Four other birds were on the pole, one looking into the hole."

The above extracts from his notes, made at frequent intervals and often for several days in succession, would seem to indicate that at least two, and possibly three, pairs of woodpeckers assisted in the excavation of that nest, but evidently their work was not very efficient, as the time involved was unusually long. The same cooperative behavior continued during incubation of the eggs and the feeding of the young, several different birds working in relays; and this continued during the rearing of three broods of young that season. He says that "in the case of the second brood, on eight different occasions I saw three different old birds feed the young ones in the nest, and at one time I witnessed a fourth one delivering food to them."

Referring to the third brood, he says:

In the large oak tree standing so near the trolley pole that some of its outer branches nearly reached the pole, there were almost always from six to eight mature woodpeckers, all of which seemed to be interested in the welfare of the nestlings in the pole. I repeatedly saw three of them feed the youngsters, and on two occasions noted four different old birds perform this parental service. I was satisfied from the actions of the birds that a majority of the flock, if not all of them, participated in the care of the young woodpeckers. * * * For others than the parent birds to feed the young was a custom that was not confined to this group or flock at the trolley pole. At about the time the young were leaving that nest, I discovered another nest in a large oak tree situated about a quarter of a mile distant from the pole, where I found from one to five old birds, and possibly more, very busy feeding the nestlings.

Major Bendire (1895) remarks: "The California woodpecker is by far the most social representative of this family found within the United States, and it is no unusual occurrence to see half a dozen or more in a single tree. It is also a well-disposed bird, and seldom quarrels or fights with its own kind or with smaller species; but it most emphatically resents the thieving propensities of the different jays, magpies, and squirrels, when caught trespassing on its winter stores, attacking these intruders with such vigor and persistency that they are compelled to vacate the premises in a hurry."

According to some other observers, its behavior toward other species is not always as friendly as it might be. M. P. Skinner writes to me: "Once I found a California woodpecker and a California jay peaceably perched in the top of a dead cottonwood. But at other times I have noted much fighting between these woodpeckers and the jays, with the woodpeckers apparently able to hold their own. On May 1, 1933, at old Fort Tejon, I saw a California woodpecker make a vicious dive at a plain titmouse that was clinging to the bark on the trunk of an oak. On May 31 I saw one make a dive at an Arkansas kingbird on a fence and drive it away. In May 1933 I found a pair of house finches that had attempted to nest in a cavity high up in a dead stub of a black oak. When I appeared, I found a California woodpecker throwing out the straws and other nest material. The two finches were only a foot or two distant, but they made no attempt to save their home, although it is probable that they were scolding. Old acorn stores in the same stub indicated that some woodpecker had an earlier claim to that stub than the finches had."

Howard W. Wright (1908) says:

January 18, while collecting at Newhall, California, I wounded a Lewis woodpecker. The bird was able to fly to another tree, and I noticed that some California woodpeckers in a nearby tree became very much excited. As the Lewis woodpecker lit on the tree trunk four California woodpeckers attacked him evidently with the intent of driving him off. The Lewis started for another tree but a California flew at him from in front, and they both fell in the struggle that ensued. At this the other California woodpeckers, which were joined by a few more, set up a violent chattering and when I ran up, to my amazement I found that the Lewis had hold of the California by the skull, two of its claws entering the latter's eyes and the other two entering the skull in front and behind. The Lewis woodpecker was dead and the California so nearly so that it died while I was removing the former's claws.

Voice.—Mr. Skinner says in his notes: "In May, at least, these woodpeckers are sometimes noisy while calling to their mates. One gave a ringing *cleep-ep, cleep-ep* call on May 25, 1933. It was somewhat similar to a flicker's call." Ralph Hoffmann (1927) says: "When a bird lights on a pole or limb already occupied, there is always mild excitement, fluttering of the wings, bowing and scraping, and always a lively interchange of harsh calls, like the syllables *chák-a, chák-a, chák-a chak,* dying off at the end." W. L. Dawson (1923) gives the following interpretations of its notes: "A jeering, raucous voice, * * * *Jacob, Jacob, Jacob;* * * * *Kerack Kerack;*" and "*chaar chaar tchurrup.*"

Field marks.—The California woodpecker is conspicuously marked and need not be mistaken for anything else from any angle. When flying away, it looks like a black bird with an extensive white rump and with a white patch in each wing; when flying over or when perched facing the observer, the white abdomen and the broad black band across the chest are distinctive; if near enough, the color pattern of the head is easily seen.

BALANOSPHYRA FORMICIVORA ANGUSTIFRONS (Baird)

NARROW-FRONTED WOODPECKER

HABITS

The Cape region of southern Baja California is the home of this subspecies. It is a well-marked race, which Ridgway (1914) describes as "similar to *B. f. formicivora,* but wing averaging much shorter, bill relatively larger, white frontal band decidedly narrower, lower throat usually much more strongly yellow, white area on proximal portion of remiges smaller, and the adult female with black area on crown much narrower."

William Brewster (1902) says of its haunts:

This woodpecker, which seems to be confined to the Cape Region proper, is exceedingly abundant throughout the pine forests on the higher mountains south of La Paz and common in many places in the oaks at the bases of the mountains and among their foot-hills, ranging downward, according to Mr. Belding, to an elevation of about 700 feet. Mr. Frazar found it most numerous on the Sierra de la Laguna, during the last week of April and the first week of May. After that its numbers decreased perceptibly. It began breeding on this mountain the first week in June, but the breeding season was not at its height until the middle of that month. * * *

Only one specimen was seen at Triunfo during the last two weeks of June, but the bird was common and presumably breeding at Pierce's Ranch in July. At the latter place it fairly swarmed in December, the resident colony being probably augmented by large numbers of winter visitors from La Laguna, where Mr. Frazar found only a few birds lingering in late November and early December. Along the road between San José del Cabo and Miraflores it was seen in considerable numbers on November 15, and three were observed in some evergreen oaks at Santiago on November 23.

Nesting.—There is a set of four eggs in the Thayer collection, apparently the same set referred to by Mr. Brewster, collected by M. Abbott Frazar in the Sierra de la Laguna, on June 3, 1887; the nest is described as 10 feet up in a dead pine stump; the entrance measured 1¾ inches in diameter, and the cavity was 18 inches deep. The measurements of these 4 eggs are 24.13 by 19.05, 22.61 by 19.56, 22.61 by 19.30, and 23.88 by 18.80 millimeters.

The food and general habits of this woodpecker do not seem to differ materially from those of the species elsewhere. It has similar acorn-storing habits, for Mr. Frazar found "many dead pines literally stuffed full of acorns."

BALANOSPHYRA FORMICIVORA ACULEATA (Mearns)

MEARNS'S WOODPECKER

Plate 28

HABITS

Along our southwestern border, from Arizona, New Mexico, and western Texas southward over northwestern Mexico to Durango, we find this race of ant-eating woodpecker. It was separated, named, and described by Dr. Edgar A. Mearns (1890a) as follows: "General size and coloring intermediate between *M. formicivorus* and *M. formicivorus bairdi*; throat less yellow than in either of them; bill shorter, more slender, and less arcuate than in either of the other forms of *M. formicivorus*; white striping of chest more than in the Pacific coast form, less than in *formicivorus*."

He says of its haunts (1890b): "A very common resident through the pine belt, breeding plentifully. I have found it as high as the spruce forests, but never in them. It is essentially a bird of the pines, only occasionally descending to the cottonwoods of the low valleys. The oaks which are scattered through the lower pine zone supply a large share of its food."

Henry W. Henshaw (1875) writes: "This woodpecker was first observed when we neared Camp Apache, and, so far as my own observations go, its range in Arizona is coincident with that of the oaks, the acorns of which appear to constitute a very important item in its bill of fare. We noticed it to the southward in every locality where oaks were found in sufficiently large groves to afford it at once a place of shelter and an inexhaustible source whence to draw food."

Harry S. Swarth (1904), writing of the Huachuca Mountains, Ariz., says: "A most abundant summer resident in the lower parts of the mountains; a few winter here but they are scarce during the cold weather. I saw but two or three during February and the early part of March, about the middle of March they began to arrive in numbers, and by April 1 were most abundant. Primarily a bird of the oak woods they seldom venture into the higher parts of the mountains, breeding almost entirely below 6,000 feet."

Courtship.—We found this woodpecker quite common on the steep slopes of the Huachuca Mountains in May 1922, especially in the vicinity of Ramsay Canyon, between 5,000 and 6,000 feet elevation. They were usually seen in the open groves of tall pines mixed with oaks. A tall dead pine seemed to be one of their favorite resorts for their courtship displays, which were both showy and noisy. They reminded me of flickers as they dodged about the branches, chasing each other and displaying their conspicuous markings.

Nesting.—I have the records of four sets of eggs, all taken in the Huachuca Mountains but in a variety of nesting sites. There are two sets in the Thayer collection; one, containing six eggs, was taken on May 10, 1897, from a hole 8 inches deep in the dead limb of a sycamore, 30 feet from the ground; the other set of five eggs was taken on June 1, 1902, from a cavity 10 inches deep in an ash stump, 20 feet from the ground. A set of three eggs, in my collection, was collected by O. W. Howard on May 31, 1901; the nest was 6 feet above ground in a dead oak stump. Frank C. Willard took a set of five eggs on May 31, 1899, from a cavity 15 inches deep, 35 feet up in a large dead pine stub.

Eggs.—Mearns's woodpecker evidently lays three to six eggs. Major Bendire (1895) mentions a set of ten eggs, taken by F. H. Fowler, which were "evidently the product of two females." The eggs are pure white, of course, and vary from short-ovate to rounded-ovate, with only a slight gloss. The measurements of 20 eggs average 24.07 by 18.91 millimeters; the eggs showing the four extremes measure 26.8 by 17.8 (a long narrow egg), 23.9 by 20.8, and 22.4 by 19.5 millimeters.

Plumages.—Mr. Swarth (1904) writes:

About July 1 the young birds begin to make their appearance so like the adults in general appearance that it is difficult to distinguish between them. The young of both sexes usually have the entire crown red, as in the adult male, but of a duller color, more of a brick red; but one young female secured has the red area very limited and coming to a point behind, so as to form a small, triangular shaped patch on the crown. Of seventeen specimens collected in the Huachucas, three show, more or less distinctly, white markings on the outer tail feathers. In one of these, an adult female, the marks consist of indistinct white spots, mostly on the inner web. The other two, juvenile females, have the outer feathers distinctly, though irregularly, barred with white for about half their length.

Food.—The food of this woodpecker is evidently similar to that of other races of the species. Dr. Mearns (1890b) remarks: "Its habit of industriously hoarding food in the bark of pines, and in all sorts of chinks and hollows, is well known. These stores are the source of unending quarrels between this woodpecker and its numerous pilfering enemies; and I have laid its supplies under contribution myself, when short of provisions and lost from the command with which I had been traveling, by filling my saddlebags with half-dried acorns from under the loose bark of a dead pine."

Behavior.—Mrs. Bailey (1928) says: "An odd habit of the woodpeckers was happened on by Mr. Ligon in the Black Range. At dark, on March 15, 1913, seeing a bird enter a hole about eight feet up in an oak he closed it after it, and in the morning when he returned was surprised to find six birds in the one hole. As the woodpeckers do not nest until the last of May, and then in high dead pines, it was, of course, a night roost."

Ed. S. Steele (1926) tells the following story:

I was camping in a pine forest not many miles from Reserve, N. Mex., accompanied by a small English terrier. In front of my tent stood a large dead pine, near the top of which there were a number of holes, evidently the homes of four pairs of Ant-eating Woodpeckers (*Balanosphyra formicivora aculeata*). A gray tassel-eared squirrel came scampering along, and was at once spied by the dog, which gave chase. The squirrel ran up the dead tree mentioned above, to be instantly assailed by the woodpeckers. Their constant cries and their sharp bills made things so uncomfortable for the squirrel that it ran down the tree to within a few feet of the dog, who sent him scampering to the top again with his eight antagonists constantly flaying him.

About this time there was a swish of wings, and a sharp-shinned hawk (*Accipiter velox*) darted like a streak among the woodpeckers. For an instant it seemed that one of them was doomed, but by a small margin it managed to escape, and in an instant they had all darted to cover among the green boughs of surrounding trees. All was quiet for a few brief seconds, when the woodpeckers returned to the attack, except one which perched on the topmost bough of a near-by tree, as guard or lookout, watching for the hawk. The other seven took up the fight with the squirrel.

In a few minutes the hawk again appeared on the scene, the guard gave a shrill call of warning, and all the woodpeckers were under cover before their enemy could reach them. The hawk, then, finding the birds on their guard, left and did not return. The terrier soon abandoned the tree, and the squirrel hurried down and scampered away; the woodpeckers quickly quieted down and went peacefully about their home affairs. I believe that the birds recognized in the squirrel a danger to their eggs or young.

BALANOSPHYRA FORMICIVORA MARTIRENSIS Grinnell and Swarth

SAN PEDRO WOODPECKER

HABITS

The acorn-storing woodpecker of the Sierra San Pedro Martir, northwestern Baja California, has been separated and described by Grinnell and Swarth (1926) under the above name, to which they have added the long common name "San Pedro Martir acorn-storing woodpecker." Its distinguishing characters are given as follows:

Most nearly like *B. f. bairdi.* Distinguished from that species primarily by shorter wing, and by slightly shorter and notably weaker, more slender bill; also by average differences in head markings as set forth below. * * *

The relatively feeble bill of this bird, as compared with that of the upper California *bairdi*, is the most conspicuous character of this subspecies. In bill structure it is closely similar to *B. f. aculeata*, of Arizona.

The character of the head markings in the female is suggestive again of *aculeata*, the red area being usually more nearly square, as in that form, rather than shorter than wide, as in *bairdi*. The white frontal band averages slightly narrower than in *bairdi*, an approach toward the condition in *angustifrons*, of the Cape San Lucas region. The yellowish white (more dilutely yellow than in *bairdi*) U-mark on the lower throat in both sexes averages very much narrower in our specimens of *martirensis* than in a large series of *bairdi* usually only about half the width of the former as in the latter. This we are not quite confident of as a real character, in that there is a chance that "make" of specimen (whether or not the skin of the throat was stretched) affects the width of the white band. * * *

In character of the markings on the feathers of the breast there is no departure from the condition in *bairdi*. The upper breast is broadly and solidly black, the black band not penetrated posteriorly with white streaks to such an extent as in *aculeata* and *angustifrons*.

The range is given as, "so far as now known, only parts of the Sierra San Pedro Martir, in northern Lower California, between latitudes 30° and 31°30''; altitude 5,800 to 7,200 feet; life-zone mainly Upper Sonoran (live-oak association), but also Transition locally or sporadically."

The eggs are similar to those of other races of the species. The measurements of 12 eggs average 26.19 by 18.35 millimeters; the eggs showing the four extremes measure **25.1** by **19.4, 19.0** by 18.5, and 22.8 by **16.8** millimeters.

ASYNDESMUS LEWIS (Gray)

LEWIS'S WOODPECKER

PLATE 29

HABITS

My first impression of this curious and interesting woodpecker was of a large, black bird that looked more like a crow than a woodpecker and that flew with the strong, steady flight of a crow or a jay, with none of the undulations common to so many woodpeckers. I made the same comment the second time I saw it, and am interested to see that the same impressions were made on many others.

It is essentially a bird of the more open country and among scattered large trees, rather than of the heavily forested regions. S. F. Rathbun writes to me of its haunts in western Washington: "In this section of the State are many tracts of land commonly known as 'old burns.' At one time all were forested, then later they were swept by fire and in some instances more than once; but even now, on many, still stand the scarred and blackened trunks of what formerly were large, tall trees; and it is in or about these unattractive places that this woodpecker is more apt to be found, although by no means is it restricted to them."

Major Bendire (1895) says: "I have rarely seen Lewis's woodpecker in deep forests; far more frequently just on the outskirts of the pines, in juniper groves on the table-lands bordering the pines, as well as in the deciduous timber along streams in the lowlands, and occasionally even in solitary cottonwoods or willows, near some little spring, in the drier sagebrush-covered flats, miles away from the nearest forest."

Winton and Donald Weydemeyer (1928) say that in northwestern Montana it is—

a common summer resident throughout most of the Transition zone. It occurs most regularly in mixed broadleaf and conifer woods in river valleys, and in open forests of yellow pine along the foothills. It rarely ranges into the higher mountains, although we observed one individual in a Canadian zone forest of lodgepole pine and alpine fir, at an altitude of 6,160 feet. In cut-over or burned woods, it ranges to a higher elevation than in virgin forests.

In the eastern part of the county, this woodpecker is most common around farms and slashings, and in the more open woods of fir, larch, and yellow pine. Near Libby, in the western part, it seems to prefer creek-bottom woods of aspen, spruce, and cottonwood.

Johnson A. Neff (1928) says that his "acquaintance with this exotically brilliant woodpecker began in the mountains of Colorado, and even now the thought of it calls to mind that bleak, wind-blown area at an elevation of 8,500 feet, where these birds were very much at home in the dead trunks of spruce and hemlock that had once covered the mountains with living verdure."

Nesting.—Mr. Rathbun says in his notes: "In western Washington this woodpecker nests in June. Almost invariably the excavation for its nesting place is in a dead tree, the trunk of which is more or less blackened by fire, and this may be one reason why the bird is partial to the old burns. The tree may be one of several scattered about, or, infrequently, somewhat isolated. But in any event, this woodpecker shows a liking for a good-sized tree, broken off at quite a height, the outside of which has been charred or blackened by the flames. We have found many of its nesting places, and among these was one we shall not forget. In this case, the tree was a very large one, was broken off at a height of about 175 feet, and, as usual, had its outer surface burnt. Not far below its top was the entrance to the nest of a pair of these woodpeckers. Because it was so high it could be distinctly seen only by the use of glasses, but often we had noticed one of the birds enter it or come out of it. This nesting place was used for a number of years, and when it was in use we have gone out of our way more than once just to see these woodpeckers; for the top of the tree was used as a lookout station by the pair of birds, from which at times one or both would sail into the air after a flying insect."

Major Bendire (1895) says that—

it is by no means as particular in the choice of a nesting site as the majority of our Woodpeckers. Shortly after arriving on their breeding grounds a suitable site is selected for the nest, and not infrequently the same excavation is used for successive years. In most cases the nesting sites are excavated either in the tops of tall pines or in dry cottonwoods, and in tall rotten tree trunks, occasionally in partly decayed limbs of sycamores, oaks, and less frequently in junipers and willows. The nests, as a rule, are not easily gotten at, and quite a number are practically inaccessible, varying in height from 6 to fully 100 feet from the ground.
* * * [At Camp Harney, Oreg.] these birds nested mostly in junipers. * * * The junipers which are selected for nesting sites were invariably decayed inside, and after the birds had chiseled through the live wood, which was usually only from 1 to 2 inches thick, the remainder of the work was comparatively easy; the same site, if not disturbed, was occupied for several seasons, and in such the inner cavity was much deeper, some being fully 30 inches deep and generally about 4 inches wide at the bottom. The entrance hole varies from 2 to 2½ inches in diameter, and when this is made by the birds it is always perfectly circular; but occasionally a pair will take advantage of an old knot hole, if it and the cavity it leads to are not too large.

The Weydemeyers (1928) say that in northwestern Montana this species exercises a wide range of selection for nesting trees; of four nests that they record, two were in larch stubs, one in a dead cottonwood, and one in a live yellow pine; these nests were in the Transition Zone at elevations between 2,000 and 3,100 feet.

Ed. S. Currier (1928) found Lewis's woodpeckers nesting in what he called "colonies," near Portland, Oreg.; in each of two dead cottonwoods, less than a mile apart, he found three occupied nests all on the same day.

Eggs.—Bendire (1895) says:

From five to nine eggs are laid to a set; those of six or seven are the most common, but sets of eight are not very rare; I have found several of that number, and a single set of nine.

The eggs of Lewis's woodpecker vary greatly in shape and also in size. They are mostly ovate or short ovate in shape, but an occasional set is decidedly rounded ovate, while others are elliptical ovate; the shell is close grained and, in most cases, dull, opaque white, without any gloss whatever. Some sets, however, are moderately glossy, but scarcely as much so as the better-known eggs of the red-headed woodpecker, and none are as lustrous as the eggs of the flicker.

The measurements of 58 eggs average 26.22 by 19.99 millimeters; the eggs showing the four extremes measure **30.48** by 21.34, 26.67 by **24.38**, and **23.37** by **17.27** millimeters.

Young.—Major Bendire (1895) says of the young:

Both sexes assist in incubation, and this lasts about two weeks. The young leave the nest about three weeks after they are hatched, and are readily tamed. I kept a couple for several days, but they had such enormous appetites that I was glad to give them their liberty, as they kept me busy providing suitable food. They were especially fond of grasshoppers, but also ate raw meat, and climbed everywhere over the rough walls of my house. A considerable share of the food of these birds is picked up off the ground, and they appear to be much more at home there than woodpeckers generally are. The young are fed on insects, and I believe also on berries; I have seen one of these birds alight in a wild strawberry patch, pick up something, evidently a strawberry, fly to a tree close by in which the nest was situated, and give it to one of the young which was clinging to the side of the tree close to the nesting site.

Plumages.—The young Lewis's woodpecker is hatched naked and blind, but the juvenal plumage is acquired before the young bird leaves the nest. In fresh juvenal plumage the red "face" of the adult is replaced by black or dusky, though a young bird taken on July 22 shows some red mixed with the black in this area; the bill is small and weak; the crown and occiput are dull brownish black, without any greenish luster; the silvery-gray nuchal collar of the adult is wholly lacking; the under parts are mostly dull pale gray or dull grayish white, more or less suffused on the central breast and abdomen with dull red or orange-red; the whole plumage is softer and more blended in texture. Dr. J. A. Allen (Scott, 1886) says of some young birds that he examined: "The back and upper surface of the wings are bronzy green nearly as in the adult, with, however, in addition, broad bars of steel-blue on the scapulars and quills. These bars are especially prominent on the secondaries and inner vanes of the primaries, and are seen also in some specimens on the rectrices. The steel-blue edging the outer vanes of the quill feathers in the adult is absent; and the inner secondaries and longest primaries are tipped more or less prominently with white."

This juvenal plumage is worn through the summer and into September, when the molt into the first winter plumage begins with a sprinkling of the silvery, bristly feathers appearing on the breast and in the collar, with the increase of red in the "face," and with metallic-green feathers showing on the head. This molt is apparently prolonged and is not finished until early in winter, when young birds and adults are practically alike. Adults have a complete annual molt late in summer and fall; I have observed it as late as October 12.

Food.—Referring to the food of Lewis's woodpecker, Major Bendire (1895) writes:

In summer its food consists mainly of insects of different kinds, such as grasshoppers, large black crickets, ants, beetles, flies, larvæ of different kinds, as well as of berries, like wild strawberries and raspberries, service berries and salmon berries, acorns, pine seeds, and juniper berries, while in cultivated districts cherries and other small fruits enter into its daily bill of fare. Here, when common, it may occasionally do some little damage in the orchards, but this is fully compensated by the noxious insects it destroys at the same time. In localities where grasshoppers are abundant they live on these pests almost exclusively while they last. Mr. Shelly W. Denton tells me he noticed this Woodpecker gathering numbers of May flies (*Ephemera*) and sticking them in crevices of pines, generally in trees in which it nested, evidently putting them away for future use, as they lasted but a few days. It is an expert flycatcher, and has an extremely keen vision, sallying forth frequently after some small insect when this is perhaps fully 100 feet from its perch.

On this latter subject, Mr. Rathbun writes to me:

Lewis's woodpecker is an expert at catching insects on the wing. When in this act, its perch is some vantage spot, such as the top of a dead tree or a bare limb in the open. Here it sits motionless, except to turn its head from side to side on the lookout for its prey; and when this is seen, the bird glides from its resting place to make a capture. On one occasion for more than an hour, we watched a pair of these woodpeckers seize flying insects, and in that length of time not less than 35 were taken. Through our field glasses we kept a close watch on the birds and soon learned from their actions when an insect was sighted, thus it was easy for us to anticipate its capture, and in not a single instance was a failure made by either of the birds. Once, a light puff of air changed the course of the insect just at the time it was about to be taken, but the woodpecker made a quick turn upward at the same time, dropped its legs straight down, and neatly made the take. When busy catching insects on the wing, this bird leaves its perch by easy wing beats or a long, slow, graceful glide; then, after its prey is caught, rises in its flight and, quickly wheeling, returns to its lookout station.

But, as if not content with hunting insects after the manner of a flycatcher, sometimes this bird mingles with the swallows as they hawk over the ground. On one occasion in summer, as we came to a very open pasture, we noticed numbers of barn and cliff swallows in flight over it after insects, and in company with them was a pair of Lewis's woodpeckers. Back and forth over the meadow flew these dark birds, busy in an attempt to catch flying insects, and their actions as they flew were in marked contrast to those of the graceful swallows. Although we watched the woodpeckers for more than half an hour, throughout that time neither one alighted; and when we left the place both still coursed busily above the field.

About one-third of the food of Lewis's woodpecker consists of acorns. It shares with the California woodpecker the interesting habit of storing acorns, though its method of storing them is quite different, for it seldom, if ever, makes the neat round holes to fit the acorns, so characteristic of the other species; and its stores of acorns are never so extensive, so systematic, or so conspicuous as those of the California woodpecker. Charles W. Michael (1926) writes:

Recently we watched a Lewis Woodpecker making trips back and forth between a Kellogg oak and his home tree, a cottonwood. He was busy storing away his winter supply of acorns. Occasionally he picked a fallen acorn from the ground; more often he flew into the lesser branches of the oak, and hanging like a great black chickadee he plucked the acorn from the cup. With crow-like flappings, his broad wings carried him back to the dead cottonwood with his prize in his bill. Alighting somewhat below the summit of his tree he would, by a series of flight jumps, come to a certain shattered stub where a fissure formed a vise. Into this he would wedge the acorn.

With the acorn held firmly in place he would set about cutting away the hull, and strong strokes of his bill would soon split away the shell and expose the kernel. But he was not satisfied in merely making the kernel accessible, he must go on with his pounding until he had broken it into several pieces, and then with a piece in his bill he would dive into the air like a gymnast, drop twenty or thirty feet and come with an upward swoop to perch on the trunk of the same tree. A few hitching movements would bring him to a deep crack that opened into the heart of the tree. Here he would carefully poke away, for future reference, his morsel. Usually the acorn was cut into four parts, involving four such trips, and on the last trip to the vise he would take the empty hull in his bill, and with a jerk of his head, toss it into the air. An examination of the ground beneath the tree disclosed hundreds of empty acorn shells. Holding a watch on the Lewis Woodpecker, we found that he made five trips in five minutes and stored five acorns.

J. Eugene Law (1929) has published another illuminating paper on this subject, which is well worth reading; he describes in considerable detail the woodpeckers' methods in storing the meats of acorns in cracks in poles and indulges in some speculation as to the causes and purposes involved in the habit.

Herbert Brown (1902) found Lewis's woodpeckers quite destructive to pomegranates and quinces, near Tucson, Ariz. On September 30 he counted ten in the pomegranate groves; "they were mostly feeding on pomegranate fruit. They first cut a hole through the hard skin of the fruit and then extract the pulp, leaving nothing but an empty shell." Later, on October 13, he says: "Now that the pomegranate crop has been destroyed they have commenced to eat the quinces, of which there are large quantities. On the tops of some of the bushes I noticed that every quince had been eaten into, one side of the fruit being generally eaten away."

William E. Sherwood (1927) writes:

On June 16, 1923, while collecting near Imnaha, Wallowa County, Oregon, I frightened a Lewis woodpecker from the top of a fence post where it was evidently having a feast. On top of the post it had left a fresh egg, probably its own; for it was absolutely fresh, of the right size, and unmarked. The shell had been broken into, but the contents not yet extracted.

In a knothole on the side of the post was an eggshell (of the same kind), and a snail shell which had been broken into. Wedged into the cracks of the post were several insects (some of them still alive) of the two species commonly known as "salmon flies" and "trout flies." On the ground at the foot of the post were several snail shells, a green prune (picked into), and several cherry seeds with stems attached.

Johnson A. Neff (1928) has much to say about the economic status of this woodpecker, mainly in Oregon. A few quotations from his paper will serve to show the vast amount of damage to the fruit grower that it does in sections where it is abundant, mainly in summer and fall. He says that Prof. Beal (1911) "mentions one case in Washington wherein the birds tore the paper at the corners of packed boxes of apples left in the orchard over night, picking into every apple within reach, and necessitating the repacking of every box attacked."

S. D. Hill wrote to Mr. Neff:

In some sections and seasons they will destroy carloads of fruit, especially in orchards near timber. I have known them to do 50 percent damage to a pear crop in the Peyton district on upper Rogue River." Jackson Gyger, Ashland, wrote: "In 1924 the loss on Spitz and Delicious apples was about 75 percent, on Newtowns about 15 percent; Bosc and Anjou pears about 10 percent. The loss on trees near oak timber was nearly 100 percent. This season (1925) due to hunting them every day the loss was possibly 50 percent less. I bought $18.00 worth of ammunition to combat them this year. One man can not keep them out of a seven acre orchard, as they will work on one end while you are scaring them out of the other.

Mr. Neff goes on to say:

These complaints can not be over-looked, for stomach analyses show only the volume of fruit eaten, not the percentage of fruit damaged per tree, nor the real loss to the orchardist. * * *

In Oregon, although it sometimes becomes a nuisance in the small fruit plantings of various areas, it centers its destructive activities in the Rogue Valley; there it flocks in the greatest abundance. * * *

In this area there can be no question of the objectionable status of the Lewis woodpecker. If the birds would consume each fruit injured, there would be little complaint of their taking the quantity which probably would satisfy them. They are restless and energetic, however, and always attacking fresh fruit, which with one stroke of the bill is ruined for commercial use. If one allows only one bite to each fruit, some of the stomachs studied would have contained the samples of as high as two bushels of fruit. In the restricted areas mentioned the Lewis woodpecker is a pest.

Behavior.—Lewis's woodpecker seldom indulges in the undulating flight so common to other woodpeckers, though it sometimes swings in a long curve in a short flight from tree to tree. Its ordinary traveling flight is quite unlike the flight of other members of the family; it is strong, direct, and rather slow, with steady strokes of its long, broad wings. At first glance one would hardly recognize it as a woodpecker, for its flight and its appearance are more suggestive of a crow, a Clarke's nutcracker, or a jay. But it is far from clumsy in the air, and its skill in catching insects on the wing demonstrates

its mastery of the air in flight. It also indulges in some rather remarkable aerial evolutions, which one would hardly expect from a
member of the woodpecker family. On this subject, Robert Ridgway (1877) writes:

In its general habits and manners this beautiful species resembles quite
closely the eastern Red-headed Woodpecker (*M. erythrocephalus*), being quite
as lively and of an equally playful disposition. Some of its actions, however, are
very curious, the most remarkable of them being a certain elevated flight,
performed in a peculiar floating manner, its progress apparently laborious, as
if struggling against the wind, or uncertain, like a bird which had lost its
course and become confused. At such a time it presents the appearance of a
Crow high in the air, while the manner of its flight is strikingly similar to
that of Clarke's Nutcracker (*Picicorvus columbianus*). * * * After per-
forming these evolutions to its satisfaction, it descends in gradually contracting
circles, often to the tree from which it started.

Herbert Brown (1902) evidently saw a similar flight, of which he
says: "In flight they have little or none of that laborious undulating
movement so common to its kind, but in action and flight they seem
possessed of peculiarities supposed to belong to birds of a totally
different family. Today not less than fifty of them were circling
through the air, at an elevation of about 500 feet, with all the ease
and grace of the Falconidae. Not a stroke of the wing was apparent. * * * Those high in the air were sailing in great circles.
They kept it up indefinitely and had the appearance of being so
many miniature crows. When sailing they appear to open their
wings to the fullest extent possible."

Mr. Neff (1928) states that "these birds love the hottest sunshine,
and are commonly found perched in the tiptop of some tall partly-
dead tree, whence they can scan the air for insect food. They rarely
sit vertically upright on a branch as do most other woodpeckers, but
perch cross-wise with ease. They seldom climb up the trunk or
branches, although perfectly capable of doing so, and are rarely
heard tapping." They perch occasionally on wires, an uncommon
habit with other woodpeckers.

Major Bendire (1895) observes: "On its breeding grounds Lewis's
woodpecker appears to be a stupid and rather sluggish bird; it does
not show nearly as much parental affection as most of the other
members of this family, and is much less demonstrative. It is not
at all shy at such times, and will often cling to some convenient limb
on the same tree while its eggs are being taken, without making the
least complaint."

Voice.—Bendire (1895) says: "It is by far the most silent woodpecker I have met, and, aside from a low twittering, it rarely utters a
loud note. Even when suddenly alarmed, and when it seeks safety
in flight, the shrill 'huit, huit' given on such occasions by nearly all
of our woodpeckers is seldom uttered by it. Only when moving about

in flocks, on their first arrival in the spring and during the mating season, which follows shortly afterwards, does it indulge in a few rattling call notes, resembling those of the Red-shafted Flicker, and it drums more or less, in a lazy sort of way, on the dead top of a tall pine, or a suitable limb of a cottonwood or willow."

Ralph Hoffmann (1927) writes: "For a great part of the year the Lewis woodpecker is a silent bird, uttering not even a call note, but in the mating season it utters a harsh *chirr* and a high-pitched squalling *chee-up*, repeated at rather long intervals. Adult birds utter near the nest a series of sharp metallic cries like the syllable *ick, ick, ick*, which when rapidly repeated become a rattle. The young in the nest utter the usual hissing sound of young woodpeckers."

Field marks.—Lewis's woodpecker should be easily recognized. At a distance it appears likes a black bird, the back and the upper and lower surfaces of the wings being black, with no conspicuous white showing anywhere, and with a crowlike flight, broad wings and black tail. At short range, the greenish sheen of the back may glisten in the sunlight, and the silvery gray collar and pinkish underparts may be seen, as well as the gray upper breast and perhaps the red face.

Fall.—This woodpecker seems to be a highly migratory species. From the northern parts of its range it disappears almost entirely during winter; and throughout its entire range it is given to extensive wanderings, being very abundant in certain localities during fall and winter in certain seasons and at other seasons entirely absent. The species is highly gregarious in fall, wandering about in large flocks in search for suitable food supplies.

Mr. Rathbun tells me that this woodpecker is found in Washington from April to about November and occasionally is seen in winter, and says: "In this part [western] of the State the fall migration of this bird seems to begin early in September. Once, very early in the month, on our arrival at a lake not far from Seattle, we noticed a large number of these woodpeckers in three or four deciduous trees along the shore. Occasionally, a few of the birds would make short flights after insects in the air, but by far the larger number were more or less inactive and appeared to be resting, as some remained motionless where perched. And when one did change its position, it did this in a listless manner. Our arrival at the lake was rather late in the afternoon, and from the actions of the birds as a whole we gained the impression that they must have made quite an extended flight that day on their movement southward. On several other occasions in September we have seen this woodpecker as it was migrating. In each case a good many were in company, though rather loosely associated. And once, moving in a southerly direction with them for a very brief time, were numbers of nighthawks, swallows, and Vaux's swifts flying around for insects."

Mr. Neff (1928) writes:

This species, more than all its kin, moves in flocks in autumn. After the nesting season it gathers into flocks of from 10 to 300 or more. In such numbers it drops down into the fruit districts of southern Oregon and of northern California, and disaster results. * * *

On August 29, the writer, accompanied by Mr. Richardson, made a trip to Lake of the Woods, Klamath County. Just south of Ashland a few scattered individuals were seen. As the Cascade summit was approached many were seen in the open fields and meadows. In the flats near the lake, and in the open meadows near Rainbow Creek, numbers were found feeding on the mountain huckleberries. Returning to Ashland on September 1, huge flocks of these birds could be seen moving steadily toward the lower Valley. * * *

On September 7, also, the growers in the vicinity of Medford reported the arrival of the first birds there. Flocks were present until September 19, when almost every bird in the area disappeared. A few scattering individuals were left in various foothill areas, but these left during November. The areas in which they wintered so abundantly during the 1924-5 season were totally deserted during the 1925-6 season, and not until spring did they return to this area.

Herbert Brown (1902) states that Lewis's woodpeckers appeared in large numbers, during the fall of 1884, in the Santa Cruz Valley, Ariz., the first he had seen there for 20 years. He saw the first one on September 28 and ten on the 30th. They were very abundant at times during October but disappeared at intervals. They were last seen on November 16.

Winter.—W. E. D. Scott (1886) says of its winter habits in Arizona:

About my house it generally appeared about the 20th of September, and some years was very abundant. It stays as late as April 20, and then is not seen again till fall, though I have seen the species in the pine region above me late in the spring. In 1884, there was an unprecedented abundance of the species throughout the entire region under consideration. They came in countless numbers about the ranches, both on the San Pedro and near Tucson. Arriving early in September, they did great injury to the fruit crops raised in these regions, and I heard much complaint of them. In the oak woods they were equally abundant, living almost altogether on acorns, but spending much of the warmer portion of the day catching insects on the wing, very much as any of the larger flycatchers do, only that on leaving the perch of observation or rest, the flight is much more prolonged than in the flycatchers that I have seen.

Lewis's woodpeckers sometimes remain in winter, in small numbers, as far north as the Okanagan Valley in British Columbia. According to Suckley and Cooper (1860), they are "constant winter residents" near Fort Dalles on the Columbia River. Of their winter habits, Suckley writes:

They seem in winter to be semi-gregarious, flying singly, yet still keeping more or less in each other's company. Their flight at this season is high and very erratic, resembling much, in its characteristic peculiarities, that of the swallow. On warm days they keep up a lively chattering noise, unlike, in character, that of any other woodpecker that I have heard. During the cold season they are so shy that it is difficult to shoot them, as at the least alarm they betake themselves to the tops of the highest trees in the vicinity. They at that season subsist principally upon the larvae of insects, found in the cracks and fissures of the "red pine" of the country. I dissected a specimen killed at Fort Dalles, January 9, 1855, finding the coats of the stomach (gizzard) very thick and muscular, its cavity filled with the white larvae of insects, together with fine gravel.

DISTRIBUTION

Range.—Western United States, southwestern Canada, and northwestern Mexico; migratory in the northern areas.

Breeding range.—Lewis's woodpecker breeds **north** to southern British Columbia (Courtenay, Okanagan Landing, and Arrow Lake); Montana (Fortine, Flathead Lake, and Great Falls); and southwestern South Dakota (Elk Mountains). **East** to southwestern South Dakota (Elk Mountains); southeastern Wyoming (Laramie Hills and Laramie); eastern Colorado (Boulder, Denver, Colorado Springs, Boone, and Rouse Junction); and New Mexico (Bojuaque and Sacramento Mountain). **South** to southern New Mexico (Sacramento Mountain); Arizona (San Francisco Mountain and Fort Whipple); and southern California (Paso Robles). **West** through the coast ranges of California, Oregon, Washington, and British Columbia (Victoria, Comox, and Courtenay).

Winter range.—On the Pacific coast the species is resident **north** to the Columbia River (Portland and The Dalles, Oreg.) and is found **south** at this season to northern Baja California (Catavina and Guadalupe Valley). During two different winters these woodpeckers were recorded wintering in southern British Columbia (Alowna in 1920–21, Vernon in 1928–29, and Summerland 1928–29).

In the Rocky Mountain region it winters **north** to north-central Colorado (Boulder and Denver) and is found **south** to central Texas (San Angelo); southern New Mexico (Guadalupe Mountains); and northern Sonora (5 miles southwest of Nogales, Ariz.).

Spring migration.—At neither season is the migratory movement extensive, but the following early dates of arrival in the northern parts of the breeding range may be considered typical: Wyoming—Wheatland, April 15; Laramie, May 5; Yellowstone Park, May 14. Montana—Fortine, April 27; Big Hole River, May 1; Corvallis, May 6. Washington—Grand Dalles, April 23; Prescott, April 26; Tacoma, April 27. British Columbia—Okanagan Landing, April 20; Arrow Lakes, April 28; Sumas, May 3.

Fall migration.—The following are late dates of departure in autumn: British Columbia—Arrow Lakes, October 16; Kelowna, October 23; William Head, November 23. Washington—Prescott, September 18; North Dalles, October 10; Yakima, October 29. Montana—Columbia Falls, September 9; Missoula, September 17; Gold Creek, September 21. Wyoming—Laramie, September 24; Careyhurst, September 26; Wheatland, October 4.

Casual records.—Lewis's woodpecker has been taken on several occasions at points east of its normal range. Among these records are Alberta, Castor, May 7 and 9, 1924; Big Hay Lake, October 12, 1930; and Lesser Slave Lake, May 22, 1928; Saskatchewan, one specimen at Herschel on September 23, 1914, three in the Qu'Appelle Valley, one from near Eastend on September 19, 1915, two in the same vicinity on September 24, 1929, and two in the summer of 1931; North Dakota, a specimen was taken at Neche, on October 13, 1916, and one was noted at Grafton on October 10, 1926; Nebraska, recorded at Long Pine during the winter of 1898–99; Kansas, a specimen at Ellis on May 6, 1878, and another near Lawrence on November 7, 1908; eastern Oklahoma, one was carefully observed near Tulsa on December 24, 1922; Iowa, recorded at Sioux City from November 28, 1928, to April 7, 1929; Illinois, one recorded from Chicago on May 24, 1923, and another from Argo on May 14, 1932; and Rhode Island, a specimen collected at Mount Pleasant, near Providence, on November 16, 1928.

Egg dates.—California: 19 records, April 18 to June 10; 10 records, May 3 to 28, indicating the height of the season.

Colorado: 30 records, May 8 to August 6; 15 records, June 2 to 20.

Oregon: 18 records, May 17 to June 24; 9 records, May 30 to June 10.

British Columbia: 6 records, May 31 to June 15.

CENTURUS CAROLINUS (Linnaeus)

RED-BELLIED WOODPECKER

PLATES 30, 31

HABITS

This showy and noisy woodpecker enjoys a wide distribution throughout much of the eastern half of the United States, except the most northern and northeastern States. Throughout much of this range, it is one of the commonest and most conspicuous of the woodpeckers. Arthur H. Howell (1932) writes: "In Florida, red-bellied woodpeckers are found chiefly in hammocks, groves, and wet bottomland timber, less commonly in the pine woods and the cypress swamps. * * * These woodpeckers are not particularly shy, and they often visit dooryards and orchards." In Texas, according to George Finlay Simmons (1925), its favorite haunts are "heavily timbered bottom lands or swampy woods; open deciduous or mixed coniferous woodlands with very large trees; heavy woods of oak and elm along river and creek bottoms; shade trees and dead trees in town." Major Bendire (1895) says: "Throughout the northern portions of its range it prefers deciduous or mixed forests to coniferous, but in the south it is apparently as common in the flat, low pine woods as in the oak hammocks. Newly cleared lands in which numbers of girdled trees still remain standing are favorite resorts for this as well as other species."

Nesting.—Bendire (1895) writes:

Birds that migrate from the northern portions of their range usually arrive on their breeding grounds rather early, sometimes by March 20, and shortly afterwards preparations for nesting are commenced. A suitable site is readily found in the decayed top of some tree, or in an old stump, near a stream along the edges of a pasture, or close to some road, and less often farther in the center of a forest. Deciduous trees, especially the softer wooded ones, such as elms, basswood, maple, chestnut, poplar, willow, and sycamore, are preferred to the harder kinds, such as ash, hickory, oak, etc. In northern Florida they nest frequently in pines. Several excavations are often found in the same tree in which the nest is located, and occasionally the same site, with slight repairs, is used for more than one season. * * *

Both sexes assist in excavating the nesting site, as well as in incubation, which lasts about fourteen days. The sites selected are usually from 5 to 70 feet from the ground, and resemble those of our Woodpeckers in every respect, averaging about 12 inches in depth. It takes from seven to ten days to excavate a nest, and frequently the birds rest a week afterwards before beginning to lay; an egg is deposited daily, and from three to five are usually laid to a set, rarely more.

Mr. Howell (1932) says that in Florida "almost any kind of a tree will satisfy the birds for a nesting site, but a partly decayed stub seemingly is preferred. Where cabbage palms occur, a dead stub of that tree is often chosen, and cavities in oaks, cypresses, pines, and other trees are frequently utilized, the nesting hole being anywhere from 5 to 70 feet from the ground, usually, however, under 40 feet. Nesting begins in April and continues until June." The only nest I ever examined in Florida was found on April 25, 1903, on one of the Bowlegs Keys, in the Bay of Florida; it was placed in a dead branch of a black mangrove; the cavity was about 14 inches deep and contained four fresh eggs.

Mr. Simmons (1925) says that in Texas this woodpecker nests in "dead limbs of stumps of hackberry, Chinaberry, cedar elm, pecan, and American water elm trees, particularly the rotten, shaky, skeleton upper-parts of living hackberry trees in backyards, or in telegraph poles along city streets and alleys." In a small village in Texas I once found a nest containing three eggs in a fencepost near one of the houses.

Various observers have given quite different measurements of the nesting cavity. Mr. Simmons (1925) says: "Entrance, diameter 1.75 to 1.96. Cavity, depth 10 to 12; widest diameter near bottom (3 above eggs) 5.25." William H. Fisher (1903) found a nest in Maryland in which "the opening measured 2 by 2¼ inches and it was 5 inches from the outer edge of the hole to the back wall."

Charles R. Stockard (1904) located a nest in Mississippi, of which he says:

In the spring of 1900 a nest of this species was located in a dead cottonwood tree which stood in an open pasture. The nest was a burrow fifteen inches deep with a perfectly circular entrance about forty feet above the ground. A set of five eggs was taken from it on April 24. The entrance being small it was found necessary to cut it larger so as to admit my hand. Twenty-three days later the same nest contained a second set of five eggs, slightly incubated. The enlarging of the entrance evidently had no ill effect except for the fact that the burrow had been deepened several inches, probably to prevent an extra amount of light on the floor of the nest. These birds seem to gauge the depth of their excavations more by the amount of light admitted than from any instinct to dig a certain distance. For example, burrows that had their entrance just below a limb or were situated in shady woods were noticed, as a rule, to be shallower than those located in exposed fields or on the sunny side of the tree.

Bayard H. Christy (1931) describes a nest found in Pennsylvania as follows:

The hole was in the top of a great primeval white oak, standing in the bottom of a wooded ravine and at the edge of a neglected clearing, in southern Beaver County. I had discovered it a month or six weeks before, attracted by the calls of the bird. The hole was drilled in a dead and vertically standing bough about eight inches in diameter, in the very centre of the crown of the oak, and was, I should say, about eighty feet above the ground; it was drilled in the northern side of the bough, and beneath the talus of a branch which had died and fallen away, leaving a knot-hole a few inches above. The woodpeckers' hole was newly cut, and the bark around and beneath it had been trimmed by use or by design, so that the region about formed a tawny patch upon the grey of the bough.

S. A. Grimes (1932) mentions four cases that have come under his observation, in which red-bellied woodpeckers have occupied old nests of red-cockaded woodpeckers in Florida. F. M. Phelps (1914) mentions another similar case.

Eggs.—The red-bellied woodpecker lays three to eight eggs, usually four or five. It is a persistent layer; if the first set is taken, it will lay a second set within a week or two, generally in the same nest. Mr. Stockard (1904) reports his experience with a pair that laid four sets of eggs, 19 eggs in all, and all in the same nest.

Bendire (1895) says that "the eggs are white, mostly ovate in shape; the shell is fine grained and rather dull looking, with little or no gloss, resembling in this respect the eggs of Lewis's woodpecker more than those of the red-headed species." I have seen eggs that are elliptical-ovate in shape, and decidedly glossy; eggs that have been incubated for some time become more glossy than when first laid. The measurements of 50 eggs average 25.06 by 18.78 millimeters; the eggs showing the four extremes measure **27.00** by 19.79, 25.15 by **23.62, 23.00** by 18.70, and 23.11 by **16.76** millimeters.

Young.—The period of incubation is said to be about 14 days. Both sexes assist in this and in the feeding and care of the young.

In the more northern portions of its range, probably only one brood is reared in a season, but in the South this woodpecker is said to raise two and sometimes three broods.

Plumages.—Like other woodpeckers, the young are hatched naked and blind, but the juvenal plumage is acquired before the young leave the nest. In this the young male closely resembles the adult female, but the colors are duller, the barring is less distinct, and the white bars are suffused with brownish white; there are indistinct dusky shaft streaks on the chest and little or no red on the abdomen, which, if present, is more orange or yellowish; there is no clear red on the head, but the gray crown is sometimes suffused centrally with dark red mixed with the gray; the hind neck is often suffused with pinkish or yellowish. The juvenal female is similar to the young male, but the top of the head is darker gray, or dusky, and there is less reddish or yellowish suffusion anywhere. The juvenal plumage is apparently worn through the first fall; I have seen it as late as December 20, but Forbush (1927) says that it is shed between August and October. In the first winter plumage, there is an advance toward maturity, young males acquiring more red on the crown and occiput, and young females on the latter. There is probably a more or less continuous molt during winter, or a partial prenuptial molt in early spring, by which young birds become practically indistinguishable from adults. Adults have a complete postnuptial molt late in summer and early in fall.

Food.—Bendire (1895) says:

> Its food consists of about equal proportions of animal and vegetable matter, and it feeds considerably on the ground. Insects, like beetles, ants, grasshoppers, different species of flies, and larvae are eaten by them, as well as acorns, beech-nuts, pine seeds, juniper berries, wild grapes, blackberries, strawberries, poke-berries, palmetto and sour-gum berries, cherries, and apples. In the South it has acquired a liking for the sweet juice of oranges and feeds to some extent on them; but as it always returns to the same one, until this ceases to yield any more juice, the damage done in this is slight. It has also been observed drinking the sweet sap from the troughs in sugar camps. The injury it commits by the little fruit it eats during the season is fully atoned for by the numerous insects and their larvae which it destroys at the same time, and I therefore consider this handsome Woodpecker fully worthy of protection.

An examination of 22 stomachs by Professor Beal (1895) showed: "Animal matter (insects) 26 percent and vegetable matter 74 percent. A small quantity of gravel was found in 7 stomachs, but was not reckoned as food. Ants were found in 14 stomachs, and amounted to 11 percent of the whole food. Adult beetles stand next in importance, aggregating 7 percent of all food, while larval beetles only reach 3 percent. Caterpillars had been taken by only 2 birds, but they had eaten so many that they amounted to 4 percent of the whole food. The remaining animal food is made up of small quantities of bugs (*Hemiptera*), crickets (*Orthoptera*), and spiders, with a few bones of a small tree frog found in 1 stomach taken in Florida."

The red-bellied woodpecker eats some corn, which it has been seen to steal from corncribs and from bunches of corn hung up to dry. Various berries have been recorded in its food, besides those mentioned above, mulberries, elderberries, bayberries, blueberries, and the berries of the Virginia creeper, cornel, holly, dogwood, and poison ivy, also the seeds of ragweed and wild sarsaparilla, hazelnuts, and pecans. N. M. McGuire (1932) saw one feeding at the borings of a yellow-bellied sapsucker on a sugar maple tree, driving the latter away; he "would fly at the Sapsucker, causing him to dodge around a limb in order to keep out of the way."

Dr. B. H. Warren (1890) first called attention to the orange-eating habit of the red-bellied woodpecker in Florida, where it is called the "orange sapsucker" or "orange borer." He found on inquiry that these birds often destroyed large numbers of oranges when they were ready for picking and that "they damaged the orange trees by boring holes in them and sucking the sap." He collected 26 of these woodpeckers in one orchard, 11 of which had "fed to a more or less extent on oranges."

William Brewster (1889) saw a red-bellied woodpecker eating the pulp of a sweet orange at Enterprise, Fla. He says that it attacked the orange on the ground, pecking at it in a slow and deliberate way for several minutes. On examining the orange he found it to be decayed on one side. "In the sound portion were three holes, each nearly as large as a silver dollar, with narrow strips of peel between them. The pulp had been eaten out quite to the middle of the fruit. Small pieces of rind were thickly strewn about the spot. Upon searching closely I discovered several other oranges that had been attacked in a similar manner. All were partially decayed, and were lying on the ground. I was unable to find any on the trees which showed any marks of the Woodpecker's bill."

Certainly the habit of eating fallen and partially decayed oranges does no injury to the orange groves, but D. Mortimer (1890) tells a different story:

While gathering fruit or pruning orange trees, I frequently found oranges that had been riddled by this woodpecker, and repeatedly saw the bird at work. I never observed it feeding upon fallen oranges. It helped itself freely to sound fruit that still hung on the tree, and in some instances I have found ten or twelve oranges on one trees that had been tapped by it. Where an orange accidentally rested on a branch in such a way as to make the flower end accessible from above or from a horizontal direction the Woodpecker chose that spot, as through it he could reach into all the sections of the fruit, and when this was the case there was but one hole in the orange. But usually there were many holes around it. It appeared that after having once commenced on an orange, the woodpecker returned to the same one repeatedly until he had completely consumed the pulp, and then he usually attacked another very near to it. Thus I have found certain clusters in which every orange had been bored, while all the others on the tree were untouched.

The red-bellied woodpecker shares with other species, formerly included in the genus *Melanerpes*, the habit of storing acorns, nuts, insects, and other articles of food for future use. Ben. J. Blincoe (1923) writes:

The red-bellied woodpecker is a heavy feeder on beech and oak mast. In the early fall its incessant "Cha-cha-cha" was a familiar sound in the beech woods about Cherry Hill. I never observed it in the act of storing beech mast though on numerous occasions red-bellied woodpeckers were seen carrying beechnuts to a considerable distance from the trees from which they were secured. Very likely many of these nuts were wedged in cracks or crevices for future use. However, in the fall of 1913, a red-belly was seen storing the acorns from a Chinquapin Oak (*Quercus acuminata*) which stood over the wood-pile at Cherry hill. The acorns were carried, one at a time, to fence posts ranging from twenty-five to three hundred yards distant from the oak tree, and were generally wedged in a crack in the post, usually near the top. One acorn was placed in a cavity caused by decay, and laid loosely on the rotten wood. As far as my observations went, but one acorn was placed in a single post.

While Mr. Blincoe was shelling walnuts, he saw one of these woodpeckers carry off the shells, and apparently eat the remaining meat out of them. Several times he saw one stealing corn from his corncrib or flying off with cherries from a tree in his garden and sometimes carrying them to a fence post to eat. Again he watched one eating a hole in an apple, and "found that the apple on which it had been working bore a decayed spot near the stem and just at the edge of it, but entirely in the solid part of the apple, was a hole about half an inch across, and three-quarters deep. The bottom of this cavity contained several tiny holes, markings made by the woodpecker's mandibles. In the early winter, frequently, a red-belly would be seen feeding on an apple that remained on the tree, though decayed and practically dried up."

Lester W. Smith writes to me that it seems to be a habit of the red-bellied woodpecker in Florida to store away insects and other food. "After digging into and capturing an insect, I see it fly to a small hole, commonly in the trunk of the cabbage palmetto, and place the insect in it. At a hole 5 feet from the ground I found a male *carolinus* inserting the badly mutilated body of a cockroach. A large portion of his catches or finds he seems to prefer to hide away. A tree of small, late tangerines was visited almost daily during the latter half of May, and sections of the pulp, taken from fruit torn open by the mockingbird, were carried off and hidden in various places. On June 3 I saw *carolinus* go to the base of banana leaves, take out a section of pulp, and fly away with it. Examination showed other pieces similarly hidden, some with ants on them."

M. P. Skinner (1928) says: "Although other woodpeckers carry off and store bits of food, the red-bellied woodpeckers appear to do it more than any others in the Sandhills. These birds are rather easily attracted to artificial feeding stations, especially if suet be offered them. They will eat nuts and bread crumbs, also, but not as greedily."

Behavior.—Mr. Skinner (1928) writes: "In flight, these woodpeckers are apt to progress step by step from tree to tree. In this respect, and in that it is undulating, their flight is much like that of other woodpeckers. In approaching a perch, the red-bellied woodpeckers usually glide and sweep up to it with the impetus already gained. * * * These woodpeckers work and hammer on the trunks of trees, on the boles of oaks, on boles high up in live or blasted pines, and on both living and dead limbs, usually working up, but working down also if they want to, using a peculiar partly-sidewise drop downward."

Voice.—Mr. Simmons (1925) gives the following elaborate interpretations of the various calls of this noisy bird:

In fall and winter, a soft scolding *chuh; chuh-chuh; chow-chow; cherr-cherr;* or *chawh-chawh.* At other seasons, a variety of calls: a slow, harsh *crer-r-r-r-r-r r r r r r r r* or *chur-r-r-r-r r r r r r r;* a noisy *charr-r-r* or *chawh-chawh;* a rather slow, regular *chuh-chuh-chuh-chuh-chuh,* sometimes uttered in a series of a dozen or more as rapidly as the syllables can be plainly pronounced; a very rapid *chuck-a-chuck-a-chuck-a-chuck-a-chuck-a-chuck-a-chuck-a;* a slow, harsh *sherr, cherr, cherr* or *crerr, crerr, crerr, crerr, crerr;* an alarmed *cha-cha-cha;* at intervals, a loud, bold, running, connected *koo er-r-r-r; qu er-r-r-r;* *qui er-r-r-r-r;* or *k-r-r-ring,* uttered with a distinct rolling of the *r*'s; in the nesting season, an additional *whicker.*

Bendire (1895) says: "The Red-bellied, like the majority of our Woodpeckers, is a rather noisy bird. Its ordinary call note resembles the 'tchurr, tchurr' of the red-headed very closely; another sounds more like 'chawh, chawh,' and this is occasionally varied with a disagreeable creaking note, while during the mating season peculiar, low, mournful cooing sounds are sometimes uttered, which somewhat resemble those of the Mourning Dove."

Various other observers have given somewhat similar descriptions of some of the above interpretations. When I first saw this woodpecker, many years ago in Florida, climbing up the trunk of a cabbage palmetto, its rolling notes sounded to me like those of a tree toad, as heard before a rain.

Field marks.—The red-bellied woodpecker is so conspicuously marked that it could hardly be overlooked. It is a medium-sized woodpecker, about the size of the hairy; the entire back and rump are conspicuously barred transversely with black and white; the wings are spotted or barred with white; the under parts are uniform gray, except for the inconspicuous reddish tinge on the abdomen; in the male the entire crown and nape are brilliant scarlet, and a large patch of the same color adorns the nape of the female.

Winter.—The migrations of this woodpecker are, apparently, not so extensive or so regular as those of most migratory birds; they seem to consist more of irregular wanderings and to depend more on the abundance of the food supply. The species occurs, in small numbers at least, more or less irregularly in winter even in the northern portions of its range. There is, however, usually a general southward movement in fall, which greatly increases its abundance in the Southern States in winter. William H. Fisher (1897) says of its winter occurrence in Maryland: "I have only met with about half a dozen individuals outside of Somerset County, but there, for the last fourteen years, in either November, December or January, I have found them to be very abundant. According to my observations, they prefer the low, swampy woodlands and clearings, only occasionally being found in the isolated tree in the field."

W. E. Saunders tells me that it was formerly quite common in southern Ontario and came regularly to the feeding stations in winter; evidently some of these birds did not migrate. On the other hand, Audubon (1842) says: "In winter I have found the red-bellied woodpecker the most abundant of all in the pine barrens of the Floridas, and especially on the plantations bordering the St. John's river, where on any day it would have been easy to procure half a hundred." And C. J. Maynard (1896) writes: "I found the red-bellied woodpeckers quite abundant in winter in the piney woods which border the plantations on the Sea Islands off the Carolinas but as I proceeded south, their numbers increased and in Florida, they fairly swarmed, actually occurring in flocks. They accompany the cockaded woodpeckers in the piney woods and also associate with the yellow-bellies in the swamps and hummocks; in fact, it is difficult to remain long in any portion of Florida where there are trees, without hearing the discordant croak of these woodpeckers and I even found them on the Keys."

DISTRIBUTION

Range.—Chiefly the Eastern United States, casual west to Arizona and Colorado; nonmigratory.

The range of the red-bellied woodpecker extends **north** to southeastern Nebraska (Lincoln and Nebraska City); southeastern Minnesota (St. Peter and Minneapolis); southern Michigan (Grand Rapids, Howell, and Plymouth); and southern Ontario (Coldstream, Toronto, and Twin Lakes). **East** to southeastern Ontario (Twin Lakes); western New York (Canandaigua, Potter, and probably Ithaca); southern Pennsylvania (Fulton County); eastern Maryland (Marydel and Church Creek); Virginia (Dismal Swamp); North

Carolina (Mattamuskeet Lake and Orton); South Carolina (Columbia and Frogmore); Georgia (Savannah, Cumberland Island, and Blackbeard Island); and Florida (New Smyrna, Eldred, Cape Florida, and Upper Matecumbe Key). The **southern** limits extend westward along the Gulf coast to eastern Texas (Giddings and Austin). **West** to eastern Texas (Austin, Cameron, and Waco); Oklahoma (Caddo, Norman, and Arnett); eastern Kansas (Harper, Wichita, and Manhattan); and southeastern Nebraska (Lincoln).

Although not a migratory species, there appears to be some retreat from the northern parts of the range, particularly during severe winters.

Casual records.—Red-bellied woodpeckers have been taken or observed on numerous occasions in New Jersey and eastern New York (including Long Island). The northernmost records on the Atlantic seaboard are several from Massachusetts, among which are the following: Springfield, May 13, 1863; Newton, November 25, 1880; Cohasset, May 28, 1881; and Clinton, July 17, 1896. One was noted at Sault Ste. Marie, Michigan, on August 29, 1920; two were reported from Yankton, S. Dak., on April 14, 1923; one was seen in Monroe Canyon, Sioux County, northwestern Nebraska (date ?); in Colorado, a specimen was taken at Fountain in 1873 and another at Limon in May 1899, while one was seen at Greeley in 1895 and another at Yuma on October 1, 2, and 3, 1906. According to Ridgway (1914), the species is "accidental in Arizona (Fort Grant)," but no information is available to indicate the authority for this statement.

Egg dates.—Alabama: 9 records, April 17 to July 11.

Florida: 20 records, April 10 to June 20; 10 records, April 16 to May 13, indicating the height of the season.

Illinois: 8 records, April 1 to June 3.

Texas: 8 records, April 8 to July 9.

CENTURUS AURIFRONS (Wagler)

GOLDEN-FRONTED WOODPECKER

HABITS

The golden-fronted woodpecker is found, in suitable localities, from central Texas southward to the Valley of Mexico. It is not, however, evenly distributed, being common in certain regions that suit its requirements and entirely absent from other types of surrounding country. For example, E. M. Hasbrouck (1889) says: "In the single locality in Eastland County where they are found, they may be said to be fairly common, but outside of an area of twenty-five square miles they are unknown in the County. * * * This section of country presents peculiar characteristics; the timber is entirely of post-oak, and the ground more or less thickly covered with 'shinnery,' and differs from the surrounding country in that the tops of the trees were affected some years ago with a blight, and now this entire area is one mass of dead-topped trees, and this is what apparently suits the present species."

George F. Simmons (1925) says of its haunts in the Austin region: "Mesquite forests with large trees, and mesquite flats; partial to large timber near mesquite growth, particularly among post oak and mixed oaks on gravel uplands, and in pecan groves on open and semi-open bottoms."

D. B. Burrows (Bendire, 1895) says that, in Starr County, on the lower Rio Grande, "the golden-fronted woodpecker is a common resident species in this locality, and much more abundant than Baird's woodpecker, the only other variety that I have found here. They may be found wherever there is a growth of trees sufficiently large to afford nesting places, but are most numerous in the river bottoms where there is a heavy growth of old mesquite timber."

Nesting.—Major Bendire (1895) writes: "Nidification commences sometimes in the latter part of March, but usually not much before the middle of April; both sexes assist in this labor, and it takes from six to ten days to excavate a proper nesting site; both live and dead trees are used for this purpose, as well as telegraph poles and fence posts; the holes are rarely over 12 inches deep, and are situated at no great distances from the ground, mostly from 6 to 25 feet up." As to its nesting in Starr County, he quotes from Mr. Burrows: "The nest is by preference made in the live trunks of large trees, usually the mesquite, but sometimes in a dead stump or limb, the same cavity being used year after year, and it is quite a rare thing to see a fresh excavation. The nesting season begins in April, and most of the nests contain fresh eggs by May 10. I took a set of six eggs from a cavity in a live mesquite tree, the opening being but 2 feet 9 inches from the ground, but usually they are placed from 8 to 20 feet up." And H. P. Attwater wrote to him that "near San Antonio, Texas, where the golden-fronted woodpecker is a common resident, it nests in all kinds of tall live timber, pecan, oak, and large mesquite trees being preferred, but telegraph poles furnished favorite sites here also. A line running out of San Antonio to a ranch nine miles distant was almost destroyed by these birds; they came from all sides, from far and near, and made fresh holes every year, sometimes as many as five or six in a single pole. Here it also nests occasionally in artificial nesting sites, like bird boxes, etc., in yards and gardens."

My only experience with the nesting habits of this woodpecker was in Cameron County, Tex., where we found this noisy and conspicuous bird quite common in the trees about the ranches. On May 24, 1923, we found two nests quite near the buildings on a well-kept Mexican ranch and collected two sets of four fresh eggs; one was about 8 feet up in an anaqua tree and the other about 12 feet from the ground in a willow.

Eggs.—The golden-fronted woodpecker lays four to seven eggs to a set, usually four or five. The eggs are pure white and vary from ovate to short or rounded-ovate, with very little or no gloss when fresh.

The measurements of 59 eggs average 25.82 by 19.50 millimeters; the eggs showing the four extremes measure 28.45 by 20.07, 27.94 by 20.83, 22.86 by 17.78, and 25.91 by 18.03 millimeters.

Young.—Major Bendire (1895) says: "Incubation lasts about fourteen days, and both sexes share this duty. * * * It is probable that two broods are occasionally raised in a season, as there are sets of eggs in the collection taken in June, and two of these in the latter part of this month." But Mr. Simmons (1925) says "probably only one brood." Both parents assist in the care of the young. In summer and fall the young may be seen traveling about with their parents in family parties, but they separate before winter.

Plumages.—Probably the young are hatched naked and blind, as with other woodpeckers, and the juvenal plumage is acquired before the young bird leaves the nest. The young male, in juvenal plumage, is similar to the adult male but is everywhere duller, with the markings less clearly defined; the red crown patch is smaller and consists of somewhat scattered red feathers; there is usually more or less indistinct dusky barring on the forehead, which is duller yellow than in the adult; the yellow of the hind neck is paler and duller; the chest is usually more or less streaked with dusky, and the yellow on the abdomen is paler. The young female is similar to the young male but without any red on the head, the yellow band on the hind neck paler, and the under parts all paler. This juvenal plumage is apparently worn all through fall and early winter; I have seen it as late as January 5; but probably a protracted molt during fall and winter produces a gradual change into a plumage that is practically adult. Adults have a complete postnuptial molt late in summer and fall, mainly in August and September, according to what few molting specimens I have seen.

Food.—Bendire (1895) says: "Their food consists of insects of various kinds, such as beetles, ants, grasshoppers, also larvae, acorns, Indian corn, and different kinds of wild berries and fruit. Considered from an economic point of view, this woodpecker certainly does more good than harm, and the only thing that can be said against it is that in certain localities where it is common it may make itself more or less of a nuisance by injuring telegraph poles." In this connection, George B. Sennett (1879) makes the following interesting remark: "The numerous holes which I observed the previous season in the telegraph poles, and which I inferred might be nests of Woodpeckers, I found to be excavations made by the birds in search of a large species of borer that works in the dry wood."

Roy W. Quillin writes to me that "this species has an odd habit of placing shelled mesquite beans in the nesting holes. I have not yet found any reason for this which seemed plausible."

Behavior.—In general habits and behavior, the golden-fronted woodpecker is much like the red-bellied woodpecker, to which it is closely related; and it reminded me also of our more familiar red-headed woodpecker. It is a lively, active, noisy bird, being much in evidence wherever it is found. It loves to perch for many minutes in the dead top of some tall tree or on some telegraph or telephone pole, where it can obtain a good outlook. Mr. Burrows (Bendire, 1895) says: "During the fall and winter they may be found traveling about from place to place in pairs, and are easily located by the call note, which somewhat resembles that of the red-bellied woodpecker, the habits of the two birds being in many respects quite similar. In the spring, when nesting, they become very noisy, and when approached, utter their alarm note with great vigor. I have never known this species to drum on a dead limb, as most of the other woodpeckers do. When searching for food they may be seen very diligently at work near the base of old trees, among the thick bushes, or even on the ground."

Voice.—Mr. Simmons (1925) says that this bird is "extremely noisy," and describes its notes as "a harsh, rapid, scolding *chuh-chuh-chuh-chuh-chuh-chuh-chuh;* a metallic *whah-whah;* a loud, long-drawn *sk-k-k-k-ah-er-r-r-r* or *tcher-r-r-r, tcher-r-r-r;* a short *check, check-check.* Both this species and the red-bellied woodpecker have the same *chow, chow, chow, chow* call; however, there is a striking difference in the tone; the call of the Red-bellied Woodpecker may be imitated by completely filling the mouth with air and keeping the lips pushed well forward, while that of the golden-fronted woodpecker—*choogh-choogh*—is best given by pulling the lips back tightly, tautening the vocal cords, and making a hoarse, croupy noise in the throat, since the bird at times sounds as if it had a bad cold."

Mr. Hasbrouck (1889) writes: "Their note is peculiar, combining the 'chirp, chirp' of *carolinus* with a certain shrillness and accent of their own, while the call note, either flying or at rest, is similar to that of *M. erythrocephalus* and at the same time not unlike that of *Colaptes auratus.* While their notes once learned are readily recognized, still it takes not a little practice to distinguish between a red-head in one tree and the gold-front in the next, or between a gold-front and a flicker when both are on the opposite side of a ravine and hidden from view; and I have more than once shot *carolinus* even when morally certain it was what I wanted."

Field marks.—The golden-fronted woodpecker might easily be confused with the red-bellied woodpecker, for they are often found in the same general region, and both have the back and wings barred with black and white; but all the lower part of the rump is white, instead of barred, in the golden-fronted and the gray under parts are tinged with yellow, instead of red; the male red-bellied has the whole upper part of the head, from forehead to hind neck, bright scarlet, and the female has an extensive patch of red on the posterior half of the upper head; whereas the male golden-fronted has a much smaller patch of red on the crown, a yellow forehead, and an orange-yellow band on the hind neck; and the female golden-fronted has no red on the head at all. The voice is said to be more distinctive than the color pattern.

Enemies.—Mr. Quillin writes to me: "While this species is still fairly abundant in southern Texas, it was much more plentiful ten or more years ago. Because of the damage the birds wrought to telephone and telegraph poles, the various concerns owning such property secured passage of a law placing all woodpeckers on the unprotected list. This done, they gave section crews of the railroads shotguns, and the killing was on in earnest. Hunters and others helped, and the result has been a marked decrease in the ranks of this species. The killing, or controlling still continues. However, pressure is now being brought to place the birds back on the protected list, and this will be done sooner or later. There is no getting around the fact that the birds did cause considerable damage. In this species we have a woodpecker which for centuries had been pecking into hard mesquite trees. Along came the soft pine poles and these same birds immediately literally ate them up. I have seen 16 holes, three of which were deep enough for nesting sites, in one small pole, not over 10 inches in diameter."

DISTRIBUTION

Range.—North-central Texas south to Central Mexico; nonmigratory.

The golden-fronted woodpecker ranges **north** to central Texas (San Angelo and Dallas). **East** to Texas (Dallas, Giddings, Cuero, Corpus Christi, and Brownsville); Tamaulipas (Matamoros, San Fernando, Ciudad Victoria, and Tampico); southeastern San Luis Potosi (Valles); Hidalgo (Ixmiquilipam and Tula); and the Federal District of Mexico (near Mexico City). **South** to the Federal District of Mexico (near Mexico City); Michoacan (Querendero, Morelia, and Patzcuaro); and Jalisco (Ocotlan and Guadalajara). **West** to Jalisco (Guadalajara); Zacatecas (Calvillo, Aguas Calientes, and Chicalote); northwestern Durango (Boquilla, Sestin, and Rosario);

eastern Chihuahua (Julimes); and central Texas (Eagle Pass, Fort Clark, Kerrville, and San Angelo).

Egg dates.—Texas: 66 records, March 30 to June 29; 33 records, April 24 to May 17, indicating the height of the season.

CENTURUS UROPYGIALIS UROPYGIALIS Baird

GILA WOODPECKER

PLATES 32–34

HABITS

In the desert regions of our southwestern borders, this gay little woodpecker is one of the commonest, noisiest, and most conspicuous birds, always much in evidence, and always seeming to protest, in whining tones, the intrusion of strangers. Its center of abundance seems to be on the great desert mesas of southern Arizona, where the infertile soil is scantily covered with a scattered growth of creosote bushes, low mesquites, an occasional cholla or barrel cactus and dotted with single specimens or little groups of the giant cactus, or saguaro. But it is also common in the river bottoms, covered with a heavier growth of mesquite, and in the canyons of the foothills among the cottonwoods, willows, and sycamores. It ranges from an elevation of 2,500 feet on the mesas up to 4,000, or even 4,500, feet in the canyons and foothills.

In this region, it is a dominant species and a very useful neighbor, even if unintentionally, for the many species of birds and small mammals for which it provides homes. M. French Gilman (1915) puts it very well as follows:

Were it not for the Gila woodpecker (*Centurus uropygialis*) what would become of the several species of birds that use already prepared cavities for their domiciles? In some cases these tenants do not even await the pleasure of the excavators, but take forcible possession. In holes excavated by Gila woodpeckers there may regularly be found nesting the elf owl, ferruginous pigmy owl, ash-throated flycatcher, and Arizona crested flycatcher. Occasionally a cactus wren makes use of the handy hollow, and once I saw one occupied by a Lucy warbler. A big "rough-neck" scaly lizard frequents the holes when not too high in the cactus, and in two holes in willow trees I found snakes. It is not pleasant to insert one's hand and have a big lizard or snake crawl up the arm to escape. Rats and mice are sometimes found in the deserted holes, especially if the tree be much decayed and with cracks and hollows connecting holes at different heights in the tree or branch. So these woodpeckers may be considered among the class of innocent or unintentional benefactors.

In addition to the species mentioned by Mr. Gilman above, we found saguaro screech owls, desert sparrow hawks, and western martins nesting in the old holes made by woodpeckers. Some of these holes were doubtless made by Mearns's gilded flickers, perhaps those that were used by the larger species, as this woodpecker is fairly common in the same region and nests regularly in the saguaros. These old holes make ideal nesting sites, for the sap of the cactus hardens around the excavations, making them fairly permanent nesting boxes; I have seen these gourd-shaped pockets still persisting in fallen saguaros, where the pulp had all rotted away, leaving only the skeleton ribs of the dead giant.

Nesting.—While collecting with the late Frank C. Willard in southern Arizona in 1922, we examined seven occupied nests of the Gila woodpecker. The first of these was found on May 17, at Fairbank, in the valley of the San Pedro River; the nest was a cavity 15 inches deep in a dead branch of a cottonwood, 15 feet above ground. Five days, May 19 to 23, were spent in Pima County, in the vicinity of Tucson, between the mesquite forest in the valley of the Santa Cruz River and the southern end of the Santa Catalina Mountains. Two nests were found in the mesquite forest on May 19, both in mesquite trees, one 20 and one 25 feet from the ground; one contained only a single fresh egg and the other held a brood of young. We had an interesting experience here the next day. While crossing the forest, I saw a Gila woodpecker fly out from what I supposed was its nesting hole, about 15 feet up in a mesquite stub; the bird made such a great fuss about it that I felt sure that we had a set of woodpecker's eggs within easy reach, and I called Mr. Willard to investigate it. He climbed the stub and chopped out the hole, while the woodpecker was flying about, scolding us and showing the greatest concern. But, much to our surprise, he pulled out an elf owl and three unmistakable elf owl's eggs. I killed the owl and shot the woodpecker, which still seemed much interested; and, on skinning and sexing both specimens, I found that the woodpecker was a male and the owl a female. We were naturally much puzzled to figure out the relationship between the two birds and their interest in the nest. But, since reading Mr. Gilman's remarks, quoted above, that sometimes the woodpecker's tenants "do not even await the pleasure of the excavators, but take forcible possession," it has occurred to me that probably this was a case in point. The owl may have appropriated the finished burrow of the woodpecker, and the latter was trying to evict an unwelcome tenant.

The remaining four nests found in this vicinity, and one found by Mr. Willard on June 11, were all in saguaros on the desert mesa; the heights from the ground varied from 16 to 20 feet; and the cavities varied in depths from 15 to 20 inches; there was one set of five eggs, two nests held four and one three eggs; and in one nest were two young and an addled egg.

Referring to the nesting habits of this woodpecker in the vicinity of the Gila River, in Arizona, Mr. Gilman (1915) writes:

Nesting sites in this locality are restricted to giant cactus (*Cereus gigan-teus*), cottonwood and willow, as they are the only suitable material for a nest excavation. More nests are found in the giant cactus, as these plants are more numerous than the others, and more "peckable," though the willows and cottonwoods along the river and the canals are well patronized when sufficiently decayed. Of the nests I examined I should say that fifty per cent were in the cactus, and the rest equally divided between the other trees mentioned. * * *

As to the size of the holes in the cactus as compared with those in cottonwood and willow, I found no appreciable difference. I expected the holes in the cactus to average a little larger owing to possible greater ease in excavating but the difference was too slight to be sure of in measuring. Of eighteen holes measured, the average diameter was 1.95 inches; the largest was 2.25 inches and the smallest 1.87 inches. The deepest hole was 16 inches, with the entrance 2 inches in diameter. The shallowest one was 9 inches, with entrance a little less than 2 inches in diameter. The average depth of holes measured was a little more than 12 inches. Many of the holes were not exactly circular, there being a difference of from ⅛ to nearly ½ inch between the long and short diameter if it be allowable to use the term in that way. Usually the nest hole runs straight in for a short distance before turning downward, the distance seemingly depending on the texture of the wood. In one case the hole went straight back for nine inches before turning downward. It was in a big cottonwood stump, and the bird excavated horizontally until decayed wood was reached, when the hole turned downward. This was an extreme case, as the depth horizontally is usually about three inches. In the giant cactus it varies according to the diameter of the trunk, the smaller the trunk the less distance before turning downward. * * *

The same nest hole is used more than one season, both in cactus and other locations. In 1913 I found a nest in a big cottonwood stump containing young. The next year it had young again, and I cut into it to measure the hole and count them.

Frank C. Willard (1912) says: "I think it is their habit to dig fresh holes after raising their brood of young. These fresh holes are not occupied that year but are made use of the next year when the sap has had a chance to dry and form the hard lining which coats the inside of all the cavities. I have found but one fresh hole occupied as a nest." Bendire (1895) also says that "most of their nesting sites are used for several years in succession; in fact, I doubt very much if a freshly excavated hole in a giant cactus is fit to nest in the same season. Both sexes assist in excavating the nesting site."

In the heavily incrusted nest cavity in a giant cactus, the eggs lie on the bare, hard floor of the nest, there being no chips to furnish a soft bed.

In addition to the trees mentioned above, the Gila woodpecker has been found nesting more rarely in oaks and palo-verdes.

Eggs.—The Gila woodpecker lays three to five eggs, three or four being much oftener found than five. The eggs are pure white and not very glossy when fresh, but sometimes quite glossy when heavily incubated; they vary from ovate to elliptical-ovate and are sometimes quite pointed. The measurements of 52 eggs average 25.14 by 18.56 millimeters; the eggs showing the four extremes measure 27.43 by 18.80, 26.6 by 20.1, 22.86 by 17.27, and 23.9 by 16.6 millimeters.

Young.—Incubation is said to last about two weeks, and is probably shared by both parents. Mr. Gilman (1915) writes:

It is not easy to determine just what food the young in the nest are given, but insects play a prominent part, as I have seen them frequently carried to the young. Fruit is also used, as I watched one parent carry ripe Lycium berries several times to the nest; after emerging from the hole she would halt at the entrance each time and "lick her chops." * * *

The young are fed by the parents for a long time after leaving the nest, and they are regular little beggars. One pair stayed around our house for several months, and became quite tame. They were missed during the breeding season but soon came back with three youngsters to share the good things found on the bird tables in the yard. The young, though as large as their parents, would flutter their wings and sit with open beak as though the old ones told them to "open your mouth and shut your eyes," etc. The old ones would try to get them to eat watermelon placed on the tables, but the babies would not be shown; the parents had to put it in their mouths. They followed the parents from perch to perch, begging for food until I expected to see them chastised. The pair in question stayed with the three juvenals until they had them broken to eat for themselves, and then left. After a proper interval they came back with two more young ones, thus indicating that a second brood is sometimes raised. The abundant supply of food may have been a determining factor in the number of broods raised.

Plumages.—The nestlings are naked and blind at first but become fully clothed in the juvenal plumage before leaving the nest. The young male, in juvenal plumage, is much like the adult male, but the colors are generally paler, the head and under parts grayer, the barring on the upper parts less distinct, and the white bars are suffused with brownish buff; the red patch on the crown is smaller and often consists of only a few red feathers; and the bill is somewhat smaller and weaker. The young female is like the young male but has no red on the head. I have been unable to trace the postjuvenal molt, but young birds in the following spring are apparently like the adults. Adults have a complete postnuptial molt in August, September, and October.

Food.—Major Bendire (1895) says: "Its food consists of insects of various kinds, such as ants, beetles, grasshoppers, and larvæ, and in season largely on the sweet, fig-like fruit of the sahuaras, the giant cactus, and also, to a considerable extent, on the viscous berries of a species of mistletoe which is commonly found on most of the larger cottonwoods, oaks, and mesquite trees in these regions. These sticky, whitish-looking berries are a favorite food of many Arizona birds."

Mr. Gilman (1915) writes:

The food of this woodpecker is varied, nearly everything being grist that comes to his mill. He pecks around decayed and dying trees as well as green ones, and presumably get the insects usually found and eaten by such birds. The giant cactus is pecked into very frequently, and I believe some of the pulp is eaten. The small punctures made are not enlarged, and in some cases quite an area is bitten into. The fruit of the giant cactus is eaten as long as it lasts, and the berries of the Lycium are also freely eaten. The Gila woodpecker frequents corn fields, and pecks through the husks into the ears of corn. The birds may peck in at first to get a worm, but it is a case similar to the discovery of roast pig as portrayed by Lamb. They alight on the ground and feed upon table scraps thrown to chickens, three of them being regular morning visitors, star boarders, to a pen of chickens I fed. They are very fond of peaches and pears, and volubly resent being driven from a tree of the fruit. They peck holes in ripening pomegranates and then the green fruit beetle helps finish the fruit. They relish grapes, both white and colored, and will spear one with their bill and carry it to a convenient crevice where it may be eaten at leisure. On bird tables I have tried them with various articles of food and found very little that they rejected. They would not eat cantaloupe at all but were regular watermelon fiends, eating it three times a day and calling for more. They did not care for oranges, and I had no success in trying to teach them to eat ripe pickled olives. I tried the olive diet on them because two Mocking-birds in our yard learned to eat this fruit. Meat, raw and cooked, was eaten, and they ate suet greedily. Their favorite cut of beef was the T-bone steak and we always left some meat on the bone for them. They picked it clean, and if a new supply was slow in coming the softer parts of the bone were devoured. * * * Mr. Frank Pinkley, custodian of the Casa Grande Ruins told me of a pair of these woodpeckers that stayed around his home and became quite tame, coming into the shed to drink from a can of water. He said they got into the habit of sucking the eggs in the chicken house, or at least pecking into them and eating of the contents. * * *

The Indians store corn in the ear on the flat tops of their houses and sheds, * * * and each home has one or more of woodpecker retainers or pensioners hanging about most of the time. This corn provides an abundant and sure source of food, and the birds make the most of it. I have never seen any indication of food-storage on the part of the Gila woodpecker, as with the California Woodpecker, for they live in a claw-to-beak fashion. They peck at a kernel until it comes off the cob, when it is carried to a post or tree and placed firmly in a crack. Here it is pecked to pieces and eaten. They seem never to swallow a kernel whole but always break it up.

W. L. Dawson (1923) says that this woodpecker indulges in "a systematic search for birds' eggs, especially those of the Lucy warbler, yellow warbler, and Arizona Least Vireo. In case of the first-named, the eggs are devoured in spite of the most emphatic protests of the tiny parents; but eggs of Cardinal, Cooper Tanager and Towhee must be obtained by stealth."

A. H. Anderson (1934) writes:

In the Tucson, Arizona, area a gall-insect (*Pachypsylla venusta*) frequently attacks the leaves of the hackberry tree (*Celtis reticulata*). The galls form on the leaf petiole, becoming from a quarter to half an inch in diameter. During the winter the outer shell hardens like a nut.

I have often seen the Gila woodpeckers tear the galls loose from the twigs and, flying to a fence post, proceed to chisel out the contents. The hard gall is wedged into a crack on the post and then opened by repeated hammering. Around the base of one fence post I counted nearly 300 empty shells. Sometimes cracks in nearby trees are used. At one time five of these woodpeckers were seen in a single tree, all of them feeding on the galls.

Behavior.—The Gila woodpecker is not only the most abundant woodpecker, in fact one of the most abundant birds, in the region it inhabits, but it is more conspicuous, noisier, and more active than any of its neighbors. It is always much in evidence, always protesting the intrusion of a stranger, and shows the greatest concern when its nest is approached, especially if it has young. It is a close sitter and will often remain in the nest hole to peck viciously at an investigating hand; while the nest is being robbed, it flits nervously about, scolding vociferously with all the vile epithets it can muster. As to its behavior with other species, Mr. Gilman (1915) writes:

This woodpecker has not the best disposition in the world, for he is very quarrelsome and intolerant. He fights his own kin and all the neighbors that he dares. He, or she, is a great bluffer however and when "called", frequently side-steps, subsides, or backs out entirely. I saw one approach a Bendire Thrasher that was eating, and suddenly pounce on him. He had the thrasher down and I was thinking of offering my friendly services as a board of arbitration, when the under bird crawled from beneath and soon gave the woodpecker the thrashing of his career. Several times I have seen the woodpeckers start to attack Bendire and Palmer thrashers, but they were always bluffed or beaten at the game. With the Bronzed Cowbirds it is a drawn battle, sometimes one and then the other backing down. Most other birds, such as Cardinals, Abert Towhees, Dwarf Cowbirds and Cactus Wrens do not attempt to assert their rights, but always take a rear seat. But when it is woodpecker versus woodpecker it seems not to be a case of "Thrice armed is he who hath his quarrel just", but rather, "Four times he who gets his blow in fust".

I had two bird tables about twenty feet apart, and frequently one woodpecker might be peacefully assimilating watermelon, when another one would come hurrying up and make a dive at him, causing a retreat to the other table. Frequently the new-comer would then follow and drive him from the second table. He seemingly would rather fight than eat if another was eating at the same time. One day I saw him, or her, I forget which, hanging to the edge of the table busily eating steak, when another one perched on the table and made a vicious stab at him. He dodged backward clear under the table, though retaining his hold, and then bobbed up again, just like the Punch and Judy show. The attack was renewed, and the dodging as well, but this time he did not "come back". Another day one of them was at work on a piece of melon when one of his fellows came and perched on the end of the table. The diner made a pass at the new comer, and seizing him by the feathers of the neck held him suspended over the end of the table for a few seconds.

Voice.—Major Bendire (1895) says: "Its ordinary call note, sounding like 'dchürr, dchürr,' can be heard in all directions in the spring; when flying from one point to another it usually utters a sharp, shrill 'huit' two or three times, resembling the common call note of the Phainopepla, and which may readily be mistaken for it. It is also more or less addicted to drumming on the dead tops of cottonwood, sycamore, and mesquite trees."

Mr. Gilman (1915) writes:

As a neighbor, the Gila Woodpecker is permanently on the map, and is afraid neither of being seen nor heard. He is much in the public ear with a variety of notes and calls. His sociable conversational notes somewhat resemble those of the California Woodpecker but are shriller. In such of his notes as are directed at humanity there is a peevish complaining tone, especially if closely approached when feeding on fruit or some other delicacy. In such cases there is only one term that exactly describes his attitude and utterances, and that is the phrase "belly-aching." In fact all of his talk at us has a distinctly "colicky" tone and one feels like giving him something to whine about. His ordinary call slightly resembles that of the Flicker but is not quite so loud; altogether he is quite a conversationalist.

Field marks.—The Gila woodpecker should be easily recognized as a medium-sized woodpecker, about the size of a hairy woodpecker, with a grayish-brown head, neck, and under parts and a báck narrowly barred with black and white; in flight a white patch shows in the wing and basal half of the primaries, and the black and white barring on the central tail feathers is rather conspicuous; the red crown patch of the male is conspicuous only at short range.

Fall.—This woodpecker is apparently somewhat given to wandering in fall and spring, for W. E. D. Scott (1886) says that he does not see it about his house, at an elevation of 4,500 feet in Pinal County, Ariz., in summer, but that it is rather common there in fall and spring.

DISTRIBUTION

Range.—Southwestern United States and western Mexico; nonmigratory.

The range of the Gila woodpecker extends **north** to extreme southern Nevada (Clark County); southern Arizona (Sacaton, Rock Canyon, and Tombstone); and southwestern New Mexico (Red Rock and probably Gila). **East** to New Mexico (probably Gila); eastern Sonora (Fronteras, Boca de Huachy, and Nuri); southwestern Chihuahua (Batopilas); western Durango (Chacala); and western Zacatecas (Calvillo). **South** to southwestern Zacatecas (Calvillo); and Jalisco (Guadalajara, Santa Ano, and Rio Ameca). **West** to Jalisco (Rio Ameca); Nayarit (Tepic and San Blas); southwestern Sinaloa (Escuinapa, Labrados, and Mazatlan); Baja California (Cape San Lucas, Santa Margarita Island, San Ignacio, Rosario, San Quintin, Las Palmas, and the Alamo River); southeastern California (Calexico, probably Brawley, Palo Verde, and Needles); and southern Nevada (Clark County).

This species has been separated into three geographic races, or subspecies. Typical *C. u. uropygialis* is the form found in that part of the range lying in the United States, and this race also is the one found in the western mainland of Mexico. The cardon woodpecker (*C. u. cardonensis*) is found in the northern part of Baja California south to about latitude 28° N. Brewster's woodpecker (*C. u. brewsteri*) occupies the cape district of Baja California north to San Ignacio and including also Santa Margarita Island.

Egg dates.—Arizona: 26 records, April 7 to May 30; 13 records, May 5 to 25, indicating the height of the season.

Baja California: 10 records, April 21 to June 2.

CENTURUS UROPYGIALIS CARDONENSIS Grinnell

CARDON WOODPECKER

HABITS

In describing and naming this race, Dr. Joseph Grinnell (1927a) says:

In its main characters similar to *Centurus uropygialis uropygialis*, but general coloration much darker: whole head (except for red patch on crown) and anterior lower surface strongly tinged with snuff brown rather than pale drab; and white barring on closed wings, tail, dorsum, rump, flanks, and lower tail coverts, narrower, leaving the black-barring correspondingly broader. Similar to *C. u. brewsteri*, but size larger, and coloration darker, in the same respects though not to quite so great a degree as shown in comparison with *uropygialis*. In other words, the new form differs from both the previously known races in the deeper brown tinge of the head and lower surface and in the greater degree of predominance of black over white in the barring.

He says of its range: "So far as now known, only the giant cactus (cardon) association in the northern section of the Lower Californian peninsula, from about latitude 30° to latitude 31°. Life-zone, Lower Sonoran." The 1931 Check-list extends the range northward "along the western rim of the Colorado Desert to about latitude 32°."

A. W. Anthony (1895a) says of the haunts of this woodpecker in Baja California: "The range of this species along the Pacific slope is exactly coextensive with that of *Cereus pringlei*, becoming common with that cactus a short distance below Rosario and seldom if ever being seen at any distance from the shelter of its mighty branches. At the mission, where the cardons were very large and abundant, to within a short distance of the mesquite thickets, this Woodpecker delighted in making frequent forays into the lesser growth, spending hours in hammering on the mesquite trunks and hunting through their branches, always beating a precipitate retreat to the cactus on the hillsides above at the first sign of danger."

I can find nothing further of consequence published on the habits of the cardon woodpecker, which doubtless do not differ materially from those of its Arizona relative.

The eggs are similar to those of the Gila woodpecker. The measurements of 11 eggs average 23.59 by 18.30 millimeters; the eggs showing the four extremes measure 25.6 by 18.1, 24.5 by **19.8**, **21.9** by 17.8, and 22.1 by **17.3** millimeters. Griffing Bancroft has a still larger egg, which measures 26.4 by 21.8 millimeters.

CENTURUS UROPYGIALIS BREWSTERI Ridgway

BREWSTER'S WOODPECKER

HABITS

In the Cape region of Baja California, we find this local race, which Ridgway (1914) describes as "similar to *C. u. uropygialis* but smaller, with relatively (often absolutely) larger bill, bars on back, etc., averaging decidedly narrower (the white ones about 1.5–2 mm. wide), black bars on lower rump and upper tail-coverts narrower or more numerous, and white bars on lateral rectrices as well as black ones on inner web of middle rectrices narrower."

William Brewster (1902) says: "In the Cape Region the Gila Woodpecker has apparently much the same distribution as *Dryobates lucasanus*. Neither Mr. Belding nor Mr. Frazar found it in the higher mountains, but both note its abundance throughout the low country, and Mr. Frazar obtained many specimens at Triunfo which is within the lower edge of the oak belt."

Griffing Bancroft (1930) referred the woodpeckers of this species that he found breeding in central Lower California to this southern race. Probably they are intermediate between this and *cardonensis*. He says of it:

The most abundant bird of its order, ranging throughout the territory examined. It is to be found in the suburban gardens of Santa Rosalia, among the palms of San Ignacio, and everywhere through the desert cactus belt. Its favorite choice of a home is a site high in a candelebra cardón; but it will also nest, even when not driven by necessity, in palms and tree yucca.

Its breeding season is quite long, fresh eggs being found from the latter part of April until well into June. The number laid is irregular. About half the sets are of two, but there are four's and even five's. Sixteen eggs taken in the vicinity of San Ignacio average 24.0 by 18.9 mm.

The birds are quite tame and often cannot be flushed. More than once, on opening cavities, we have lifted an adult from eggs or young, or even from an empty hole. Repeatedly a bird has been seen flying into a nest, either to feed young or to go onto eggs, while people were standing at the foot of the tree. When their homes are being examined the birds often approach within a few feet to voice their protests. Such fearlessness is unusual on this desert.

COLAPTES AURATUS AURATUS (Linnaeus)

SOUTHERN FLICKER

PLATE 35

HABITS

The type name *auratus* is now restricted to the flickers of the South Atlantic and Gulf States, from North Carolina to southern Florida and central Texas north to extreme southern Illinois and Indiana, southeastern Missouri, and southeastern Kansas, because the above Linnaean name was based on birds described by Catesby, which belonged to the smaller southern race.

The habits of the southern flicker are so similar to those of the northern flicker that the following account given for the northern race will serve very well for both. It is a common bird, widely distributed and well known throughout its range. In Florida we found it rather partial to open, burned-over tracts in the flat pine woods, nesting in the charred stumps, but it was also common in more open country in thinly settled regions, where we often found it nesting in isolated trees or dead stubs of palmettos or pines.

W. J. Erichsen (1920) says of its haunts in Chatham County, Ga.: "Wherever there are areas of cut-over lands on which remain an abundance of dead trees this species will be found in large numbers. At all seasons it exhibits a preference for open pine barrens, but, particularly during the breeding season, is occasionally met with about the edges of swamps if they contain suitable nesting sites. It is abundant on all of the wooded islands, particularly Ossabaw island, where I observed it in large numbers in May, 1915. Here it is oftenest seen in the woods close to the salt marsh or adjoining the beach, apparently not frequenting in any numbers the more heavily forested interior of the island."

Nesting.—Capt. H. L. Harllee writes to me that southern flickers raise two broods in a season in South Carolina and are not very particular as to their nesting sites. They nest in holes of their own excavation in dead trees of many species, 3 to 100 feet from the ground, either in thick woods or in a lone dead tree in an open cultivated field; they also nest in natural cavities in trees. He found one pair of these birds nesting in a hole made by fire in an old burned-out stump; the cavity was about two feet deep and eight inches in diameter; "the opening was slightly arched over with grass growing around it; a small quantity of pine straw was the only lining."

Arthur H. Howell (1932) says: "The nests are placed in pines, oaks, cabbage palms, or other trees, at heights varying from a few feet to 60 feet above the ground. At Ponce Park, in May, 1925,

I observed a Flicker using a hole in a palmetto pile under the dock on the shore of the Halifax River, only 2 feet above the salt water at high tide. Nicholson found a nest 12 inches above the ground in a sawed-off stump of a palmetto on a ditch bank."

Alexander Sprunt, Jr. (1931), mentions a concentration of hole-nesting birds in a tree in a yard in Beaufort, S. C.; the tree measured only 20 feet in height and contained nests of two pairs of flickers, and one nest each of crested flycatcher, screech owl, and downy woodpecker. "All five cavities were contained in a radius of ten feet, and four were within six feet of each other."

A. F. Ganier (1926) writes:

While in the suburbs of Chattanooga, Tennessee, last spring, I noticed a Flicker engaged in what appeared to be a hopeless task in the way of nest excavation. An iron water tank, supported by steel columns forty feet high, was fed by a large iron pipe through its bottom, and, to keep this pipe from freezing in winter, it had been encased with a plank shaft two feet square that was filled with cedar sawdust. Our friend *Colaptes auratus* had evidently sounded the boards, and, sensing easy digging, had drilled a hole in the middle of one side about thirty feet up. When espied, he was enthusiastically pitching out quantities of sawdust, which I presume caved in about as fast as he dug, but during the half hour I was engaged near by there was no let up in the work. About a month later I was again in the vicinity and made it a point to go by the tank. On the ground below the hole was at least a bushel of sawdust, and in a few minutes I had the pleasure of seeing a Flicker enter the hole with food in its mouth, presumably to feed the young that had come to reward his perseverance.

Eggs.—The southern flicker lays five to ten eggs, ordinarily, but shares with its northern relative its reputation as a prolific egg layer; it will continue to lay again and again after being robbed, as many as 30 or 40 eggs and often three or four sets. The eggs are similar to those of the northern flicker, except for a slight difference in size. The measurements of 44 eggs from South Carolina average 28.57 by 22.01 millimeters; the eggs showing the four extremes measure **30.15** by **24.56** and **24.13** by **20.32** millimeters. These seem to run larger than eggs from farther north.

In all other respects, the habits of the southern flicker are similar to those of the species elsewhere, with due allowance for the difference in environment. Two items of interest, however, are worth quoting. Charles R. Stockard (1904) writes from Mississippi:

On April 18 a burrow of a Flicker containing only one fresh egg was found. The egg was not disturbed. When visiting the nest again on April 28 a flying squirrel was found in possession. On my arrival the bird was at the entrance of the burrow peering in at the intruder. It was supposed that the squirrel was eating the eggs, but on examining the nest it was found to contain one spoilt egg. The squirrel had then probably been in possession for the ten days since the nest was observed, so the bird had been unable to enter and lay. * * * The Flicker must then have remained about her nest for this length of time, and as soon as the squirrel was removed she again took charge. On visiting the nest May 5, seven days later, it contained seven fresh eggs and the old one that had been left. * * * This was undoubtedly a case of discontinuous laying unless she had dropped her eggs on the ground while the squirrel was occupying the nest.

Mrs. Sanford Duncan (1932), of Nashville, Tenn., tells an interesting story of a flicker that was captured by a bullsnake. She heard a great commotion among the birds in her yard and went out to investigate the cause of the excitement. "The Flickers were leading the battle, dashing and darting at a bundle of something on the ground. Closer inspection with field glasses showed it was a snake, all tied up in a curious knot. He was too big for me to attack with the hoe I had, so I shot into the 'bundle' with a shotgun. As if by magic the snake flung himself into the air and fell, straightened out, over five feet long, and disclosed a full-grown Flicker that he had wrapped himself around many times. The Flicker was still alive, but died very shortly, probably from the gunshot that killed the bullsnake."

Lester W. Smith writes to me that he watched a southern flicker digging white grubs out of a lawn and killing them by repeated blows and shaking; meantime a loggerhead shrike was attempting to rob the flicker of its prey.

DISTRIBUTION

Range.—North America, chiefly east of the Rocky Mountains, and from the limit of trees south to the Gulf coast.

Breeding range.—The breeding range of the flicker extends **north** to Alaska (Circle); northwestern Mackenzie (probably Fort Mc-Pherson, Fort Anderson, McVicar Bay, Fort Rae, and Hill Island Lake); northern Saskatchewan (Reindeer Lake); northern Manitoba (probably Lake Du Brochet and Fort Churchill); Ontario (Lac Seul and probably Moose Factory); Quebec (probably Fort George, probably Lake Mistassini, Godbout, and Mingan Island); and Labrador (Cartwright). From this northeastern point the range extends **southward** through Newfoundland, along the Atlantic coast to Key West, Fla. The **southern** limits of nesting are the Gulf coasts of Florida and Alabama, thence in the interior to Louisiana (St. Francisville and Genoa); and Oklahoma (Okmulgee and Norman). **West** to Oklahoma (Norman); central Kansas (Harper, Hay, and Stockton); Nebraska (Red Cloud, Alda, and Chadron); eastern Wyoming (Midwest and Newcastle); Montana (Terry, Fairview, and Great Falls); Alberta (Morrin, Henry House, and Lesser Slave Lake); northwestern British Columbia (Telegraph Creek and Atlin); Yukon (Caribou Crossing and Selkirk); and eastern Alaska (Circle). This species, more or less crossed with the red-shafted flicker (*Colaptes c. collaris*), also is found occasionally in eastern Colorado (Hallvale, Denver, and Fort Morgan).

Winter range.—During the winter season the flicker is found with more or less regularity **north** to southeastern South Dakota (Yankton, Vermillion, and Sioux Falls); southern Minnesota (Hutchinson and Minneapolis); southern Wisconsin (North Freedom and Milwaukee); southern Michigan (Kalamazoo, Jackson, Ann Arbor, and Detroit); southern Ontario (Plover Mills, Hamilton, and Toronto); New York (Rochester, Syracuse, and Rhinebeck); and rarely Maine (Waterville). From this point it is found **south** along the Atlantic coast to southern Florida (St. Lucie and Fort Myers). The southern limits of the winter range are found on the Gulf coast from Florida (Fort Myers) to Texas (Brownsville). **West** to Texas (Brownsville, San Antonio, San Angelo, and Abilene); central Oklahoma (Norman, Oklahoma City, and Tonkawa); Kansas (Wichita and rarely Hay); Nebraska (Red Cloud and North Loup); and southeastern South Dakota (Yankton). It also has been taken or observed at this season north to southern Saskatchewan (Eastend); Quebec (Montreal); New Brunswick (St. John); and Nova Scotia (Bridgetown).

The range as outlined is for the entire species, of which two subspecies are currently recognized. The typical form, known as the southern flicker (*C. a. auratus*), is found from southern Florida and Texas north to southeastern Kansas, southeastern Missouri, southern Illinois and Indiana, and North Carolina. It probably is nonmigratory. The rest of the range is occupied by the northern flicker (*C. a. luteus*).

Spring migration.—Early dates of arrival in regions north of the winter range as outlined, are: Nova Scotia—Wolfville, March 26; Halifax, April 7. New Brunswick—Scotch Lake, April 5; Grand Manan, April 12. Quebec—Quebec City, April 27; Godbout, May 2; Paradise, June 5. North Dakota—Fargo, March 29; Charlson, March 30; Grand Forks, April 2. Manitoba—Winnipeg, March 30; Alexander, April 14; Raeburn, April 15. Saskatchewan—Eastend, April 3; McLean, April 3. Wyoming—Cheyenne, April 7; Laramie, April 12. Montana—Great Falls, April 1; Terry, April 4; Jackson, April 14. Alberta—Banff, April 4; Flagstaff, April 13; Edmonton, April 17. Mackenzie—Fort Simpson, May 4; Fort Reliance, May 2. Alaska—Fairbanks, April 25; Fort Yukon, May 1.

Fall migration.—Late dates of fall departure are: Alaska—Wrangell, October 11; Craig, October 21. Mackenzie—near McVicar Bay, September 10; Great Slave Lake, September 11; Fort Simpson, October 16. Alberta—Lac La Biche, September 25; Glenevis, October 2; Calgary, October 10. Montana—Bozeman, September 24; Saskatchewan—Eastend, October 14. Manitoba—Alexander, October 22; Aweme, October 27. North Dakota—Arlington, October 19; Argusville, October 21; Fargo, October 21. Northern Michigan—Sault

Ste. Marie, October 24. Quebec—Montreal, November 25. New Brunswick—St. John, November 5; Scotch Lake, November 22. Nova Scotia—Wolfville, November 19.

The records of flickers that have been banded and subsequently recovered throw much light upon the migrations of this species. In the files of the Biological Survey there are long series of cases where birds banded at their nests in the northern parts of the breeding range (Alberta, Saskatchewan, Manitoba, Michigan, New York, and Massachusetts) have returned to the same point one to four years later. These birds probably all belonged to the subspecies *luteus*. Similarly, similar data also are available for areas (Missouri, Kentucky, Tennessee, and Florida) within the range of *C. a. auratus*, which probably is nonmigratory.

Definite migrations of individual banded birds are indicated by the records of flickers banded in Saskatchewan and recovered in Iowa, Oklahoma, and Texas; banded in Missouri and recovered in Texas; banded in Iowa and recovered in Louisiana; banded in South Dakota and recovered in Arkansas and Oklahoma (4); banded in Illinois and recovered in Kentucky, Tennessee, Missouri, Arkansas (2), and Louisiana (3); banded in Indiana and recovered in Mississippi; banded in Michigan and recovered in Arkansas and Louisiana; banded in Ohio and recovered in Alabama and Mississippi; banded in Pennsylvania and recovered in Georgia; and banded in Nova Scotia and recovered in North Carolina.

Casual records.—In southern British Columbia a specimen was collected at Sumas on April 8, 1903, and two were seen at Vernon on December 26, 1906; a specimen was taken at Orcas Island, Wash., on October 15, 1907; one was collected at Blaine, Oreg., on November 3, 1921; and one was taken at Cliff Spring, Nev., on September 29, 1931. There are several records for California as follows: Furnace Creek, April 12, 1917; St. Geronimo, December 18, 1893, and January 14, 1895; Point Lobos, December 14, 1934; Los Angeles, February 20, 1901; San Diego, December 4, 1931; and Eldridge, January 4, 1913.

At least four occurrences well north of the breeding range in Alaska have been recorded: St. George Island, fall of 1904; Cape Etolin, September 14, 1927; Wainwright, a specimen in 1924; and Cape Halkett, in the fall of 1927.

A specimen was collected on Okpatok Island in Hudson Strait in October 1882, one was taken in Sandwich Bay in August 1908, and a specimen has been reported from Cape Wolstenholme on the Ungava Peninsula. The species also has been recorded from Bermuda where at least one specimen was collected in 1871.

Egg dates.—Arctic America: 6 records, June 3 to 16.

Florida: 18 records, March 25 to July 18; 9 records, April 16 to May 18, indicating the height of the season.

Illinois: 22 records, April 30 to May 30; 11 records, May 13 to 21.

Michigan: 16 records, April 17 to June 24; 8 records, May 12 to 30.

New York: 15 records, May 13 to June 15; 8 records, May 25 to 29.

COLAPTES AURATUS LUTEUS Bangs

NORTHERN FLICKER

PLATE 36

HABITS

I can remember as clearly as if it were only yesterday my boyish, enthusiastic admiration for this beautiful bird, though it was between 50 or 60 years ago that my father first showed me a freshly killed flicker. I was simply entranced with the softly blended browns, the red crescent on the head, the black crescent and bold spotting on the breast, and, above all, with the golden glow in the wings and tail. Few birds combine such charming colors and pleasing contrasts. I have never lost my admiration for it, and still consider it one of nature's gems.

It, and its close relative, the red-shafted flicker, together are widely distributed over nearly all the wooded regions of North America. Consequently it is widely known and over most of its range is a common and familiar species. Its prominence and popularity are attested by the long list of vernacular names by which it is locally known. Franklin L. Burns (1900), in his monograph of the species, lists 123 such names; and later he adds nine more, bringing the list up to 132 names. These are far too many to be quoted here, and many of them are "very local or very slight orthographical or cacographical variants." I have always loved our local name "partridge woodpecker," suggestive of my boyhood days, when flickers, meadowlarks, and robins were considered legitimate game. But now the name yellow-shafted flicker seems appropriate to distinguish it from the red-shafted flicker.

The haunts of the flicker are almost everywhere in open country or lightly wooded regions; it can hardly be called a forest-loving species, though I have often found it nesting in more or less extensive deciduous woods; its favorite haunts during the summer seem to be in the rural districts among the farms, orchards, and scattered woodlots; it seems to be at home, also, in villages and small towns, and even in some of the smaller cities, where spacious grounds and gardens provide suitable surroundings. In fall and winter it is more apt to wander about in open woodlands, fields, and meadows or seek shelter in coniferous woods or swamps.

Spring.—Although many flickers remain all winter in the Northern States, there is a decided spring migration of the great bulk of northern-bred birds that have wintered in the Southern States. These birds gather in flocks during the late winter, and the northward movement starts with the first mild weather, the migration being largely performed during the night. Mr. Burns (1900) says that at Berwyn, Pa., the forerunners, consisting of solitary old males, appear "as early as Feb. 2 or as late as April 6, according to the promises of the season, correlating in a measure with the date at which the first frog is heard peeping. * * *

"It becomes common soon after the hardy willow has unfolded its leaves, and about the time the fragrant spicewood blossoms, when the ants, spiders and beetles become active once more, and just in the height of the arbutus season. The northward movement is far from being steady or regular, being largely governed by weather conditions; Mr. Burns calculates from his mass of data that the average distance traveled daily is about 12 miles, "varying according to season and weather conditions from 7 to 48 miles per night. It is absolutely certain that it does not move steadily night after night, but only as the weather permits or necessitates and its physical condition allows."

Flickers often migrate in companies of considerable size, in loose, scattered flocks, noisy and active, flying from tree to tree and calling excitedly. Their arrival is announced by the loud challenge-call, given from the top of some tall tree, *wicker*, *wicker*, *wicker*, or *wake-up*, *wake-up*, *wake-up*, as the male challenges his rivals or invites his prospective mate to join him in courtship. This, one of the most welcome sounds of early spring, is indeed a call to "wake up," for all nature is awakening, buds are swelling on the trees, verdure is appearing in the woods and fields, the early flowers are beginning to blossom, the hylas are peeping in the warming pools, insects are becoming active, and the songs of the early birds announce that spring is here. Another spring sound soon strikes our ears, a loud, far-reaching, vibrant sound, the long, almost continuous roll of the flicker's drumming, another challenge-call, a preliminary of the courtship performance; at frequent intervals, often repeated over a long period in early morning, he beats his loud tattoo on some hollow, resonant limb.

Courtship.—The courtship of the flicker is a lively and spectacular performance, noisy, full of action, and often ludicrous, as three or more birds of both sexes indulge in their comical dancing, nodding, bowing, and swaying motions, or chase each other around the trunk or through the branches of a tree. From the time of Audubon to the present day, many observers have noted and described the curious antics of this star performer. But I prefer to quote first from some extensive notes recently contributed by Francis H. Allen, as follows: "The courtship of the flicker is an elaborate and somewhat puzzling performance. Two birds face each other on the branch of a tree or cling side by side, though at a little distance apart, on the trunk, and spread their tails and jerk their heads about in a sort of weaving motion, frequently uttering a note that is peculiar to this performance, a *wick-up* or *week-up*. The head motion is a series of backward jerks with the bill pointing up at an angle of perhaps 60° and the head at the same time swinging from side to side. Sometimes a short, low *wuck* is uttered from time to time during the performance. These bouts occur not only between male and female, but frequently between two males or two females.

"In April 1934, for more than a week I saw a trio of flickers about my house. Invariably the two females went through courtship antics together, while the male fed on the ground nearby, apparently completely indifferent to them. One of the females was much more active than the other, which usually kept a stiff pose with head drawn in, only occasionally responding with feeble head-waggings. At no time did the active female use any other display than the head-wagging, and there was never any suggestion of combat or intimidation.

"A year later, 1935, the flickers near my house behaved differently. In the afternoon of April 24, the two males were singing loudly and frequently in the woods, about an eighth of a mile away and at some distance apart. By singing I mean, of course, the prolonged laughing call of *wick-wick-wick*, etc. Presently they stopped singing, and one flew toward the other, stopping about halfway. Very soon the other joined him, and a long period of posturing and *wick-up*-ing ensued. Both birds had the black mustaches of the male. The posturing was the regular 'weaving' of the head and the fanning of the tail. The notes, after the first at least, were much subdued in tone. There were frequent intervals of quiet. The birds kept close together most of the time, often with heads only two or three inches apart, or perhaps less. They flitted about frequently, sometimes clinging to the trunk of an oak, sometimes perched on a horizontal branch, and once or twice they alighted on the stems of underbrush. After a long period of posturing, they met in a momentary tilt, and presently there was another clash after more posturing, then a third clash, and after that they separated. The same bird was the aggressor in at least two of the clashes. As often in such encounters, the attacked bird stood his ground and the attacker veered off. It was very mild warfare, if it was really serious at all.

"Two days after the bout of the two males, I saw two females engaged in the dance in one of our pear trees. It lasted only a few minutes, and I heard no notes. Not long after the dance of the two females a prolonged 'sexual flight' took place. It lasted five or ten minutes, as nearly as I could tell, with a few short intervals of resting. I could at no time determine the sexes of the two birds thus engaged, but occasionally a snatch of faint song was heard (*wick-wick-wick*), and I assume that they were male and female. They flew rather slowly and kept only a few feet apart. It was evident that the spacing was intentional and that the pursuer made no attempt to catch up with the other. The flight covered a territory of several acres. It was a graceful and interesting performance.

"I supposed at the time that this sexual flight indicated that the affair was completed, but later that afternoon I several times saw a male and two females together, the females posturing and *wick-up-ing*, the male motionless. The females showed no enmity toward each other and did not face each other, as the males of two days before did. They kept rather farther apart. At one time a second male appeared and stayed about for a time, but he disappeared, apparently without becoming a serious factor in the situation.

"Three days later a pair of flickers, male and female, were feeding peacefully together on the lawn in the morning and in the afternoon, and I judged that the marital arrangements of at least two of my flickers had been completed."

More active courtship on the part of a female flicker is thus described in some notes from Lewis O. Shelley: "On April 24, coincident with a male flicker's message from the elm stub, a female and a second male appeared. All three were later in the cherry tree by our garden, perched on branches some three feet apart. The female took the initiative in the following activities and, perched crosswise of the branch, often bobbed and ducked up and down, then crosswise of the branch jerked to left, right, left, right, head cocked erect and with tail fully spread. At times the males, less actively, did likewise, but for the most part perched noncommittally, silent and still, giving but few calls. At one time, after the female had displayed intermittently several times, and when the males had been still for some five minutes, she sidled up to the nearest male and again displayed with much wing-fluttering and tail-spreading and sidewise twitchings; then the same to the other male who flew when her actions of bobbing and bowing face to face commenced. Not to be outdone, or so affronted, she flew after him, then the second male followed."

C. W. Leister (1919) noticed an aerial courtship evolution of the flicker, of which he says: "When first noticed, he was about fifty feet from the ground and ascending in peculiar, bumpy, and jerky spirals. This was maintained until a height of about 350–400 feet was reached, when, after a short pause, a reverse of practically the same performance was gone through. The Flicker (*Colaptes auratus luteus*), for as such he was identified by this time, then alighted in a cherry tree, just above a female that we had previously failed to notice, and completed the performance by going through his more familiar courting antics."

A recrudescence of the amatory instinct is sometimes seen in fall. On September 22, 1933, a clear, warm morning, a pair of flickers, male and female, were watched for some time as they performed their courtship dance on the top of one of my chimneys, where there might have been some warmth remaining from a fire that had since died out. They danced around on all four sides of the chimney, always facing each other, both of them bowing and swaying the head and neck, or whole body, from side to side, with the neck extended and the bill pointing almost straight upward. Sometimes they stopped for a few seconds, holding the upright posture, or one performed while the other posed. There was no wing or tail display that I could see. Lewis O. Shelley tells me that he has seen flickers in courtship display while the young were just leaving the nest.

Nesting.—Soon after mating is accomplished the choice for a nesting site is made, and often the selection is made during courtship, especially if a nesting cavity of the previous year is to be used. Probably the female usually makes the final decision, though there is some evidence to indicate that in many cases the male selects the site and persuades his mate to accept it.

Miss Althea R. Sherman (1910) made some very thorough studies of the nesting habits of the northern flicker at National, Iowa, in some boxes so arranged on her barn that she could observe the home life of the birds at close range. The male and the female had been occupying two different boxes as roosting places, and the eggs were laid in the box occupied by the male, from which it became evident "that the male bird chose the nesting place, and persuaded his mate to lay her eggs there, even when she was inclined to nest elsewhere, and when she had a box quite as good as his."

Often the male "stakes out his claim," so to speak, in the vicinity of an old nest, where, during the courtship period, he utters his loud mating call for several days, or even weeks, before the female answers the invitation. Then, after mating is accomplished, his chosen mate may or may not accept his choice of a nesting site. The desirability of the nesting site may in such cases influence the female's choice of a mate, for she is as much interested in having a comfortable and safe home as in choosing a handsome husband.

Having chosen the site, the pair set about repairing the old cavity or excavating a new one, at which both birds work diligently for anywhere from a week to three weeks, depending on the conditions they find. Mr. Shelley tells me that, in his experience with several nests, the nesting cavity is completed from a week to a fortnight before the eggs are laid. The chips are usually, but not always, carried away to some distance from the nest tree, but often chips are merely scattered about the base of the tree. William Brewster (1936) gives the following account of rather peculiar behavior of a flicker while excavating its nest:

Found a Flicker at work excavating a hole in an apple-tree in Bensen's orchard. I was passing the tree within six feet when I heard a low tapping, accompanied by a continuous muffled whining sound. Turning, I at once saw the bird's tail projecting from the hole, which was not over five feet above the ground. For a minute or more the pecking and whining continued uninterruptedly, the tail wriggling violently the while. Evidently the bird had carried in the hole to just that point where she had less room to work than she had had before or would have afterwards. In other words, she had just about reached the point where the entrance hole must begin to be expanded into a chamber and to turn downward. It seemed to me that the whining sound expressed rage or impatience. Perhaps it was the Flicker's form of swearing!

The northern flicker seems to show no very decided preference for any one species of tree in its choice of a nesting site, though I believe it does prefer a dead tree, or a dead stub on a living tree, or a tree that has a soft or partially decayed heart. It has always seemed to me that in New England we find more nests in large apple trees in old orchards than elsewhere, the nest being excavated in the main trunk, or large upright branch, at no great height from the ground. Such trees may have a hard outer shell, but the interior is often more or less soft. Old orchards are becoming scarce in my vicinity, which forces the flickers to look elsewhere. Next in importance here as a common nesting site is the trunk or stub of a dead white pine tree. Mr. Burns (1900) mentions one dead pine "perforated with 25 or 30 holes, most of which were in use at one time or another." He lists, as favorite trees in the Middle and Eastern States, "apple, sycamore, oak, butternut, cherry, elm, chestnut, maple, poplar, beech, ash, pine, hickory, etc." In Pennsylvania, he says that J. Warren Jacobs has "found the sycamore to be the favorite, with the apple and maple second, the beech and locust third, oak and cherry fourth, and all other varieties fifth."

Mr. Burns continues: "From Ohio westward the apple orchard is a favorite with the poplar, willow, maple, oak, elm, walnut, cottonwood, etc., more or less resorted to, according to availability. It very seldom nests in a living coniferous tree, though it has been known to nest in a living red cedar and in dead hemlocks and spruces."

Telegraph, telephone, and other tall poles, as well as fenceposts, are favorite nesting sites in the prairie regions and other parts of the West, where trees are scarce. Frank L. Farley writes to me that in the timbered country of northern Alberta, "where there are many suitable nesting trees and stubs, the telephone and telegraph poles are frequently used for nesting. These poles are usually cedar and it is assumed that the birds prefer these for nesting, because of the ease with which they can excavate."

Flickers quite often nest in boxes erected for that purpose and in buildings, much to the annoyance of the owners. I have frequently seen nests in icehouses; these have double walls, the intervening space being filled with sawdust; the birds drill through the outer walls and make their nests in the sawdust. The cornices and walls of many buildings on the farms, as well as the towers of churches and schoolhouses, are perforated, and the eggs laid on the beams or boarding within. Mr. Burns (1900) records the following interesting case:

Mr. Burke H. Sinclair found a nest containing eggs in the garret of the town high school. The birds obtained entrance to this large three-story brick building by means of a displaced brick. As in all infloored lofts it consists of nothing but the parallel rafters, with attached lath and plaster, which forms the ceiling of the room below. This frail floor is about ten inches below the entrance hole, and the nest was situated about one foot from and directly in front of the entrance. The place had evidently been used for several years, there being at least a peck of wood chippings, some fresh, but a large quantity old and discolored with age. The nest was placed between two of the parallel rafters and composed of these chippings, being about six inches thick by eighteen inches in diameter. This material had been all cut from the rafters on the floor and the roof overhead.

A number of other unusual nesting sites have been recorded. F. A. E. Starr tells me of a nest that "was in an old stump two feet high; the six eggs were on a bed of rotten wood at ground level." Dr. Jonathan Dwight, Jr. (1893), reports a nest that he found on Prince Edward Island; the "nest with fully fledged young was examined in the top of a hollow fence post. No excavation had been made by the bird, and the young were entirely exposed to the weather." Flickers occasionally nest in natural cavities in trees, where no excavation is needed beyond enlarging the opening, if necessary, or cleaning out the interior. Ned Hollister (1918) reports that a pair of flickers and a pair of house wrens nested in holes in an old stump in a lion's cage in the National Zoological Park in Washington. Mr. Burns (1900) writes: "It has been found breeding far out on the prairie in an old wagon hub, surrounded by weeds; also in barrels, and one instance of an excavation of the regulation size in a hay stack is on record; another nested in a crevice of an unused chimney for several years; and stranger yet it has been found more than once occupying Kingfisher's and enlarged Bank Swallow's burrows."

The haystack nest is reported by Major Bendire (1895), on the authority of William A. Bryant, of New Sharon, Iowa, as follows:

On a small hill, a quarter of a mile distant from my home, stood a haystack which had been placed there two years previously. The owner, during the winter of 1889–'90, had cut the stack through the middle and hauled away one portion, leaving the other standing with the end smoothly trimmed. The following spring I noticed a pair of yellow-shafted flickers about the stack showing signs of wanting to make it a fixed habitation. One morning a few days later I was amused at the efforts of one of the pair. It was clinging to the perpendicular end of the stack and throwing out chipped hay at a rate to defy competition. This work continued for nearly a week, and in that time the pair had excavated a cavity 20 inches in depth. The entrance was located 8½ feet above ground, and was 2½ inches in diameter and dug back into the stack for 6 inches, where it turned sharply downward and was slightly enlarged at the bottom. On May 28 I took a handsome set of seven eggs from the nest, the eggs lying on a bed of chipped hay. The birds lingered about the stack and by June 14 had deposited another set of eggs. * * * I never could quite understand the philosophy of their peculiar choice of this site, as woodland is abundant here. A well-timbered creek bottom was less than half a mile distant, while large orchards and groves surround the place on every hand.

Kumlien and Hollister (1903) and J. A. Farley (1901) record instances of flickers nesting on hay; in each case the birds bored a hole through the walls of a barn and laid their eggs in a hollow in a pile of hay near the entrance hole. William Brewster (1909) published an account of a flicker's nest on the open ground, found by some ladies on Cape Cod and seen by him. Beside a sandy road, "fully a quarter of a mile from the nearest house and bordered on both sides by dense woods of pitch pines, the ladies found five eggs of the Flicker lying together in a hollow in the ground within a few feet of the deeply rutted wagon track." The nest "was a circular, saucer-shaped depression, measuring 21¼ inches across the top, by 3 inches in depth. Dry yellowish sand mixed with fine gravel and wholly free from vegetation of any kind, living or dead, formed its bottom and the gently sloping sides, as well as the surface of the level ground about it for two or three yards in every direction, but a little further back there were weeds and grasses growing sparingly, in slightly richer soil." Photographs of two nests similarly located may be seen in Bird-Lore, volume 18, page 399, and volume 36, page 105.

Mr. Burns's data show that the height of the nest from the ground varies in middle and eastern States from 2 to 60 feet, and in central western States from ground level to 90 feet. His accumulated data on the measurements of nesting cavities show that the depth of the excavation is "greatest in New York and New England (10 to 36 inches), Illinois (14 to 24 inches), Pennsylvania (10 to 18 inches), and Minnesota (9 to 18 inches)." Probably the depth of the cavity depends on the quality of the wood and the age of the nest; when an old cavity is used, it is usually deepened somewhat. Dr. H. C. Oberholser (1896) gives the measurements of four Ohio nests; the total depth varied from 7 to 18 inches; the diameter of the entrance varied from 2.00 by 2.00 to 4.00 by 4.00 and averaged 2.94 by 2.72 inches. Mr. Burns (1900) says the diameter of the cavity near the bottom varies from 4.50 to 10.00, and averages 7.67 inches. No nesting material is taken in from outside, but enough fine chips are left in the bottom of the hole to make a soft bed, in which the eggs are partially buried. Carl W. Buchheister tells me that he once found a nest "the bottom of which was 6 inches below the ground level and 12 inches below the opening, a round hole which was 6 inches above the ground. There was but one egg."

Eggs.—The flicker is notorious as a prolific egg layer, but under ordinary circumstances, when not disturbed, the average set consists of six to eight eggs. Incubated sets of as few as three or four have been found, sets of nine and ten are not very rare, and as many as 17 have been found in a nest at one time; the large numbers may be products of two females. Mr. Burns (1900) records the contents of 169 sets of the northern flicker as 11 sets of four, 16 sets of five, 35 sets of six, 34 sets of seven, 38 sets of eight, 17 sets of nine, 13 sets of ten, 3 sets of twelve, and one each of thirteen and fourteen. Major Bendire (1895) states that Steward Ogilby, of Staten Island, N. Y., reports "finding a brood of not less than nineteen young Flickers in one nest, all alive and apparently in good condition."

If robbed of its eggs, the flicker will continue to lay new sets for a long time. Dr. Barton W. Evermann (1889) "obtained thirty-seven eggs in forty-nine days from a 'yellowhammer' which had its nest near my house. The eggs were in seven sets, five, five, five, six, seven, four, and five eggs respectively." J. Parker Norris (1888) took five sets of six eggs each from a nest in Pennsylvania between May 16 and June 18. Several other similar cases of persistent laying have been reported, all of which indicate that an egg is laid each day and that the birds begin at once to replace the lost set. Mr. Burns (1900) lists a number of such cases, where no nest egg was left to induce the bird to keep on laying; the largest number reported was 48 eggs in 65 days. My neighbor, Charles L. Phillips, tried the experiment of taking one egg each day, leaving one as a nest egg; he holds the extraordinary record of having taken 71 eggs from one nest in 73 days; the poor bird rested only two days in the long strain of over two months.

Eggs of the flicker have sometimes been found in the nests of other birds. In an old orchard, not far from my home, I once found a flicker's egg in a bluebird's nest, with five eggs of the latter; and in another cavity in the same tree was a tree swallow's nest containing five eggs of the swallow and an egg of the flicker. As this was in a remote locality, it is hardly likely that the eggs were placed there artificially, and the chances are that the flicker's nest had been destroyed and she was forced to lay in the nearest available cavity. Mr. Burns (1900) says: "A similar instance is recorded by E. G. Elliot, Bradford, Mass., May 16th, '84, of a set of five eggs of bluebird and one of flicker, nest of grass and feathers. Records of European house sparrow and red-headed woodpecker eggs in freshly excavated quarters with one or more eggs of the Flicker are not uncommon, and upon investigation the latter proved to be the aggrieved party in every instance." He also tells of a flicker that laid an egg in a mourning dove's nest.

The eggs of the flicker are pure lustrous white, with a brilliant gloss; the shell is translucent, and, when fresh, the yolk shows through it, suffusing the egg with a delicate pinkish glow, which is very beautiful.

The shape is quite variable, but the majority are ovate; some are short-ovate or elliptical-ovate, some nearly oval, and some rarely somewhat pointed. The measurements of 57 eggs average 26.85 by 20.58 millimeters; the eggs showing the four extremes measure **30.48** by 22.86, 28.19 by **24.38**, **24.45** by 21.34, and 27.68 by **19.05** millimeters.

Young.—The period of incubation of the flicker has been said to be from 14 to 16 days. Miss Sherman's (1910) careful observations on marked eggs, laid on known dates, indicate a shorter period. From some former nests she had learned "that sometimes the eggs hatched in nine days, but more frequently in ten days after the laying of the last egg." In these cases, incubation may have begun before the set was complete, or the eggs may have received some heat from the body of the male, for she said that, in at least one case, "while the eggs were being laid, and before incubation began the male roosted in the box with the eggs." According to a later observation, "the exact time for incubation had been twelve days, three hours and fifty-two minutes. The seventh egg hatched four hours later making its period of incubation eleven days and eight hours nearly." After another similar experience with the hatching of nine marked eggs, which extended over a period from 5:40 a.m. one day until 10:48 a.m. the next day, she says: "Roughly speaking, then, the time that our Flickers take for incubation is from eleven to twelve days."

Her observations showed that the duties of incubation are shared by both sexes, that the male usually incubates during the night, but "by day the duties of incubation seem to be shared about equally between the two birds, who are close sitters, the eggs seldom being found alone. Of the length of the sittings no adequate record has been kept, but those lasting from one hour and a half to two hours have been noted."

Miss Sherman (1910) noted that "the usual time for depositing the eggs in the nest appears to be the hour between five and six o'clock in the morning," though in one case an egg was laid between 11 a.m. and 4 p. m.

Some of her observations on the young follow:

Until the young are about eleven days old, they lie in a circle in the nest, their long necks stretched over each other, then for nearly a week they press against the side of the nest. At seventeen or eighteen days of age, their claws having acquired a needlelike sharpness, they begin to cling to the wall of the nest, and when three weeks old they are able to climb to the hole and be fed while the parent hangs outside.

Although the eyes of the nestlings are not open until they are ten days old yet these organs are by no means dormant. An easy proof of this is made by placing the hand noiselessly over the entrance hole when they are no more than three or four days old, and are lying apparently asleep; up comes every head and they beg for food, getting none they soon sleep, when the experiment may be repeated, gaining from the young the same response that is given when a parent darkens the hole.

That cry of the young which is so often described as a hissing sound, begins very soon after they are hatched. At first exceedingly faint it soon grows stronger, and is uttered day and night for two weeks. A parent upon taking its place to brood these wailing nestlings begins to croon a lullaby and continues this musical murmur until it falls asleep, which is often quite soon. It has no effect in lessening the noise of the youngsters, yet the parent faithfully renders its cradle song until the young cease to make this noise which is about the time they begin to show fear. Of other cries that they make, there is the chuckling noise uttered when the little one is in the act of seizing the food-bearing bill, and there is a cry that sounds like a whine. Still another one is a note of alarm given when the young are disturbed by some such thing as the opening of the trap door. This uttered in unison has a very theatrical effect strongly suggesting the chorus of the stage. After they have commenced to move about freely in the nest they make much of the time a pleasant sound like a chatter or quack, as if talking to each other. And lastly comes the grown-up Flicker "pe-ap", which they begin to call as soon as they climb to the hole. * * *

Some broods are much more quarrelsome than others. Their battle ground is in the vicinity of the hole. The one in possession of the hole maintains his supremacy there by occasional withdrawals of his head from the hole in order to deliver vigorous blows on the heads of all within his reach. This is the case with the stronger ones, the weaker ones frequently are driven from the vantage place. When the hole is large enough for two to thrust out their heads together, they draw within after the serving of a meal and fight furiously, while a waiting third may slip up and gain the coveted hole. But all their fighting days seem to be confined to a few in the fourth week of their lives.

  * * * In very early life a meal is served to baby Flicker with many insertions of the parent's bill, as many as thirty-four have been counted, but from eight to twenty are the ordinary number, decreasing to three or four before the young leave the nest. A record made during a continuous watch of six hours and thirty-two minutes shows that each parent fed five times; that the father delivered his supply with eighty-two insertions of the bill, while the mother used but forty-one. Probably the father brought more food since on every count he proved himself the more devoted parent. In grasping the bill the point of the youngster's bill is at right angles with that of the parent's, thus the opening between the food-bearing mandibles is covered after the young have attained a few days of age, and any over-dropping of food is prevented. This accident frequently happens in the early days of the nest, then the mussed up ants that fall are carefully picked up by the frugal parent when the feeding is over. * * *

Experiments show that to a nestling weighing 743 grains was given a break-fast that weighed 76 grains, to one weighing 1,430 grains a dinner of 118 grains, and to another that tipped the scales at 1,530 grains a supper of 103 grains. Probably the weight of the average load is not far from one hundred grains. * * *

When the young were eighteen days old during a watch of four and one-half hours twenty-five meals were given to five nestlings that wore dis-tinguished marks. Three of these are positively known to have received five meals apiece, and two received four apiece. * * * At this age the young Flickers every hour partake of food to the amount of one-sixteenth of their own weight, or in one day consume their full weight of food.

She says that flickers are very solicitous to keep a clean nest; for the first nine or ten days the parents eat the excrements, but after that the dejecta are carried out in the tough white sacks in which they are enclosed. If no sacks of excrement are found in the nest after feeding, the parent solicits them; "this is done by biting the heel joints sometimes, but more often the fleshy protuberance that bears that budding promise of the tail."

She says that the male "staid with the young every night until they were three weeks old, brooding all of them until nearly two weeks of age, when they began pressing their breasts against the side of the nest, and he could cover the tails of two or three only, after which for two or three nights he sat upon the bottom of the nest apart from the young; then for four nights he hung upon the wall of the nest near the hole; thereafter he staid with them no more."

Her records show that the young remained in the nest nearly or quite four weeks, or from 25 to 28 days. During the last three or four days nearly all of them lost weight; this may have been due to the period of the heaviest feather growth, or because the parents may have let up on the feeding to induce the young to leave the nest. Miss Sherman's statements, as to the period of incubation and the length of time that the young remain in the nest, are quite at variance with statements made by others, but her observations were so care-fully and thoroughly made under such favorable circumstances that they are more convincing than less accurate observations of others.

Some others have also described the method of feeding the young by regurgitation in a manner that differs from that observed by Miss Sherman. Mr. Brewster (1936), for example, says:

Standing on the edge of the hole, the parent would select one—usually the nearest, I thought—and bending down would drive his bill to its base into the gaping mouth which instantly closed tightly around it, when the head and bill of the parent was worked up and down with great rapidity for from one to one and one-half seconds (timed with a stop watch), the young mean-while holding on desperately and apparently never once losing its grasp, although its poor little head was jerked up and down violently. The first, or entering downward thrust of the parent's bill looked like a vicious stab, the bird ap-parently striking with all its force and as if with the design of piercing his offspring to the vitals. The subsequent up and down motion was invariably rapid and regular and resembled the bill movement of a woodpecker while "drumming." It also suggested the stroke of a piston.

In this case the top of the stump had been broken off, leaving the nest open and exposed, so that every motion could be clearly seen from a distance of not over 15 feet. After the young had left the nest, he discovered that "the nest was left in a terribly foul state, the bottom being a disgusting mass of muddy excrement alive with wriggling worms. * * * These young, however, managed to keep very clean and all, so far as I could discover, were perfectly free from vermin." Apparently the old birds find it difficult to clean the nest after the young reach a certain size.

W. I. Lyon (1922) tells an interesting story of a screech owl that adopted and brooded a family of young flickers, after its own nest in the same tree had been broken up twice; the owl even brought in part of a small bird, perhaps intending to feed it to the young flickers, which were all the time being fed by their parents and were successfully raised.

Plumages.—Miss Sherman (1910) gives a very good description of the naked and blind nestling, as follows: "The pellucid color of the newly hatched Flicker resembles that of freshly sun-burned human skin, but so translucent is the nestling's skin that immediately after a feeding one can see the line of ants that stretches down the bird's throat and remains in view two or three minutes before passing onward. This may be witnessed for several days while the skin assumes a coarser red, until it begins to thicken and become a bluish hue, before the appearance of the pin-feathers. These may be detected under the skin on the fifth day at the same time that bristle-like projections about one-sixteenth of an inch long announce the coming of the rectrices and remiges."

Mr. Burns (1900) says: "It is not known when the white membranous process which extends from either side of the base of the lower mandible disappears, but it probably goes at a very early age. This formation is apparently peculiar to all young woodpeckers, as suggested by Frank A. Bates, in the *Ornithologist and Oologist*, Vol. XVI, p. 35, but its use is unknown." A photograph, published by E. H. Forbush (1927), shows that this does not wholly disappear until the young bird is nearly fledged; its function is probably to help guide the regurgitated food from the mouth of the adult into the throat of the young bird during the feeding method noted by Miss Sherman (1910).

The young flicker is fully fledged in its juvenal plumage when it leaves the nest; and, contrary to the rule among birds, this plumage more nearly resembles the plumage of the adult male than that of the old female, as the young of both sexes have the black malar patches. The black bands on the upper parts are much broader, the vinaceous portions of the head and neck are more tinged with gray, the malar patches are duller black, and the lower parts are paler with duller and larger black spots than in the adult. The crown is usually more or less suffused with dull red, especially in young males, and sometimes the red nuchal crescent is somewhat wider or more extensive; the crescent on the breast is usually smaller; the yellow on the under sides of the wings and tail is duller and more greenish; the black tips in the tail are duller and not so sharply defined against the yellow; and the upper tail coverts are black with white spots, instead of being white and boldly barred with black, as in the adult. The plumage is soft and loose in texture and the bill is small and weak.

This plumage is worn but a short time, as a complete molt begins in July and is usually finished in September or October, producing a first winter plumage that is practically adult. Adults have a complete postnuptial molt at about the same time of year. A detailed account of the progress of the molt of young birds is given by William Palmer (1901) and one of the adults by Burns (1900); both accounts are too long to be quoted here. Fall adults in fresh plumage are very handsome birds, more deeply and richly colored than spring birds; the upper parts are deeper brown and the lower parts are suffused with yellowish buff; wear and fading produce a more contrasted plumage in the spring in which the dark markings are less obscured and the soft suffusion has disappeared.

The interesting and extensive hybridizing with the red-shafted flicker will be discussed under the latter species.

Food.—The flicker is more terrestrial in its feeding habits than any of our other woodpeckers. It is a common sight to see one of them hopping about on a lawn, or in an open place in the woods and fields, probing in the ground for ants or picking up ground insects or fallen berries. It is one of our most useful birds, worthy of the fullest protection. Professor Beal (1911) has shown that 60.92 percent of its food consists of animal matter and 39.08 percent of vegetable matter. About 75 percent of the animal food, or 45 percent of the entire food, consists of ants. The flicker eats more ants than any other bird; ants were found in 524 of the 684 stomachs examined, and 98 stomachs contained no other food; one stomach contained over 5,000 ants, and two others held over 3,000 each. If it had no other beneficial habit, the flicker would deserve protection for the good it does in keeping in check these injurious and annoying insects. Ants protect plant lice of various species, which may become very injurious to many kinds of cultivated plants, inflicting serious losses for the agricultural interests; the plant lice, or aphids, secrete a sweet honey-dew juice, of which the ants are very fond; consequently these tiny insects are herded by the ants

and milked like cows. The ants take good care of their honey-pro-
ducing "cattle," driving them away from ladybugs and other enemies,
leading them to new pastures, if the old ones dry up, sheltering the
aphid eggs in their nests, and carrying the young aphids out onto
the plants to feed. Mr. Forbush (1927) also says: "Ants riddle
posts set in the ground or any timber or lumber resting upon or
in contact with the ground. They destroy the sills of buildings set
close to the ground and often ruin living trees, especially such as
have a few dead roots. They infest lawns and buildings, destroying
grass on the lawns and food in the house, and are difficult to eradi-
cate. They sometimes eat alive the young of certain ground-nesting
birds. They are very prolific and require a severe check on their
numbers. Otherwise they would become unbearable pests."

The flicker explores the ground, often scratching away leaves or
rubbish, to locate the ant nests, digs into the nest with its long bill,
and, as the ants come pouring out, it laps them up in quantities or
inserts its long, sticky tongue deep down into the nest to get the
young and eggs. Early in spring it digs into the large mounds of
the mound-building ants, while the ants are less active, or tears open
some rotten stump to uncover a nest. Only a few days ago, I dug
into an old apple-tree stump for some rotten wood to put on some of
my wildflowers and uncovered a large nest of ants; within a very
few minutes my pair of flickers were on the job cleaning up the ants
and their pupae.

Other insect food of the flicker includes a variety of beetles, wasps,
grasshoppers, crickets, mole crickets, chinch bugs, wood lice, caterpillars, grubs, and various flying insects, which it sometimes catches
on the wing, darting after them like a flycatcher (Burns, 1900).

According to Beal (1911), 39.08 percent of its food is vegetable
matter. Most of this consists of wild fruits and berries, such as the
berries of the dogwood (*Cornus*) and Virginia creeper, hackberries,
blueberries, huckleberries, pokeberries, serviceberries (*Amelanchier*),
elderberries, barberries, mulberries, blackberries, wild grapes, wild
black cherries, choke cherries, cultivated cherries, and the berries of
the black alder, sour gum, black gum, greenbrier (*Smilax*), spicebush
(*Benzoin*), red cedar, hawthorn, mountain ash, and woodbine. Harold H. Bailey (1913) says that while the fall migration is at its
height in Virginia, about October first, "they are particularly fond
of the blue berry of the black-gum tree, and after once finding a tree
with fruit, will continue to come to it until every berry is gone, even
though continually shot at. I remember a case a few years back, when
a local gunner killed fifty-seven flickers from one black-gum tree
in one forenoon. After the gumberries are gone, they take to the
dogwood berry for their main article of food, a fine red berry and
always plentiful in Tidewater."

The flicker feeds freely on the seeds of the poison ivy and poison sumac and perhaps does some harm in distributing the seeds of these noxious plants. Professor Beal (1895) also includes the seeds of other sumacs, clover, grasses, pigweed, mullein, ragweed, and other unidentified seeds, and the seeds of the magnolia and knotweed. Mr. Burns (1900) adds wild strawberries, dewberries, raspberries, and wild plums, also acorns, beechnuts, corn from shocks, and oats, wheat, and rye from stacks.

The birds that Miss Sherman (1910) watched in their nesting box ate considerable sawdust. "That at one time the male ate three tablespoonfuls is deemed a modest estimate. An attempt to measure the amount both ate by a fresh supply daily showed the consumption of three or more handfuls. The sawdust came from sugar maple, white and red oak wood." She seemed to think that flickers have "little use for water," having seen them drink only twice, during many hours of watching from a blind, "all of which taken together would amount to weeks." Owen Durfee speaks in his notes of having seen three flickers drinking, or eating, snow on a cold day in winter; he saw one drop down onto a patch of snow on a stone wall and begin eating the snow. "His motions were just like a chicken drinking water—the partly closed bill was dipped into the snow and then held up in the air and the mandibles worked as though chewing or dissolving it, when another dip would be made. Soon two other flickers flew down in the same manner and secured some snow water. On approaching, I found the footprints and several little round holes somewhat smaller than a pencil."

I have often seen them drinking water and so have other observers; perhaps they drink copiously but not often.

Francis H. Allen says in his notes: "I have seen one feeding in the manner of a chickadee among the twigs of a tree, perching crosswise of the twig and flitting about actively, gleaning some minute food. Mr. Brewster told me that he had seen a flicker feeding this way."

Joseph J. Hickey tells me that he has seen a flicker feeding after the manner of an Arctic three-toed woodpecker, deliberately scaling off the bark in search for food; this bird had denuded about half the bark of a hemlock.

Behavior.—In ordinary short flights, the flicker proclaims its relationship to the other woodpeckers by its rhythmic bounding flight, the wings beating more rapidly on the rises and much less so on the dips, which are usually followed by a short sail on motionless wings. Mr. Burns (1900) noted that the dips occur about every 15 or 20 feet and that the bird drops about 3 feet on each dip. On more prolonged flights the flight is steadier, more direct, strong, and fairly swift. It does not ordinarily fly at any great height, except when migrating. When alighting on a tree trunk, there is a graceful upward glide, the trunk is grasped with the feet, and the tail is used as a prop in true woodpecker fashion; but the flicker is more apt to alight on a horizontal branch than other woodpeckers, when there is less upward glide and an upright posture is assumed, as balance is acquired.

On the ground, the flicker proceeds slowly by short hops, but sometimes it runs rapidly for a few steps and then stops; it seems content to confine its foraging to a rather limited area and does not appear very active.

Spring drumming on a resonant limb, or inside a nesting cavity, is an essential part of the call to courtship or mating, and perhaps a signal call for other purposes; but it is used at other times, perhaps for sheer amusement. This habit sometimes becomes a nuisance, since the bird has discovered that the tin roof of a house serves as the best kind of a drum; here he comes morning after morning while we are enjoying our slumbers, from which we are rudely awakened at an unseemly hour. Mr. DuBois writes to me that, on an afternoon in June, "a flicker was drumming on the lid of a large galvanized iron ash or garbage can at the corner of the back porch of a residence; he stood on the top of the lid and, at intervals, after looking around, he beat an extremely rapid roll on this metallic drum; the effect was startling."

As to the roosting habits of flickers, Miss Sherman (1910) writes: "Of all our birds the flickers are the earliest to retire at night, sometimes going to their lodgings an hour before sundown, the customary time being about a half hour before sunset. Generally they go out soon after sunrise, but on cool autumn mornings they have been known to linger much longer. During a rainstorm in the middle of the day they have been seen to seek their apartments, also in fine weather they have been found there enjoying the seclusion thus afforded."

Frank R. Smith, of Hyattsville, Md., sends me the following note, dated February 28, 1936: "For some nights, a flicker has been roosting in the shell of a dead tree, from which one side has decayed away, leaving a troughlike section of its trunk standing. He roosts about 12 feet from the ground. This morning it was cloudy and he left the roosting place at 7:25, although official sunrise is at 6:37." Mr. Shelley tells me that he flushed a male from the nest tree, "where he clung each night about 3 feet above the nest hole, with the female brooding the young within." Flickers will roost in any open cavity in a tree, or even in a partially sheltered spot on the open trunk; they often drill holes in barns or under the eaves of houses for winter roosts; a favorite winter roosting place is in the sawdust between the double walls of icehouses. Sometimes they dig a hole into a vacant building and fail to find their way out; I once found one dead inside the garage at my summer cottage, which had been closed all winter. Mr. Forbush (1927) says that "during one winter at Wareham one apparently slept on the wall of my summer cottage under the eaves, clinging to one of the ornamental battens in an upright position as it would cling to a tree trunk. This bird for some unaccountable reason chose the north side of the cottage. He was there night after night at dusk and also at daylight each morning. Mr. R. F. Carr tells of a flicker that was accustomed to pass winter nights in a chimney of an unoccupied dwelling in a thickly settled neighborhood which undoubtedly was a more comfortable roosting place than the north side of my cottage."

Dr. Lynds Jones told Mr. Burns (1900) that "at Oberlin College a single bird roosted between the vertical water pipe and wall of Spear Library for two successive winters, and another occupied the cupola of the Theological Seminary the succeeding winter."

Flickers are generally regarded as peaceful harmless birds, but the following two quotations indicate that they are sometimes otherwise.

O. P. Allert (1934) writes from Giard, Iowa: "On June 4, 1933, while in the yard of my home, I was attracted by the cries of a pair of Robins and saw a female Flicker in the act of killing the two young that the Robins' nest contained. One was killed in the nest, and the other either fell or was thrown to the ground, where the Flicker followed and dispatched it."

Dr. Dayton Stoner (1932) writes: "While the flicker is not habitually belligerent, it does on occasion show some aggressiveness. This most frequently occurs during the breeding season. For example, on July 11, 1929, in the Parker woods south of Lakeport, I came upon several flickers and two or three crows that were tormenting a red-shouldered hawk. The flickers were pecking excitedly on the limbs of the tree on which the hawk perched, and clamoring loudly at it. When the hawk flew off the flickers darted after it, pecking it unmercifully until it lit again, when they were cautious about approaching close to the harassed hawk. This quarrel was continued for more than half an hour."

Voice.—The flicker has an elaborate vocabulary; no other woodpecker, and few other birds, can produce a greater variety of loud striking calls and soft conversational notes. A number of its many vernacular names are based on a fancied resemblance to some one of its notes, and in most cases these names give a very fair idea of the note. A few of such names are "flicker," "yucker," "wacup," "hittock," "yarrup," "clape," and "piute"; and there are other modifications of these in different combinations of letters.

The commonest and most characteristic note is the loud spring call, of which Eugene P. Bicknell (1885) says: "Its long rolling call may be taken as especially representative of song, and is a characteristic sound of the empty woodland of early spring. It is usually given from some high perch, and has a free, far-reaching quality, that gives it the effect of a signal thrown out over the barren country, as if to arouse sleeping nature. This call continues irregularly through the summer, but then loses much of its prominence amid the multitude of bird voices. It is not infrequent in September, but later than the middle of October I have not heard it."

This is a sharp, penetrating note, which can be heard at a long distance; the syllables *wick, wick, wick, wick,* or *yuck, yuck, yuck, yuck,* are very rapidly uttered and repeated in long series. Dr. Elon H. Eaton (1914) says that "it may be heard for more than half a mile and has been variously syllabized, usually written as *'cuh-cuh-cuh-cuh',*" which hardly represents my idea of the song.

A softer note, heard during active courtship and display, sounds like *wake-up, wake-up, wake-up,* or *yarrup, yarrup, yarrup,* given more deliberately in subdued tones and not so prolonged. This has been referred to as the scythe-sharpening, or rollicking, song and has also been written as *yucker, yucker, yucker,* or *wicker, wicker, wicker,* or *hick-up, hick-up, hick-up,* or *flicker, flicker, flicker.* Mr. Bicknell (1885) has recorded these notes from April 8 to September 5; there seems to be no seasonal regularity about them, as they are probably affectionate notes of greeting. Mr. Burns (1900) "heard an apparently rare variation, a metallic *Ka-wick-wick-wick-wick-wick-wick-wick-wick-wick-wick-wick-ka* by the male while close to the nest."

He gives as conversational, or soliloquizing notes, "commonly a scanny, gurgling, almost involuntary *chur-r-r-r* as danger seems to threaten it when on the wing, or when flushed from the ground or just before a-lighting, which may be interpreted as a note of warning or announcement of arrival according to the circumstances. I have heard a low guttural *who-del* as it endeavored to balance itself on a slender branch immediately after arrival." A bird on a house roof, in December, "uttered an odd guttural call of *huck-a-woó-ah* or again only *woo woo* evidently for his own edification." Other soft conversational notes sound like *ouit-ouit,* or *puir-puir,* or a cooing *yu-cah-yu-cah.*

Dr. Eaton (1914) says: "When the flicker flies up from the ground and alights on a stub or fence post, he frequently bobs and bows to an imaginary audience and immediately thereafter jerks his head high upward giving voice to a sharp note like the syllable 'clape.'" This is a loud, explosive note and may indicate defiance or surprise.

A common note, oftenest heard during summer and fall, is a plaintive call suggesting one of the notes of the blue jay or the red-shouldered hawk. It is a loud and rather musical note, which has been variously interpreted as *pee-ut, ye-a-up, pee-up, que-ah, kee-yer,* etc., given singly or repeated two or three times, as a ringing call of considerable carrying power.

Field marks.—While hopping about on the lawn, the flicker may be recognized as a brown bird somewhat larger than a robin and with a rather long bill; if facing the observer, the black crescent on the spotted breast is rather conspicuous, but the red crescent on the nape does not show up much except at short range, nor does the black malar patch of the male. The most conspicuous field mark is the white rump, which shows plainly as the bird rises from the ground and flies away; this probably serves as a direction mark, or a warning to the companions with which it is often associated. Then, of course, the flash of bright yellow in the wings and tail marks the bird in flight, chiefly when high in the air, but somewhat also in straightaway flight.

Enemies.—When I was a boy, 50 or 60 years ago, flickers, meadow-larks, and robins were considered legitimate game, and they were very good to eat. Bunches of these birds were often seen hanging in the game dealers' stalls. During our fall vacations on the coast, when the weather was unfavorable for coot shooting, my father and uncle used to resort to the uplands to shoot "partridge woodpeckers" and "brown backs" (robins) among the bayberry bushes and sumacs. And flickers were slaughtered in large numbers in the South. Man was then the flicker's worst enemy, but that is now all ancient history, as these birds are now protected. But a new enemy has been intro-duced, which is probably worse than the old one. The European starling has come to compete with the flicker in its search for a food supply. The starlings are now so abundant that they swoop down in flocks on the formerly plentiful supply of wild fruits and berries, stripping the trees and bushes clean of the fruits on which the flickers and robins depended for their summer and fall food. They also compete for nesting sites, fighting for or usurping every avail-able cavity, even driving the flickers from the homes that they had made. Lester W. Smith writes to me: "For several years after the starling became common in Connecticut, other birds, especially the flicker, were seldom ejected, or not until all available nesting possibil-ities about buildings were used and filled up. Never have I seen the flickers actually fight to retain their hole or bird house. On the sanctuary they were exceptionally noisy whenever starlings at-tempted to take or had taken possession. On one occasion three starlings took part; one remained in the entrance hole of the box and took dry grass that a second brought to it; the third chased off either of the pair of flickers, as it flew near the nest box, which was about 8 feet from the ground on a sawed-off tree in a white-pine grove. On shooting one of the starlings, the other four birds flew away temporarily, and, on examination, I found a thin layer of grass over the flicker's eggs. In 15 minutes the starlings returned and a second was shot. I removed the grass, and, hiding nearby, I saw nothing more of the third starling; but the flickers returned soon, took possession of the box, and later raised the five young."

Sydney R. Taber (1921) tells an interesting story of a battle between a male flicker and a pair of starlings for the possession of the flickers' nest. The flicker had once pulled one of the starlings out of the hole, but, during his absence, both of the starlings entered the hole.

On this second occasion, despairing of being able to pull the two out at long range, so to speak, the Flicker also plunged into the hole. Then followed a battle royal, lasting for what seemed minutes. It was rather ghastly to imagine the blows that were being dealt at closest quarters; not a sound was emitted, but one could imagine what was going on within the hole by the feathers that flew from it. The first bird to emerge—that is, to be pushed out, by fractions of an inch—was one of the Starlings, which then flew away. The fight between the other two birds then continued out of sight until something appeared at the mouth of the hole. This proved to be the tail of the Flicker. When he had backed out of the hole into view once more, it appeared that he and the remaining Starling had clinched in a desperate grapple. With the latter gripping one of the wings of the Flicker, they fell, fluttering and fighting, a distance of nearly 40 feet; but just before touching the ground, they parted and flew in different directions. * * *

The above events occurred a fortnight ago. Since then the Starlings have been in full possession of the hole of contention.

Flickers figure largely in the food of duck hawks; their brightly colored feathers are often found about the aeries. Other hawks take their toll. O. A. Stevens sends me the following note on a sharp-shinned hawk attacking a flicker, perhaps only in sport: "The hawk settled in a partially dead, spreading pine tree, some 8 feet from the top. A flicker perched about 6 feet above him, apparently from curiosity. For some time they remained, the hawk sitting quietly, preening, occasionally casting a glance at the flicker. The latter teetered about on his perch, craning his neck at the hawk and even dropping down a foot or so. After at least 10 minutes, the hawk suddenly darted at the flicker and away they went, the flicker twisting and escaping. It seems odd that an apparently heavy flier like a flicker would escape so easily."

Mr. Burns (1903) adds the broad-winged hawk to the flicker's enemies; "a nest of lusty young hawks examined in July, '01, contained the primaries and rectrices of one or two young Flickers, probably just out of the nest. * * * To the above Mr. Benj. T. Gault adds the Blacksnake—one having been killed and cut open by a farmer's lad at a place he was stopping at in Reynolds county, Missouri, contained the body of one of these woodpeckers." I have positively recorded flickers in the food of the marsh hawk, Cooper's hawk, and red-shouldered hawk; probably they are killed by all the larger hawks and owls. Taverner and Swales (1907) say that the sharpshin flights at Point Pelee discommoded the flickers less than any other species of small birds. "Though at times they seemed uneasy and restless, they were perfectly able to take care of themselves and easily made their escape when attacked. * * * The usual course of procedure of the Flicker, when attacked by a hawk, was to wait until the last minute, when the hawk, in its swoop, was just about to seize its victim, and then dodge quickly to the other side of the limb. In every case observed the ruse worked perfectly, and we found only once the feather remains which proved that once in a while the hawk was a little too quick for the Flicker."

Mr. Burns (1900) says that the eggs and young are sometimes destroyed by squirrels, weasels, mice, crows, jays, and the red-headed woodpecker. Fred. H. Kennard records in his notes that a pair of flickers, nesting in one of his boxes, were robbed of their eggs by some red squirrels, who ate the eggs in the box, built their own nest in the box, and brought in their young from another nest.

Fall.—As soon as the young are strong on the wing and the molting season is over, the flickers, old and young, begin to gather into loose flocks or scattered parties, perhaps family parties, late in summer and early in fall. On cold, windy autumn days they may be found in close companionship in hollows and sheltered localities in woodland clearings, protected from the cold winds, and feeding in the bayberry patches and clumps of staghorn sumac. At such times, they lie close and can be easily approached.

In southern Canada and the Northern States, the great bulk of the flickers start to migrate in September, continuing to pass southward during October. Mr. Burns (1900) says of the fall migration: "While the retrograde movements are conducted in larger numbers, being re-cruited by great numbers of birds of the year, it is scarcely as notice-able, lacking the noise and bustle of Spring arrivals. Like the Robin, its whole nature seems to have undergone a change. It no longer solic-its notice by song or display, but becomes shy and suspicious, and while gregarious to a great extent, in flight every one is capable of looking out for itself. The mature birds are the most wary, and by example prepare the young for the dangers of migration and Winter residence in the South, where it is constantly menaced by hunters."

During migration, they fly rather high, well above the treetops, in widely detached flocks, often far apart, but keeping more or less in touch with each other and sometimes fairly close together; hundreds may be counted, as they pass in a steady stream for hours at a time. Taverner and Swales (1907) report heavy flights across Lake Erie from Point Pelee: "During September it has always been one of the most abundant birds of the Point. Keays reports a flight in 1901 when he noted four hundred September 21." Long Point, which extends well out from the north shore of Lake Erie, is another favorite crossing place; here, according to L. L. Snyder (1931), "the flight observed by Mr. James Savage on September 30, 1930, was very remarkable, individuals estimated to be from one to two hundred yards apart, forming a scattered and straggling flock, passed in an almost steady stream throughout the morning hours."

Mr. Burns (1903) writes:

In south New Jersey, in the region of the Upper Delaware Bay, which runs due south, some time in October of every year the migrating Flickers are found flying north just previous to and during a northwest storm. At this time the wind is generally high and the birds fly against it. This peculiarity of flight affects a large territory extending inland from the east shore of the bay some fifteen or twenty miles. While the birds prefer to breast a wind, it is also probable that they are reluctant to cross the lower part of the bay during such a storm which would tend to drive them seaward, rather preferring to return northwad to the more narrow river where they could cross in comparative safety.

Winter.—Winter finds most of the flickers gone from the northern States and southern Canada. Most of the birds wintering in New England seek the milder climate of the seacoast, where they feed in the extensive bayberry patches and on the semidormant insect life in the rows of drift seaweed along the beaches. The few that remain inland during mild winters are usually to be found in sheltered hollows or along the sunny sides of the woods, feeding on the ground or on what berries and dry fruits still remain on the bushes, often in company with merry little winter parties of juncos, tree sparrows, chickadees, nuthatches, and perhaps a downy or hairy woodpecker. Favorite resorts at that season are the southern slopes of the hills overgrown with thick stands of red cedars, mixed with staghorn sumacs, barberries, and other berry-bearing bushes. They probably seek shelter at night in the dense cedar swamps or in the holes excavated for that purpose in icehouses or other buildings, or in hollow trees.

L. H. Walkinshaw, of Battle Creek, Mich., writes to me that there, "in deep winter, flickers can be found in the deep tamarack swamps, coming to the edge during periods of the day. They often flush, even when snow is deep, from mounds on the ground or from dead or dying stubs along the border."

O. A. Stevens says in his notes: "At my farm home in Kansas, the flickers caused some annoyance by seeking entrance to the barn for winter nights. They enlarged other openings for this purpose and sometimes started openings which would not lead them inside. One bird at least, enlarged the opening about the hayfork track and roosted on the iron track just inside the door."

Dr. Paul L. Errington (1936) writes an interesting story on the winter-killing of flickers in central Iowa. By a careful study of the droppings of the three birds that he studied, it appeared that they were much weakened by improper food, too large a proportion of indigestible seeds, mainly those of the sumac, and not enough animal food, which ordinarily amounts to more than half of the average food supply.

M. P. Skinner (1928), writing of the Sandhills of North Carolina, says: "Flickers stay in the Sandhills all winter, but the infrequent snowstorms cause them lots of trouble in finding food. On January 10, 1927, I found quite a little coterie of birds had scratched the leaves under a dogwood tree until they had a space twelve feet in diameter more or less cleared of snow. Here, among other species of birds, were two Flickers foraging among the leaves for fallen dogwood berries. These berries were probably eaten until weather conditions became better for insect catching. Even during winter, ants are fairly plentiful for the Sandhill Flickers, especially on warm days."

COLAPTES CAFER COLLARIS Vigors

RED-SHAFTED FLICKER

PLATE 37

HABITS

This western representative of our well-known eastern flicker is so closely related to it and so similar to it in all its habits that practically all that has been written about the northern flicker would apply equally well to the red-shafted species. The two differ strikingly in coloration, but the color pattern is similar in both, and the fact that they interbreed so freely and extensively where their ranges come together shows their close relationship. The only differences in their habitats, nesting, and feeding habits are due to the differences in environments.

The red-shafted flicker is a wide-ranging species through many types of open country or sparsely wooded regions, from the Rocky Mountains to sea level on the Pacific coast. It is a common bird near human habitations in thinly settled towns and villages and in agricultural regions, as well as in the wilder foothills and mountain slopes up to timberline, but not on the treeless plains or deserts. The Weydemeyers (1928), referring to its haunts in northwestern Montana, give a good idea of its habitat there, which would doubtless apply equally well throughout its range elsewhere; they say: "The Flicker is most abundant about farms and in cut-over woods, nesting commonly near barnyards and in pastures. An observer will note fewer and fewer individuals as he passes from cultivated farms into stump-lands; from there to virgin forests of fir, larch, and yellow pine; thence into the lodgepole pine and white pine woods of the lower part of the Canadian zone; and onward into denser forests of alpine fir, spruce, and arborvitae. But he will find the birds increasing in numbers on the rocky mountain slopes and upward through the Hudsonian zone, where the species ranges to timberline."

Milton P. Skinner says in his Yellowstone Park notes: "This bird is found at all elevations from the lowest at 5,300 feet to timberline at 9,500 feet, and in practically all kinds of habitat except the largest opens, and even there I have seen it flying across from side to side. It is in the sagebrush areas, in the borderland between forest and open, in detached groves, and even in heavy forest.

"They are often seen on the ground, especially in May, but also in June and July. Sometimes they are in the road. I have seen them frequently in the grass and perched on a bowlder or a prostrate log. In addition to these treeless and brushless localities, I often see flickers on the ground under sagebrushes and greasewood; on the ground in a grove of cedars and limber pines; under aspens, willows, cedars, firs; and on the ground amid the stumps of a former fir forest. I have seen them in groves of mixed lodgepole pines and aspens and in meadows where there were only groves of willow bushes."

Courtship.—In the same notes Mr. Skinner says: "On April 29, 1915, I saw a pair of flickers 'dancing.' They were on a dead lodgepole, and although there was not much movement of the feet, the body was bent from side to side and there was a constant 'juggling' or 'jigging' motion. The head was tilted back and the bill pointed up at an angle of sixty degrees, with the neck outstretched. The neck, head, and bill were in constant motion; the motion of the bill reminded me of a musical director's baton. Intervals of rest alternated with periods of motion; the whole thing lasted perhaps 5 minutes."

Nesting.—Major Bendire (1895) says on this subject:

Its favorite nesting sites are old rotten stubs or trees, such as cottonwoods, willows, sycamores, junipers, oaks, and pines. It nests also in holes in banks, in the sides of houses, in gate posts, etc. * * *

Among some peculiar nesting sites of this species the following deserve mention:

Mr. Walter E. Bryant gives the following: "One of these was in a bridge bulkhead, a few feet above the Carson River, Nevada. The interior of the structure was filled with gravel and large stones, among which the eggs were deposited. Another pair used a target butt, at a much-frequented range, as a substitute for a stump. A third nest was in a sand bank, 3 feet from the top and 10 from the creek. This hole was apparently specially prepared, and not one made by a ground squirrel, such holes being sometimes used by these birds."

Mr. Charles A. Allen, of Nicasio, Calif., found a pair of red-shafted flickers nesting in a similar situation in a creek bank, the burrow containing seven eggs, which he took. About ten days later, happening to pass the same spot, he examined the hole again and found it occupied by a California Screech Owl, which in the meantime had deposited four eggs. Some two weeks subsequently he examined it for a third time, and on this occasion the tenant proved to be a Sparrow Hawk, which was setting on five handsome eggs. There was no nesting material present on any occasion, the eggs lying on some loose dirt.

Others have noted the bank-nesting habit of this flicker, which seems to be rather common. Most of the nests, however, are excavated in trees or stubs, at heights varying from ground level to 100 feet above the ground. We found them nesting commonly in the Huachuca Mountains, Ariz., in the sycamores in the canyons and in the tall pines near the summits at 9,000 feet. A large majority of the nests will be found between 8 and 25 feet above the ground. Dawson (1923) mentions a nest "in a stump only two feet high, and its eggs rested virtually upon the ground." Walter P. Taylor (1912) mentions a nest in a cavity in a haystack, in the desert regions of Humboldt County, Nev., where there were practically no trees. This flicker also nests frequently in telegraph and other poles, also far too often in buildings, where it drills a hole through the outer wall and lays its eggs on a beam or other flat surface, accumulating enough chips to keep the eggs from rolling.

Florence A. Merriam Bailey (1896) watched a red-shafted flicker excavating its nest-hole, of which she says: "The flicker hung with claws planted in the hole, and with its tail braced at an angle under it, leaned forward to excavate. Using its feet as a pivot, it gradually swung in farther and farther; and when it had gone so far that it had to reach back to throw out its chips, it swung in and out on its feet like an automatic toy wound up for the performance. When it had been building for a week, only the tip of its tail protruded from the nest hole as it worked."

Mrs. Irene G. Wheelock (1904) says: "The site having been chosen, the male clings to the surface and marks with his bill a more or less regular circle in a series of dots, then begins excavating inside this area, using his bill, not with a sidewise twist, as do many of the woodpecker family, but striking downwards and prying off the chips as with a pickaxe. When his mate has rested and wishes to share in the labor, she calls from a near-by tree and he instantly quits his task."

Dr. and Mrs. Grinnell (Grinnell, Dixon, and Linsdale, 1930) made the following observations on this species, while excavating its nest-hole:

The bird entered the hole, entirely out of view, at 8:54, reappeared from within at 9:05, when it rested a minute with the head partly out; then it proceeded to bring out from within load after load of chips, which showered down as if of fine, almost sawdust-like size. Forty-five such loads were counted to 9:10, delivered with striking regularity. Twelve loads delivered were counted in one sixty-second period. At 9:10 the bird disappeared again till 9:15, when its head appeared and twenty-seven loads were flipped out in three minutes; then after a long pause, till 9:19, the other flicker arrived, with scythe-whetting note, and both birds flew off. One of them returned at 9:29, flipped out several loads of chips and left at 9:31. Digging in this particular stump must have been easy and hence rapid.

Eggs.—The red-shafted flicker lays five to twelve eggs to a set. Probably, if the experiment were tried, it would prove to be as prolific an egg layer as its eastern relative, though I have found no evidence to that effect. The eggs are indistinguishable from those of the northern flicker. The measurements of 57 eggs average 28.18 by 21.85 millimeters; the eggs showing the four extremes measure 35.56 by 20.32, 27.94 by 24.89, 25.40 by 20.83, and 27.68 by 19.30 millimeters.

Young.—Mrs. Wheelock (1904) says of the young: "For nearly three weeks they are fed by regurgitation, and after that time the insects brought are masticated by the parents. * * *

"After they are old enough to leave the nursery, they follow their parents about for nearly two weeks, begging to be fed and gradually learning to hunt for themselves. This lesson is wisely taught by the parents, who place the food under a crevice in the bark, in full sight of the young, who must pick it out or go hungry. The baby cocks his head wisely, looks at it, and proceeds to pull it out and dine."

Plumages.—The sequence of plumages and molts, from fledgling to adult, in the red-shafted flicker is similar to that of the northern flicker, but there is one marked difference in the color pattern in the juvenal plumage; whereas in *auratus* young birds of both sexes have black malar patches, in *cafer* only the young male has the red malar patches. Ridgway (1914) describes the juvenal male of the red-shafted flicker as "similar to the adult male, but coloration duller, gray of throat, etc., duller, more brownish, black jugular patch smaller and less sharply defined, black spots on under parts less sharply defined, less rounded, feathers of pileum indistinctly tipped with paler, and red malar stripes less bright, less uniform, and black terminal area on under side of tail not sharply defined." The young female is similar to the young male, but the malar region is grayish brown instead of red. The juvenal plumage is worn through summer, and a complete molt during fall produces a first-winter plumage that is practically adult. Adults have a complete annual molt late in summer and fall.

A most interesting and unique case, among American birds at least, of hybridizing on an extensive scale over a wide region occurs between *Colaptes auratus* and *Colaptes cafer*. We found this most beautifully illustrated in southwestern Saskatchewan, where pureblooded birds of both species were taken, together with quite a series of hybrid birds showing all the intermediate grades of plumage. Almost all the males showed some traces of the red malar stripes of *cafer*, and nearly all showed some traces of the red nuchal crescent of *auratus;* the other characters seemed to be less constant. I collected a pure-blooded male *auratus* and a nearly pure-blooded *cafer* female, which were apparently mated. And two young in juvenal plumage, one almost pure *cafer* and the other equally near *auratus*, were taken from the same family.

Although the general color *patterns* of the two species are strikingly similar, or parallel, the characters that separate them are radically qualitative rather than quantitative, so that the numerous hybrids cannot by any means be considered as intermediates between subspecies. No two species of a genus could well present more striking contrasts in *coloration* in such similar patterns.

In one species the quills are red, in the other yellow; the male has a red malar stripe in one and a black stripe in the other; neither sex in *cafer* has the red nuchal crescent, while both sexes have it in *auratus; cafer* has the throat and fore neck gray and the top of the head and hind neck brown, while these colors are reversed in *auratus*. These contrasting colors may be blended or mixed in an almost endless variety of patterns in the hybrids; and the patterns are often asymmetrical, the opposite sides of the bird being quite different. Some specimens of *cafer* show the first traces of *auratus* blood by the presence of a few black feathers in the malar stripe, or traces of the red nuchal crescent. Slight traces of *cafer* blood in *auratus* appear with a mixture of red in the black malar strip, or with a tinge of orange or reddish·in the wings or tail. Between these two extremes there is every degree of blending or mixture of the characters.

For many years after these interesting hybrids were discovered and described by Baird (1858), they were known only from the upper Missouri and Yellowstone River region. Later they were found to be widely distributed from the western border of the Great Plains westward to the Pacific coast, and from Texas to southern Canada. While the center of abundance of birds showing thoroughly mixed characters seems to lie between the Great Plains and the Rocky Mountains, evidence of hybrid blood is much more widely dispersed in a gradually diminishing degree, more strongly westward and to a lesser degree eastward. Dr. J. A. Allen (1892), in his excellent paper on this subject, says: "Specimens with a slight amount of red in the malar stripe are represented in the material I have examined from Massachusetts, Long Island, New Jersey (five specimens), Pennsylvania, Virginia, Florida (several), Louisiana (several), Tennessee, Ohio, Indiana, Illinois (several), Michigan (two), and Minnesota. They seem to be quite as frequent along the Atlantic seaboard as at any point east of the Mississippi River."

Food.—Professor Beal's (1910) study of 118 stomachs of the two western races of the red-shafted flicker showed that 54 percent of the food was animal and 46 percent vegetable matter. Of the animal food, beetles constituted 3 percent, most of which were harmful; there were only a few predatory carabids; ants made up 45 percent of the year's food; other Hymenoptera totaled 1 percent, and miscellaneous items, such as caterpillars, crickets, and spiders, amounted to 5 percent of the food.

Of the vegetable food, acorns formed 10 percent of the yearly food; grains, including rye, corn, barley, and oats, amounted to 4 percent; fruits, averaging 15 percent, included pears, apples, grapes, cherries, and prunes; and the other 17 percent was made up of wild fruits, such as pepperberries, elderberries, and gooseberries and the seeds of the poison oak and sumac and of a few weeds. He says of the poison-oak seeds:

> The consumption of these seeds would be a decided benefit to man if they were ground up and destroyed in the stomachs. Unfortunately they are either regurgitated or pass through the intestinal tract uninjured and ready to germinate. The action of the stomach simply removes the outer covering, a white, wax-like substance, which is probably very nutritious, and is evidently relished by many birds. Birds are probably the most active agents in the dissemination of these noxious shrubs. On the other hand, these seeds, which are wonderfully abundant, afford food for thousands of birds during the winter, when other food is hard to obtain, and thus enable the birds to tide over the cold season to do their good work of destroying insects the next summer.

Johnson A. Neff (1928) says that "in a great many instances they are known to feed on the larvæ of the codling moth"; and that "ants were the largest item of food for the year, averaging 40.30%, taken during every month; several stomachs held over 2,000 each, and many of them contained over 500." Among the vegetable food he lists manzanita berries and seeds and such wild fruits as madrona, dogwood, haw, serviceberry, elderberry, Oregon crab, and huckleberry; seeds of poison oak averaged 7.5 percent, but in December the percentage was 33.3.

Referring to the fruit-eating habits of this flicker in Los Angeles County, Calif., Robert S. Woods (1932) writes:

> Fortunately for the grower, and perhaps for the birds as well, the rind of an orange is impervious to the attacks of any ordinary bird, though when once opened the fruit is well liked by many of them. Only the Red-shafted Flicker (*Colaptes cafer collaris*) is able to chisel through the tough skin; after making a round opening large enough for the insertion of its bill, it scoops out a large portion of the pulp with its tongue. Examples of this sort of damage, however, are infrequent and usually, as it seems, in oranges which have fallen to the ground, where they are more easily reached.
>
> The flicker's attacks on avocados appear more serious, though this is partly due to the smaller numbers of the fruit available. Avocados which hang near a convenient perch are often found to have a roughly circular hole extending through to the seed. In a few of the fruits these holes have been considerably enlarged, but usually they are not much larger than the base of the bird's bill.

Jack C. von Bloeker, Jr. (1935), saw three red-shafted flickers capture scarab "beetles in flycatcher fashion. In each case, the bird attained a position behind its intended victim, then, taking up the erratic zigzag course of the beetle, suddenly swooped down and captured it in mid-air."

Major Bendire (1895) also says: "Besides the usual insects and larvæ upon which this species feeds, I have seen it catch grasshoppers, both on the ground and on the wing, and it is likewise very fond of wild strawberries."

Behavior.—I can find nothing in the behavior or general habits of the red-shafted flicker that is essentially different from the habits of the northern flicker. It has the same annoying habit of drumming on the resonant parts of dwellings at early hours in the morning, which is quite disturbing to sleepers. It also does considerable damage to buildings by drilling holes in the eaves or walls for nesting or roosting places, spending winter nights or even stormy days in such sheltered retreats. John G. Tyler (1913) says on this subject:

Unfortunately these handsome birds have fallen into disfavor among a large number of both city dwellers and country residents, on account of their habit of drilling holes in the gable ends of buildings. When once a house has been selected it seems that nothing short of death will cause them to cease their drilling operations until one, and in some cases three or four, holes have been cut through the outer wall of the building. Whether these holes, which are generally made in the winter, are excavated for roosting places or simply through a sort of nervous energy seems a matter of doubt; but certain it is that the birds spend much time in them as soon as they succeed in completing their work. It is a common sight, on rainy days, to see a Flicker's head peering out from his open doorway.

The speed in flight of the red-shafted flicker has been recorded as from 25 to 27 miles an hour, as measured with the speedometer of an automobile.

Grinnell and Storer (1924) write of its habits:

The tramper in almost any part of the Yosemite region can hardly fail to at least hear one or more Red-shafted Flickers in a half-day's circuit. Although these birds are never seen in true flocks, he may flush from favorable places as many as 6 of them within a few yards. This is particularly true on the floor of Yosemite Valley during the autumn months. This omnivorous woodpecker then almost completely forsakes the timber and forages in the brush patches, eating berries of various sorts, especially cascara; it often seeks the open meadows where it gathers ants and grasshoppers.

The birds flush one or two at a time, often not until the observer is almost upon them; then the sudden flapping of broad pinkish-red wings, the view of the white rump patch fully displayed, leave no doubt in the observer's mind as to the identity. A bird seldom flies far before alighting, not against an upright tree trunk as with most other woodpeckers, but perching on a branch, to bow deeply this way and that and perhaps utter its explosive *claip*.

Voice.—The notes of the red-shafted flicker are almost identical with those of the northern flicker, though George F. Simmons (1925) evidently thinks that the voice is "much coarser, rougher, and heavier, * * * easily distinguished when the two are heard calling near each other."

Field marks.—The white rump is the most conspicuous recognition mark for both species, and the color *pattern* is similar for both, but the flashing colors in the wings and tail, as well as the other contrasting colors, will serve to distinguish the red-shafted from the yellow-shafted species.

Winter.—During the winter that I spent in Pasadena, flickers were common or abundant all winter in an arroyo on the outskirts of the city. I could always find them picking up food among the dry leaves on the ground, or flying about among the large sycamores and live oaks. On a bright, sunny morning, after a frosty night, they could be seen perched in the topmost branches of the tallest trees, which were the first to catch the warmth of the rising sun. On February 14, 1929, I saw two males perched close together facing each other, bowing and nodding, or bobbing up and down, as if beginning to feel the urge of spring.

DISTRIBUTION

Range.—Western North America south to the Isthmus of Tehuantepec.

Breeding range.—The red-shafted flicker breeds **north** to southeastern Alaska (Sitka and Portage Cove); central British Columbia (158-mile House and Horse Lake); west-central Alberta (Jasper House); southern Saskatchewan (Cypress Hills); and North Dakota (Fort Union, Oakdale, and Fort Clark). **East** to central North Dakota (Fort Clark); South Dakota (Reliance and Yankton); northwestern Nebraska (Chadron); Colorado (Fort Morgan, Denver, Colorado Springs, and Beulah); extreme western Oklahoma (Kenton); central New Mexico (Santa Fe, Cloudcroft, and Mesilla); western Chihuahua (San Luis Mountains and Pinos Altos); Durango (Rio Sestin, Arroyo del Buey, and Durango City); Tamaulipas (Ciudad Victoria); Hilaygo (Real del Monte); Vera Cruz (Jalapa and Orizaba); and eastern Oaxaca (Villa Alta and Totontepec). **South** to Oaxaca (Totontepec); Guerrero (Omilteme); and Jalisco (Zapotlan and Volcan de Colima). From this southwestern point the species ranges north through the mountains of western Mexico, including northern Baja California and (formerly) Guadalupe Island, California, Oregon, Washington, and British Columbia, to southeastern Alaska (Sitka).

Winter range.—The red-shafted flicker is a resident species over most of its range, withdrawing from the more northern parts only during severe winters. At this season it is found **north** regularly to southern British Columbia (Comox, Okanagan, and Edgewood); northern Montana (Fortine and Great Falls); eastern Wyoming (Midwest); and rarely southeastern South Dakota (Yankton).

The range as outlined applies to the entire species, of which four subspecies or geographic races are now recognized. The typical form, known as the northwestern flicker (*Colaptes c. cafer*), is found in the northern Pacific coast regions from southeastern Alaska and western British Columbia south to northern California. The red-shafted flicker (*C. c. collaris*) occurs over all the remaining parts of the range except for certain mountainous areas in northern Baja California and Guadalupe Island, occupied by the San Pedro flicker (*C. c. martirensis*) and the now extinct Guadalupe flicker (*C. c. rufipileus*).

Migration.—Such migratory movements as are made by this species cannot be satisfactorily portrayed by the use of dates. The most conspicuous migration is vertical rather than lateral, for during fall and winter in the eastern part of the range there is a more or less well-defined movement east from the Rocky Mountain region onto the Great Plains. At these seasons the species may travel eastward to Iowa (Forest City, Boone, and Des Moines); Missouri (Kansas City); Arkansas (Van Buren); southeastern Oklahoma (Caddo); and eastern Texas (Gainesville, Waco, Somerset, and Brownsville).

Spring migration.—In the northern part of the breeding range, from which the species appears to withdraw in winter with more or less regularity, the following are early dates of spring arrival: South Dakota—White River, March 28; Yankton, April 1. North Dakota—McKenzie County, March 31; Arnegard, April 11. Alberta—Banff, April 3; Warner, April 24; Edmonton, April 29. Alaska—Kupreanof Island, April 12.

Fall migration.—Late dates of departure from northern areas are: Alaska—Wrangell, November 26. Alberta—Jasper, September 8; Henry House, September 22. North Dakota—Grafton, October 7 (one was collected in the Red River Valley on December 6, 1924). South Dakota—Faulkton, October 15.

Although red-shafted flickers have been banded in considerable numbers, the Biological Survey files do not contain any data indicative of an extensive flight from the point of banding. There are, however, many cases of recapture in succeeding seasons at the banding station.

Casual records.—Among the few records where this species has been collected or observed outside its normal range are the following: One was taken at Grafton, N. Dak., April 19, 1925, and another was shot near Winnipeg, Manitoba, September 30, 1904. There are two records for northern Alberta, one at Fort Chipewyan, May 21, 1893, and the other at Smiths Portage, June 8, 1908. Other records, some of which are from points farther east (as Minnesota), are for hybrids between this species and *C. auratus*.

Egg dates.—British Columbia: 13 records, May 8 to June 7; 7 records, May 14 to 26, indicating the height of the season.

California: 75 records, April 9 to July 2; 38 records, May 3 to 28.

Colorado: 22 records, May 5 to July 1; 11 records, May 22 to 31.

Guadalupe Island: 6 records, April 8 to June 8.

Oregon: 33 records, May 3 to June 12; 17 records, May 12 to June 1.

Washington: 17 records, April 29 to June 10; 9 records, May 12 to 24.

COLAPTES CAFER CAFER (Gmelin)

NORTHWESTERN FLICKER

PLATE 38

HABITS

The northwestern flicker was formerly known as *Colaptes cafer saturatior* Ridgway, type locality Neah Bay, Wash. But it has since been learned that Gmelin's name *Picus cafer* was based on a bird taken at Bay of Good Hope, Nootka Sound, British Columbia. As this locality is well within the range of the northwestern flicker, Gmelin's name has priority over Ridgway's *saturatior.*

This larger and more richly colored race of *Colaptes cafer* inhabits the humid Northwest coast region, from Sitka, Alaska, to northern California, Humboldt County, including most of southern British Columbia east to the Kootenay district. It is not only larger than *Colaptes cafer collaris*, but its upper parts are browner and its under parts are more strongly suffused with vinaceous.

D. E. Brown writes to me that this "is the common woodpecker of western Washington. It will outnumber all the other woodpeckers two to one." Referring to its haunts on Mount Rainier, Taylor and Shaw (1927) say: "As the noisiest and most conspicuous, adaptable, and broadly distributed woodpecker in the park, the flicker is bound to achieve some notoriety. It avoids the dark woods, and undoubtedly prefers the tracts of dead stubs which are encountered at fairly frequent intervals around the mountain; for here both nesting sites and food are present in great abundance."

Major Bendire (1895) says that "in western Oregon, and probably also in northwestern California, it appears to be found only on the summits of the different mountains between the Cascades and the coast during the breeding season, where the same moist climate prevails as is found in the immediate vicinity of the coast, while in the drier lowlands, such as the Umpqua, Rogue, and Willamette river valleys, it is replaced by" *Colaptes cafer collaris.*

Nesting.—The nesting habits of the northwestern flicker do not seem to differ materially from those of its close relative farther south.

D. E. Brown tells me that this bird "will nest anywhere where there is room to dig out a cavity large enough for the nest. I have found them in large stumps and in fenceposts and from 18 inches from the ground to 100 feet up. They will nest in birdboxes of suitable size and will use them for winter homes. The eggs are from 5 to 10 in number and may be found May 1 to August. Both birds incubate and, when incubation is advanced, sit very close; sometimes they are removed by hand."

Harry S. Swarth (1911a) reports a nest, found at Portage Cove, Revillagigedo Island, Alaska, that "was in a dead stub, some fifty feet from the ground. The stump was so rotten that an attempt to climb it brought down the whole upper portion, including the nest, in a mass of disintegrated punk. * * * The nest tree was in a valley bordering a stream, in fairly open country, with clumps of scattered timber interspersed between the open meadows."

Eggs.—The eggs of this race are indistinguishable from those of the red-shafted flicker, except for a slight average difference in size. The measurements of 47 eggs average 29.37 by 22.37 millimeters; the eggs showing the four extremes measure **32.0** by 23.4, 30.6 by **24.3**, and **26.4** by **20.8** millimeters.

Food.—What has been said about the food of the red-shafted flicker, and to a large extent that of the northern flicker, would apply equally well to the northwestern. D. E. Brown says in his notes: "It puts in most of its time feeding on the ground and becomes quite tame around houses. I once placed some cornmeal on the back porch for some small birds. A flicker lit on the porch and, approaching the meal, laid its head sideways nearly on the floor and ran its long tongue through the meal several times; it then turned its head over and repeated the operation from the other side, leaving a checkered effect on the meal."

Theed Pearse writes to me from Vancouver Island that he has seen "a flicker picking up grains of rolled-oats off a flat surface by a sideways action of the beak." Flickers at his feeding station fed on apples, but seemed to prefer suet or fat.

S. F. Rathbun, of Seattle, has sent me the following interesting note: "On one occasion in November I watched a northwestern flicker for more than an hour feeding on a closely cut lawn in our yard. At different times it had visited the spot, and I became somewhat curious to know what the food represented that the bird found. This time as soon as the woodpecker alighted it commenced tapping rapidly with its beak the surface of the lawn, from time to time driving its bill into the earth. Then when this was withdrawn oftener than not it held an earthworm or some large grub, which at once was eaten and then the tapping recommenced. On two occasions I could plainly see that its prey was cutworms. But what was of particular interest was the painstaking way in which the flicker worked over every inch of the small space to which it confined its attentions, for the spot was not larger than 10 by 15 feet, and this was gone over again and again. During the time I watched the flicker it captured more than a dozen earthworms, all of which were of good size, and also eight cutworms. Another action of the bird while it was hunting caught my attention. At odd times it would vigorously scratch the surface of the lawn as if to uncover some prey, and I noticed that each time this took place, a worm would be pulled from the earth by the bird."

He says further, in a letter, regarding this observation: "At the time we watched it, the bird was so close we had difficulty at times in using the field glasses, so could readily see what it obtained. Sometimes it would pull an angleworm from the ground very much as a robin does, the worm stretched out to quite an extent."

Behavior.—There is nothing peculiar in the behavior of this flicker that would not apply to its close relatives equally well. But J. Hooper Bowles (1926) had his attention called in an interesting way to the regularity of its habits in going to roost. He was calling on a friend one afternoon in the fall of 1924, of which he writes: "I happened to remark that it was half past three, when my friend answered quickly, 'In five minutes it will be bedtime for our Flicker.' This somewhat astonished me, but we went outside the house and took a station where we could command a good view of a certain section of the eaves of the house. Sure enough, in about five minutes a Northwestern Flicker swooped up and hung itself woodpecker-fashion against a board under the eaves, where it composed itself for spending the night. The bird had been doing this with absolute regularity for some time, although it was of course broad daylight and bright sunshine."

COLAPTES CAFER MARTIRENSIS Grinnell

SAN PEDRO FLICKER

HABITS

Under the above name, Dr. Joseph Grinnell (1927b) has separated and described the red-shafted flicker of the Sierra San Pedro Martir region of northern Baja California. He describes it as follows:

Similar in general characters to *Colaptes cafer collaris* Vigors (topotypes from Monterey, California), but averaging slightly smaller, bill more attenuated (especially more compressed in terminal half), and tone of ground color on head and on upper and lower surfaces in fresh plumage much more gray (rather than brown or vinaceous). * * *

The relative depth and clearness of the gray on the throat and sides of head and neck in *martirensis* is a nearly constant character, as is also the deep fuscous (of Ridgway, Color Standards and Color Nomenclature, 1912, pl. XLVI) tone of the back and of the top of the head, in fresh, new plumage:

on the sides of the body, and on the chest surrounding the big black bar, there is little hint of the bright vinaceous tinting that characterizes *collaris* from throughout upper California. Weathering of the plumage toward spring tends to rob *martirensis* of its most characteristic color tones, especially on the top of the head which then becomes warmer brown, but not, however, to the degree of brightness seen in *rufipileus*. The latter is even browner than *collaris*.

He gives, as its range: "Sierra San Pedro Martir (San José, 2,500 feet, near La Grulla at 7,200 feet, and near Vallecitos at 7,500 feet) and Sierra Juarez (Laguna Hanson, 5,200 feet)." Elsewhere (1928b), he calls it a "common resident on the western slopes of the Sierra Juárez and Sierra San Pedro Martír; in winter invading westwardly to the seacoast. Breeds in Upper Sonoran and Transition zones."

Its habits are probably similar to those of the species elsewhere.

Griffing Bancroft has sent me the measurements of a set of eight eggs, which average 26.87 by 22.16 millimeters; the eggs showing the four extremes measure 28.2 by 22.0, 26.8 by 22.8, and 26.2 by 20.7 millimeters.

COLAPTES CHRYSOIDES CHRYSOIDES (Malherbe)

CAPE GILDED FLICKER

HABITS

Because Malherbe's name was given to the first gilded flicker to be described, and because his type came from the Cape region of Baja California, this race becomes the type race of the species. Its range extends from about latitude 28° N. to the southern extremity of Baja California. It is about the same size as its nearest relative to the northward, *brunnescens*, but is decidedly lighter in coloration. It is smaller than *mearnsi* and somewhat darker in coloration. William Brewster (1902) says of its haunts: "Mr. Belding and Mr. Frazar agree as to the rarity of the Gilded Flicker on the higher mountains, where only a few individuals were seen by the former, and but two (both females, taken on the Sierra de la Laguna, April 29) obtained by the latter. The bird's true home is evidently at the bases of the mountains, and among the foothills extending thence to the shores of the Pacific on the south and west, and to the Gulf on the east. Throughout this region it is a common species, although not so numerously represented as *Melanerpes uropygialis*. On the arid plains near the coast it breeds in the stems of the giant cactus."

Griffing Bancroft (1930) says of this species in central Baja California, south of latitude 28°:

The birds are extremely wild, often flushing from a distance of a quarter of a mile. They lay in old cavities and, probably, also in those that are new; scarred sahuaro dries so rapidly that a definite determination on this point was not possible. The nests are usually twenty feet or more above the ground and the cavities are generous; an eight-inch diameter and a two-foot depth are not unusual. Occasionally they will use natural openings in the cardón or holes that have been chopped open by honey gatherers.

The flickers lay from early April until well into June. The number of eggs in a clutch is normally three. With the single exception of one set of five we found none larger, and none smaller in which incubation had commenced.

The eggs of the Cape gilded flicker are apparently similar to those of other flickers, except in size. Mr. Bancroft (1930) gives the measurements of 18 eggs as averaging 26.3 by 20.9 millimeters. The measurements of 8 other eggs average 28.49 by 21.15 millimeters; the eggs, in this series, showing the four extremes measure **31.35** by 21.83, 30.15 by **22.22**, **25.90** by 20.70, and 26.70 by **20.00** millimeters.

Its habits in general are apparently similar to those the gilded flicker of Arizona, on which more has been published, and the reader is referred to the following account of *Colaptes chrysoides mearnsi*.

DISTRIBUTION

Range.—Southern Arizona, southeastern California, and northwestern Mexico; nonmigratory.

The range of the gilded flicker extends **north** to extreme southeastern California (Duncan Flats); and southern Arizona (Antelope Peak, Bigbug, and the Salt River Bird Reservation). **East** to southeastern Arizona (Salt River Bird Reservation, Desert Wells, Picacho, Oracle, and Tombstone); central Sonora (Magdalena, Opodepe, Hermosillo, Cedros, and Camoa); and central Sinaloa (Culiacan). **South** to Sinaloa (Culiacan); and southern Baja California (Cape San Lucas). **West** to Baja California (Cape San Lucas, Todos Santos, Triunfo, Santa Margarita Island, San Javier, San Quintin, and the Alamo River); and southeastern California (Duncan Flats).

The range as outlined is for the entire species, which has been separated into three geographic races. The typical race, known as the Cape gilded flicker (*C. c. chrysoides*), is found in the Cape district of Baja California and north to about latitude 28° N. The San Fernando flicker (*C. c. brunnescens*) occurs only within a range of two degrees latitude in Baja California (lat. 28° to 30° N.). Mearns's gilded flicker (*C. c. mearnsi*) is the race found in the southwestern United States, northwestern Baja California, and the mainland of Mexico.

Egg dates.—Arizona: 24 records, April 1 to June 11; 12 records, April 21 to May 20, indicating the height of the season.

Baja California: 16 records, April 6 to May 20; 8 records, April 10 to May 17.

COLAPTES CHRYSOIDES MEARNSI Ridgway

MEARNS'S GILDED FLICKER

PLATE 39

HABITS

Mearns's gilded flicker is the best known of the three races of this handsome species. Its range is along our southwestern border in southwestern Arizona, extreme southeastern California, and in Sonora, Mexico. It is confined almost entirely, especially in the breeding season, to the giant cactus region in this area; its distribution seems to be mainly governed by the distribution of this cactus, on which it seems to depend for most of the necessities of life. M. French Gilman (1915) puts it very well, as follows: "The giant cactus is to this Flicker and the Gila Woodpecker, what the bamboo is to the inhabitants of some of the eastern islands. * * * The cactus furnishes the birds with home, shelter, food and possibly drink. They roost in the holes and seek them as retreat from rain storms." But he says that this flicker is also "found in cottonwood and willow groves as well as wherever the giant cactus grows."

W. E. D. Scott (1886) writes: "A rather common resident wherever the giant cactus occurs throughout the region, but is much more common in the giant cactus of the southern part of the area under consideration [southern Arizona] than to the northward. They are common all about Tucson in such localities as I have indicated, but are more rare in the San Pedro Valley. I have met with the species in early spring and fall on the San Pedro slope of the Catalinas as high up as 3,000 feet. I have now and then seen single individuals in the mesquite timber, far from any giant cactus. All that I have ever met with breeding have been in giant cactus."

Nesting.—We spent three days, May 21, 22, and 23, 1922, collecting on the giant-cactus plains near Tucson, Ariz., between the mesquite forest to the southward and the Catalina Mountains to the eastward from Tucson. Here we found Mearns's gilded flicker very common; we climbed to and examined seven nests and probably passed by a number of others. The nests were all in the giant cactus, at heights ranging from 12 to 20 feet from the ground; the only cavity measured was about 24 inches deep. We were rather too late for eggs of this species, as many of the nests held large young, two in each nest examined, never more nor fewer. On May 22 we found a nest containing two fresh eggs and another nest with four addled eggs, probably deserted. At one of the first nests that I examined I was surprised, when I inserted my hand, to feel something cold and clammy; my hand was quickly withdrawn and the hole was chopped out, revealing a large gopher snake that had killed and half swallowed, head first, one of the large young. At another nest, containing two large young, I shot the adult male for a specimen, after which I found the female dead in a nearby hole, which necessitated taking the two young also. After I had left for home, my companion, Frank C. Willard, took a set of three fresh eggs on June 11, from a nest 14 feet up in a small giant cactus; this was probably a second laying.

Mr. Gilman (1915), who has had considerable experience with this species, writes:

The nests are found in giant cactus, cottonwood and willow, and in that order as to frequency, the giant cactus leading. Nests are in the giant cactus or Saguaro as it is called, far from water, and in cottonwood and willow along the river, on banks of the canals, or even standing in stagnant water pools. Of twenty-seven nests examined, containing eggs or young, twenty-one were in the Saguaro, four in willow, and two in cottonwood. Others were seen in cottonwood but too difficult of access, and many in the cactus were out of reach. If careful count were made I believe about ninety per cent would be found in the cactus. Nests in cottonwood and willow ranged from five to twenty-five feet from the ground, and in Saguaros from eleven to twenty-five or thirty feet. * * *

The entrance to the nest holes varies much, as may be seen from the figures given. The smallest entrance measured 2¾ inches and the largest 4¾ inches. The shallowest hole was ten inches, and the deepest eighteen inches. * * * The entrance to the eighteen inch hole was three and one-half inches in diameter, and while the ratio is not constant, the shallower holes tend to have smaller entrances, and the deeper holes have larger entrances. * * * From the few measurements taken it may be stated that the bottom of the nest hole is from four and one-half to six inches in diameter. It is hardly correct to use the term diameter, as many of the hole bottoms were not nearly circular, one I measured being four inches one way and six the other. This variation seemed to be governed by the size of the cactus, as in the smaller plants there was not room to excavate a large circular bottom, and it had to be stretched one way.

In the lower Colorado Valley, Dr. Joseph Grinnell (1914) found that "at least two pairs were nesting in dead cottonwood stumps in the drowned-out area of the river bottom. A nesting hole located here was eighteen feet above the ground, in a large stub." He also mentions the following nests found in the saguaro belt: "On the Arizona side, April 22, excavation sixteen and one-half feet above ground in cactus thirty-one feet high, contained two fresh eggs; April 24, excavation twenty feet above the ground, not investigated. On the California side, April 23, excavation ten and one-third feet above the ground, in cactus twenty-eight feet high, contained on infertile egg and two small young."

Major Bendire (1895) writes:

It nests at varying distances from the ground from 8 to 40 feet, generally at heights of about 15 feet. I have the indurated form of a nesting cavity of this species now before me, showing its exact shape. The hardened walls are about one-fourth of an inch thick, and show the inner contour of the cavity perfectly. The entrance is nearly 3 inches in diameter; inside it is about 7 by 4 inches wide and 5½ inches deep. The sides and bottom of the cavity are quite smooth, considering the nature of the substance (the soft inner pulp of the cactus) out of which it is excavated. It occupied only one-half of the trunk of one of these giant cacti, and the rear of the cavity did not quite reach the center of the plant. The eggs lay on the hardened floor, and not, as usual, on a layer of chips. I am inclined to believe that a freshly excavated nesting site is not habitable for some weeks, as it must require some time for the exuding sap to harden. The mold before me somewhat resembles a wasp's nest, both in color and shape, and if suspended from the limb of a tree might easily be mistaken for one.

Eggs.—As to the number of eggs laid by the gilded flicker, Mr. Gilman (1915) writes: "Of the twenty-seven nests examined, eight had five eggs, or young plus eggs, to make count of five for the set; eleven had four eggs or young, or young plus eggs; six nests contained three eggs or three young; and two nests had two young each. In no case did I find five young in a nest, and from the fact that infertile eggs were found with three and four young in a nest, it may be inferred that in many of the nests containing two, three or four young, more eggs had been laid. In no nest did I find more than five eggs, and I conclude that the set is from three to five eggs."

The gilded flicker evidently lays fewer eggs than its northern and eastern relatives, and the surprising thing is that there are so many cases of infertile eggs, often one and sometimes two in a set. I have had sets of six and seven eggs reported in collections, but these may have been products of two females, where nesting holes were scarce or the region overcrowded by the many birds that use these holes. The few eggs that I have seen are like other flickers' eggs but either dull white or only slightly glossy; this may not be the universal rule, however. The measurements of 50 eggs average 27.86 by 21.34 millimeters; the eggs showing the four extremes measure **32.0** by **22.0**, **27.78** by **22.22**, and **24.61** by **20.04** millimeters.

Plumages.—Mr. Gilman (1915) says: "The young when first hatched are not very prepossessing to any one, except perhaps the parents. At first glance they remind one of the pictured restoration of the Plesiosaurus, with their long twisting naked necks. The lower mandible was more than an eighth of an inch longer than the upper, and on the tip of each was the hard white growth used in opening the shell."

In the juvenal plumage, which is acquired before the young bird leaves the nest, the young male is similar to the adult male, but the forehead is usually tinged with dark red; the red malar patch is duller and less uniform; the upper parts are grayer, less brownish, and more heavily barred; the primaries are tipped with brownish white; the under parts are grayish white, more profusely, but less distinctly, spotted; the black patch on the breast is smaller and more central;

the yellow in the wings and tail is duller; the black tips on the under side of the tail are duller and not so well defined; and the bill is much smaller and weaker. The young female is similar to the young male, but there is no red in the crown or in the malar patches, the latter being pale brown.

I have not seen enough material, taken at the proper seasons, to work out the molts, but these are probably the same as in other flickers.

Several apparent hybrids with *cafer* have been reported. Dr. Grinnell (1914), who has made a study of this subject, seems to doubt if there is any hybridizing between these species; he writes:

> The salient fact shown by this comparative examination is that in *all other characters* the specimens aberrant in colors of wing and tail, are perfectly typical of *chrysoides* (that is, of its subspecies *mearnsi*). None of the phenomena consequent upon hybridization is evidenced in other particulars, such as general size, proportional dimensions, extent of dorsal barring, colors of body and head. In all these characters there is no nearer approach of the red-shafted *chrysoides* to *collaris*, than of the yellow-shafted *chrysoides*.
>
> My conclusion is that the strain of *chrysoides* occurring at the present time in the lower Colorado Valley shows proneness to replacement of yellow by red, without there having been any interbreeding with another species. This may be accounted for chemico-physiologically, as in the case of the linnet of the Hawaiian Islands, where, however, the change has been from red to yellow. * * * It is quite evident that the aberrant examples described by Brewster and Swarth from central Arizona, as referred to above, are of the same nature as the Colorado Valley specimens. The chances are that they were not hybrids. So far as shown by the literature at hand, no unquestioned hybrids have been found between *chrysoides* (or any of its subspecies) and *collaris* or *cafer*.

Food.—The food of Mearns's gilded flicker seems to be much like that of the other flickers, including ants and various other insects and such wild fruits and berries as are available in its territory. Dr. Grinnell (1914) reports that the stomachs of two birds, taken in the Colorado Valley, "had their gullets distended with a mass of small black ants and ant larvae." Mr. Gilman (1915) says:

> They resort regularly to the Indian corncribs and are seen in corn fields though I have never noticed them actually engaged on an ear of green corn as I have the Gilas. They probably attack the green corn but are quiet about the work instead of advertising their presence. They eat largely of the cactus fruit and possibly of the pulp at certain lean seasons. They are very fond of watermelon, and eat freely of it when it is placed on bird tables or on the ground in shade of tree or shed. They appear to feed frequently on the ground in the way the red-shafted does, and are probably after ants most of the time. I have seen them at work on an ant hill and even pecking into the ground after the insects.

Behavior—The same writer says on this subject:

> The Gilded Flickers are much quieter than the Gilas, and are not so much in evidence around homes, though they do not appear to be very timid. They are simply less sociable I presume. * * *

They are peaceable and impress me as being eminently practical and matter of fact. Each one minds his own business and seems willing to live and let live. They do not assemble in numbers as the Gilas do sometimes, but are solitary or in pairs. They have the same habit of pecking the walls of buildings as have the red-shafted flickers, and one has worked spasmodically at the shingled gable of the school house here for the past three years. I take it to be the same individual, for he is rather tame and roosts each night above one of the window casings. * * *

They are not close sitters, and usually leave the nest before the tree is reached or the ladder placed against the trunk. As soon as an intruder's footsteps become audible the landlady pokes her head from the entrance, and soon after departs, never giving opportunity for capturing her on the nest.

Voice.—The gilded flicker apparently possesses as good a vocabulary as any other flicker, uttering practically all the varied notes common to the genus, but evidently it is not quite so noisy as its relatives. Mr. Gilman (1915) thinks that its notes are "not so frequent nor quite so loud" as those of the red-shafted flicker.

Field marks.—The gilded flicker can be recognized easily as a flicker by the characteristic markings of the genus, by its flight and by its voice. It looks like an eastern flicker with a red malar patch (in the male) instead of a black one, and with no red crescent on the nape in either sex. It looks like a pale red-shafted flicker with yellow, instead of red, in the wings and tail. Its smaller size is hardly noticeable in the field.

COLAPTES CHRYSOIDES BRUNNESCENS Anthony

SAN FERNANDO FLICKER

HABITS

The gilded flicker of middle Baja California, between latitude 28° and latitude 30° N., is a well-marked subspecies. A. W. Anthony (1895b), naming it, characterized it as "differing from *C. chrysoides* in darker upper parts and slightly smaller size." He says further: "It would be quite natural to expect specimens of *Colaptes* from the northern half of Lower California to be more or less intermediate between those of Arizona and Cape St. Lucas. They are, however, further removed from the type form from the Cape than are those from Arizona and northern Mexico, and in the series I have examined the Arizona skins are exactly intermediate in the color of the upper parts betwen a series from Cape St. Lucas and my skins from San Fernando."

Ridgway (1914) describes *brunnescens* as "similar to *C. c. chrysoides,* but coloration decidedly darker and browner, color of pileum more rufescent (russet, or between russet and mars brown, in typical specimens), immaculate area of rump more restricted (sometimes whole rump spotted with black), wing and tail averaging shorter, and bill longer."

Mr. Anthony wrote to Major Bendire (1895) : "The Gilded Flicker is rather common in the heavy growth of giant cactus, *Cereus pringlei*, but not adverse to the candlewood forests which cover a large part of the peninsula between latitudes 28° and 30°." The general habits of this flicker do not seem to differ from those of the species elsewhere.

The eggs of the San Fernando flicker are similar to those of the preceeding subspecies. Griffing Bancroft (1930) gives the average measurements of 24 eggs as 27.1 by 21.3 millimeters. I have the measurements of 5 others, which average 28.9 by 22.1 millimeters.

COLAPTES CAFER RUFIPILEUS Ridgway

GUADALUPE FLICKER

HABITS

This insular race of the red-shafted flickers is another member of the unique avifauna of that interesting island that has followed the Guadalupe caracara, and other species peculiar to Guadalupe Island, into extinction. It was discovered by Dr. Edward Palmer in 1875 and was described and named by Robert Ridgway (1876) as *Colaptes mexicanus rufipileus*. In his description of it, he remarks: "In the closed tail, only about half an inch of red is exposed on the under surface beyond the lower coverts, the remaining 2.50 being uniform black. The main differences from the continental form consist in the longer bill, more pinkish rump, and bright tawny forehead. In the latter feature, the resemblance is closer to *C. chrysoides*, the crown and nape having about the same gradation from bright cinnamon-tawny anteriorly to dull grayish-cinnamon posteriorly." Although it has a decidedly longer bill than the mainland forms, it has a much shorter wing and tail. The collector's notes state that, even then, it was "rare, and apparently only found in the pine-woods of the north end of the island."

Walter E. Bryant (1887), who visited Guadalupe in 1885 and 1886, gives us the best account we have of this little-known bird. He says of its status and haunts at that time: "Comparatively speaking, this bird was not rare in the restricted area of the large cypress grove, but apart from this locality less than a dozen were seen. Three specimens were taken among some palms within a short distance from the beach on the eastern side of the island. One only was heard among the pines at the northern portion, and in the vicinity of the large palm grove on the northwestern slope they were occasionally seen." He collected ten specimens, whereas Dr. Palmer took only three.

In the spring of 1906, W. W. Brown, Jr., with two assistants, collected for two months on the island for the Thayer Museum, of which

Thayer and Bangs (1908) say: "This well-marked island form is in all probability doomed to speedy extinction, and will be the next of the Guadalupe birds to go. Brown and Marsden found in all not more than forty individuals in the island. In the small cypress grove near the cabins there were four and in the large cypress woods about thirty-five.

"Mr. Brown tells us that in the breeding season, at least, the species is wholly confined to the cypresses, none being seen in the pine woods. The bird is very tame and unsuspicious and falls an easy prey to the cats."

Courtship.—Mr. Bryant (1887) noted Guadalupe flickers in courtship antics in January and in February. According to his description of their actions and their notes at such times, these performances are evidently similar to those of other flickers elsewhere.

Nesting.—Apparently Dr. Palmer found no nests and collected no eggs of this flicker, but Mr. Bryant (1887) has this to say about its nesting habits:

By March 16, the birds were invariably found in pairs, and my wish to secure a setting of eggs before departing seemed in a fair way of being fulfilled. Strolling among the cypresses on the 27th of March, I found four trees upon which the birds were at work or had been recently, and in such cases the birds themselves were always to be found in the immediate vicinity. Passing a half-dead tree I heard the sounding taps of a woodpecker at work, and as I neared the spot, the slight noise which I made as I carefully picked my way over the rock-strewn ground caused a handsome male bird to suddenly appear at an opening about four feet high. With a foot grasping either side of the entrance he gazed upon the intruder. Having comprehended the situation, he flew to another tree, where he quietly awaited my inspection and departure. The hole was then down about fifteen inches. By April 7, it had reached a depth of about twenty inches and contained six fresh eggs, upon which the female was then sitting.

Mr. Brown collected, for the Thayer Museum, six sets of eggs, one set of five, two sets of four, one set of three, and two single eggs, all of which are now in the Museum of Comparative Zoology in Cambridge, Mass. The eggs were collected on dates ranging from May 8 to June 8, 1906; the nests were all in cypresses, mostly old or dead trees or stumps, at heights ranging from 4 to 20 feet above the ground, and at altitudes of from 3,700 to 4,500 feet above sea level; one of the cavities was only 2 inches deep, but some of the others were 18 or 20 inches deep and from 3½ to 4 inches in diameter.

Eggs.—The number of eggs laid by the Guadalupe flicker apparently ranged from four to six. The eggs that I have seen, in Cambridge, are ovate, pure white, and decidedly glossy, like other flickers' eggs. The measurements of 23 eggs average 27.8 by 21.7 millimeters; the eggs showing the four extremes measure 30.2 by 21.1, 28.0 by 22.5, and 26.8 by 20.5 millimeters.

Food.—Mr. Bryant (1887) says: "The food of this species during a portion of the year consists largely of smooth-skinned caterpillars, besides numerous beetles and ants; the latter are always obtainable and growing to a large size figure as an important item of their diet."

Behavior.—He also remarks: "Of all the species of this family I have ever met with, none have been so tame and unsuspicious or less frightened by the report of a gun."

Voice.—The notes of the Guadalupe flicker are also similar to those of the mainland forms, for Mr. Bryant (1887) says: "In addition to the familiar scythe-whetting notes they have the peculiar 'wake-up' call and its rapid prelude of monosyllables. By imitating this call I decoyed a distant female to within short range, the bird coming through the thickest of the cypress grove, stopping at short intervals to call and listen for a reply."

LITERATURE CITED

ACHILLES, LAURENCE.
1906. Nesting of the Arctic three-toed woodpecker in the Adirondacks.
Bird-Lore, vol. 8, pp. 158–160.
AGERSBORG, GILBERT SMITH.
1881. Novel nesting-sites of woodpeckers (*Colaptes auratus* and *Melanerpes erythrocephalus*). Bull. Nuttall Orn. Club, vol. 6, p. 120.
ALDERSON, V. A.
1890. Hairy woodpecker and potato bugs. Oologist, vol. 7, p. 147.
ALLEN, ARTHUR AUGUSTUS.
1928. Downy woodpecker's story. Bird-Lore, vol. 30, pp. 415–424.
1937. Hunting with a microphone the voices of vanishing birds. Nat. Geogr. Mag., vol. 71, pp. 697–706.
ALLEN, ARTHUR AUGUSTUS, and KELLOGG, P. PAUL.
1937. Recent observations on the ivory-billed woodpecker. Auk, vol. 54, pp. 164–184.
ALLEN, JOEL ASAPH.
1892. The North American species of the genus *Colaptes*, considered with special reference to the relationships of *C. auratus* and *C. cafer*. Bull. Amer. Mus. Nat. Hist., vol. 4, pp. 21–44.
ALLERT, OSCAR PAUL.
1934. Flicker kills young robins. Iowa Bird Life, vol. 4, p. 20.
AMERICAN ORNITHOLOGISTS' UNION.
1910. Check-list of North American birds. Ed. 3.
1931. Check-list of North American birds. Ed. 4.
ANDERSON, ANDERS HAROLD.
1934. Food of the Gila woodpecker (*Centurus uropygialis uropygialis*). Auk, vol. 51, pp. 84–85.
ANDERSON, MALCOLM P., and GRINNELL, JOSEPH.
1903. Birds of the Siskiyou Mountains, California: A problem in distribution. Proc. Acad. Nat. Sci. Philadelphia, vol. 55, pp. 4–15.
ANTHONY, ALFRED WEBSTER.
1895a. Birds of San Fernando, Lower California. Auk, vol. 12, pp. 134–143.
1895b. New races of *Colaptes* and *Passerella* from the Pacific coast. Auk, vol. 12, pp. 347–349.
ARTHUR, EDMUND WATTS.
1934. Courtship dance of the pileated woodpecker. Cardinal, vol. 3, p. 173.
ATTWATER, HENRY PHILEMON.
1892. List of birds observed in the vicinity of San Antonio, Bexar County, Texas. Auk, vol. 9, pp. 229–238.
AUDUBON, JOHN JAMES.
1842. The birds of America, vol. 4.
BACON, C. C.
1891. A large set or series of the red-headed woodpecker. Oologist, vol. 8, p. 32.

BAILEY, FLORENCE AUGUSTA MERRIAM.
1896. Notes on some of the birds of southern California. Auk, vol. 13, pp. 115–124.
1902. Handbook of birds of the Western United States.
1923. Birds recorded from the Santa Rita Mountains in southern Arizona. Pacific Coast Avifauna, no. 15.
1928. Birds of New Mexico.

BAILEY, HAROLD HARRIS.
1913. The birds of Virginia.
1925. The birds of Florida.

BAILEY, HARRY BALCH.
1878. Some new traits for the red-headed woodpecker (*Melanerpes erythrocephalus*). Bull. Nuttall Orn. Club, vol. 3, p. 97.
1883. Memoranda of a collection of eggs from Georgia. Bull. Nuttall Orn. Club, vol. 8, pp. 37–43.

BAIRD, SPENCER FULLERTON.
1858. Pacific Railroad Reports, vol. 9, pt. 2. Birds.

BAIRD, SPENCER FULLERTON; CASSIN, JOHN; and LAWRENCE, GEORGE NEWBOLD.
1860. The birds of North America.

BANCROFT, GRIFFING.
1930. The breeding birds of central Lower California. Condor, vol. 32, pp. 20–49.

BANGS, OUTRAM.
1898. Some new races of birds from eastern North America. Auk, vol. 15, pp. 173–183.
1900. A review of the three-toed woodpeckers of North America. Auk, vol. 17, pp. 126–142.
1910. A new race of the pileated woodpecker. Proc. New England Zool. Club, vol. 4, pp. 79–80.

BARROWS, WALTER BRADFORD.
1912. Michigan bird life.

BATCHELDER, CHARLES FOSTER.
1889. An undescribed subspecies of *Dryobates pubescens*. Auk, vol. 6, pp. 253–255.
1908. The Newfoundland hairy woodpecker. Proc. New England Zool. Club, vol. 4, pp. 37–38.

BAYNARD, OSCAR EDWARD.
1913. Breeding birds of Alachua County, Florida. Auk, vol. 30, pp. 240–247.

BEAL, FOSTER ELLENBOROUGH LASCELLES.
1895. Preliminary report on the food of woodpeckers. U. S. Dept. Agr. Div. Orn. and Mamm. Bull. 7.
1910. Birds of California in relation to the fruit industry, pt. 2. U. S. Dept. Agr. Biol. Surv. Bull. 34.
1911. Food of the woodpeckers of the United States. U. S. Dept. Agr. Biol. Surv. Bull. 37.

BENDIRE, CHARLES EMIL.
1895. Life histories of North American birds. U. S. Nat. Mus. Spec. Bull. 3.

BEYER, GEORGE EUGENE.
1900. The ivory-billed woodpecker in Louisiana. Auk, vol. 17, pp. 97–99.

BEYER, GEORGE EUGENE; ALLISON, ANDREW; and KOPMAN, HENRY HAZLITT.
1908. List of the birds of Louisiana. Auk, vol. 25, pp. 173–180, 439–448.

BICKNELL, EUGENE PINTARD.
1885. A study of the singing of our birds. Auk, vol. 2, pp. 249–262.

BLACKWELDER, ELIOT.
1909. Summer birds of Iron County, Michigan. Auk, vol. 26, pp. 363–370.
BLINCOE, BENEDICT JOSEPH.
1923. Random notes on the feeding habits of some Kentucky birds. Wilson
    Bull., vol. 35, pp. 63–71.
BOLLES, FRANK.
1891. Yellow-bellied woodpeckers and their uninvited guests. Auk, vol. 8,
    pp. 256–270.
1892. Young sapsuckers in captivity. Auk, vol. 9, pp. 109–119.
BOWLES, JOHN HOOPER.
1926. Regularity in habits of the northwestern flicker. Murrelet, vol. 7,
    p. 42.
BRASHER, REX.
1926. Secrets of the friendly woods.
BREWSTER, WILLIAM.
1876a. The yellow-bellied woodpecker (Sphyrapicus varius). Bull. Nuttall
    Orn. Club, vol. 1, pp. 63–70.
1876b. Some observations on the birds of Ritchie County, West Virginia.
    Ann. Lyc. Nat. Hist. New York, vol. 11, pp. 129–146.
1882. Impressions of some southern birds. Bull. Nuttall Orn. Club, vol. 7,
    pp. 94–104.
1889. Melanerpes carolinus eating oranges. Auk, vol. 6, pp. 337–338.
1897. On the nomenclature of certain forms of the downy woodpecker.
    (Dryobates pubescens). Auk, vol. 14, pp. 80–82.
1898. Notes on the American three-toed woodpecker (Picoides americanus).
    Osprey, vol. 2, pp. 73–76.
1902. Birds of the Cape region of Lower California. Bull. Mus. Comp. Zool.,
    vol. 41, pp. 1–241.
1906. Birds of the Cambridge region. Mem. Nuttall Orn. Club, no. 4.
1909. Eggs of the flicker (Colaptes auratus luteus) found in an odd place.
    Bird-Lore, vol. 11, pp. 73–74.
1936. October Farm.
1937. Concord River.
BROOKS, MAURICE.
1934. Some traits of the northern pileated woodpecker. Bird-Lore, vol. 36,
    pp. 347–351.
BROWN, HERBERT.
1902. Unusual abundance of Lewis's woodpecker near Tucson, Arizona, in
    1884. Auk, vol. 19, pp. 80–83.
BRYANT, HAROLD CHILD.
1916. A note on the food of the northern pileated woodpecker. Condor,
    vol. 18, p. 32.
1921. California woodpecker steals eggs of wood pewee. Condor, vol. 23,
    p. 33.
BRYANT, WALTER (PIERO) E.
1887. Additions to the ornithology of Guadalupe Island. Bull. California
    Acad. Sci., vol. 2, pp. 269–318.
BRYENS, OSCAR MCKINLEY.
1926. Actions of the northern pileated woodpecker. Auk, vol. 43, p. 98.
BURLEIGH, THOMAS DEARBORN.
1931. Notes on the breeding birds of State College, Centre County, Pennsyl-
    vania. Wilson Bull., vol. 43, pp. 37–42.

BURMEISTER, CARL HERMANN CONRAD.
    1856. Systematische Uebersicht der Thiere Brasiliens welche während einer
        Reise durch die Provinzen von Rio de Janeiro und Minas Geraës
        gesammelt oder beobachtet wurden.
BURNS, FRANKLIN LORENZO.
    1900. Monograph of the flicker. Wilson Bull., vol. 7, pp. 1–82.
    1903. A few additional notes on the flicker. Wilson Bull., vol. 10, pp. 24–26.
    1915. Comparative periods of deposition and incubation of some North
        American birds. Wilson Bull., vol. 27, pp. 275–286.
    1916. One hundred and thirty-two vernacular names for the flicker. Wil
        son Bull., vol. 28, pp. 90–91.
BURTCH, VERDI.
    1923. Red squirrel eating young hairy woodpecker. Auk, vol. 40, pp.
        340–241.
CARRIGER, HENRY WARD, and WELLS, GURNIE.
    1919. Nesting of the northern pileated woodpecker. Condor, vol. 21, pp.
        153–156.
CASSIN, JOHN.
    1852. Descriptions of birds of the genera Laniarius, Dicrurus, Graucalus,
        Manacus and Picus, specimens of which are in the collection of
        the Academy of Natural Sciences of Philadelphia. Proc. Acad. Nat.
        Sci. Philadelphia, vol. 5, pp. 347–349.
    1854. Illustrations of the birds of California, Texas, Oregon, British and
        Russian America, pt. 7.
CATESBY, MARK.
    1731. The natural history of Carolina, Florida and the Bahama Islands,
        vol. 1.
CHRISTY, BAYARD HENDERSON.
    1931. Nesting of the red-bellied woodpecker in Beaver County. Cardinal,
        vol. 3, pp. 44–45.
COOPER, JAMES GRAHAM.
    1870. Geological survey of California. Ornithology, vol. 1. Land birds.
COUES, ELLIOTT.
    1874. Birds of the Northwest.
CURRIER, EDMONDE SAMUEL.
    1928. Lewis woodpeckers nesting in colonies. Condor, vol. 30, p. 356.
DAWSON, WILLIAM LEON.
    1903. The birds of Ohio.
    1923. The birds of California, vol. 2.
DAWSON, WILLIAM LEON, and BOWLES, JOHN HOOPER.
    1909. The birds of Washington, vol. 1.
DICE, LEE RAYMOND.
    1918. The birds of Walla Walla and Columbia Counties, southeastern
        Washington. Auk, vol. 35, pp. 40–51.
DINGLE, EDWARD VON SIEBOLD.
    1926. Red-cockaded woodpecker in cornfields. Bird-Lore, vol. 28, pp.
        124–125.
DIXON, JOSEPH SCATTERGOOD.
    1927. Black bear tries to gnaw into a woodpecker's nest. Condor, vol. 29,
        pp. 271–272.
DORSEY, GEORGE ANDREW.
    1926. A red-headed woodpecker storing acorns. Bird-Lore, vol. 28, pp. 333–
        334.

DUNCAN, MRS. SANFORD.
 1932. Flicker captured by a bullsnake. Migrant, vol. 3, p. 9.
DWIGHT, JONATHAN, JR.
 1893. Summer birds of Prince Edward Island. Auk, vol. 10, pp. 1–15.
EATON, ELON HOWARD.
 1914. Birds of New York. New York State Mus. Mem. 12, pt. 2.
ECKSTROM, FANNIE HARDY.
 1901. The woodpeckers.
EIFRIG, CHARLES WILLIAM GUSTAVE.
 1906. Notes on some northern birds. Auk, vol. 23, pp. 313–318.
 1919. Notes on birds of the Chicago area and its immediate vicinity. Auk,
   vol. 36, pp. 513–524.
EMERSON, WILLIAM OTTO.
 1893. Random bird-notes from Merced Big Trees and Yosemite Valley.
   Zoe, vol. 4, pp. 176–182.
 1899. Fall notes from Haywards, Cal. Bull. Cooper Orn. Club, vol. 1,
   p. 28.
ERICHSEN, WALTER JEFFERSON.
 1920. Observations on the habits of some breeding birds of Chatham County,
   Georgia. Wilson Bull., vol. 32, pp. 133–139.
ERRINGTON, PAUL LESTER.
 1936. Winter-killing of flickers in central Iowa. Auk, vol. 53, pp. 334–335.
EVERMANN, BARTON WARREN.
 1889. Birds of Carroll County, Indiana. Auk, vol. 6, pp. 22–30.
FARLEY, JOHN AUSTIN.
 1901. Massachusetts bird notes. Auk, vol. 18, pp. 398–400.
FISHER, WALTER KENRICK.
 1902. The downy woodpeckers of California. Condor, vol. 4, pp. 68–70.
FISHER, WILLIAM HARMANUS.
 1903. Nesting of the red-bellied woodpecker in Harford County, Maryland,
   Auk, vol. 20, pp. 305–306.
FLANAGAN, JOHN HENRY.
 1911. Some Colorado woodpecker and sapsucker notes. Oologist, vol. 28,
   pp. 69–71.
FLEMING, JAMES HENRY.
 1901. A list of the birds of the Districts Parry Sound and Muskoka, Ontario. Auk, vol. 18, pp. 33–45.
FORBUSH, EDWARD HOWE.
 1913. Useful birds and their protection.
 1927. Birds of Massachusetts and other New England States, vol. 2.
FOWLER, FREDERICK HALL.
 1903. Stray notes from southern Arizona. Condor, vol. 5, pp. 68–71, 106–107.
FRITZ, EMANUEL.
 1937. Sapsuckers on redwood. Condor, vol. 39, pp. 36–37.
GANIER, ALBERT FRANKLIN.
 1926. An unusual flicker's nest. Wilson Bull., vol. 38, p. 116.
GIBBS, MORRIS.
 1902. The movements of birds. Oologist, vol. 19, pp. 83–85.
GIGNOUX, CLAUDE.
 1921. The storage of almonds by the California woodpecker. Condor, vol.
   23, pp. 118–121.
GILMAN, MARSHALL FRENCH.
 1915. Woodpeckers of the Arizona lowlands. Condor, vol. 17, pp. 151–163.

GOODPASTURE, A. V.
   1909. Woodpeckers and June-bugs. Bird-Lore, vol. 11, pp. 196–197.
GRIMES, SAMUEL ANDREW.
   1932. Notes on the 1931 nesting season in the Jacksonville region. Florida
      Nat., vol. 5, pp. 57–63.
GRINNELL, JOSEPH.
   1900. Birds of the Kotzebue Sound region, Alaska. Pacific Coast Avifauna,
      no. 1.
   1901. Two races of the red-breasted sapsucker. Condor, vol. 3, p. 12.
   1902. The southern white-headed woodpecker. Condor, vol. 4, pp. 89–90.
   1908. The biota of the San Bernardino Mountains. Univ. California Publ.
      Zool., vol. 5, pp. 1–170.
   1909. Birds and mammals of the 1907 Alexander expedition to south-
      eastern Alaska. Univ. California Publ. Zool., vol. 5, pp. 171–264.
   1910. Birds of the 1908 Alexander Alaska expedition. Univ. California Publ.
      Zool., vol. 5, pp. 361–428.
   1914. An account of the mammals and birds of the lower Colorado Valley
      with especial reference to the distributional problems presented.
      Univ. California Publ. Zool., vol. 12, pp. 51–294.
   1927a. A new race of Gila woodpecker from Lower California. Condor, vol.
      29, pp. 168–169.
   1927b. Six new subspecies of birds from Lower California. Auk, vol. 44,
      pp. 67–72.
   1928a. Do willow woodpeckers ever drill in tree-bark? Condor, vol. 30,
      pp. 253–254.
   1928b. A distributional summation of the ornithology of Lower California.
      Univ. California Publ. Zool., vol. 32, pp. 1–300.
GRINNELL, JOSEPH; DIXON, JOSEPH SCATTERGOOD; and LINSDALE, JEAN MYRON.
   1930. Vertebrate natural history of a section of northern California through
      the Lassen Peak region. Univ. California Publ. Zool., vol. 35,
      pp. 1–594.
GRINNELL, JOSEPH, and STORER, TRACY IRWIN.
   1924. Animal life in the Yosemite.
GRINNELL, JOSEPH, and SWARTH, HARRY SCHELWALDT.
   1926. A new race of acorn-storing woodpecker, from Lower California.
      Condor, vol. 28, pp. 176–178.
GRISCOM, LUDLOW.
   1929. Changes in the status of certain birds in the New York City region.
      Auk, vol. 46, pp. 45–57.
HARGITT, EDWARD.
   1886. Notes on woodpeckers—no. 11. On a new species from Arizona. Ibis,
      ser. 5, vol. 4, pp. 112–115.
HARLOW, RICHARD CRESSON.
   1914. Nesting of the northern pileated woodpecker. Oologist, vol. 31, pp.
      82–85.
HARTERT, ERNST.
   1912. Die Vögel der paläarktischen Fauna, Heft 7 (Band 2, I).
HASBROUCK, EDWIN MARBLE.
   1889. Summer birds of Eastland County, Texas. Auk, vol. 6, pp. 236–241.
HELME, ARTHUR HUDSON.
   1882. Red-headed woodpeckers. Ornithologist and Oologist, vol. 7, p. 107.
HENDERSON, JUNIUS.
   1927. The practical value of birds.

HENSHAW, HENRY WETHERBEE.
1875. Report upon the ornithological collections obtained from portions of Nevada, Utah, California, Colorado, New Mexico, and Arizona, during the years 1871, 1872, 1873 and 1874.
1921. The storage of acorns by the California woodpecker. Condor, vol. 23, pp. 109–118.
HOFFMAN, RALPH.
1927. Birds of the Pacific States.
HOLLAND, HAROLD MAY.
1931. Doves and woodpeckers. Oologist, vol. 48, pp. 61–63.
HOLLISTER, NED.
1918. A sanctuary within a sanctuary. Bird-Lore, vol. 20, pp. 158–159.
HOWELL, ARTHUR HOLMES.
1924. Birds of Alabama.
1932. Florida bird life.
HOYT, ROBERT DAY.
1905. Nesting of the ivory-billed woodpecker in Florida. Warbler, ser. 2, vol. 1, pp. 52–55.
HUEY, LAURENCE MARKHAM.
1927. A discussion of the zonal status of the Sierra San Pedro Martir, Lower California, Mexico, with descriptions of a new kangaroo rat and a new woodpecker from that region. Trans. San Diego Soc. Nat. Hist., vol. 5, pp. 1–10.
INGERSOLL, ERNEST.
1906. The wit of the wild.
JENKS, RANDOLPH.
1934. Unusual nesting records from northern Arizona. Condor, vol. 36, pp. 172–176.
JENSEN, JENS KNUDSEN.
1923. Notes on the nesting birds of northern Santa Fe County, New Mexico. Auk, vol. 40, pp. 452–469.
JONES, HOWARD.
1883. An unrecorded habit of the red-headed woodpecker. Ornithologist and Oologist, vol. 8, p. 56.
KENNARD, FREDERIC HEDGE.
1895. January occurrence of the "sapsucker" in Brookline, Mass. Auk, vol. 12, pp. 301–302.
KING, FRANKLIN HIRAM.
1883. Economic relations of Wisconsin birds. Geology of Wisconsin, Survey of 1873–1879, pp. 441–610.
KLUGH, A. B.
1909. A remarkable migration of yellow-bellied sapsuckers. Ottawa Nat., vol. 23, pp. 115–116.
KNIGHT, ORA WILLIS.
1908. The birds of Maine.
KOPMAN, HENRY HAZLITT.
1915. List of the birds of Louisiana, pt. 6. Auk, vol. 32, pp. 15–29.
KUMLIEN, LUDWIG, and HOLLISTER, NED.
1903. The birds of Wisconsin. Bull. Wisconsin Nat. Hist. Soc., new ser., vol. 3, pp. 1–143.
KYLER, Mrs. JOHN FRANKLIN.
1927. Bob, the redhead. Bird-Lore, vol. 29, pp. 335–338.
LAING, HAMILTON MACK, and TAVERNER, PERCY ALGERNON.
1929. Notes on birds collected and observed in Chitina River region, Alaska. Ann. Rep. Nat. Mus. Canada, 1927, pp. 72–95.

LATHAM, JOHN.
    1783. A general synopsis of birds, vol. 1.
LAW, JOHN EUGENE.
    1929. Another Lewis woodpecker stores acorns. Condor, vol. 31, pp. 233-238.
LEACH, FRANK A.
    1925. Communism in the California woodpecker. Condor, vol. 27, pp. 12-19.
LEISTER, CLAUDE WILLARD.
    1919. Aerial evolutions of a flicker. Auk, vol. 36, p. 570.
LINNAEUS, CARL.
    1758. Systema naturae. Ed. 10.
LLOYD, HOYES.
    1932. The birds of Ottawa—Addenda. Canadian Field-Nat., vol. 46, pp.
        123-127.
LYON, WILLIAM ISAAC.
    1922. Owl kidnaps young flickers. Wilson Bull., vol. 34, pp. 230-231.
MACFARLANE, RODERICK ROSS.
    1908. List of birds and eggs observed and collected in the northwest Terri-
        tories of Canada, between 1880 and 1894. In, Through the Macken-
        zie Basin, by Charles Mair.
MACOUN, JOHN.
    1909. Catalogue of Canadian birds. Ed. 2.
MAYNARD, CHARLES JOHNSON.
    1896. The birds of eastern North America. Revised edition.
MCATEE, WALDO LEE.
    1911. Woodpeckers in relation to trees and wood products. U. S. Dept.
        Agric. Biol. Surv. Bull. 39.
MCGUIRE. N. M.
    1932. A red-bellied woodpecker robs a sapsucker. Wilson Bull., vol. 44, p. 39.
MEARNS, EDGAR ALEXANDER.
    1890a. Descriptions of a new species and three new subspecies of birds from
        Arizona. Auk, vol. 7, pp. 243-251.
    1890b. Observations on the avifauna of portions of Arizona. Auk, vol. 7,
        pp. 251-264.
MERRIAM, CLINTON HART.
    1878. Remarks on some of the birds of Lewis County, northern New York.
        Bull. Nuttall Orn. Club, vol. 3, pp. 123-128.
    1879. Remarks on some of the birds of Lewis County, northern New York.
        Bull. Nuttall Orn. Club, vol. 4, pp. 1-7.
MERRIAM, ROBERT OWEN.
    1920. Snow bathing. Bird-Lore, vol. 22, p. 348.
MERRILL, JAMES CUSHING.
    1888. Notes on the birds of Fort Klamath, Oregon. Auk, vol. 5, pp. 139-
        146, 251-262.
MICHAEL, CHARLES WILSON.
    1926. Acorn storing methods of the California and Lewis woodpeckers. Con-
        dor, vol. 28, pp. 68-69.
    1928. The pileated woodpecker feeds on berries. Condor, vol. 30, p. 157.
    1935. Nesting of the Williamson sapsucker. Condor, vol. 37, pp. 209-210.
MINOT, HENRY DAVIS.
    1877. The land and game birds of New England.
MOORE, WILLIAM H.
    1902. Notes on some Canadian birds. Ottawa Nat., vol. 16, pp. 130-134.

MORRELL, CLARENCE HENRY.
1901. Notes on the pileated woodpecker. Journ. Maine Orn. Soc., vol. 8, p. 32.
MORSE, GEORGE WASHINGTON.
1927. Notes on a red-cockaded woodpecker. Oologist, vol. 44, pp. 22–23.
MORTIMER D. [=B. (BENJAMIN.)].
1890. Notes on habits of a few birds of Orange County, Florida. Auk, vol. 7, pp. 337–343.
MOUSLEY, HENRY.
1916. Five years personal notes and observations on the birds of Hatley, Stanstead County, Quebec—1911–1915. Auk, vol. 33, pp. 57–73.
MUNRO, JAMES ALEXANDER.
1919. Notes on some birds of the Okanagan Valley, British Columbia. Auk, vol. 36, pp. 64–74.
1923. The pileated woodpecker. Canadian Field-Nat., vol. 37, pp. 85–88.
1930. Miscellaneous notes on some British Columbia birds. Condor, vol. 32, pp. 65–68.
MYERS, HARRIET WILLIAMS.
1915. A late nesting record for the California woodpecker. Condor, vol. 17, pp. 183–185.
NAUMAN, E. D.
1930. The red-headed woodpecker. Bird-Lore, vol. 32, pp. 128–129.
1932. The red-headed woodpecker as a mouser. Wilson Bull., vol. 44, p. 44.
NEFF, JOHNSON ANDREW.
1928. A study of the economic status of the common woodpeckers in relation to Oregon horticulture.
NEHRLING, HENRY.
1882. List of birds observed at Houston, Harris Co., Texas, and in the Counties Montgomery, Galveston and Fort Bend. Bull. Nuttall Orn. Club, vol. 7, pp. 166–175.
NELSON, EDWARD WILLIAM.
1887. Report upon natural history collections made in Alaska between the years 1877 and 1881. U. S. Signal Service, Arctic ser., no. 3.
NEWBERRY, JOHN STRONG.
1857. Report upon the zoology of the route. U. S. Pacific Railroad Reports, vol. 6, pt. 4, pp. 35–110.
NORRIS, JOSEPH PARKER.
1888. Five sets of eggs from one bird in one season. Ornithologist and Oologist, vol. 13, p. 102.
NUTTALL, THOMAS.
1832. A manual of the ornithology of the United States and of Canada, vol. 1. Land birds.
NYE, HARRIET AUGUSTA.
1918. The sapsucker wintering in central Maine. Auk, vol. 35, pp. 353–354.
OBERHOLSER, HARRY CHURCH.
1896a. Descriptions of two new subspecies of 'the downy woodpecker, *Dryobates pubescens* (Linnaeus). Proc. U. S. Nat. Mus., vol. 18, pp. 547–550.
1896b. A preliminary list of the birds of Wayne County, Ohio. Bull. Ohio Experiment Sta., vol. 1, pp. 243–353.
1911a. A revision of the forms of the hairy woodpecker (*Dryobates villosus* [Linnaeus]). Proc. U. S. Nat. Mus., vol. 40, pp. 595–621.
1911b. A revision of the forms of the ladder-backed woodpecker (*Dryobates scalaris* [Wagler]). Proc. U. S. Nat. Mus., vol. 41, pp. 139–159.

OSGOOD, WILFRED HUDSON.
    1901. Natural history of the Queen Charlotte Islands, British Columbia.
        North Amer. Fauna, no. 21, pp. 7–50.
PALMER, WILLIAM.
    1901. The malar stripe of young flickers and the molt. Osprey, vol. 5, pp.
        102–104.
PEARSE, THEED.
    1934. Display of Harris woodpecker. Murrelet, vol. 15, pp. 25–26.
PEARSON, THOMAS GILBERT.
    1909. Nesting of the red-cockaded woodpecker. Bird-Lore, vol. 11, pp. 265–
        266.
PENNANT, THOMAS.
    1785. Arctic zoology, vol. 2.
PHELPS, FRANK MILLS.
    1914. The resident bird life of the Big Cypress Swamp region. Wilson Bull.,
        vol. 26, pp. 86–101.
PHILIPP, PHILIP BERNARD, and BOWDISH, BEECHER SCOVILLE.
    1917. Some summer birds of northern New Brunswick. Auk, vol. 34, pp.
        265–275.
    1919. Further notes on New Brunswick birds. Auk, vol. 36, pp. 36–45.
PIERCE, WRIGHT MCEWAN.
    1916. More bird notes from Big Bear Valley, San Bernardino Mountains.
        Condor, vol. 18, pp. 177–182.
POTTER, JULIAN KENT.
    1912. Red-headed woodpecker at Camden, N. J. Bird-Lore, vol. 14, pp.
        216–217.
PURDY, JAMES BRITTON.
    1900. The red-headed and other woodpeckers in Michigan in winter. Auk,
        vol. 17, p. 174.
REID, SAVILE GREY.
    1884. The birds of Bermuda. U. S. Nat. Mus. Bull. 25, pp. 163–279.
RIDGWAY, ROBERT.
    1876. Ornithology of Guadeloupe Island. Bull. Hayden Surv. Terr., vol.
        2, pp. 183–195.
    1877. United States geological exploration of the fortieth parallel. Part 3.
        Ornithology.
    1881. An unaccountable migration of the red-headed woodpecker. Bull.
        Nuttall Orn. Club, vol. 6, pp. 120–122.
    1898. The home of the ivory-bill. Osprey, vol. 3, pp. 35–36.
    1914. The birds of North and Middle America. U. S. Nat. Mus. Bull. 50,
        pt. 6.
RITTER, WILLIAM EMERSON.
    1921. Acorn-storing by the California woodpecker. Condor, vol. 23, pp.
        3–14.
    1922. Further observations on the activities of the California woodpecker.
        Condor, vol. 24, pp. 109–122.
    1938. The California woodpecker and I.
ROBERTS, THOMAS SADLER.
    1932. The birds of Minnesota, vol. 1.
SAMPSON, ELIZABETH.
    1934. Downy goes visiting. Bird-Lore, vol. 36, pp. 356–360.
SAUNDERS, ARETAS ANDREWS.
    1921. A distributional list of the birds of Montana. Pacific Coast Avifauna,
        no. 14.

1929. The summer birds of the northern Adirondack Mountains. Roosevelt Wild Life Bull., vol. 5, no. 3.

1935. A guide to bird songs.

SCOTT, WILLIAM EARL DODGE.

1881. On birds observed in Sumpter, Levy and Hillsboro Counties, Florida. Bull. Nuttall Orn. Club, vol. 6, pp. 14–21.

1886. On the avi-fauna of Pinal County, with remarks on some birds of Pima and Gila Counties, Arizona. Auk, vol. 3, pp. 421–432.

1888. Supplementary notes from the Gulf coast of Florida, with a description of a new species of marsh wren. Auk, vol. 5, pp. 183–188.

SCOVILLE, SAMUEL, Jr.

1920. The pileated woodpecker. Cassinia, for 1919, no. 23, p. 14.

SEMPLE, JOHN BONNER.

1930. Red-headed woodpeckers in migratory flight. Auk, vol. 47, pp. 84–85.

SENNETT, GEORGE BURRITT.

1879. Further notes on the ornithology of the lower Rio Grande of Texas, from observations made during the spring of 1878. Bull. U. S. Geol. and Geogr. Surv., vol. 5, pp. 371–440.

SETON, ERNEST THOMPSON.

1890. The birds of Manitoba. Proc. U. S. Nat. Mus., vol. 13, pp. 457–643.

SHARPE, VERNON, Jr.

1932. The pileated wodpecker. Migrant, vol. 3, pp. 40–41.

SHELLEY, LEWIS ORMAN.

1932. Inbreeding downy woodpeckers. Bird-Banding, vol. 3, pp. 69–70.

1933. Some notes on the hairy woodpecker. Bird-Banding, vol. 4, pp. 204–205.

SHERMAN, ALTHEA ROSINA.

1910. At the sign of the northern flicker. Wilson Bull., vol. 22, pp. 135–171.

SHERWOOD, WILLIAM E.

1927. Feeding habits of Lewis woodpecker. Condor, vol. 29, p. 171.

SIMMONS, GEORGE FINLAY.

1915. On the nesting of certain birds in Texas. Auk, vol. 32, pp. 317–331.

1925. Birds of the Austin region.

SIMPSON, RALPH B.

1910. The northern pileated woodpecker. Oologist, vol. 27, pp. 147–149.

SKINNER, MILTON PHILO.

1928. A guide to the winter birds of the North Carolina sandhills.

SMITH, AUSTIN PAUL.

1908. Some data and records from the Whetstone Mountains, Arizona. Condor, vol. 10, pp. 75–78.

SNYDER, LESTER LYNNE.

1923. On the crown markings of juvenile hairy and downy woodpeckers. Canadian Field-Nat., vol. 37, pp. 167–168.

SNYDER, LESTER LYNNE, and LOGIER, E. B. S.

1931. A faunal investigation of Long Point, and vicinity, Norfolk County, Ontario. Contrib. no. 4, Royal Ontario Mus. Zool. Reprint from Trans. Royal Canadian Inst., vol. 18, pp. 117–236.

SPIKER, CHARLES JOLLEY.

1935. A popular account of the bird life of the Finger Lakes section of New York, with main reference to the summer season. Roosevelt Wild Life Bull., vol. 6, no. 3.

SPRUNT, ALEXANDER, Jr.

1931. Unusual nesting concentration in a single tree. Auk, vol. 48, pp. 621–622.

STEARNS, WINFRID ALDEN.
1883. New England bird life. (Edited by Elliott Coues.)
STEELE, EDWARD SIMON.
1926. A three-cornered fight. Condor, vol. 28, p. 272.
STOCKARD, CHARLES RUPERT.
1904. Nesting habits of woodpeckers and vultures in Mississippi. Auk,
vol. 21, pp. 463-471.
STODDARD, HERBERT LEE.
1917. Notes on a few of the rarer birds of Sauk and Dane Counties, Wisconsin. Auk, vol. 34, pp. 63-65.
STONE, WITMER.
1909. The birds of New Jersey. Ann. Rep. New Jersey State Mus., 1908.
STONER, DAYTON.
1932. Ornithology of the Oneida Lake region: With reference to the late
spring and summer seasons. Roosevelt Wild Life Ann., vol. 2, nos.
3, 4.
STONER, EMERSON AUSTIN.
1915. Unusual red-headed woodpecker's nest. Oologist, vol. 32, p. 54.
SUCKLEY, GEORGE, and COOPER, JAMES GRAHAM.
1860. The natural history of Washington Territory and Oregon.
SUTTON, GEORGE MIKSCH.
1928a. Notes. Cardinal, vol. 2, pp. 104-105.
1928b. The birds of Pymatuning Swamp and Conneaut Lake, Crawford
County, Pennsylvania. Ann. Carnegie Mus., vol. 18, pp. 19-239.
1930. Notes on the northern pileated woodpecker in Pennsylvania. Cardinal, vol. 2, pp. 207-217.
SWAINSON, WILLIAM, and RICHARDSON, JOHN.
1831. Fauna Boreali-Americana, vol. 2. Birds.
SWARTH, HARRY SCHELWALDT.
1904. Birds of the Huachuca Mountains, Arizona. Pacific Coast Avifauna,
no. 4.
1911a. Birds and mammals of the 1909 Alexander Alaska expedition. Univ.
California Publ. Zool., vol. 7, pp. 9-172.
1911b. Description of a new hairy woodpecker from southeastern Alaska.
Univ. California Publ. Zool., vol. 7, pp. 313-318.
1917. Geographical variation in *Sphyrapicus thyroideus*. Condor, vol. 19,
pp. 62-65.
1922. Birds and mammals of the Stikine River region of northern British
Columbia and southeastern Alaska. Univ. California Publ. Zool.,
vol. 24, pp. 125-314.
1924. Birds and mammals of the Skeena River region of northern British
Columbia. Univ. California Publ. Zool., vol. 24, pp. 315-394.
1929. The faunal areas of southern Arizona: A study in animal distribution.
Proc. California Acad. Sci., vol 18, pp. 267-382.
TABER, SYDNEY RICHMOND.
1921. A bird battle. Bird-Lore, vol. 23, p. 243.
TAVERNER, PERCY ALGERNON, and SWALES, BRADSHAW HALL.
1907. The birds of Point Pelee. Wilson Bull., vol. 19, pp. 133-153.
TAYLOR, WALTER PENN.
1912. Field notes on amphibians, reptiles and birds of northern Humboldt
County, Nevada, with a discussion of some of the faunal features
of the region. Univ. California Publ. Zool., vol. 7, pp. 319-436.

TAYLOR, WALTER PENN, and SHAW, WILLIAM THOMAS.
1927. Mammals and birds of Mount Rainier National Park. National Park Service.

THAYER, JOHN ELIOT, and BANGS, OUTRAM.
1908. The present state of the ornis of Guadaloupe Island. Condor, vol. 10, pp. 101–106.

THOMPSON, JAMES MAURICE.
1885. By-ways and bird notes.
1896. An archer's sojourn in the Okefinoke. Atlantic Monthly, vol. 77, pp. 486–491.

THOMS, CRAIG S.
1927. A close-up of downy. Bird-Lore, vol. 29, pp. 417–419.

THOREAU, HENRY DAVID.
1906. Journal, 1857, edited by Bradford Torrey.

TIBBETS, ELLIOTT R.
1911. A clever trick of the downy woodpecker. Bird-Lore, vol. 13, p. 251.

TOWNSEND, CHARLES WENDELL.
1925. Notes on the nesting habits of the northern pileated woodpecker. Auk, vol. 42, pp. 132–134.
1932. Are rings of holes in tree bark made by downy woodpeckers? Condor, vol. 34, pp. 61–65.

TROTTER, SPENCER.
1903. The red-headed woodpecker as a Pennsylvania and New Jersey bird. Cassinia, no. 7, pp. 6–10.

TYLER, JOHN GRIPPER.
1913. Some birds of the Fresno District, California. Pacific Coast Avifauna, no. 9.

VAN ROSSEM, ADRIAAN, and PIERCE, WRIGHT MCEWAN.
1915. Further notes from the San Bernardino Mountains. Condor, vol. 17, pp. 163–165.

VAN TYNE, JOSSELYN.
1926. An unusual flight of Arctic three-toed woodpeckers. Auk, vol. 43, pp. 469–474.

VICKERS, ERNEST WATERS.
1910. The pileated wodpecker. Bird-Lore, vol. 12, pp. 57–59.
1915. The rolling call of the pileated woodpecker. Oologist, vol. 32, pp. 44–48.

VON BLOEKER, JACK C., Jr.
1935. Flickers and jays feeding on scarab beetles in flight. Condor, vol. 37, pp. 288–289.

WALTER, ALICE HALL.
1912. The hairy and downy woodpeckers. Bird-Lore, vol. 14, 66. 127–130.

WARD, BILLY.
1930. Red-cockaded woodpeckers on corn. Bird-Lore, vol. 32, pp. 127–128.

WARREN, BENJAMIN HARRY.
1890. Report on the birds of Pennsylvania.

WARREN, EDWARD ROYAL.
1912. Some north-central Colorado bird notes. Condor, vol. 14, pp. 81–104.

WAYNE, ARTHUR TREZEVANT.
1906. A contribution to the ornithology of South Carolina, chiefly the coast region. Auk, vol. 23, pp. 56–68.
1910. Birds of South Carolina. Contributions from the Charleston Museum, I, pp. 87–94.

WEYDEMEYER, WINTON.
    1926. Sapsuckers feeding sap to young. Auk, vol. 43, p. 236.
WEYDEMEYER, WINTON, and WEYDEMEYER, DONALD.
    1928. The woodpeckers of Lincoln County, Montana. Condor, vol. 30, pp.
        339–346.
WEYGANDT, CORNELIUS.
    1912. The summer of fire and bird adaptation. Cassinia, no. 15, pp. 28–34.
WHEELOCK, IRENE GROSVENOR.
    1904. Birds of California.
    1905. Regurgitative feeding of nestlings. Auk, vol. 22, pp. 54–70.
WHITTLE, CHARLES LIVY.
    1920. A colony of three-toed woodpeckers. Bird-Lore, vol. 22, pp. 351–352.
WILLARD, FRANCIS COTTLE.
    1912. A week afield in southern Arizona. Condor, vol. 14, pp. 53–63.
    1918. Evidence that many birds remain mated for life. Condor, vol. 20,
        pp. 167–170.
WILSON, ALEXANDER.
    1832. American ornithology, vol. 1. (1811 edition also cited.)
WOOD, JOHN CLAIRE.
    1905. Some nesting sites of the hairy woodpecker (Dryobates villosus).
        Wilson Bull., vol. 17, p. 66.
WOODS, ROBERT S.
    1932. Acquired food habits of some native birds. Condor, vol. 34, pp.
        237–240.
WRIGHT, ALBERT HAZEN, and HARPER, FRANCIS.
    1913. A biological reconnaissance of Okefinoke Swamp: The birds. Auk,
        vol. 30, pp. 477–505.
WRIGHT, HORACE WINSLOW.
    1911. The birds of the Jefferson region in the White Mountains, New
        Hampshire. Proc. Manchester Inst. Arts and Sci., vol. 5, pt. 1.
    1912. Morning awakening and even-song. Auk, vol. 29, pp. 307–327.
WRIGHT, HOWARD W.
    1908. A death struggle. Condor, vol. 10, p. 93.

INDEX

abieticola, Ceophloeus pileatus, 164, 165, 170, 171, 191.
Achilles, Laurence, on Arctic three-toed woodpecker, 106, 108, 110, 113.
aculeata, Balanosphyra formicivora, 211, 212, 223, 226.
Agersborg, G. S., on red-headed woodpecker, 196, 200.
Alaska three-toed woodpecker, 122.
albolarvatus, Dryobates albolarvatus, 97. Xenopicus, 101, 105.
albolarvatus albolarvatus, Dryobates, 97.
albolarvatus gravirostris, Dryobates, 104, 105.
Alderson, V. A., on eastern hairy woodpecker, 18.
Allen, A. A., viii, 179.
on ivory-billed woodpecker, 1.
on northern downy woodpecker, 57, 62, 64.
Allen, A. A., and Kellogg, P. P., on ivory-billed woodpecker, 3–6, 8, 10, 12.
Allen, C. A., 288.
on Cabanis's woodpecker, 34.
on northern red-breasted sapsucker, 153.
on willow woodpecker, 70.
Allen, F. H., on Arctic three-toed woodpecker, 113.
on eastern hairy woodpecker, 13, 20.
on northern downy woodpecker, 53, 64.
on northern flicker, 265–267, 279.
on northern pileated woodpecker, 174–175.
Allen, J. A., on hybrid flickers, 291.
on Lewis's woodpecker, 229.
Allen, R. P., on southern pileated woodpecker, 169.
Allert, O. P., on northern flicker, 281.
Alpine three-toed woodpecker, 124.
Amadon, Dean, viii.
American three-toed woodpecker, 116.
americanus, Picoïdes, 108, 119.
Anderson, A. H., on Gila woodpecker, 254.
Anderson, M. P., and Grinnell, Joseph, on Gairdner's woodpecker, 50.
angustifrons, Balanosphyra formicivora, 211, 212, 222.
Melanerpes, 82.
Ant-eating woodpecker, 211.
Anthony, A. W., on cardon woodpecker, 257.
on San Fernando flicker, 305, 306.

Arctic three-toed woodpecker, 106.
arcticus, Picoïdes, 106, 118, 119.
Arizona woodpecker, 91.
arizonae, Dryobates arizonae, 91.
Picus, 91.
arizonae arizonae Dryobates, 91.
arizonae fraterculus, Dryobates, 97.
Arthur, E. W., on northern pileated woodpecker, 174.
Asyndesmus lewis, 226.
Attwater, H. P., on golden-fronted woodpecker, 246.
Audubon, J. J., 30.
on Gairdner's woodpecker, 49.
on ivory-billed woodpecker, 2, 4, 5, 8, 10.
on northern downy woodpecker, 53, 57.
on pileated woodpecker, 172, 188.
on red-bellied woodpecker, 244.
on red-cockaded woodpecker, 73.
on red-headed woodpecker, 199, 203, 205.
on southern hairy woodpecker, 28.
on southern pileated woodpecker, 167, 169.
on yellow-bellied sapsucker, 127, 133.
auduboni, Dryobates villosus, 23, 27.
auratus, Colaptes, 290, 291, 295.
Colaptes auratus, 259.
auratus auratus, Colaptes, 259.
auratus luteus, Colaptes, 262–264.
aurifrons, Centurus, 245.
bacatus, Picoïdes tridactylus, 116.
Bachman, John, on southern pileated woodpecker, 169.
Bacon, C. C., on red-headed woodpecker, 197.
Bagg, C. L., 207.
Bailey, A. M., viii.
Bailey, C. E., 22.
on northern downy woodpecker, 63.
Bailey, Mrs. Florence M., on alpine three-toed woodpecker, 126.
on cactus woodpecker, 85.
on Mearns's woodpecker, 225.
on Natalie's sapsucker, 162.
on northern pileated woodpecker, 187.
on northern white-headed woodpecker, 101, 103.
on Nuttall's woodpecker, 90.
on red-shafted flicker, 289.

323

PLATES

PLATE 1

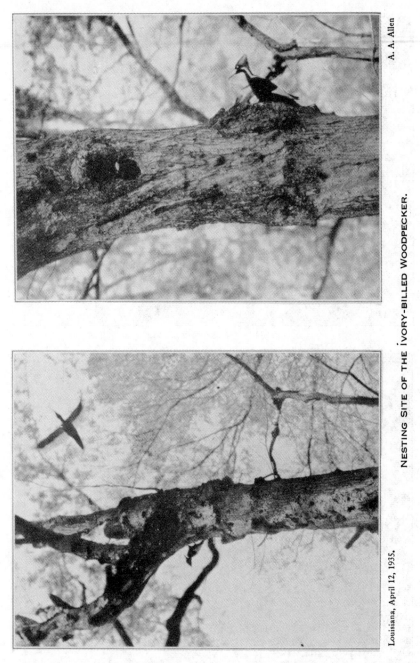

A. A. Allen

Louisiana, April 12, 1935.   NESTING SITE OF THE IVORY-BILLED WOODPECKER.

PLATE 2

Louisiana, April 12, 1935.   A. A. Allen.

IVORY-BILLED WOODPECKERS AT THEIR NEST.

PLATE 3

A. A. Allen.

Adult at nest.

EASTERN HAIRY WOODPECKER.

Owen Durfee.

Nesting site.

Rehoboth, Mass., May 10, 1907.

PLATE 4

G. D. Sprot.

Nesting site.

HARRIS'S WOODPECKER.

Vancouver Island, British Columbia, May 23, 1928.

Adult at nest.

PLATE 5

Oregon.   W. L. Finley and H. T. Bohlman.

YOUNG HARRIS'S WOODPECKER.

Duval County, Fla., May 13, 1931.   S. A. Grimes.

YOUNG SOUTHERN HAIRY WOODPECKERS.

PLATE 6

A. C. Bent.

Huachuca Mountains, Ariz., May 15, 1922.

NESTING SITES OF CHIHUAHUA WOODPECKERS.

PLATE 7

Logan County, Ill., June 10, 1913.   A. D. DuBois.

Nestling looking out and adult with food.

NORTHERN DOWNY WOODPECKER.

PLATE 8

Ithaca, N. Y.   A. A. Allen.

EGGS AND YOUNG OF NORTHERN DOWNY WOODPECKER.

PLATE 9

S. A. Grimes.

Duval County, Fla.

NESTING SITES OF RED-COCKADED WOODPECKERS.

PLATE 10

S. A. Grimes.

Duval County, Fla., May 17, 1933.

Adult at nest.

A. A. Allen.

Adult at nest.

RED-COCKADED WOODPECKERS.

PLATE 11

San Diego County, Calif., April 9, 1929.   A. C. Bent.

Nesting site.

                                                    W. L. and Irene Finley.

Adult at nest.

NUTTALL'S WOODPECKER.

PLATE 12

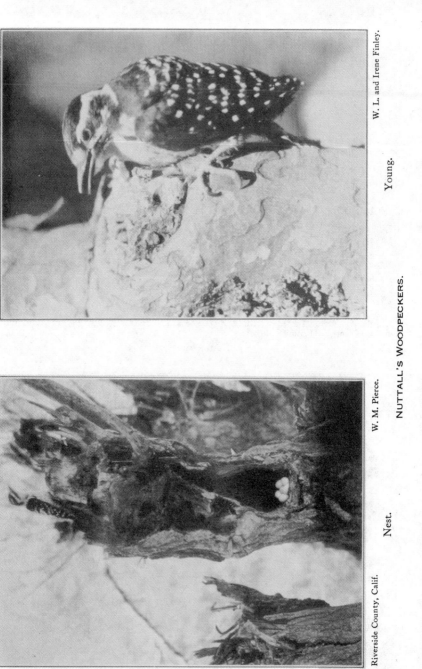

W. L. and Irene Finley.

Young.

NUTTALL'S WOODPECKERS.

W. M. Pierce.

Nest.

Riverside County, Calif.

PLATE 13

Jackson County, Oreg., May 10, 1931.

J. E. Patterson.

NESTING OF NORTHERN WHITE-HEADED WOODPECKER.

PLATE 14

Tuolumne County, Calif., June 28, 1936.   C. F. Smitl.

YOUNG NORTHERN WHITE-HEADED WOODPECKERS.

PLATE 15

J. E. Patterson.

Jackson County, Oreg., May 27, 1928.

Klamath County, Oreg., June 10, 1929.

J. E. Patterson.

NESTING OF ARCTIC THREE-TOED WOODPECKERS.

PLATE 16

New Brunswick. B. S. Bowdish.

Female at nest.

Penobscot County, Maine, June 4, 1918. F. H. Kennard.

Nesting site.

ARCTIC THREE-TOED WOODPECKER.

PLATE 17

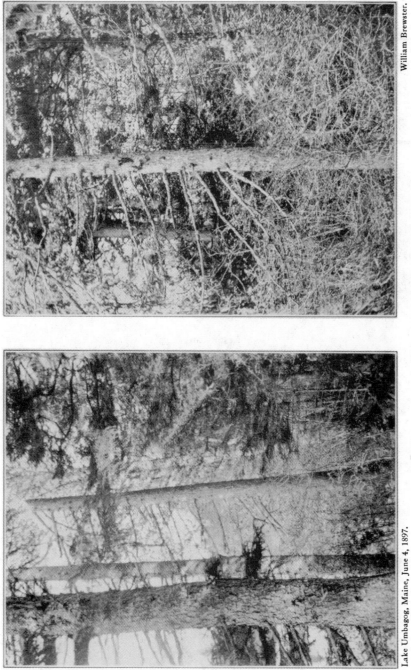

William Brewster.

Lake Umbagog, Maine, June 4, 1897.

NESTING SITE OF AMERICAN THREE-TOED WOODPECKER.

PLATE 18

A. C. Bent.

Nesting site.

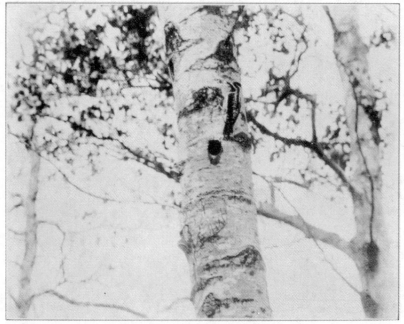

Lake Winnipegosis, Manitoba, June 1, 1913.

H. K. Job.

Adult at nest.

YELLOW-BELLIED SAPSUCKER.

PLATE 19

New Brunswick. B. S. Bowdish.

Ithaca, N. Y. A. A. Allen.

YELLOW-BELLIED SAPSUCKERS.

PLATE 20

Carver County, Minn., May 29, 1926.   A. D. DuBois.

NESTING SITE OF NORTHERN PILEATED WOODPECKER

PLATE 21

Carver County, Minn., May 8, 1936.   A. D. DuBois.

WORK OF NORTHERN PILEATED WOODPECKER.

PLATE 22

A. D. DuBois.

The entrance hole.

NORTHERN PILEATED WOODPECKER.

Carver County, Minn., June 15, 1936.

Feeding young.

PLATE 23

Near Belvidere, Alberta, June 19, 1924. R. H. Rauch.

Adult at nest.

Coos County, N. H., May 18, 1903. Owen Durfee.

Nesting site.

NORTHERN PILEATED WOODPECKER.

PLATE 24

Ithaca, N. Y.   A. A. Allen.

Approaching the nest.

Hennepin County, Minn., June 9, 1929   S. A. Grimes

Young.

NORTHERN PILEATED WOODPECKERS.

PLATE 25

A. D. DuBois.

Hennepin County, Minn., July 20, 1935.

F. R. Smith.

Fredericktown, Pa., July 18, 1920.

NESTING OF RED-HEADED WOODPECKERS.

PLATE 26

Ithaca, N. Y. A. A. Allen

NESTING OF RED-HEADED WOODPECKER.

PLATE 27

Baltimore County, Md., June 26, 1936.   M. B. Meanley, Jr.

Duval County, Fla., July 6, 1925.   S. A. Grimes.

YOUNG RED-HEADED WOODPECKERS.

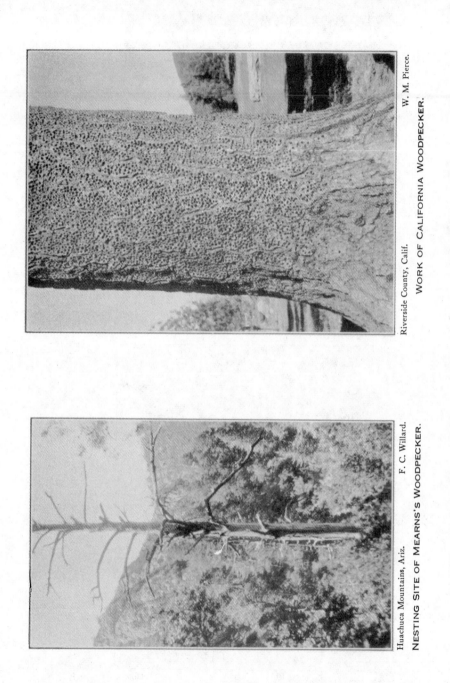

PLATE 28

Riverside County, Calif.   W. M. Pierce.

WORK OF CALIFORNIA WOODPECKER.

Huachuca Mountains, Ariz.   F. C. Willard.

NESTING SITE OF MEARNS'S WOODPECKER.

PLATE 29

Jefferson County, Colo. R. B. Rockwell.

FEMALE NATALIE'S SAPSUCKER.

W. L. Finley and H. T. Bohlman.

YOUNG LEWIS'S WOODPECKERS.

PLATE 30

S. A. Grimes.

Duval County, Fla.

NESTING SITES OF RED-BELLIED WOODPECKERS.

PLATE 31

F. N. Irving.

RED-BELLIED WOODPECKER.

PLATE 32

W. L. and Irene Finley.

Arizona.

Female at nest.

F. C. Willard.

Pima County, Ariz.

Nesting site.

GILA WOODPECKER.

PLATE 33

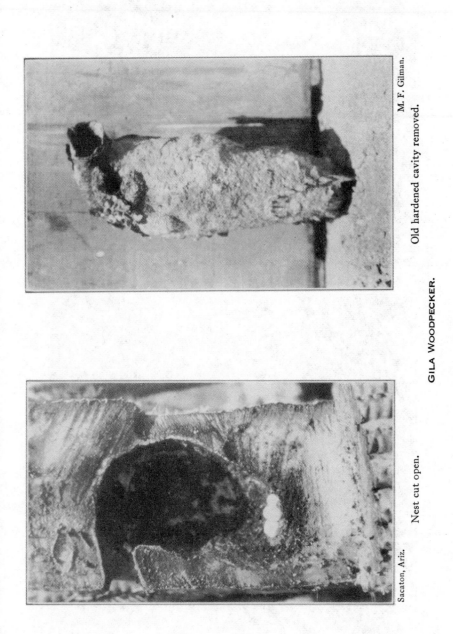

M. F. Gilman.

Old hardened cavity removed.

Sacaton, Ariz.   Nest cut open.

GILA WOODPECKER.

PLATE 34

Oracle, Ariz., December 9, 1903.   E. R. Forrest

Adult male.

W. L. and Irene Finley.

Adult female.

GILA WOODPECKER

PLATE 35

Adult male.

F. N. Irving.

St. Cloud, Fla.

A. A. Allen.

Nest in palmetto stub.

SOUTHERN FLICKER.

PLATE 36

Brunswick, Maine, June 18, 1932.   R. S. Palmer.

Nestling 26 hours old.

Illinois.   Cordelia J. Stanwood.

Nestling almost ready to leave the nest.

NORTHERN FLICKERS.

PLATE 37

J. E. Patterson.

Klamath County, Oreg., May 10, 1934.

Nest.

Alexander Walker.

Mulino, Oreg., December 10, 1913.

Adult male.

RED-SHAFTED FLICKER.

PLATE 38

W. L. Finley and H. T. Bohlman.

Young just out of the nest.

NORTHWESTERN FLICKERS.

Adult female.

PLATE 39

F. C. Willard.

M. F. Gilman.

Pima County, Ariz.

Sacaton, Ariz.

Nesting site.

Nest cut open.

MEARNS'S GILDED FLICKER.

A CATALOGUE OF SELECTED DOVER BOOKS
IN ALL FIELDS OF INTEREST

A CATALOGUE OF SELECTED DOVER BOOKS
IN ALL FIELDS OF INTEREST

AMERICA'S OLD MASTERS, James T. Flexner. Four men emerged unexpectedly from provincial 18th century America to leadership in European art: Benjamin West, J. S. Copley, C. R. Peale, Gilbert Stuart. Brilliant coverage of lives and contributions. Revised, 1967 edition. 69 plates. 365pp. of text.

21806-6 Paperbound $3.00

FIRST FLOWERS OF OUR WILDERNESS: AMERICAN PAINTING, THE COLONIAL PERIOD, James T. Flexner. Painters, and regional painting traditions from earliest Colonial times up to the emergence of Copley, West and Peale Sr., Foster, Gustavus Hesselius, Feke, John Smibert and many anonymous painters in the primitive manner. Engaging presentation, with 162 illustrations. xxii + 368pp.

22180-6 Paperbound $3.50

THE LIGHT OF DISTANT SKIES: AMERICAN PAINTING, 1760-1835, James T. Flexner. The great generation of early American painters goes to Europe to learn and to teach: West, Copley, Gilbert Stuart and others. Allston, Trumbull, Morse; also contemporary American painters—primitives, derivatives, academics—who remained in America. 102 illustrations. xiii + 306pp. 22179-2 Paperbound $3.50

A HISTORY OF THE RISE AND PROGRESS OF THE ARTS OF DESIGN IN THE UNITED STATES, William Dunlap. Much the richest mine of information on early American painters, sculptors, architects, engravers, miniaturists, etc. The only source of information for scores of artists, the major primary source for many others. Unabridged reprint of rare original 1834 edition, with new introduction by James T. Flexner, and 394 new illustrations. Edited by Rita Weiss. 6⅝ x 9⅝.

21695-0, 21696-9, 21697-7 Three volumes, Paperbound $15.00

EPOCHS OF CHINESE AND JAPANESE ART, Ernest F. Fenollosa. From primitive Chinese art to the 20th century, thorough history, explanation of every important art period and form, including Japanese woodcuts; main stress on China and Japan, but Tibet, Korea also included. Still unexcelled for its detailed, rich coverage of cultural background, aesthetic elements, diffusion studies, particularly of the historical period. 2nd, 1913 edition. 242 illustrations. lii + 439pp. of text.

20364-6, 20365-4 Two volumes, Paperbound $6.00

THE GENTLE ART OF MAKING ENEMIES, James A. M. Whistler. Greatest wit of his day deflates Oscar Wilde, Ruskin, Swinburne; strikes back at inane critics, exhibitions, art journalism; aesthetics of impressionist revolution in most striking form. Highly readable classic by great painter. Reproduction of edition designed by Whistler. Introduction by Alfred Werner. xxxvi + 334pp.

21875-9 Paperbound $3.00

VISUAL ILLUSIONS: THEIR CAUSES, CHARACTERISTICS, AND APPLICATIONS, Matthew Luckiesh. Thorough description and discussion of optical illusion, geometric and perspective, particularly; size and shape distortions, illusions of color, of motion; natural illusions; use of illusion in art and magic, industry, etc. Most useful today with op art, also for classical art. Scores of·effects illustrated. Introduction by William H. Ittleson. 100 illustrations. xxi + 252pp.

21530-X Paperbound $2.00

A HANDBOOK OF ANATOMY FOR ART STUDENTS, Arthur Thomson. Thorough, virtually exhaustive coverage of skeletal structure, musculature, etc. Full text, supplemented by anatomical diagrams and drawings and by photographs of undraped figures. Unique in its comparison of male and female forms, pointing out differences of contour, texture, form. 211 figures, 40 drawings, 86 photographs. xx + 459pp. 5⅜ x 8⅜.

21163-0 Paperbound $3.50

150 MASTERPIECES OF DRAWING, Selected by Anthony Toney. Full page reproductions of drawings from the early 16th to the end of the 18th century, all beautifully reproduced: Rembrandt, Michelangelo, Dürer, Fragonard, Urs, Graf, Wouwerman, many others. First-rate browsing book, model book for artists. xviii + 150pp. 8⅜ x 11¼.

21032-4 Paperbound' $2.50

THE LATER WORK OF AUBREY BEARDSLEY, Aubrey Beardsley. Exotic, erotic, ironic masterpieces in full maturity: Comedy Ballet, Venus and Tannhauser, Pierrot, Lysistrata, Rape of the Lock, Savoy material, Ali Baba, Volpone, etc. This material revolutionized the art world, and is still powerful, fresh, brilliant. With *The Early Work,* all Beardsley's finest work. 174 plates, 2 in color. xiv + 176pp. 8⅛ x 11.

21817-1 Paperbound $3.75

DRAWINGS OF REMBRANDT, Rembrandt van Rijn. Complete reproduction of fabulously rare edition by Lippmann and Hofstede de Groot, completely reedited, updated, improved by Prof. Seymour Slive, Fogg Museum. Portraits, Biblical sketches, landscapes, Oriental types, nudes, episodes from classical mythology—All Rembrandt's fertile genius. Also selection of drawings by his pupils and followers. "Stunning volumes," *Saturday Review.* 550 illustrations. lxxviii + 552pp. 9⅛ x 12¼.

21485-0, 21486-9 Two volumes, Paperbound $10.00

THE DISASTERS OF WAR, Francisco Goya. One of the masterpieces of Western civilization—83 etchings that record Goya's shattering, bitter reaction to the Napoleonic war that swept through Spain after the insurrection of 1808 and to war in general. Reprint of the first edition, with three additional plates from Boston's Museum of Fine Arts. All plates facsimile size. Introduction by Philip Hofer, Fogg Museum. v + 97pp. 9⅜ x 8¼.

21872-4 Paperbound $2.50

GRAPHIC WORKS OF ODILON REDON. Largest collection of Redon's graphic works ever assembled: 172 lithographs, 28 etchings and engravings, 9 drawings. These include some of his most famous works. All the plates from *Odilon Redon: oeuvre graphique complet,* plus additional plates. New introduction and caption translations by Alfred Werner. 209 illustrations. xxvii + 209pp. 9⅛ x 12¼.

21966-8 Paperbound $4.50

DESIGN BY ACCIDENT; A BOOK OF "ACCIDENTAL EFFECTS" FOR ARTISTS AND DESIGNERS, James F. O'Brien. Create your own unique, striking, imaginative effects by "controlled accident" interaction of materials: paints and lacquers, oil and water based paints, splatter, crackling materials, shatter, similar items. Everything you do will be different; first book on this limitless art, so useful to both fine artist and commercial artist. Full instructions. 192 plates showing "accidents," 8 in color. viii + 215pp. 8⅜ x 11¼. 21942-9 Paperbound $3.75

THE BOOK OF SIGNS, Rudolf Koch. Famed German type designer draws 493 beautiful symbols: religious, mystical, alchemical, imperial, property marks, runes, etc. Remarkable fusion of traditional and modern. Good for suggestions of timelessness, smartness, modernity. Text. vi + 104pp. 6⅛ x 9¼.
20162-7 Paperbound $1.50

HISTORY OF INDIAN AND INDONESIAN ART, Ananda K. Coomaraswamy. An unabridged republication of one of the finest books by a great scholar in Eastern art. Rich in descriptive material, history, social backgrounds; Sunga reliefs, Rajput paintings, Gupta temples, Burmese frescoes, textiles, jewelry, sculpture, etc. 400 photos. viii + 423pp. 6⅜ x 9¾. 21436-2 Paperbound $5.00

PRIMITIVE ART, Franz Boas. America's foremost anthropologist surveys textiles, ceramics, woodcarving, basketry, metalwork, etc.; patterns, technology, creation of symbols, style origins. All areas of world, but very full on Northwest Coast Indians. More than 350 illustrations of baskets, boxes, totem poles, weapons, etc. 378 pp.
20025-6 Paperbound $3.00

THE GENTLEMAN AND CABINET MAKER'S DIRECTOR, Thomas Chippendale. Full reprint (third edition, 1762) of most influential furniture book of all time, by master cabinetmaker. 200 plates, illustrating chairs, sofas, mirrors, tables, cabinets, plus 24 photographs of surviving pieces. Biographical introduction by N. Bienenstock. vi + 249pp. 9⅞ x 12¾. 21601-2 Paperbound $5.00

AMERICAN ANTIQUE FURNITURE, Edgar G. Miller, Jr. The basic coverage of all American furniture before 1840. Individual chapters cover type of furniture—clocks, tables, sideboards, etc.—chronologically, with inexhaustible wealth of data. More than 2100 photographs, all identified, commented on. Essential to all early American collectors. Introduction by H. E. Keyes. vi + 1106pp. 7⅞ x 10¾.
21599-7, 21600-4 Two volumes, Paperbound $11.00

PENNSYLVANIA DUTCH AMERICAN FOLK ART, Henry J. Kauffman. 279 photos, 28 drawings of tulipware, Fraktur script, painted tinware, toys, flowered furniture, quilts, samplers, hex signs, house interiors, etc. Full descriptive text. Excellent for tourist, rewarding for designer, collector. Map. 146pp. 7⅞ x 10¾.
21205-X Paperbound $3.00

EARLY NEW ENGLAND GRAVESTONE RUBBINGS, Edmund V. Gillon, Jr. 43 photographs, 226 carefully reproduced rubbings show heavily symbolic, sometimes macabre early gravestones, up to early 19th century. Remarkable early American primitive art, occasionally strikingly beautiful; always powerful. Text. xxvi + 207pp. 8⅜ x 11¼. 21380-3 Paperbound $4.00

ALPHABETS AND ORNAMENTS, Ernst Lehner. Well-known pictorial source for decorative alphabets, script examples, cartouches, frames, decorative title pages, calligraphic initials, borders, similar material. 14th to 19th century, mostly European. Useful in almost any graphic arts designing, varied styles. 750 illustrations. 256pp. 7 x 10.   21905-4 Paperbound $4.00

PAINTING: A CREATIVE APPROACH, Norman Colquhoun. For the beginner simple guide provides an instructive approach to painting: major stumbling blocks for beginner; overcoming them, technical points; paints and pigments; oil painting; watercolor and other media and color. New section on "plastic" paints. Glossary. Formerly *Paint Your Own Pictures*. 221pp.   22000-1 Paperbound $1.75

THE ENJOYMENT AND USE OF COLOR, Walter Sargent. Explanation of the relations between colors themselves and between colors in nature and art, including hundreds of little-known facts about color values, intensities, effects of high and low illumination, complementary colors. Many practical hints for painters, references to great masters. 7 color plates, 29 illustrations. x + 274pp.
                                                  20944-X Paperbound $3.00

THE NOTEBOOKS OF LEONARDO DA VINCI, compiled and edited by Jean Paul Richter. 1566 extracts from original manuscripts reveal the full range of Leonardo's versatile genius: all his writings on painting, sculpture, architecture, anatomy, astronomy, geography, topography, physiology, mining, music, etc., in both Italian and English, with 186 plates of manuscript pages and more than 500 additional drawings. Includes studies for the Last Supper, the lost Sforza monument, and other works. Total of xlvii + 866pp. 7⅞ x 10¾.
                                  22572-0, 22573-9 Two volumes, Paperbound $12.00

MONTGOMERY WARD CATALOGUE OF 1895. Tea gowns, yards of flannel and pillow-case lace, stereoscopes, books of gospel hymns, the New Improved Singer Sewing Machine, side saddles, milk skimmers, straight-edged razors, high-button shoes, spittoons, and on and on . . . listing some 25,000 items, practically all illustrated. Essential to the shoppers of the 1890's, it is our truest record of the spirit of the period. Unaltered reprint of Issue No. 57, Spring and Summer 1895. Introduction by Boris Emmet. Innumerable illustrations. xiii + 624pp. 8½ x 11⅝.
                                                  22377-9 Paperbound $8.50

THE CRYSTAL PALACE EXHIBITION ILLUSTRATED CATALOGUE (LONDON, 1851). One of the wonders of the modern world—the Crystal Palace Exhibition in which all the nations of the civilized world exhibited their achievements in the arts and sciences—presented in an equally important illustrated catalogue. More than 1700 items pictured with accompanying text—ceramics, textiles, cast-iron work, carpets, pianos, sleds, razors, wall-papers, billiard tables, beehives, silverware and hundreds of other artifacts—represent the focal point of Victorian culture in the Western World. Probably the largest collection of Victorian decorative art ever assembled— indispensable for antiquarians and designers. Unabridged republication of the Art-Journal Catalogue of the Great Exhibition of 1851, with all terminal essays. New introduction by John Gloag, F.S.A. xxxiv + 426pp. 9 x 12.
                                                  22503-8 Paperbound $5.00

A History of Costume, Carl Köhler. Definitive history, based on surviving pieces of clothing primarily, and paintings, statues, etc. secondarily. Highly readable text, supplemented by 594 illustrations of costumes of the ancient Mediterranean peoples, Greece and Rome, the Teutonic prehistoric period; costumes of the Middle Ages, Renaissance, Baroque, 18th and 19th centuries. Clear, measured patterns are provided for many clothing articles. Approach is practical throughout. Enlarged by Emma von Sichart. 464pp.   21030-8 Paperbound $3.50

Oriental Rugs, Antique and Modern, Walter A. Hawley. A complete and authoritative treatise on the Oriental rug—where they are made, by whom and how, designs and symbols, characteristics in detail of the six major groups, how to distinguish them and how to buy them. Detailed technical data is provided on periods, weaves, warps, wefts, textures, sides, ends and knots, although no technical background is required for an understanding. 11 color plates, 80 halftones, 4 maps. vi + 320pp. 6⅛ x 9⅛.   22366-3 Paperbound $5.00

Ten Books on Architecture, Vitruvius. By any standards the most important book on architecture ever written. Early Roman discussion of aesthetics of building, construction methods, orders, sites, and every other aspect of architecture has inspired, instructed architecture for about 2,000 years. Stands behind Palladio, Michelangelo, Bramante, Wren, countless others. Definitive Morris H. Morgan translation. 68 illustrations. xii + 331pp.   20645-9 Paperbound .$3.00

The Four Books of Architecture, Andrea Palladio. Translated into every major Western European language in the two centuries following its publication in 1570, this has been one of the most influential books in the history of architecture. Complete reprint of the 1738 Isaac Ware edition. New introduction by Adolf Placzek, Columbia Univ. 216 plates. xxii + 110pp. of text. 9½ x 12¾.
                          21308-0 Clothbound $12.50

Sticks and Stones: A Study of American Architecture and Civilization, Lewis Mumford.One of the great classics of American cultural history. American architecture from the medieval-inspired earliest forms to the early 20th century; evolution of structure and style, and reciprocal influences on environment. 21 photographic illustrations. 238pp.   20202-X Paperbound $2.00

The American Builder's Companion, Asher Benjamin. The most widely used early 19th century architectural style and source book, for colonial up into Greek Revival periods. Extensive development of geometry of carpentering, construction of sashes, frames, doors, stairs; plans and elevations of domestic and other buildings. Hundreds of thousands of houses were built according to this book, now invaluable to historians, architects, restorers, etc. 1827 edition. 59 plates. 114pp. 7⅞ x 10¾
                          22236-5 Paperbound $4.00

Dutch Houses in the Hudson Valley Before 1776, Helen Wilkinson Reynolds. The standard survey of the Dutch colonial house and outbuildings, with constructional features, decoration, and local history associated with individual homesteads. Introduction by Franklin D. Roosevelt. Map. 150 illustrations. 469pp. 6⅝ x 9¼.   21469-9 Paperbound $5.00

THE ARCHITECTURE OF COUNTRY HOUSES, Andrew J. Downing. Together with Vaux's *Villas and Cottages* this is the basic book for Hudson River Gothic architecture of the middle Victorian period. Full, sound discussions of general aspects of housing, architecture, style, decoration, furnishing, together with scores of detailed house plans, illustrations of specific buildings, accompanied by full text. Perhaps the most influential single American architectural book. 1850 edition. Introduction by J. Stewart Johnson. 321 figures, 34 architectural designs. xvi + 560pp.
22003-6 Paperbound $5.00

LOST EXAMPLES OF COLONIAL ARCHITECTURE, John Mead Howells. Full-page photographs of buildings that have disappeared or been so altered as to be denatured, including many designed by major early American architects. 245 plates. xvii + 248pp. 7⅞ x 10¾.
21143-6 Paperbound $3.50

DOMESTIC ARCHITECTURE OF THE AMERICAN COLONIES AND OF THE EARLY REPUBLIC, Fiske Kimball. Foremost architect and restorer of Williamsburg and Monticello covers nearly 200 homes between 1620-1825. Architectural details, construction, style features, special fixtures, floor plans, etc. Generally considered finest work in its area. 219 illustrations of houses, doorways, windows, capital mantels. xx + 314pp. 7⅞ x 10¾.
21743-4 Paperbound $4.00

EARLY AMERICAN ROOMS: 1650-1858, edited by Russell Hawes Kettell. Tour of 12 rooms, each representative of a different era in American history and each furnished, decorated, designed and occupied in the style of the era. 72 plans and elevations, 8-page color section, etc., show fabrics, wall papers, arrangements, etc. Full descriptive text. xvii + 200pp. of text. 8⅜ x 11¼.
21633-0 Paperbound $5.00

THE FITZWILLIAM VIRGINAL BOOK, edited by J. Fuller Maitland and W. B. Squire. Full modern printing of famous early 17th-century ms. volume of 300 works by Morley, Byrd, Bull, Gibbons, etc. For piano or other modern keyboard instrument; easy to read format. xxxvi + 938pp. 8⅜ x 11.
21068-5, 21069-3 Two volumes, Paperbound $12.00

KEYBOARD MUSIC, Johann Sebastian Bach. Bach Gesellschaft edition. A rich selection of Bach's masterpieces for the harpsichord: the six English Suites, six French Suites, the six Partitas (Clavierübung part I), the Goldberg Variations (Clavierübung part IV), the fifteen Two-Part Inventions and the fifteen Three-Part Sinfonias. Clearly reproduced on large sheets with ample margins; eminently playable. vi + 312pp. 8⅛ x 11.
22360-4 Paperbound $5.00

THE MUSIC OF BACH: AN INTRODUCTION, Charles Sanford Terry. A fine, nontechnical introduction to Bach's music, both instrumental and vocal. Covers organ music, chamber music, passion music, other types. Analyzes themes, developments, innovations. x + 114pp.
21075-8 Paperbound $1.95

BEETHOVEN AND HIS NINE SYMPHONIES, Sir George Grove. Noted British musicologist provides best history, analysis, commentary on symphonies. Very thorough, rigorously accurate; necessary to both advanced student and amateur music lover. 436 musical passages. vii + 407 pp.
20334-4 Paperbound $4.00

JOHANN SEBASTIAN BACH, Philipp Spitta. One of the great classics of musicology, this definitive analysis of Bach's music (and life) has never been surpassed. Lucid, nontechnical analyses of hundreds of pieces (30 pages devoted to St. Matthew Passion, 26 to B Minor Mass). Also includes major analysis of 18th-century music. 450 musical examples. 40-page musical supplement. Total of xx + 1799pp.
(EUK) 22278-0, 22279-9 Two volumes, Clothbound $25.00

MOZART AND HIS PIANO CONCERTOS, Cuthbert Girdlestone. The only full-length study of an important area of Mozart's creativity. Provides detailed analyses of all 23 concertos, traces inspirational sources. 417 musical examples. Second edition. 509pp.
21271-8 Paperbound $4.50

THE PERFECT WAGNERITE: A COMMENTARY ON THE NIBLUNG'S RING, George Bernard Shaw. Brilliant and still relevant criticism in remarkable essays on Wagner's Ring cycle, Shaw's ideas on political and social ideology behind the plots, role of Leitmotifs, vocal requisites, etc. Prefaces. xxi + 136pp.
(USO) 21707-8 Paperbound $1.75

DON GIOVANNI, W. A. Mozart. Complete libretto, modern English translation; biographies of composer and librettist; accounts of early performances and critical reaction. Lavishly illustrated. All the material you need to understand and appreciate this great work. Dover Opera Guide and Libretto Series; translated and introduced by Ellen Bleiler. 92 illustrations. 209pp.
21134-7 Paperbound $2.00

BASIC ELECTRICITY, U. S. Bureau of Naval Personel. Originally a training course, best non-technical coverage of basic theory of electricity and its applications. Fundamental concepts, batteries, circuits, conductors and wiring techniques, AC and DC, inductance and capacitance, generators, motors, transformers, magnetic amplifiers, synchros, servomechanisms, etc. Also covers blue-prints, electrical diagrams, etc. Many questions, with answers. 349 illustrations. x + 448pp. 6½ x 9¼.
20973-3 Paperbound $3.50

REPRODUCTION OF SOUND, Edgar Villchur. Thorough coverage for laymen of high fidelity systems, reproducing systems in general, needles, amplifiers, preamps, loudspeakers, feedback, explaining physical background. "A rare talent for making technicalities vividly comprehensible," R. Darrell, *High Fidelity*. 69 figures iv + 92pp.
21515-6 Paperbound $1.35

HEAR ME TALKIN' TO YA: THE STORY OF JAZZ AS TOLD BY THE MEN WHO MADE IT, Nat Shapiro and Nat Hentoff. Louis Armstrong, Fats Waller, Jo Jones, Clarence Williams, Billy Holiday, Duke Ellington, Jelly Roll Morton and dozens of other jazz greats tell how it was in Chicago's South Side, New Orleans, depression Harlem and the modern West Coast as jazz was born and grew. xvi + 429pp.
21726-4 Paperbound $3.95

FABLES OF AESOP, translated by Sir Roger L'Estrange. A reproduction of the very rare 1931 Paris edition; a selection of the most interesting fables, together with 50 imaginative drawings by Alexander Calder. v + 128pp. 6½x9¼.
21780-9 Paperbound $1.50

"ESSENTIAL GRAMMAR" SERIES

All you really need to know about modern, colloquial grammar. Many educational shortcuts help you learn faster, understand better. Detailed cognate lists teach you to recognize similarities between English and foreign words and roots—make learning vocabulary easy and interesting. Excellent for independent study or as a supplement to record courses.

ESSENTIAL FRENCH GRAMMAR, Seymour Resnick. 2500-item cognate list. 159pp.
(EBE) 20419-7 Paperbound $1.50

ESSENTIAL GERMAN GRAMMAR, Guy Stern and Everett F. Bleiler. Unusual shortcuts on noun declension, word order, compound verbs. 124pp.
(EBE) 20422-7 Paperbound $1.25

ESSENTIAL ITALIAN GRAMMAR, Olga Ragusa. 111pp.
(EBE) 20779-X Paperbound $1.25

ESSENTIAL JAPANESE GRAMMAR, Everett F. Bleiler. In Romaji transcription; no characters needed. Japanese grammar is regular and simple. 156pp.
21027-8 Paperbound $1.50

ESSENTIAL PORTUGUESE GRAMMAR, Alexander da R. Prista. vi + 114pp.
21650-0 Paperbound $1.35

ESSENTIAL SPANISH GRAMMAR, Seymour Resnick. 2500 word cognate list. 115pp.
(EBE) 20780-3 Paperbound $1.25

ESSENTIAL ENGLISH GRAMMAR, Philip Gucker. Combines best features of modern, functional and traditional approaches. For refresher, class use, home study. x + 177pp.
21649-7 Paperbound $1.75

A PHRASE AND SENTENCE DICTIONARY OF SPOKEN SPANISH. Prepared for U. S. War Department by U. S. linguists. As above, unit is idiom, phrase or sentence rather than word. English-Spanish and Spanish-English sections contain modern equivalents of over 18,000 sentences. Introduction and appendix as above. iv + 513pp.
20495-2 Paperbound $3.50

A PHRASE AND SENTENCE DICTIONARY OF SPOKEN RUSSIAN. Dictionary prepared for U. S. War Department by U. S. linguists. Basic unit is not the word, but the idiom, phrase or sentence. English-Russian and Russian-English sections contain modern equivalents for over 30,000 phrases. Grammatical introduction covers phonetics, writing, syntax. Appendix of word lists for food, numbers, geographical names, etc. vi + 573 pp. 6⅛ x 9¼.
20496-0 Paperbound $5.50

CONVERSATIONAL CHINESE FOR BEGINNERS, Morris Swadesh. Phonetic system, beginner's course in Pai Hua Mandarin Chinese covering most important, most useful speech patterns. Emphasis on modern colloquial usage. Formerly *Chinese in Your Pocket*. xvi + 158pp.
21123-1 Paperbound $1.75

AGAINST THE GRAIN (A REBOURS), Joris K. Huysmans. Filled with weird images, evidences of a bizarre imagination, exotic experiments with hallucinatory drugs, rich tastes and smells and the diversions of its sybarite hero Duc Jean des Esseintes, this classic novel pushed 19th-century literary decadence to its limits. Full unabridged edition. Do not confuse this with abridged editions generally sold. Introduction by Havelock Ellis. xlix + 206pp.   22190-3 Paperbound $2.50

VARIORUM SHAKESPEARE: HAMLET. Edited by Horace H. Furness; a landmark of American scholarship. Exhaustive footnotes and appendices treat all doubtful words and phrases, as well as suggested critical emendations throughout the play's history. First volume contains editor's own text, collated with all Quartos and Folios. Second volume contains full first Quarto, translations of Shakespeare's sources (Belleforest, and Saxo Grammaticus), Der Bestrafte Brudermord, and many essays on critical and historical points of interest by major authorities of past and present. Includes details of staging and costuming over the years. By far the best edition available for serious students of Shakespeare. Total of xx + 905pp.
21004-9, 21005-7, 2 volumes, Paperbound $7.00

A LIFE OF WILLIAM SHAKESPEARE, Sir Sidney Lee. This is the standard life of Shakespeare, summarizing everything known about Shakespeare and his plays. Incredibly rich in material, broad in coverage, clear and judicious, it has served thousands as the best introduction to Shakespeare. 1931 edition. 9 plates. xxix + 792pp.   21967-4 Paperbound $4.50

MASTERS OF THE DRAMA, John Gassner. Most comprehensive history of the drama in print, covering every tradition from Greeks to modern Europe and America, including India, Far East, etc. Covers more than 800 dramatists, 2000 plays, with biographical material, plot summaries, theatre history, criticism, etc. "Best of its kind in English," *New Republic*. 77 illustrations. xxii + 890pp.
20100-7 Clothbound $10.00

THE EVOLUTION OF THE ENGLISH LANGUAGE, George McKnight. The growth of English, from the 14th century to the present. Unusual, non-technical account presents basic information in very interesting form: sound shifts, change in grammar and syntax, vocabulary growth, similar topics. Abundantly illustrated with quotations. Formerly *Modern English in the Making*. xii + 590pp.
21932-1 Paperbound $3.50

AN ETYMOLOGICAL DICTIONARY OF MODERN ENGLISH, Ernest Weekley. Fullest, richest work of its sort, by foremost British lexicographer. Detailed word histories, including many colloquial and archaic words; extensive quotations. Do not confuse this with the Concise Etymological Dictionary, which is much abridged. Total of xxvii + 830pp. 6½ x 9¼.
21873-2, 21874-0 Two volumes, Paperbound $7.90

FLATLAND: A ROMANCE OF MANY DIMENSIONS, E. A. Abbott. Classic of science-fiction explores ramifications of life in a two-dimensional world, and what happens when a three-dimensional being intrudes. Amusing reading, but also useful as introduction to thought about hyperspace. Introduction by Banesh Hoffmann. 16 illustrations. xx + 103pp.   20001-9 Paperbound $1.00

INCIDENTS OF TRAVEL IN YUCATAN, John L. Stephens. Classic (1843) exploration of jungles of Yucatan, looking for evidences of Maya civilization. Stephens found many ruins; comments on travel adventures, Mexican and Indian culture. 127 striking illustrations by F. Catherwood. Total of 669 pp.

20926-1, 20927-X Two volumes, Paperbound $5.50

INCIDENTS OF TRAVEL IN CENTRAL AMERICA, CHIAPAS, AND YUCATAN, John L. Stephens. An exciting travel journal and an important classic of archeology. Narrative relates his almost single-handed discovery of the Mayan culture, and exploration of the ruined cities of Copan, Palenque, Utatlan and others; the monuments they dug from the earth, the temples buried in the jungle, the customs of poverty-stricken Indians living a stone's throw from the ruined palaces. 115 drawings by F. Catherwood. Portrait of Stephens. xii + 812pp.

22404-X, 22405-8 Two volumes, Paperbound $6.00

A NEW VOYAGE ROUND THE WORLD, William Dampier. Late 17-century naturalist joined the pirates of the Spanish Main to gather information; remarkably vivid account of buccaneers, pirates; detailed, accurate account of botany, zoology, ethnography of lands visited. Probably the most important early English voyage, enormous implications for British exploration, trade, colonial policy. Also most interesting reading. Argonaut edition, introduction by Sir Albert Gray. New introduction by Percy Adams. 6 plates, 7 illustrations. xlvii + 376pp. 6½ x 9¼.

21900-3 Paperbound $3.00

INTERNATIONAL AIRLINE PHRASE BOOK IN SIX LANGUAGES, Joseph W. Bátor. Important phrases and sentences in English paralleled with French, German, Portuguese, Italian, Spanish equivalents, covering all possible airport-travel situations; created for airline personnel as well as tourist by Language Chief, Pan American Airlines. xiv + 204pp.

22017-6 Paperbound $2.25

STAGE COACH AND TAVERN DAYS, Alice Morse Earle. Detailed, lively account of the early days of taverns; their uses and importance in the social, political and military life; furnishings and decorations; locations; food and drink; tavern signs, etc. Second half covers every aspect of early travel; the roads, coaches, drivers, etc. Nostalgic, charming, packed with fascinating material. 157 illustrations, mostly photographs. xiv + 449pp.

22518-6 Paperbound $4.00

NORSE DISCOVERIES AND EXPLORATIONS IN NORTH AMERICA, Hjalmar R. Holand. The perplexing Kensington Stone, found in Minnesota at the end of the 19th century. Is it a record of a Scandinavian expedition to North America in the 14th century? Or is it one of the most successful hoaxes in history. A scientific detective investigation. Formerly *Westward from Vinland*. 31 photographs, 17 figures. x + 354pp.

22014-1 Paperbound $2.75

A BOOK OF OLD MAPS, compiled and edited by Emerson D. Fite and Archibald Freeman. 74 old maps offer an unusual survey of the discovery, settlement and growth of America down to the close of the Revolutionary war: maps showing Norse settlements in Greenland, the explorations of Columbus, Verrazano, Cabot, Champlain, Joliet, Drake, Hudson, etc., campaigns of Revolutionary war battles, and much more. Each map is accompanied by a brief historical essay. xvi + 299pp. 11 x 13¾.

22084-2 Paperbound $7.00

LAST AND FIRST MEN AND STAR MAKER, TWO SCIENCE FICTION NOVELS, Olaf Stapledon. Greatest future histories in science fiction. In the first, human intelligence is the "hero," through strange paths of evolution, interplanetary invasions, incredible technologies, near extinctions and reemergences. Star Maker describes the quest of a band of star rovers for intelligence itself, through time and space: weird inhuman civilizations, crustacean minds, symbiotic worlds, etc. Complete, unabridged. v + 438pp. (USO) 21962-3 Paperbound $3.00

THREE PROPHETIC NOVELS, H. G. WELLS. Stages of a consistently planned future for mankind. *When the Sleeper Wakes,* and *A Story of the Days to Come,* anticipate *Brave New World* and *1984,* in the 21st Century; *The Time Machine,* only complete version in print, shows farther future and the end of mankind. All show Wells's greatest gifts as storyteller and novelist. Edited by E. F. Bleiler. x + 335pp. (USO) 20605-X Paperbound $3.00

THE DEVIL'S DICTIONARY, Ambrose Bierce. America's own Oscar Wilde— Ambrose Bierce—offers his barbed iconoclastic wisdom in over 1,000 definitions hailed by H. L. Mencken as "some of the most gorgeous witticisms in the English language." 145pp. 20487-1 Paperbound $1.50

MAX AND MORITZ, Wilhelm Busch. Great children's classic, father of comic strip, of two bad boys, Max and Moritz. Also Ker and Plunk (Plisch und Plumm), Cat and Mouse, Deceitful Henry, Ice-Peter, The Boy and the Pipe, and five other pieces. Original German, with English translation. Edited by H. Arthur Klein; translations by various hands and H. Arthur Klein. vi + 216pp. 20181-3 Paperbound $2.00

PIGS IS PIGS AND OTHER FAVORITES, Ellis Parker Butler. The title story is one of the best humor short stories, as Mike Flannery obfuscates biology and English. Also included, That Pup of Murchison's, The Great American Pie Company, and Perkins of Portland. 14 illustrations. v + 109pp. 21532-6 Paperbound $1.50

THE PETERKIN PAPERS, Lucretia P. Hale. It takes genius to be as stupidly mad as the Peterkins, as they decide to become wise, celebrate the "Fourth," keep a cow, and otherwise strain the resources of the Lady from Philadelphia. Basic book of American humor. 153 illustrations. 219pp. 20794-3 Paperbound $2.00

PERRAULT'S FAIRY TALES, translated by A. E. Johnson and S. R. Littlewood, with 34 full-page illustrations by Gustave Doré. All the original Perrault stories— Cinderella, Sleeping Beauty, Bluebeard, Little Red Riding Hood, Puss in Boots, Tom Thumb, etc.—with their witty verse morals and the magnificent illustrations of Doré. One of the five or six great books of European fairy tales. viii + 117pp. 8⅛ x 11. 22311-6 Paperbound $2.00

OLD HUNGARIAN FAIRY TALES, Baroness Orczy. Favorites translated and adapted by author of the *Scarlet Pimpernel.* Eight fairy tales include "The Suitors of Princess Fire-Fly," "The Twin Hunchbacks," "Mr. Cuttlefish's Love Story," and "The Enchanted Cat." This little volume of magic and adventure will captivate children as it has for generations. 90 drawings by Montagu Barstow. 96pp. (USO) 22293-4 Paperbound $1.95

THE RED FAIRY BOOK, Andrew Lang. Lang's color fairy books have long been children's favorites. This volume includes Rapunzel, Jack and the Bean-stalk and 35 other stories, familiar and unfamiliar. 4 plates, 93 illustrations x + 367pp.

21673-X Paperbound $2.50

THE BLUE FAIRY BOOK, Andrew Lang. Lang's tales come from all countries and all times. Here are 37 tales from Grimm, the Arabian Nights, Greek Mythology, and other fascinating sources. 8 plates, 130 illustrations. xi + 390pp.

21437-0 Paperbound $2.75

HOUSEHOLD STORIES BY THE BROTHERS GRIMM. Classic English-language edition of the well-known tales — Rumpelstiltskin, Snow White, Hansel and Gretel, The Twelve Brothers, Faithful John, Rapunzel, Tom Thumb (52 stories in all). Translated into simple, straightforward English by Lucy Crane. Ornamented with headpieces, vignettes, elaborate decorative initials and a dozen full-page illustrations by Walter Crane. x + 269pp.

21080-4 Paperbound **$2.00**

THE MERRY ADVENTURES OF ROBIN HOOD, Howard Pyle. The finest modern versions of the traditional ballads and tales about the great English outlaw. Howard Pyle's complete prose version, with every word, every illustration of the first edition. Do not confuse this facsimile of the original (1883) with modern editions that change text or illustrations. 23 plates plus many page decorations. xxii + 296pp.

22043-5 Paperbound $2.75

THE STORY OF KING ARTHUR AND HIS KNIGHTS, Howard Pyle. The finest children's version of the life of King Arthur; brilliantly retold by Pyle, with 48 of his most imaginative illustrations. xviii + 313pp. 6⅛ x 9¼.

21445-1 Paperbound $2.50

THE WONDERFUL WIZARD OF OZ, L. Frank Baum. America's finest children's book in facsimile of first edition with all Denslow illustrations in full color. The edition a child should have. Introduction by Martin Gardner. 23 color plates, scores of drawings. iv + 267pp.

20691-2 Paperbound $3.50

THE MARVELOUS LAND OF OZ, L. Frank Baum. The second Oz book, every bit as imaginative as the Wizard. The hero is a boy named Tip, but the Scarecrow and the Tin Woodman are back, as is the Oz magic. 16 color plates, 120 drawings by John R. Neill. 287pp.

20692-0 Paperbound $2.50

THE MAGICAL MONARCH OF MO, L. Frank Baum. Remarkable adventures in a land even stranger than Oz. The best of Baum's books not in the Oz series. 15 color plates and dozens of drawings by Frank Verbeck. xviii + 237pp.

21892-9 Paperbound $2.25

THE BAD CHILD'S BOOK OF BEASTS, MORE BEASTS FOR WORSE CHILDREN, A MORAL ALPHABET, Hilaire Belloc. Three complete humor classics in one volume. Be kind to the frog, and do not call him names . . . and 28 other whimsical animals. Familiar favorites and some not so well known. Illustrated by Basil Blackwell. 156pp.

(USO) 20749-8 Paperbound $1.50

EAST O' THE SUN AND WEST O' THE MOON, George W. Dasent. Considered the best of all translations of these Norwegian folk tales, this collection has been enjoyed by generations of children (and folklorists too). Includes True and Untrue, Why the Sea is Salt, East O' the Sun and West O' the Moon, Why the Bear is Stumpy-Tailed, Boots and the Troll, The Cock and the Hen, Rich Peter the Pedlar, and 52 more. The only edition with all 59 tales. 77 illustrations by Erik Werenskiold and Theodor Kittelsen. xv + 418pp. 22521-6 Paperbound $3.50

GOOPS AND HOW TO BE THEM, Gelett Burgess. Classic of tongue-in-cheek humor, masquerading as etiquette book. 87 verses, twice as many cartoons, show mischievous Goops as they demonstrate to children virtues of table manners, neatness, courtesy, etc. Favorite for generations. viii + 88pp. 6½ x 9¼.
22233-0 Paperbound $1.50

ALICE'S ADVENTURES UNDER GROUND, Lewis Carroll. The first version, quite different from the final *Alice in Wonderland*, printed out by Carroll himself with his own illustrations. Complete facsimile of the "million dollar" manuscript Carroll gave to Alice Liddell in 1864. Introduction by Martin Gardner. viii + 96pp. Title and dedication pages in color. 21482-6 Paperbound $1.25

THE BROWNIES, THEIR BOOK, Palmer Cox. Small as mice, cunning as foxes, exuberant and full of mischief, the Brownies go to the zoo, toy shop, seashore, circus, etc., in 24 verse adventures and 266 illustrations. Long a favorite, since their first appearance in St. Nicholas Magazine. xi + 144pp. 6⅝ x 9¼.
21265-3 Paperbound $1.75

SONGS OF CHILDHOOD, Walter De La Mare. Published (under the pseudonym Walter Ramal) when De La Mare was only 29, this charming collection has long been a favorite children's book. A facsimile of the first edition in paper, the 47 poems capture the simplicity of the nursery rhyme and the ballad, including such lyrics as I Met Eve, Tartary, The Silver Penny. vii + 106pp. (USO) 21972-0 Paperbound
$1.25

THE COMPLETE NONSENSE OF EDWARD LEAR, Edward Lear. The finest 19th-century humorist-cartoonist in full: all nonsense limericks, zany alphabets, Owl and Pussycat, songs, nonsense botany, and more than 500 illustrations by Lear himself. Edited by Holbrook Jackson. xxix + 287pp. (USO) 20167-8 Paperbound $2.00

BILLY WHISKERS: THE AUTOBIOGRAPHY OF A GOAT, Frances Trego Montgomery. A favorite of children since the early 20th century, here are the escapades of that rambunctious, irresistible and mischievous goat—Billy Whiskers. Much in the spirit of *Peck's Bad Boy,* this is a book that children never tire of reading or hearing. All the original familiar illustrations by W. H. Fry are included: 6 color plates, 18 black and white drawings. 159pp. 22345-0 Paperbound $2.00

MOTHER GOOSE MELODIES. Faithful republication of the fabulously rare Munroe and Francis "copyright 1833" Boston edition—the most important Mother Goose collection, usually referred to as the "original." Familiar rhymes plus many rare ones, with wonderful old woodcut illustrations. Edited by E. F. Bleiler. 128pp. 4½ x 6⅜. 22577-1 Paperbound $1.00

TWO LITTLE SAVAGES; BEING THE ADVENTURES OF TWO BOYS WHO LIVED AS INDIANS AND WHAT THEY LEARNED, Ernest Thompson Seton. Great classic of nature and boyhood provides a vast range of woodlore in most palatable form, a genuinely entertaining story. Two farm boys build a teepee in woods and live in it for a month, working out Indian solutions to living problems, star lore, birds and animals, plants, etc. 293 illustrations. vii + 286pp.

20985-7 Paperbound $2.50

PETER PIPER'S PRACTICAL PRINCIPLES OF PLAIN & PERFECT PRONUNCIATION. Alliterative jingles and tongue-twisters of surprising charm, that made their first appearance in America about 1830. Republished in full with the spirited woodcut illustrations from this earliest American edition. 32pp. 4½ x 6⅜.

22560-7 Paperbound $1.00

SCIENCE EXPERIMENTS AND AMUSEMENTS FOR CHILDREN, Charles Vivian. 73 easy experiments, requiring only materials found at home or easily available, such as candles, coins, steel wool, etc.; illustrate basic phenomena like vacuum, simple chemical reaction, etc. All safe. Modern, well-planned. Formerly *Science Games for Children*. 102 photos, numerous drawings. 96pp. 6⅛ x 9¼.

21856-2 Paperbound $1.25

AN INTRODUCTION TO CHESS MOVES AND TACTICS SIMPLY EXPLAINED, Leonard Barden. Informal intermediate introduction, quite strong in explaining reasons for moves. Covers basic material, tactics, important openings, traps, positional play in middle game, end game. Attempts to isolate patterns and recurrent configurations. Formerly *Chess*. 58 figures. 102pp. (USO) 21210-6 Paperbound $1.25

LASKER'S MANUAL OF CHESS, Dr. Emanuel Lasker. Lasker was not only one of the five great World Champions, he was also one of the ablest expositors, theorists, and analysts. In many ways, his Manual, permeated with his philosophy of battle, filled with keen insights, is one of the greatest works ever written on chess. Filled with analyzed games by the great players. A single-volume library that will profit almost any chess player, beginner or master. 308 diagrams. xli x 349pp.

20640-8 Paperbound $2.75

THE MASTER BOOK OF MATHEMATICAL RECREATIONS, Fred Schuh. In opinion of many the finest work ever prepared on mathematical puzzles, stunts, recreations; exhaustively thorough explanations of mathematics involved, analysis of effects, citation of puzzles and games. Mathematics involved is elementary. Translated by F. Göbel. 194 figures. xxiv + 430pp. 22134-2 Paperbound $4.00

MATHEMATICS, MAGIC AND MYSTERY, Martin Gardner. Puzzle editor for Scientific American explains mathematics behind various mystifying tricks: card tricks, stage "mind reading," coin and match tricks, counting out games, geometric dissections, etc. Probability sets, theory of numbers clearly explained. Also provides more than 400 tricks, guaranteed to work, that you can do. 135 illustrations. xii + 176pp.

20335-2 Paperbound $2.00

HOW TO KNOW THE WILD FLOWERS, Mrs. William Starr Dana. This is the classical book of American wildflowers (of the Eastern and Central United States), used by hundreds of thousands. Covers over 500 species, arranged in extremely easy to use color and season groups. Full descriptions, much plant lore. This Dover edition is the fullest ever compiled, with tables of nomenclature changes. 174 full-page plates by M. Satterlee. xii + 418pp. 20332-8 Paperbound $3.00

OUR PLANT FRIENDS AND FOES, William Atherton DuPuy. History, economic importance, essential botanical information and peculiarities of 25 common forms of plant life are provided in this book in an entertaining and charming style. Covers food plants (potatoes, apples, beans, wheat, almonds, bananas, etc.), flowers (lily, tulip, etc.), trees (pine, oak, elm, etc.), weeds, poisonous mushrooms and vines, gourds, citrus fruits, cotton, the cactus family, and much more. 108 illustrations. xiv + 290pp. 22272-1 Paperbound $2.50

HOW TO KNOW THE FERNS, Frances T. Parsons. Classic survey of Eastern and Central ferns, arranged according to clear, simple identification key. Excellent introduction to greatly neglected nature area. 57 illustrations and 42 plates. xvi + 215pp. 20740-4 Paperbound $2.00

MANUAL OF THE TREES OF NORTH AMERICA, Charles S. Sargent. America's foremost dendrologist provides the definitive coverage of North American trees and tree-like shrubs. 717 species fully described and illustrated: exact distribution, down to township; full botanical description; economic importance; description of subspecies and races; habitat, growth data; similar material. Necessary to every serious student of tree-life. Nomenclature revised to present. Over 100 locating keys. 783 illustrations. lii + 934pp. 20277-1, 20278-X Two volumes, Paperbound $7.00

OUR NORTHERN SHRUBS, Harriet L. Keeler. Fine non-technical reference work identifying more than 225 important shrubs of Eastern and Central United States and Canada. Full text covering botanical description, habitat, plant lore, is paralleled with 205 full-page photographs of flowering or fruiting plants. Nomenclature revised by Edward G. Voss. One of few works concerned with shrubs. 205 plates, 35 drawings. xxviii + 521pp. 21989-5 Paperbound $3.75

THE MUSHROOM HANDBOOK, Louis C. C. Krieger. Still the best popular handbook: full descriptions of 259 species, cross references to another 200. Extremely thorough text enables you to identify, know all about any mushroom you are likely to meet in eastern and central U. S. A.: habitat, luminescence, poisonous qualities, use, folklore, etc. 32 color plates show over 50 mushrooms, also 126 other illustrations. Finding keys. vii + 560pp. 21861-9 Paperbound $4.50

HANDBOOK OF BIRDS OF EASTERN NORTH AMERICA, Frank M. Chapman. Still much the best single-volume guide to the birds of Eastern and Central United States. Very full coverage of 675 species, with descriptions, life habits, distribution, similar data. All descriptions keyed to two-page color chart. With this single volume the average birdwatcher needs no other books. 1931 revised edition. 195 illustrations. xxxvi + 581pp. 21489-3 Paperbound $5.00

AMERICAN FOOD AND GAME FISHES, David S. Jordan and Barton W. Evermann. Definitive source of information, detailed and accurate enough to enable the sportsman and nature lover to identify conclusively some 1,000 species and sub-species of North American fish, sought for food or sport. Coverage of range, physiology, habits, life history, food value. Best methods of capture, interest to the angler, advice on bait, fly-fishing, etc. 338 drawings and photographs. 1 + 574pp. 6⅝ x 9⅜.
22196-2 Paperbound $5.00

THE FROG BOOK, Mary C. Dickerson. Complete with extensive finding keys, over 300 photographs, and an introduction to the general biology of frogs and toads, this is the classic non-technical study of Northeastern and Central species. 58 species; 290 photographs and 16 color plates. xvii + 253pp.
21973-9 Paperbound $4.00

THE MOTH BOOK: A GUIDE TO THE MOTHS OF NORTH AMERICA, William J. Holland. Classical study, eagerly sought after and used for the past 60 years. Clear identification manual to more than 2,000 different moths, largest manual in existence. General information about moths, capturing, mounting, classifying, etc., followed by species by species descriptions. 263 illustrations plus 48 color plates show almost every species, full size. 1968 edition, preface, nomenclature changes by A. E. Brower. xxiv + 479pp. of text. 6½ x 9¼.
21948-8 Paperbound $6.00

THE SEA-BEACH AT EBB-TIDE, Augusta Foote Arnold. Interested amateur can identify hundreds of marine plants and animals on coasts of North America; marine algae; seaweeds; squids; hermit crabs; horse shoe crabs; shrimps; corals; sea anemones; etc. Species descriptions cover: structure; food; reproductive cycle; size; shape; color; habitat; etc. Over 600 drawings. 85 plates. xii + 490pp.
21949-6 Paperbound $4.00

COMMON BIRD SONGS, Donald J. Borror. 33⅓ 12-inch record presents songs of 60 important birds of the eastern United States. A thorough, serious record which provides several examples for each bird, showing different types of song, individual variations, etc. Inestimable identification aid for birdwatcher. 32-page booklet gives text about birds and songs, with illustration for each bird.
21829-5 Record, book, album. Monaural. $3.50

FADS AND FALLACIES IN THE NAME OF SCIENCE, Martin Gardner. Fair, witty appraisal of cranks and quacks of science: Atlantis, Lemuria, hollow earth, flat earth, Velikovsky, orgone energy, Dianetics, flying saucers, Bridey Murphy, food fads, medical fads, perpetual motion, etc. Formerly "In the Name of Science." x + 363pp.
20394-8 Paperbound $3.00

HOAXES, Curtis D. MacDougall. Exhaustive, unbelievably rich account of great hoaxes: Locke's moon hoax, Shakespearean forgeries, sea serpents, Loch Ness monster, Cardiff giant, John Wilkes Booth's mummy, Disumbrationist school of art, dozens more; also journalism, psychology of hoaxing. 54 illustrations. xi + 338pp.
20465-0 Paperbound $3.50

THE PRINCIPLES OF PSYCHOLOGY, William James. The famous long course, complete and unabridged. Stream of thought, time perception, memory, experimental methods—these are only some of the concerns of a work that was years ahead of its time and still valid, interesting, useful. 94 figures. Total of xviii + 1391pp.
20381-6, 20382-4 Two volumes, Paperbound $9.00

THE STRANGE STORY OF THE QUANTUM, Banesh Hoffmann. Non-mathematical but thorough explanation of work of Planck, Einstein, Bohr, Pauli, de Broglie, Schrödinger, Heisenberg, Dirac, Feynman, etc. No technical background needed. "Of books attempting such an account, this is the best," Henry Margenau, Yale. 40-page "Postscript 1959." xii + 285pp. 20518-5 Paperbound $3.00

THE RISE OF THE NEW PHYSICS, A. d'Abro. Most thorough explanation in print of central core of mathematical physics, both classical and modern; from Newton to Dirac and Heisenberg. Both history and exposition; philosophy of science, causality, explanations of higher mathematics, analytical mechanics, electromagnetism, thermodynamics, phase rule, special and general relativity, matrices. No higher mathematics needed to follow exposition, though treatment is elementary to intermediate in level. Recommended to serious student who wishes verbal understanding. 97 illustrations. xvii + 982pp. 20003-5, 20004-3 Two volumes, Paperbound $10.00

GREAT IDEAS OF OPERATIONS RESEARCH, Jagjit Singh. Easily followed non-technical explanation of mathematical tools, aims, results: statistics, linear programming, game theory, queueing theory, Monte Carlo simulation, etc. Uses only elementary mathematics. Many case studies, several analyzed in detail. Clarity, breadth make this excellent for specialist in another field who wishes background. 41 figures. x + 228pp. 21886-4 Paperbound $2.50

GREAT IDEAS OF MODERN MATHEMATICS: THEIR NATURE AND USE, Jagjit Singh. Internationally famous expositor, winner of Unesco's Kalinga Award for science popularization explains verbally such topics as differential equations, matrices, groups, sets, transformations, mathematical logic and other important modern mathematics, as well as use in physics, astrophysics, and similar fields. Superb exposition for layman, scientist in other areas. viii + 312pp.
20587-8 Paperbound $2.75

GREAT IDEAS IN INFORMATION THEORY, LANGUAGE AND CYBERNETICS, Jagjit Singh. The analog and digital computers, how they work, how they are like and unlike the human brain, the men who developed them, their future applications, computer terminology. An essential book for today, even for readers with little math. Some mathematical demonstrations included for more advanced readers. 118 figures. Tables. ix + 338pp. 21694-2 Paperbound $2.50

CHANCE, LUCK AND STATISTICS, Horace C. Levinson. Non-mathematical presentation of fundamentals of probability theory and science of statistics and their applications. Games of chance, betting odds, misuse of statistics, normal and skew distributions, birth rates, stock speculation, insurance. Enlarged edition. Formerly "The Science of Chance." xiii + 357pp. 21007-3 Paperbound $2.50

PLANETS, STARS AND GALAXIES: DESCRIPTIVE ASTRONOMY FOR BEGINNERS, A. E. Fanning. Comprehensive introductory survey of astronomy: the sun, solar system, stars, galaxies, universe, cosmology; up-to-date, including quasars, radio stars, etc. Preface by Prof. Donald Menzel. 24pp. of photographs. 189pp. 5¼ x 8¼.
21680-2 Paperbound $2.50

TEACH YOURSELF CALCULUS, P. Abbott. With a good background in algebra and trig, you can teach yourself calculus with this book. Simple, straightforward introduction to functions of all kinds, integration, differentiation, series, etc. "Students who are beginning to study calculus method will derive great help from this book." Faraday House Journal. 308pp.
20683-1 Clothbound $2.50

TEACH YOURSELF TRIGONOMETRY, P. Abbott. Geometrical foundations, indices and logarithms, ratios, angles, circular measure, etc. are presented in this sound, easy-to-use text. Excellent for the beginner or as a brush up, this text carries the student through the solution of triangles. 204pp.
20682-3 Clothbound $2.00

BASIC MACHINES AND HOW THEY WORK, U. S. Bureau of Naval Personnel. Originally used in U.S. Naval training schools, this book clearly explains the operation of a progression of machines, from the simplest—lever, wheel and axle, inclined plane, wedge, screw—to the most complex—typewriter, internal combustion engine, computer mechanism. Utilizing an approach that requires only an elementary understanding of mathematics, these explanations build logically upon each other and are assisted by over 200 drawings and diagrams. Perfect as a technical school manual or as a self-teaching aid to the layman. 204 figures. Preface. Index. vii + 161pp. 6½ x 9¼.
21709-4 Paperbound $2.50

THE FRIENDLY STARS, Martha Evans Martin. Classic has taught naked-eye observation of stars, planets to hundreds of thousands, still not surpassed for charm, lucidity, adequacy. Completely updated by Professor Donald H. Menzel, Harvard Observatory. 25 illustrations. 16 x 30 chart. x + 147pp.
21099-5 Paperbound $2.00

MUSIC OF THE SPHERES: THE MATERIAL UNIVERSE FROM ATOM TO QUASAR, SIMPLY EXPLAINED, Guy Murchie. Extremely broad, brilliantly written popular account begins with the solar system and reaches to dividing line between matter and nonmatter; latest understandings presented with exceptional clarity. Volume One: Planets, stars, galaxies, cosmology, geology, celestial mechanics, latest astronomical discoveries; Volume Two: Matter, atoms, waves, radiation, relativity, chemical action, heat, nuclear energy, quantum theory, music, light, color, probability, antimatter, antigravity, and similar topics. 319 figures. 1967 (second) edition. Total of xx + 644pp.
21809-0, 21810-4 Two volumes, Paperbound $5.75

OLD-TIME SCHOOLS AND SCHOOL BOOKS, Clifton Johnson. Illustrations and rhymes from early primers, abundant quotations from early textbooks, many anecdotes of school life enliven this study of elementary schools from Puritans to middle 19th century. Introduction by Carl Withers. 234 illustrations. xxxiii + 381pp.
21031-6 Paperbound $4.00

THE PHILOSOPHY OF THE UPANISHADS, Paul Deussen. Clear, detailed statement of upanishadic system of thought, generally considered among best available. History of these works, full exposition of system emergent from them, parallel concepts in the West. Translated by A. S. Geden. xiv + 429pp.

21616-0 Paperbound $3.50

LANGUAGE, TRUTH AND LOGIC, Alfred J. Ayer. Famous, remarkably clear introduction to the Vienna and Cambridge schools of Logical Positivism; function of philosophy, elimination of metaphysical thought, nature of analysis, similar topics. "Wish I had written it myself," Bertrand Russell. 2nd, 1946 edition. 160pp.

20010-8 Paperbound $1.50

THE GUIDE FOR THE PERPLEXED, Moses Maimonides. Great classic of medieval Judaism, major attempt to reconcile revealed religion (Pentateuch, commentaries) and Aristotelian philosophy. Enormously important in all Western thought. Unabridged Friedländer translation. 50-page introduction. lix + 414pp.

(USO) 20351-4 Paperbound $4.50

OCCULT AND SUPERNATURAL PHENOMENA, D. H. Rawcliffe. Full, serious study of the most persistent delusions of mankind: crystal gazing, mediumistic trance, stigmata, lycanthropy, fire walking, dowsing, telepathy, ghosts, ESP, etc., and their relation to common forms of abnormal psychology. Formerly *Illusions and Delusions of the Supernatural and the Occult.* iii + 551pp. 20503-7 Paperbound $4.00

THE EGYPTIAN BOOK OF THE DEAD: THE PAPYRUS OF ANI, E. A. Wallis Budge. Full hieroglyphic text, interlinear transliteration of sounds, word for word translation, then smooth, connected translation; Theban recension. Basic work in Ancient Egyptian civilization; now even more significant than ever for historical importance, dilation of consciousness, etc. clvi + 377pp. 6½ x 9¼.

21866-X Paperbound $4.95

PSYCHOLOGY OF MUSIC, Carl E. Seashore. Basic, thorough survey of everything known about psychology of music up to 1940's; essential reading for psychologists, musicologists. Physical acoustics; auditory apparatus; relationship of physical sound to perceived sound; role of the mind in sorting, altering, suppressing, creating sound sensations; musical learning, testing for ability, absolute pitch, other topics. Records of Caruso, Menuhin analyzed. 88 figures. xix + 408pp.

21851-1 Paperbound $3.50

THE I CHING (THE BOOK OF CHANGES), translated by James Legge. Complete translated text plus appendices by Confucius, of perhaps the most penetrating divination book ever compiled. Indispensable to all study of early Oriental civilizations. 3 plates. xxiii + 448pp. 21062-6 Paperbound $3.50

THE UPANISHADS, translated by Max Müller. Twelve classical upanishads: Chandogya, Kena, Aitareya, Kaushitaki, Isa, Katha, Mundaka, Taittiriyaka, Brhadaranyaka, Svetasvatara, Prasna, Maitriyana. 160-page introduction, analysis by Prof. Müller. Total of 670pp. 20992-X, 20993-8 Two volumes, Paperbound $7.50

JIM WHITEWOLF: THE LIFE OF A KIOWA APACHE INDIAN, Charles S. Brant, editor. Spans transition between native life and acculturation period, 1880 on. Kiowa culture, personal life pattern, religion and the supernatural, the Ghost Dance, breakdown in the White Man's world, similar material. 1 map. xii + 144pp.
22015-X Paperbound $1.75

THE NATIVE TRIBES OF CENTRAL AUSTRALIA, Baldwin Spencer and F. J. Gillen. Basic book in anthropology, devoted to full coverage of the Arunta and Warramunga tribes; the source for knowledge about kinship systems, material and social culture, religion, etc. Still unsurpassed. 121 photographs, 89 drawings. xviii + 669pp.
21775-2 Paperbound $5.00

MALAY MAGIC, Walter W. Skeat. Classic (1900); still the definitive work on the folklore and popular religion of the Malay peninsula. Describes marriage rites, birth spirits and ceremonies, medicine, dances, games, war and weapons, etc. Extensive quotes from original sources, many magic charms translated into English. 35 illustrations. Preface by Charles Otto Blagden. xxiv + 685pp.
21760-4 Paperbound $4.00

HEAVENS ON EARTH: UTOPIAN COMMUNITIES IN AMERICA, 1680-1880, Mark Holloway. The finest nontechnical account of American utopias, from the early Woman in the Wilderness, Ephrata, Rappites to the enormous mid 19th-century efflorescence; Shakers, New Harmony, Equity Stores, Fourier's Phalanxes, Oneida, Amana, Fruitlands, etc. "Entertaining and very instructive." *Times Literary Supplement.* 15 illustrations. 246pp.
21593-8 Paperbound $2.00

LONDON LABOUR AND THE LONDON POOR, Henry Mayhew. Earliest (c. 1850) sociological study in English, describing myriad subcultures of London poor. Particularly remarkable for the thousands of pages of direct testimony taken from the lips of London prostitutes, thieves, beggars, street sellers, chimney-sweepers, street-musicians, "mudlarks," "pure-finders," rag-gatherers, "running-patterers," dock laborers, cab-men, and hundreds of others, quoted directly in this massive work. An extraordinarily vital picture of London emerges. 110 illustrations. Total of lxxvi + 1951pp. 6⅝ x 10.
21934-8, 21935-6, 21936-4, 21937-2 Four volumes, Paperbound $16.00

HISTORY OF THE LATER ROMAN EMPIRE, J. B. Bury. Eloquent, detailed reconstruction of Western and Byzantine Roman Empire by a major historian, from the death of Theodosius I (395 A.D.) to the death of Justinian (565). Extensive quotations from contemporary sources; full coverage of important Roman and foreign figures of the time. xxxiv + 965pp. 20398-0, 20399-9 Two volumes, Paperbound $7.00

AN INTELLECTUAL AND CULTURAL HISTORY OF THE WESTERN WORLD, Harry Elmer Barnes. Monumental study, tracing the development of the accomplishments that make up human culture. Every aspect of man's achievement surveyed from its origins in the Paleolithic to the present day (1964); social structures, ideas, economic systems, art, literature, technology, mathematics, the sciences, medicine, religion, jurisprudence, etc. Evaluations of the contributions of scores of great men. 1964 edition, revised and edited by scholars in the many fields represented. Total of xxix + 1381pp. 21275-0, 21276-9, 21277-7 Three volumes, Paperbound $10.50

ADVENTURES OF AN AFRICAN SLAVER, Theodore Canot. Edited by Brantz Mayer. A detailed portrayal of slavery and the slave trade, 1820-1840. Canot, an established trader along the African coast, describes the slave economy of the African kingdoms, the treatment of captured negroes, the extensive journeys in the interior to gather slaves, slave revolts and their suppression, harems, bribes, and much more. Full and unabridged republication of 1854 edition. Introduction by Malcom Cowley. 16 illustrations. xvii + 448pp. 22456-2 Paperbound $3.50

MY BONDAGE AND MY FREEDOM, Frederick Douglass. Born and brought up in slavery, Douglass witnessed its horrors and experienced its cruelties, but went on to become one of the most outspoken forces in the American anti-slavery movement. Considered the best of his autobiographies, this book graphically describes the in-human treatment of slaves, its effects on slave owners and slave families, and how Douglass's determination led him to a new life. Unaltered reprint of 1st (1855) edition. xxxii + 464pp. 22457-0 Paperbound $3.50

THE INDIANS' BOOK, recorded and edited by Natalie Curtis. Lore, music, narratives, dozens of drawings by Indians themselves from an authoritative and important survey of native culture among Plains, Southwestern, Lake and Pueblo Indians. Standard work in popular ethnomusicology. 149 songs in full notation. 23 draw-ings, 23 photos. xxxi + 584pp. 6⅝ x 9⅜. 21939-9 Paperbound $5.00

DICTIONARY OF AMERICAN PORTRAITS, edited by Hayward and Blanche Cirker. 4024 portraits of 4000 most important Americans, colonial days to 1905 (with a few important categories, like Presidents, to present). Pioneers, explorers, colonial figures, U. S. officials, politicians, writers, military and naval men, scientists, inven-tors, manufacturers, jurists, actors, historians, educators, notorious figures, Indian chiefs, etc. All authentic contemporary likenesses. The only work of its kind in existence; supplements all biographical sources for libraries. Indispensable to any-one working with American history. 8,000-item classified index, finding lists, other aids. xiv + 756pp. 9¼ x 12¾. 21823-6 Clothbound $30.00

TRITTON'S GUIDE TO BETTER WINE AND BEER MAKING FOR BEGINNERS, S. M. Tritton. All you need to know to make family-sized quantities of over 100 types of grape, fruit, herb and vegetable wines; as well as beers, mead, cider, etc. Com-plete recipes, advice as to equipment, procedures such as fermenting, bottling, and storing wines. Recipes given in British, U. S., and metric measures. Accompanying booklet lists sources in U. S. A. where ingredients may be bought, and additional information. 11 illustrations. 157pp. 5⅝ x 8⅛. 22090-7 **Paperbound $2.00**

GARDENING WITH HERBS FOR FLAVOR AND FRAGRANCE, Helen M. Fox. How to grow herbs in your own garden, how to use them in your cooking (over 55 recipes included), legends and myths associated with each species, uses in medicine, per-fumes, etc.—these are elements of one of the few books written especially for Amer-ican herb fanciers. Guides you step-by-step from soil preparation to harvesting and storage for each type of herb. 12 drawings by Louise Mansfield. xiv + 334pp. 22540-2 Paperbound $2.50

MATHEMATICAL PUZZLES FOR BEGINNERS AND ENTHUSIASTS, Geoffrey Mott-Smith. 189 puzzles from easy to difficult—involving arithmetic, logic, algebra, properties of digits, probability, etc.—for enjoyment and mental stimulus. Explanation of mathematical principles behind the puzzles. 135 illustrations. viii + 248pp.

20198-8 Paperbound $2.00

PAPER FOLDING FOR BEGINNERS, William D. Murray and Francis J. Rigney. Easiest book on the market, clearest instructions on making interesting, beautiful origami. Sail boats, cups, roosters, frogs that move legs, bonbon boxes, standing birds, etc. 40 projects; more than 275 diagrams and photographs. 94pp.

20713-7 Paperbound $1.00

TRICKS AND GAMES ON THE POOL TABLE, Fred Herrmann. 79 tricks and games— some solitaires, some for two or more players, some competitive games—to entertain you between formal games. Mystifying shots and throws, unusual caroms, tricks involving such props as cork, coins, a hat, etc. Formerly *Fun on the Pool Table*. 77 figures. 95pp.

21814-7 Paperbound $1.25

HAND SHADOWS TO BE THROWN UPON THE WALL: A SERIES OF NOVEL AND AMUSING FIGURES FORMED BY THE HAND, Henry Bursill. Delightful picturebook from great-grandfather's day shows how to make 18 different hand shadows: a bird that flies, duck that quacks, dog that wags his tail, camel, goose, deer, boy, turtle, etc. Only book of its sort. vi + 33pp. 6½ x 9¼.

21779-5 Paperbound $1.00

WHITTLING AND WOODCARVING, E. J. Tangerman. 18th printing of best book on market. "If you can cut a potato you can carve" toys and puzzles, chains, chessmen, caricatures, masks, frames, woodcut blocks, surface patterns, much more. Information on tools, woods, techniques. Also goes into serious wood sculpture from Middle Ages to present, East and West. 464 photos, figures. x + 293pp.

20965-2 Paperbound $2.50

HISTORY OF PHILOSOPHY, Julián Marías. Possibly the clearest, most easily followed, best planned, most useful one-volume history of philosophy on the market; neither skimpy nor overfull. Full details on system of every major philosopher and dozens of less important thinkers from pre-Socratics up to Existentialism and later. Strong on many European figures usually omitted. Has gone through dozens of editions in Europe. 1966 edition, translated by Stanley Appelbaum and Clarence Strowbridge. xviii + 505pp.

21739-6 Paperbound $3.50

YOGA: A SCIENTIFIC EVALUATION, Kovoor T. Behanan. Scientific but non-technical study of physiological results of yoga exercises; done under auspices of Yale U. Relations to Indian thought, to psychoanalysis, etc. 16 photos. xxiii + 270pp.

20505-3 Paperbound $2.50

Prices subject to change without notice.
Available at your book dealer or write for free catalogue to Dept. GI, Dover Publications, Inc., 180 Varick St., N. Y., N. Y. 10014. Dover publishes more than 150 books each year on science, elementary and advanced mathematics, biology, music, art, literary history, social sciences and other areas.